YOUNG BELLINI

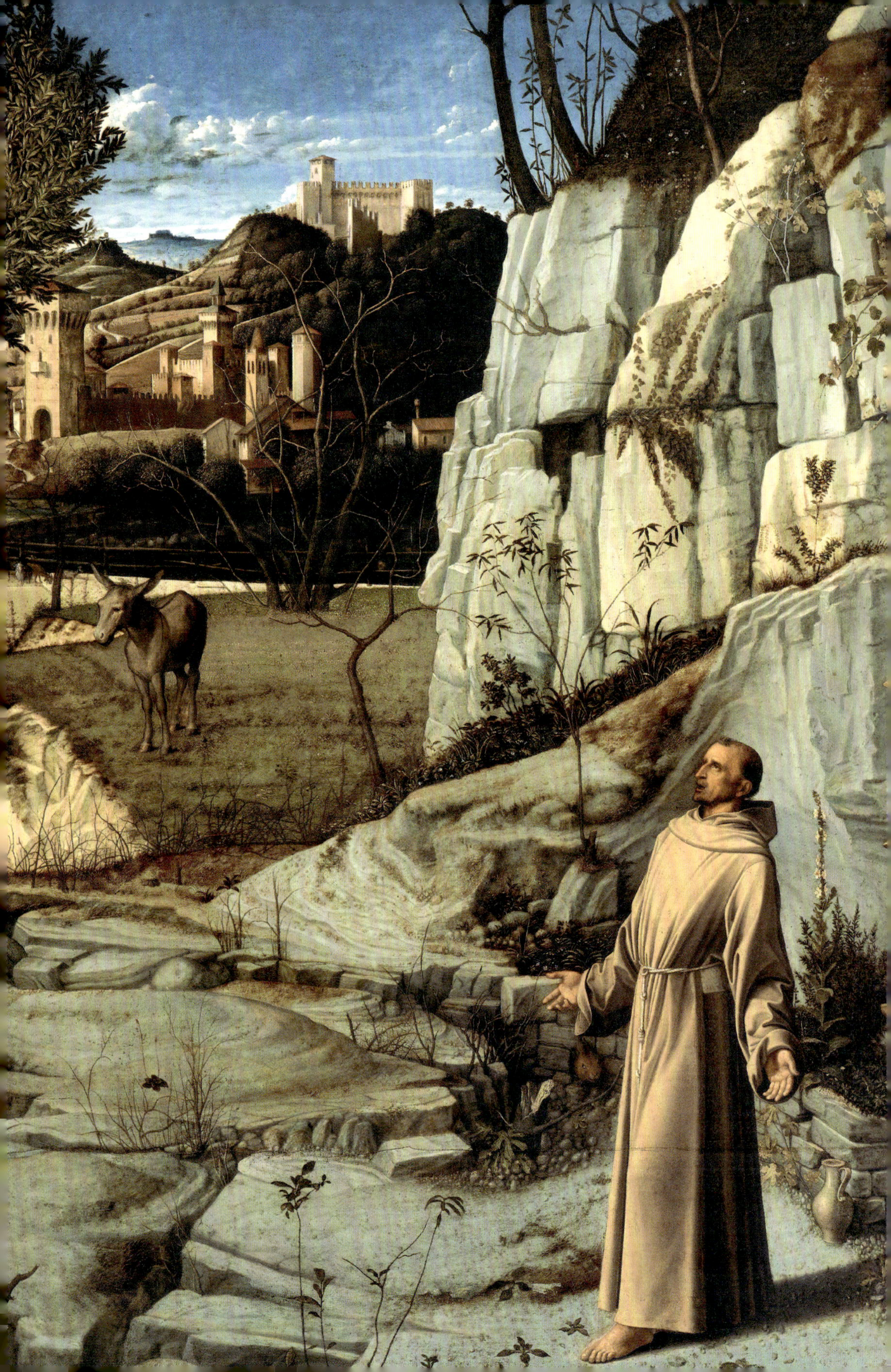

DANIEL WALLACE MAZE

YOUNG BELLINI

Yale University Press, New Haven and London

To my parents, my wife, and my two sons

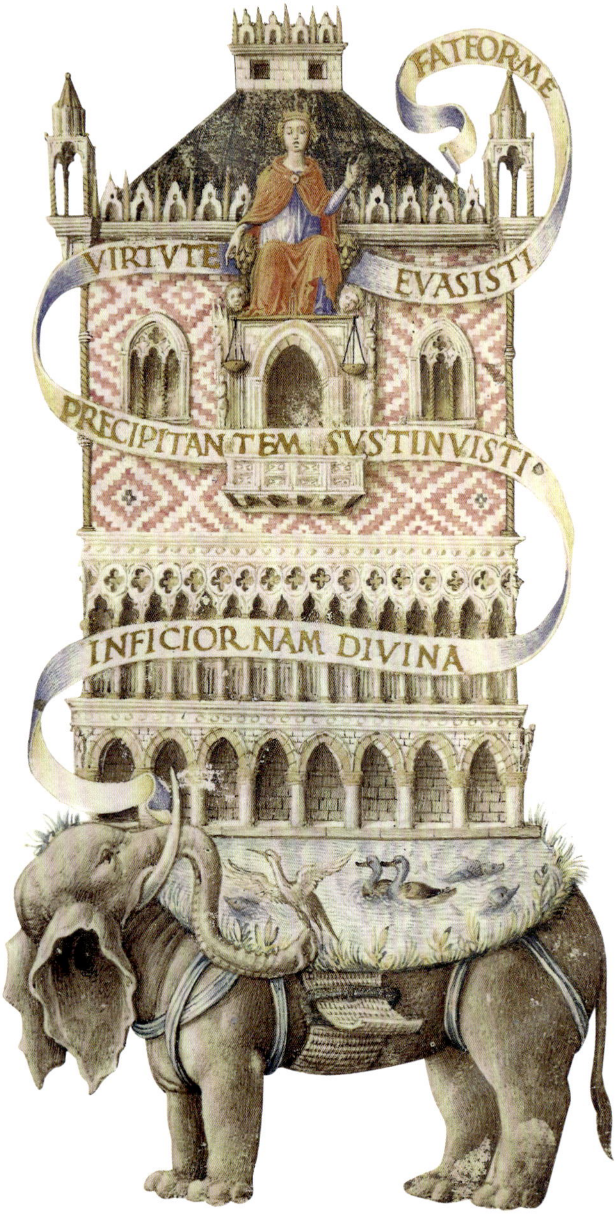

Contents

Family Tree 6

Introduction 11

1 A Tinsmith, a Felon, and an Orphan 18

2 The Bellini Family Workshop 30

3 Letters, Numbers, and Art 36

4 The First Painting 48

5 Flashes of Brilliance 64

6 Lessons for Jacopo's Assistant 80

7 A Small Masterpiece 90

Conclusions and Attributions 106

Appendix A 124
Appendix B 138
Chronology for Giovanni Bellini 148
List of Abbreviations 149
Notes 150
Bibliography 179
Index 197
Picture Credits 204
Acknowledgments 205

Family Tree

KEY

Equals sign or double line = marriage
Vertical line = parentage
Horizontal line = siblings of same parents
Dotted line = uncertain parentage

NB: Family Tree notes are located on pp. 150–52

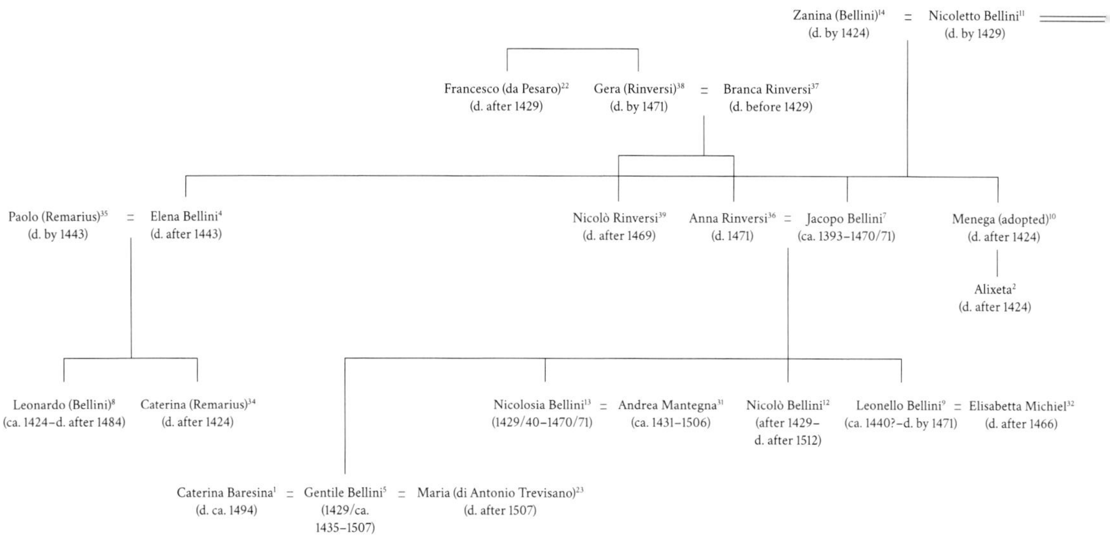

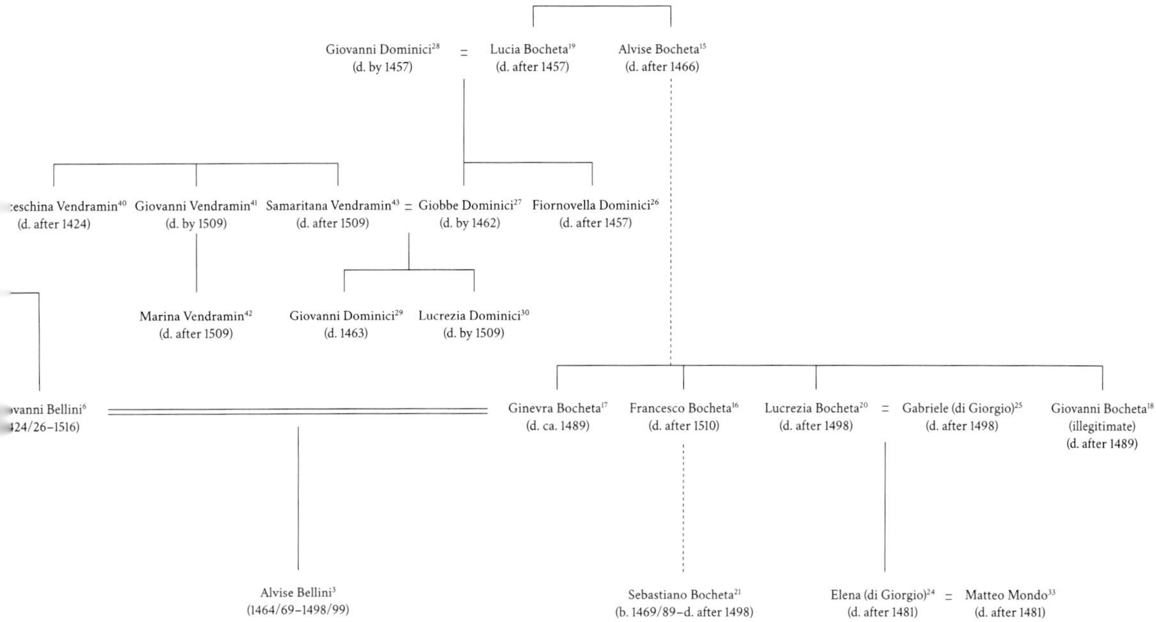

Giovanni Dominici[28] (d. by 1457)
=
Lucia Bocheta[19] (d. after 1457)
Alvise Bocheta[15] (d. after 1466)
…eschina Vendramin[40] (d. after 1424)
Giovanni Vendramin[41] (d. by 1509)
Samaritana Vendramin[43] (d. after 1509)
=
Giobbe Dominici[27] (d. by 1462)
Fiornovella Dominici[26] (d. after 1457)
Marina Vendramin[42] (d. after 1509)
Giovanni Dominici[29] (d. 1463)
Lucrezia Dominici[30] (d. by 1509)
…vanni Bellini[6] (…424/26–1516)
Ginevra Bocheta[17] (d. ca. 1489)
Francesco Bocheta[16] (d. after 1510)
Lucrezia Bocheta[20] (d. after 1498)
=
Gabriele (di Giorgio)[25] (d. after 1498)
Giovanni Bocheta[18] (illegitimate) (d. after 1489)
Alvise Bellini[3] (1464/69–1498/99)
Sebastiano Bocheta[21] (b. 1469/89–d. after 1498)
Elena (di Giorgio)[24] (d. after 1481)
=
Matteo Mondo[33] (d. after 1481)

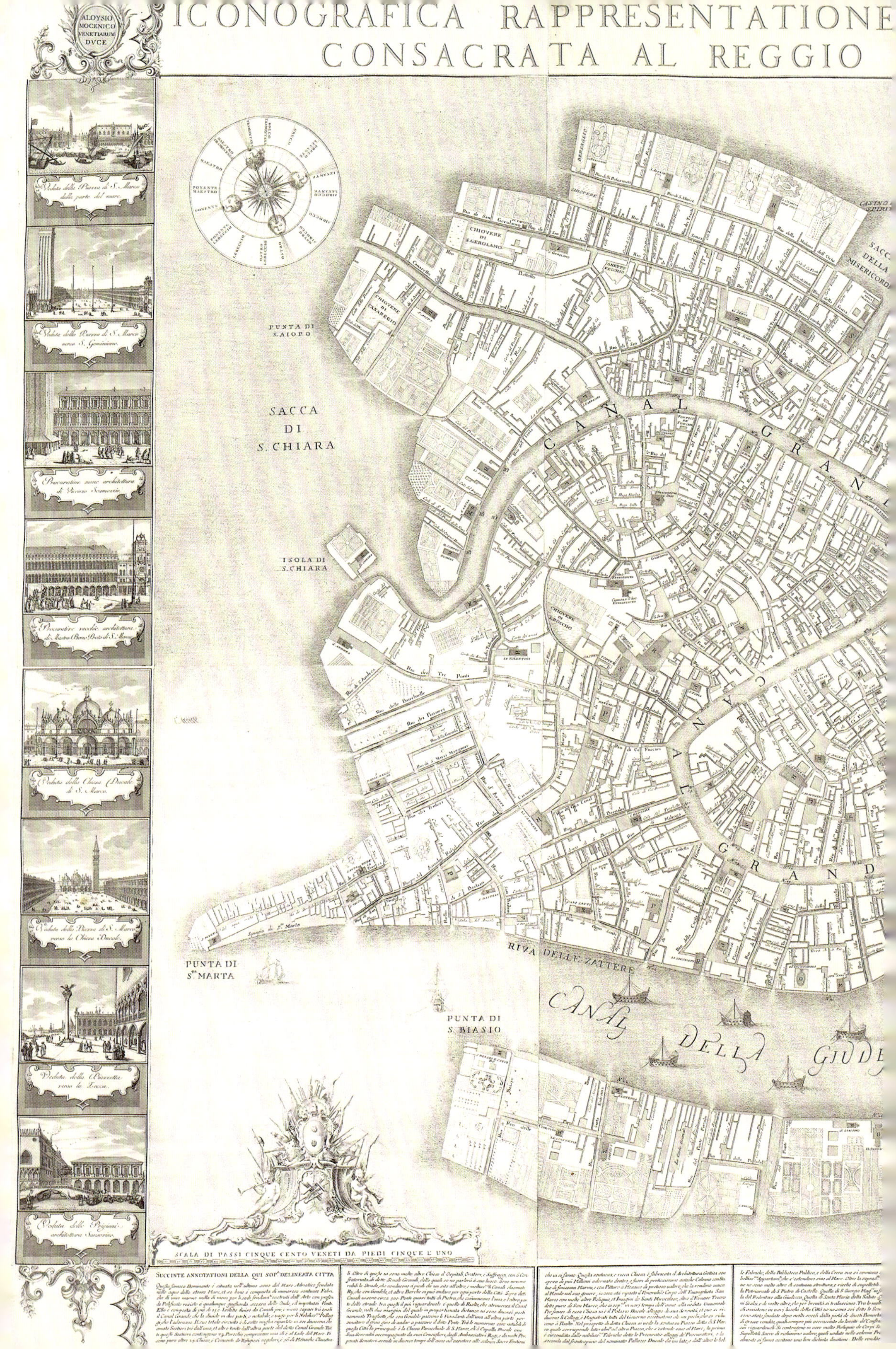
ALOYSIO MOCENICO VENETIARUM DVCE
ICONOGRAFICA RAPPRESENTATIONE
CONSACRATA AL REGGIO
Veduta della Piazza di S. Marco dalla parte del mare
Veduta della Piazza di S. Marco verso S. Geminiano
Procuratie nuove architettura di Vicenzo Scamozzi
Procuratie vecchie architettura di Mastro Bono Proto di S. Marco
Veduta della Chiesa Ducale di S. Marco
Veduta della Piazza di S. Marco verso la Chiesa Ducale
Veduta della Piazzetta verso la Zecca
Veduta delle Prigioni architettura Sansovino
PUNTA DI S. AIOPO
SACCA DI S. CHIARA
ISOLA DI S. CHIARA
PUNTA DI S.ᵗᵃ MARTA
PUNTA DI S. BIASIO
CANAL GRANDE
RIVA DELLE ZATTERE
CANAL DELLA GIUDE
CHIOVERE DI S. GEROLAMO
SACCA DELLA MISERICORD
SCALA DI PASSI CINQUE CENTO VENETI DA PIEDI CINQUE L'UNO
SUCCINTE ANNOTATIONI DELLA QUI SOP.ᵃ DELINEATA CITTÀ

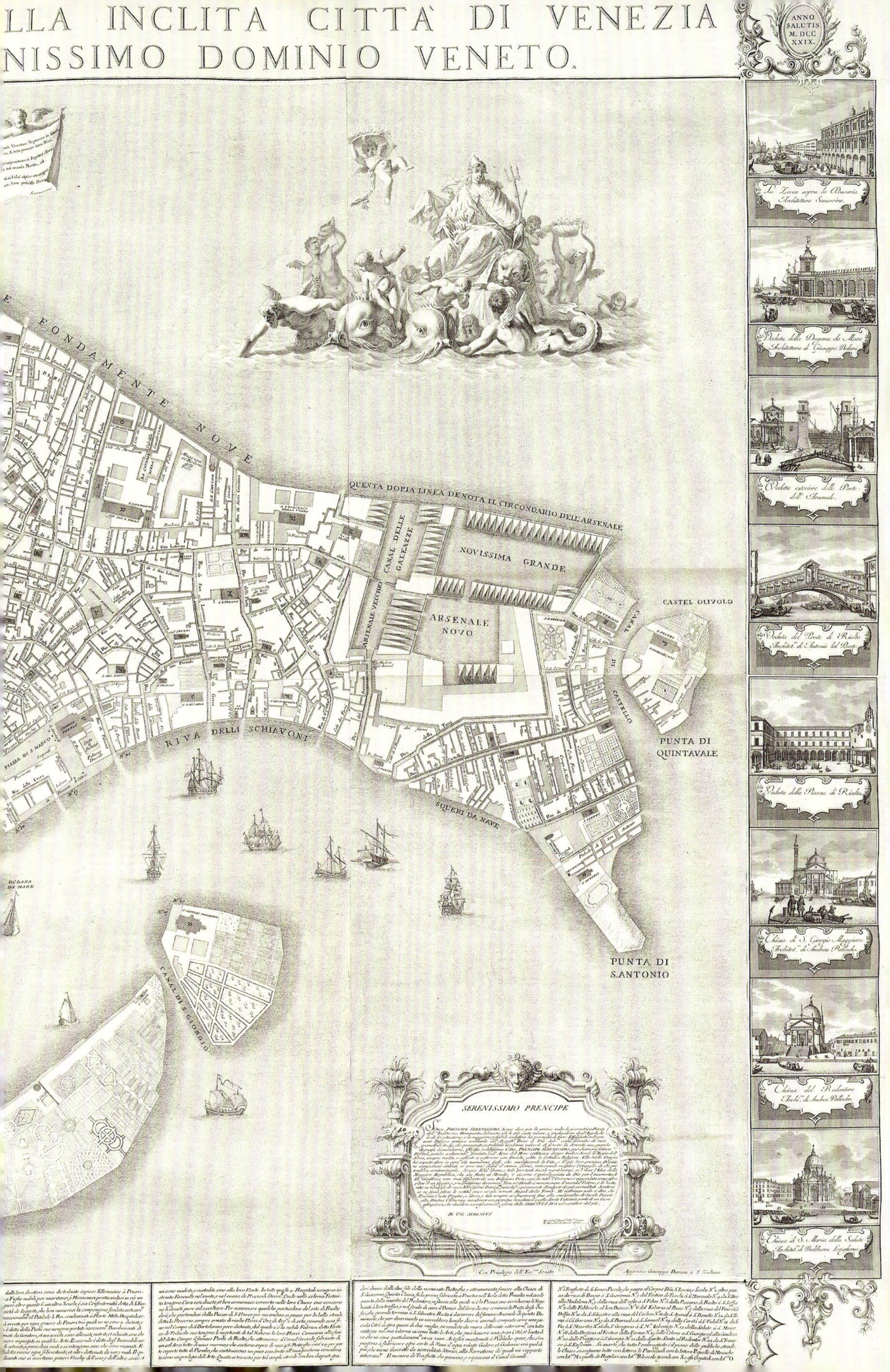
LLA INCLITA CITTÀ DI VENEZIA
NISSIMO DOMINIO VENETO.
ANNO SALUTIS M. DCC XXIX.
FONDAMENTE NOVE
QUESTA DOPPIA LINEA DENOTA IL CIRCONDARIO DELL'ARSENALE
CANAL DELLE GALEAZZE
NOVISSIMA GRANDE
ARSENALE VECCHIO
ARSENALE NOVO
CASTEL OLIVOLO
CANAL DI CASTELLO
PUNTA DI QUINTAVALE
RIVA DELLI SCHIAVONI
PIAZZA DI S. MARCO
SQUERI DA NAVE
DOGANA DA MARE
CANAL DI S. GIORGIO
PUNTA DI S. ANTONIO
SERENISSIMO PRENCIPE
Con Privilegio dell' Ecc.mo Senato
Appresso Giuseppe Baroni à S. Giuliano
Chiesa di S. Giorgio Maggiore Archit. di Andrea Palladio
Chiesa del Redentore Archit. di Andrea Palladio
Chiesa di S. Maria della Salute Archit. di Baldissera Longhena

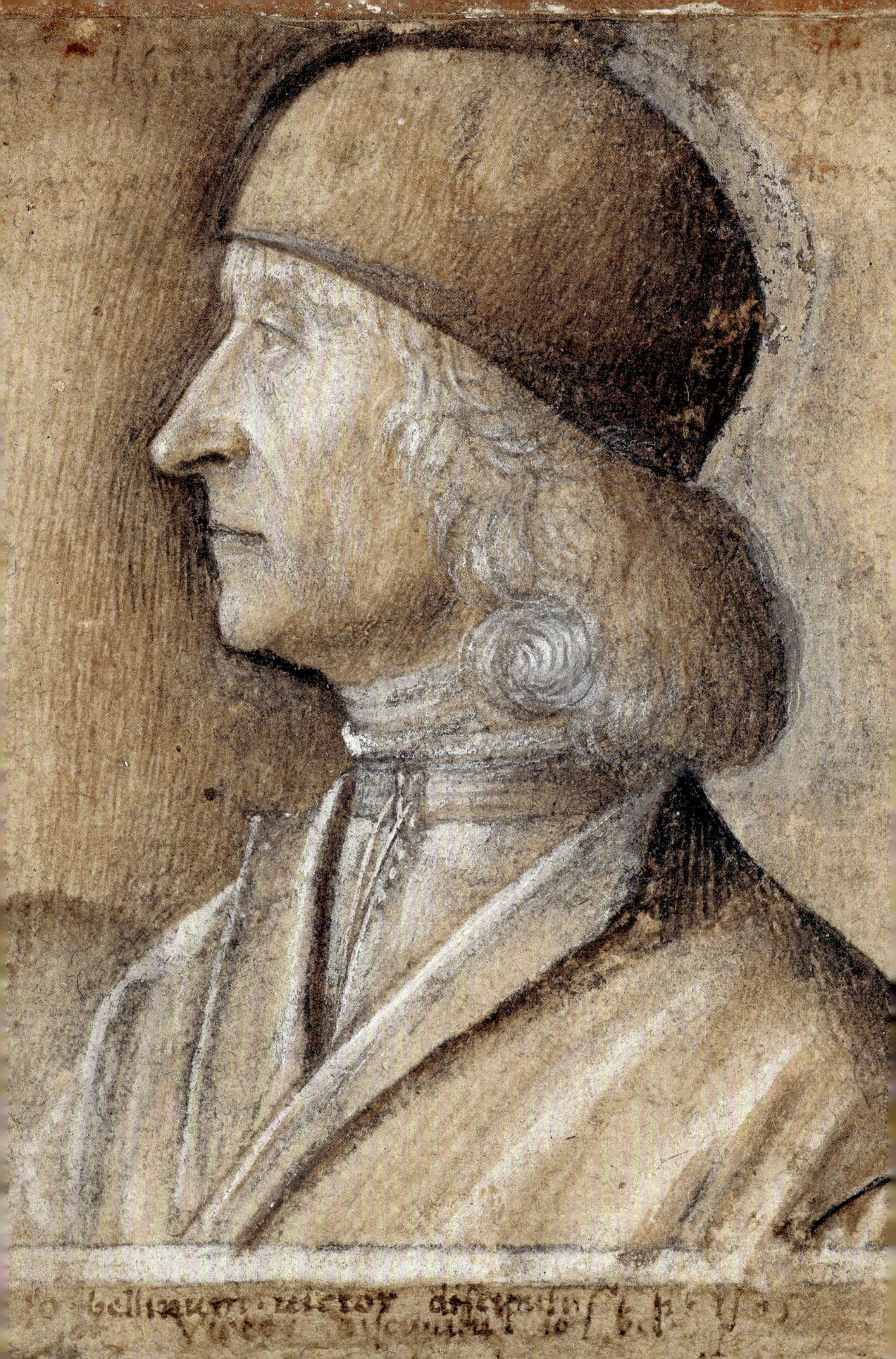

Introduction

Giovanni Bellini is generally recognized as the greatest artist of fifteenth-century Venice and a leading innovator of Italian Renaissance art (fig. 1). *Young Bellini* explores Giovanni's life up to ca. 1450, including the circumstances of his birth, his unusual upbringing in Venice, and his earliest works of art. Several paintings are here attributed to Giovanni for the first time, revealing his youthful artistic practice. Giovanni's precocity in culling from diverse visual sources is considered in depth. The revisionist history that emerges, one that illuminates various mysteries of the artist's life and proposes that his career began much earlier than currently thought, has repercussions for our understanding of the development of early Renaissance art in Northern Italy.[1]

Yet there are limitations to how far we can know Giovanni Bellini. These limits are circumscribed by the minimal evidence provided by fifteenth- and sixteenth-century primary sources. Giovanni's personality, beliefs, and particular attitudes toward politics, religion, and even the art of painting are almost entirely lost to history. During the period of Giovanni's life considered in this book, he executed few paintings, his name appears in one known document, and no other writings by him or about him exist. Nonetheless, as we shall see, there remains much to explore in the artist's early years.

New Research

One of the oldest and most contentious debates in the history of Italian art concerns Giovanni Bellini's birth.[2] Since the sixteenth century, historians have proposed dates for Giovanni's birth ranging from ca. 1425 to ca. 1440, with most Bellini specialists today arguing

FIGURE 1 Vittore Belliniano, *Portrait of a Man* (Giovanni Bellini), 1505. Brown ink and black chalk on paper, 10.9 × 8.8 cm. Musée Condé, Chantilly

for a birthdate in the mid to late 1430s. Correctly identifying the artist's birth year will enable art historians to establish a chronology for Giovanni's youthful works that would underlie an assessment of his early career. More controversially, it will allow scholars to determine whether Giovanni was older or younger than the other major figure of early Renaissance art in Northern Italy, the Paduan-trained Andrea Mantegna (ca. 1431–1506). This, in turn, will help scholars assess whether, as is currently debated, Giovanni was principally the originator or the recipient of the pictorial ideas deriving from their artistic duologue.

Research that I first published in 2013 and have updated in Appendix A (pp. 122–35) argues that Jacopo Bellini (ca. 1393–1470/71) was not Giovanni Bellini's biological father, as art historians have identified him since the sixteenth century, but instead was Giovanni's much older half-brother, the two being separated in age by over 30 years.[3] The research also suggests that Giovanni Bellini was born between the middle of 1424 and September 13, 1426.[4] This range of dates is five to fifteen years earlier than currently believed by most scholars. Nonetheless, it accords with the earliest extant identification of Giovanni's year of birth: in 1550, the art historian Giorgio Vasari (1511–1574) wrote in his *Lives of the Artists* that Giovanni had died at the age of 90 (on November 28 or 29, 1516) and thus Vasari located Giovanni's birth in late 1425 or 1426.[5] My research strengthens Vasari's proposal, which indicates that Giovanni was several years older than Mantegna. Giovanni would also have been older than Gentile Bellini (1429/ca. 1435–1507), who, according to this new research, was Giovanni's biological nephew rather than his biological brother (although they were raised and known as brothers).[6]

Youthful Ambition

Previous studies on Giovanni often begin with an analysis of his Birmingham *Saint Jerome in the Wilderness* (ca. 1450, see fig. 79), which is almost universally considered to be his first known work.[7] This book proposes that it was not. Instead, *Young Bellini* concludes its strict chronology in 1450 with a study of the *Saint Jerome*. As we shall see, the painting marks a coming-of-age for the young artist, then in his mid-twenties, with several pictorial strategies that Giovanni developed in adolescence reaching fruition in this small masterpiece. *Young Bellini* does not comprehensively examine Giovanni's subsequent works, including paintings traditionally presumed to represent the artist's earliest independent efforts, such as the *Pietà* (ca. 1453–54, Accademia Carrara, Bergamo), the *Transfiguration* (ca. 1455, fig. 2), the Davis *Virgin and Child* (ca. 1455, Metropolitan Museum of Art, New York), and the *Imago Pietatis* (1457, Museo Poldi Pezzoli, Milan), among others.[8]

Indeed, the main argument of this book is that Giovanni's pictorial style, as it emerged in his Birmingham *Saint Jerome*, may be seen as the culmination of a youthful artistic practice that included his training from Jacopo, his selection and integration of visual ideas by other artists, and his experimentation when executing his earlier paintings. After the *Saint Jerome*, Giovanni's style continued to develop, in part through his absorption of innovations by local,

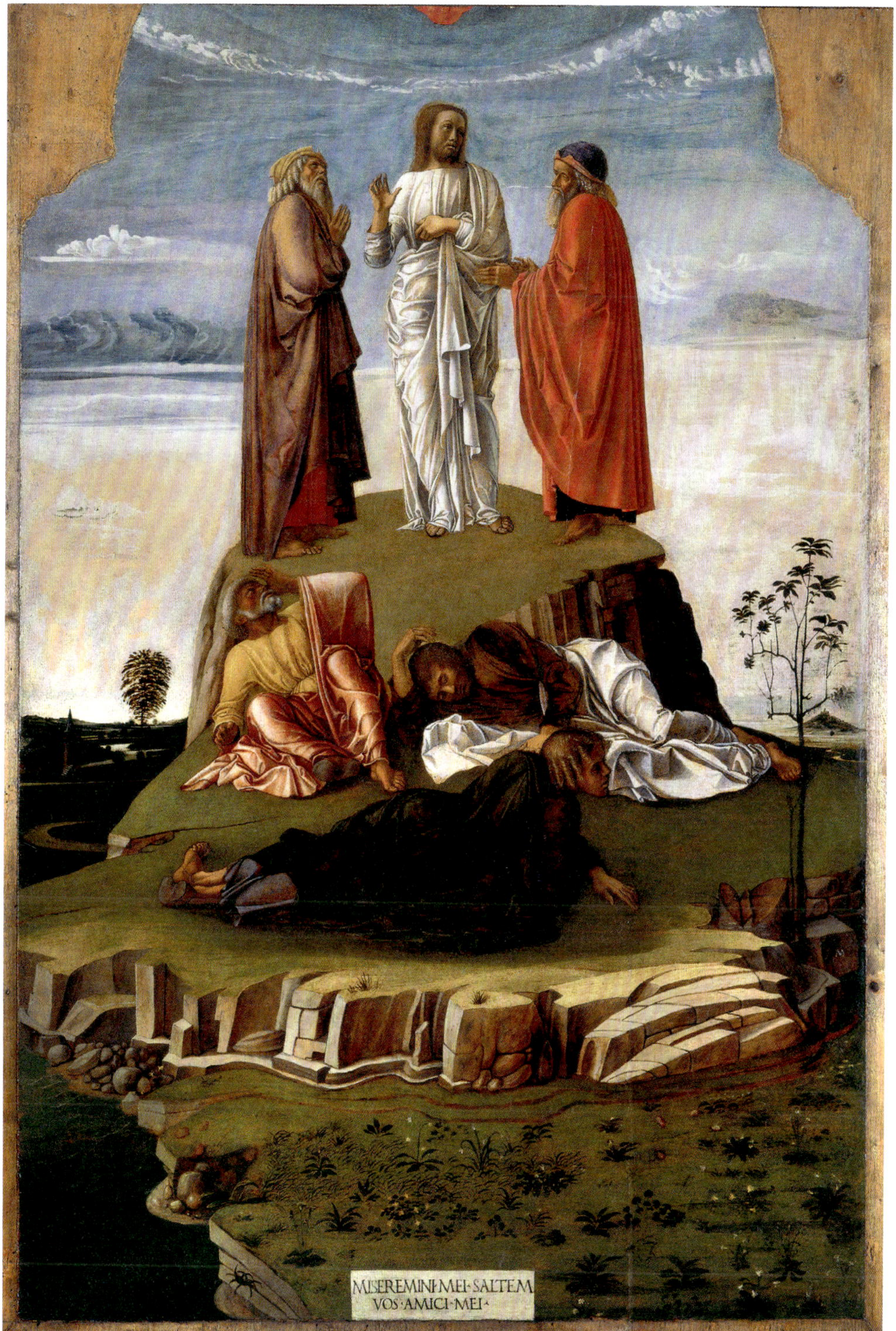

FIGURE 2 Giovanni Bellini, *The Transfiguration of Christ*, ca. 1455. Tempera and oil on panel, 133 × 90.3 cm. Museo Correr, Venice

regional, and international artists. Thus, this study contends that Giovanni's "wide-ranging looking," an often-noted aspect of his mature style, was already present in his artistic approach to his first paintings.

The events of Giovanni Bellini's early years are far messier and more fascinating than currently known. Chapter 1 begins with Jacopo Bellini in 1423, shortly before Giovanni was born. Jacopo was working in the city of Florence as the long-term assistant to Gentile da Fabriano (ca. 1370–1427), perhaps the most famous painter in Italy, when, through an unfortunate incident, Jacopo ran afoul of Florentine law and was sent to prison. Meanwhile in Venice, Jacopo's father, Nicoletto Bellini (d. by 1429), a tinsmith and widower who had recently married a young woman named Franceschina Vendramin (d. after 1424), wrote his last will and testament. The will carefully provided for his new bride and marginalized Jacopo, his only son. Nicoletto would die shortly after, as would, the evidence suggests, Franceschina, but not before she gave birth to Nicoletto's second son, Giovanni Bellini.

Jacopo was released from prison in 1425 and Gentile da Fabriano died in Rome in 1427. Chapter 2 recounts the events leading to the establishment of the Bellini workshop. By 1429, Jacopo had returned to Venice, where he would raise his half-brother Giovanni Bellini as if he were his own son. At about this time, Jacopo married Anna Rinversi (d. 1471), the daughter of a deceased silk broker. Her dowry of 250 ducats helped Jacopo found the Bellini workshop, where Giovanni came to live and would learn the art of painting.

Giovanni grew up in the Venetian parish of San Geminiano, just steps away from Piazza San Marco and its basilica, which provided Giovanni with artistic models for inspiration and later quotation. Chapter 3 explores two aspects of the artist's childhood education. While Giovanni likely received a standard schooling designed for the sons of merchants and tradesmen, his instruction in art was unique. Giovanni would have learned directly from Jacopo, witnessing his early struggles to secure commissions, serving as his assistant, and, presumably, helping with the execution of frescoes and panels in the bustling cities and illustrious courts of the Italian mainland.

New research presents a compelling argument for identifying, for the first time, the *Coronation of the Virgin* (ca. 1441–42, see fig. 25) in the Pinacoteca Nazionale in Ferrara as Giovanni's earliest known painting, executed at about age 15 or 16. The picture, considered in Chapter 4, is a rare example of an adolescent work by an Italian Renaissance master. The Ferrara *Coronation* provides a window onto Giovanni's earliest known artistic approach and new insights into his artistic development.

An examination in Chapter 5 of the predella panels from Jacopo's famous *Annunciation* Altarpiece of 1444 (Church of Sant'Alessandro, Brescia) attributes them to the young Giovanni. The five small panels reveal Giovanni's maturing artistic sensibility, which was very much in development. In his *Birth of the Virgin* predella panel (see fig. 49), Giovanni introduced pathways and avenues through which the eye might wander, which recalls one of the artist's best-known pictorial strategies. The *Visitation* panel (see fig. 56) depicts low-angled sunlight illuminating background trees and mountains, and is therefore Giovanni's earliest known

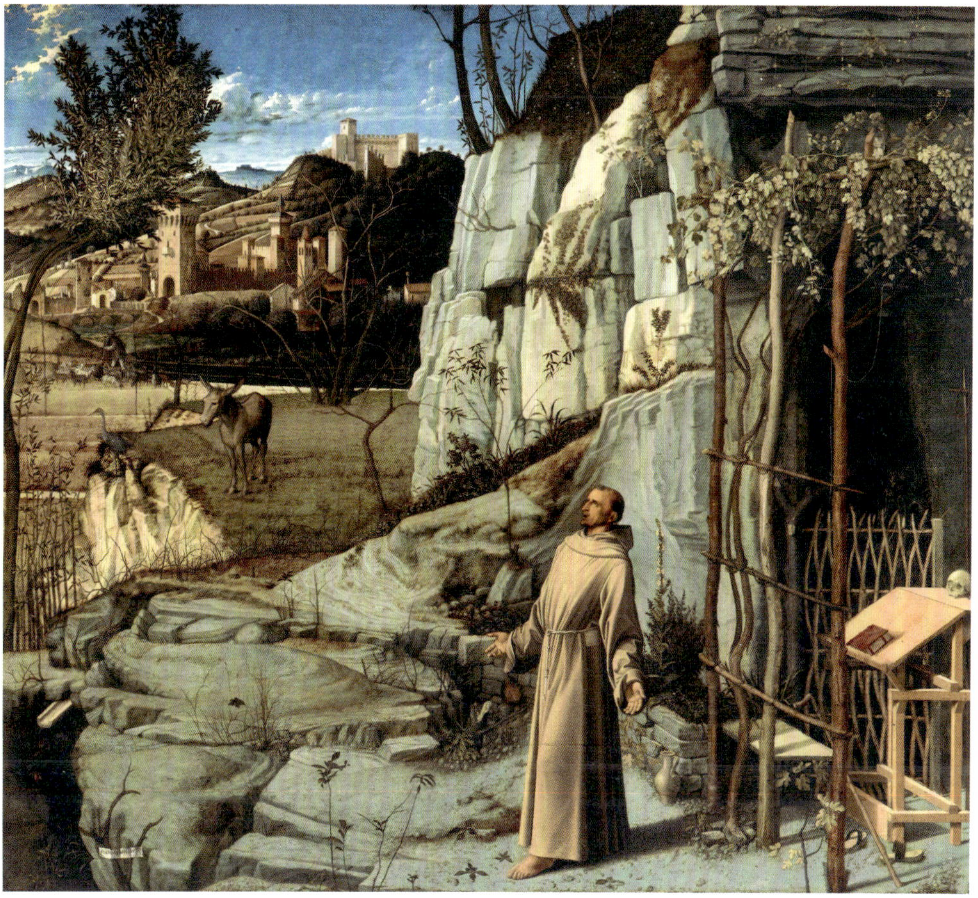

FIGURE 3 Giovanni Bellini, *Saint Francis in the Desert,* ca. 1476–78. Oil on panel, 124.6 × 142 cm. Frick Collection, New York

landscape, a type of painting that he would come to master. These panels, in which Giovanni employed a single light source to model objects and unify the composition, are the earliest known examples of the artist's approach to portraying light.

This biography must also explore the reasons for the long gap between the above works and Giovanni's early independent paintings of the 1450s, a lacuna apparently resulting from Giovanni's position as Jacopo's foremost assistant in the second half of the 1440s. Chapter 6 thus investigates Giovanni's contribution to Jacopo's now-lost decorations for the *albergo* (boardroom) of the prestigious Scuola Grande di San Marco (the Great Confraternity of Saint Mark) in Venice. This commission would help transform the Bellini workshop into the city's leading atelier. And Jacopo's entrepreneurial approach to art would later serve as a model for Giovanni when he would run one of the most successful artist's workshops in fifteenth-century Europe.

In 1450 Giovanni seems to have begun his independent career while occasionally continuing to assist Jacopo. Chapter 7 investigates Giovanni's artistic process in executing the Birmingham *Saint Jerome*, a small masterpiece now in the Barber Institute of Fine Arts that represents the blossoming of several strands in Giovanni's early artistic development. *Saint Jerome* broke radically with medieval conventions to herald the Renaissance in Venice and presage a number of Giovanni's mature masterpieces, including his renowned *Saint Francis in the Desert* (ca. 1476–78, fig. 3). *Saint Jerome* also set the stage in fifteenth-century Venice for a new type of consumer demand: small paintings intended for personal viewing and spiritual meditation, for private use in the home or possibly a monastic setting.

Young Bellini concludes by arguing that the representational strategy most characteristic of Giovanni's early artistic practice was the process he used to integrate the compositions and motifs of other artists into his own paintings. In addition, an examination of the differences between Giovanni's and Jacopo's artistic approaches can assist with the attribution of certain paintings, such as the long-debated Marcello Manuscript illuminations (1453, see figs 93–96). Lastly, a case study of the *Crucifixion with the Virgin and Saint John the Evangelist* (ca. 1457, see fig. 105) demonstrates how Giovanni's youthful process of artistic integration developed into a more mature artistic practice, one aspect of which was selecting and incorporating conceptual elements of vanguard works of art into his paintings, thus allowing Giovanni to position his pictures on the cutting edge of Italian art.

An updated version of the biographical discoveries underpinning *Young Bellini* is presented in Appendix A. The Appendix summarizes how art historians have argued for centuries over Giovanni's birth, and provides a historiographical context for assessing many of the original contributions found in this book. It also discusses the scholarly reactions to this new research. Several of these reactions are critiques based on the hypothesized existence of a so-called "Giovanni Bellini il Vecchio" or "Giovanni Bellini the Elder," supposedly Jacopo Bellini's brother and distinct from Giovanni Bellini, the famous artist. Appendix B (pp. 136–45) examines the step-by-step creation of "Giovanni Bellini il Vecchio" and shows that no documentary evidence supports this figure's existence.

Young Bellini presents a strongly revisionist history of Giovanni Bellini's early life. The chapters unfold chronologically, describing Giovanni's biography and exploring his work and artistic process. The result is a study that expands our vision of one of the most important and beloved artists of the Italian Renaissance.

1 A Tinsmith, a Felon, and an Orphan

Someone was throwing rocks at Gentile da Fabriano's paintings set out to dry in the courtyard.[1] This was in Florence on June 11, 1423.[2] Gentile's workshop, located where the Cinema Odeon stands today, once looked out onto the Piazza delle Cipolle, abutted the now-demolished Church of Santa Maria degli Ughi, and had a rear courtyard opening onto the smaller Piazza Marmor, where his paintings had been laid (fig. 4).[3] Three years earlier Gentile had arrived in the city, with his family and his long-term assistant, Jacopo of Venice, and in that time he had become the leading painter in Florence and perhaps all Italy.[4]

It was a group of local youths hurling stones. The works of art, later described in court documents as having "the utmost importance," would have been executed on panel in tempera paints and oil glazes, and finished with oil-based varnishes that needed to air-dry.[5] They might have included Gentile's altarpiece of the *Madonna and Child, with Saints Lawrence and Julian* (ca. 1423–25, fig. 5), which dates to these years, or his small painting of the *Madonna of Humility* (ca. 1423, figs 6 and 7), the reverse of which features brightly colored fictive marbles that perhaps made an enticing target.[6] Gentile, probably in his mid-fifties at the time, sent his assistant Jacopo out to the courtyard to protect the fragile works.[7]

Jacopo of Venice, as his name appears in the early sources, is with little doubt Jacopo Bellini, the future founder of the Bellini workshop and the father of Venetian Renaissance painting.[8] Some 15 or more years earlier, in the first decade of the fifteenth century, Gentile da Fabriano had arrived in Venice as an itinerant painter, and Jacopo, probably as an adolescent, had become his assistant.[9] Later, when Gentile departed Venice to execute frescoes and panels in other Italian cities and towns, Jacopo apparently had accompanied him, to Foligno in 1411, Brescia in 1414, Fabriano in 1420, and then on to Florence.[10]

By every indication, during these peripatetic years of Jacopo's long assistantship, the young Venetian had grown especially close to the older artist from the Marches. In a period when portraits of non-nobles were nearly nonexistent, Jacopo had painted a portrait of

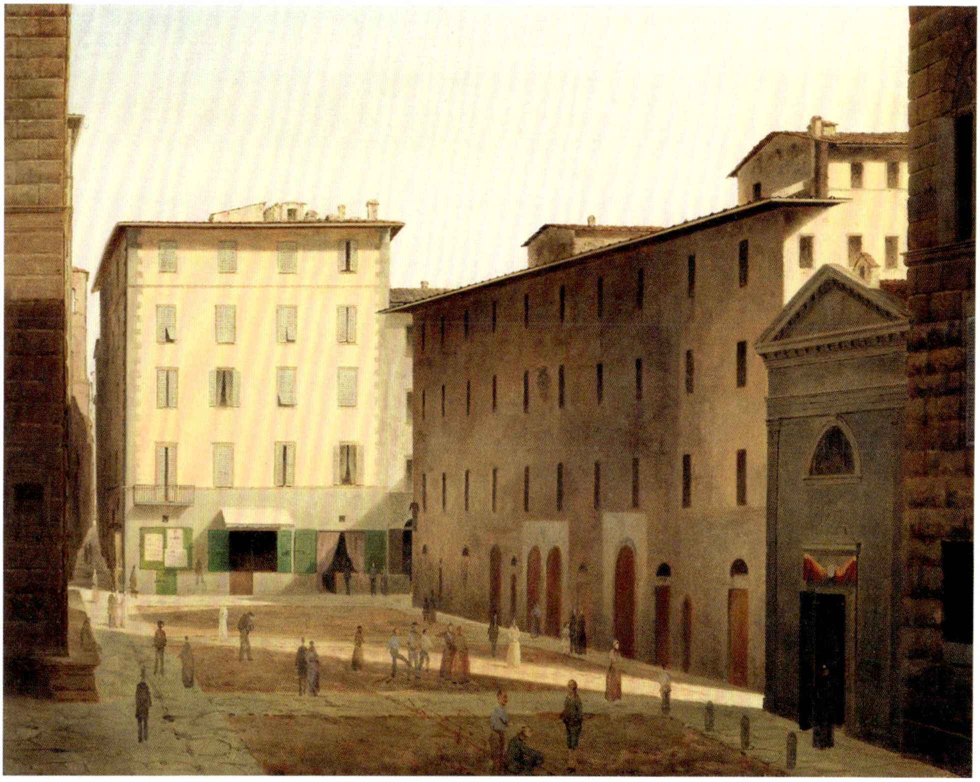

FIGURE 4 Fabio Borbottoni, *View of Piazza delle Cipolle with the Church of Santa Maria degli Ughi*, ca. 1890–95. Oil on canvas, 43 × 56 cm. Palazzo dell'Ente Cassa di Risparmio, Florence. On the far right is the Church of Santa Maria degli Ughi (deconsecrated in 1785, destroyed in the late 19th century), and adjacent to it on the reader's right would have been Gentile da Fabriano's workshop.

Gentile, presumably as a personal keepsake rather than an outside commission; the picture was later owned by the Renaissance poet and scholar Pietro Bembo (1470–1547) but is now lost.[11] Indeed, Jacopo would eventually name his son Gentile, undoubtedly in honor of his late master since Gentile was not a Venetian name.[12] And in 1436, nearly a decade after Gentile had died, Jacopo would execute his now-destroyed *Crucifixion* fresco in Verona Cathedral and inscribe it with a short encomium to Gentile, calling him *praeceptor* (teacher) and an "excellent man."[13] Thus it would seem that Giorgio Vasari was correct in 1550, some 80 years after Jacopo's death, when he wrote that Gentile da Fabriano had been not only Jacopo's master but also "like a loving father to him."[14]

In the courtyard behind Gentile da Fabriano's workshop in Florence, Jacopo, then around 30 years old, approached the troublemakers. He addressed the largest of the group, a certain Bernardo, who appeared to be the leader. "You are acting like a big lout, throwing rocks," Jacopo reportedly said, "being that you are grown like a man."[15] The young Bernardo, apparently shamed in front of his companions, became angry. He began to taunt Jacopo and ridicule him. Jacopo then grew angry. Bernardo challenged Jacopo to a fight. With bare fists

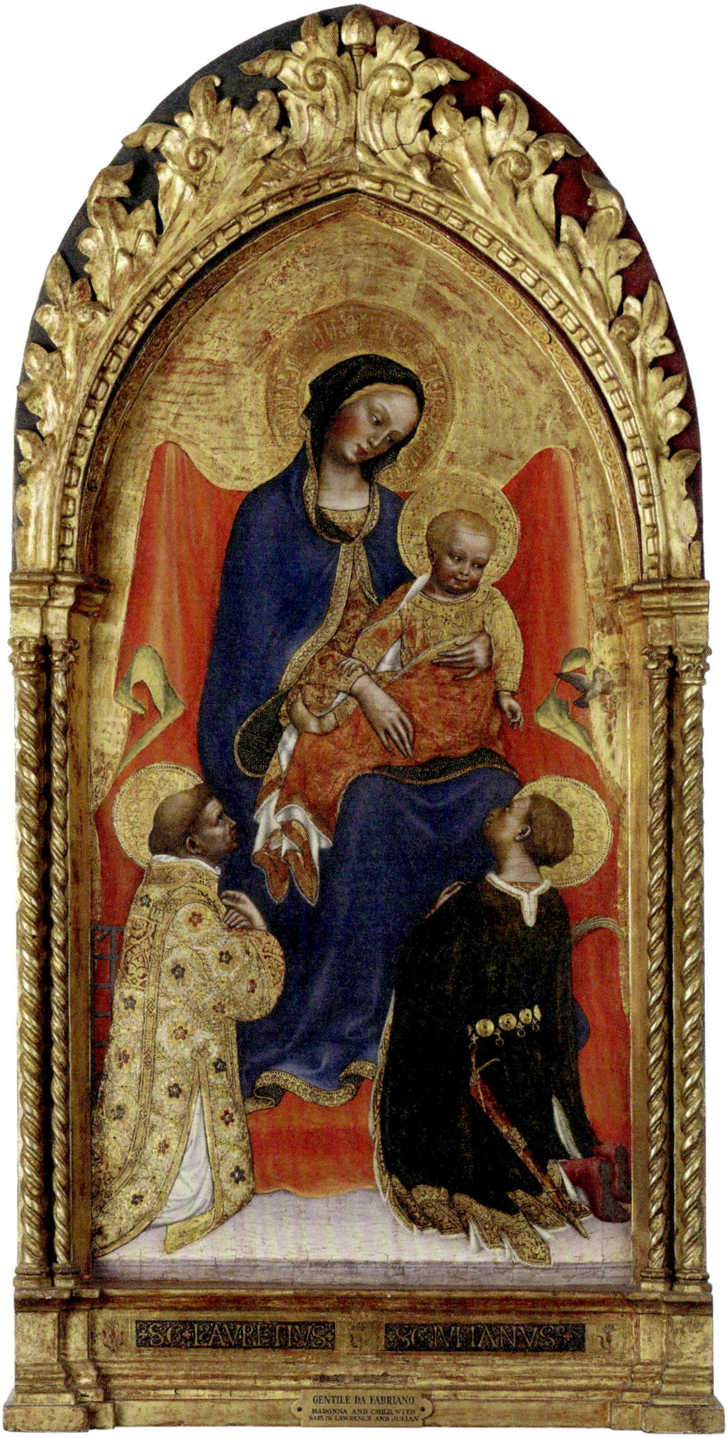

FIGURE 5 Gentile da Fabriano, *The Madonna and Child, with Saints Lawrence and Julian*, ca. 1423–25. Tempera on panel, 90.8 × 47 cm. Frick Collection, New York

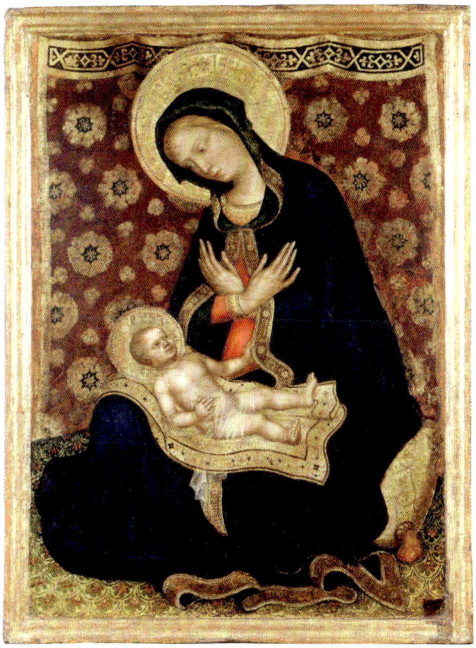

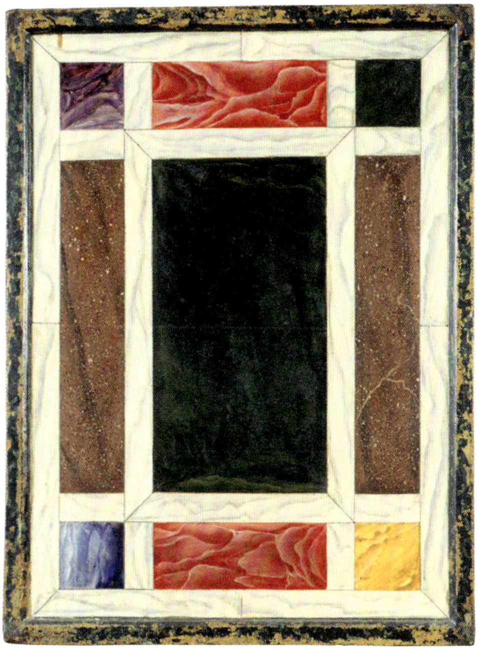

FIGURES 6 & 7 Gentile da Fabriano, *Madonna of Humility* (and reverse view), ca. 1423. Tempera on panel, 56 × 41 cm. Museo Nazionale di San Matteo, Pisa

they approached one another, and exchanged blows, Jacopo evidently not realizing whose son he was fighting.[16]

The winner of the brawl is not recorded, but subsequent events and surviving court documents suggest it was Jacopo. After serving at least 12 years as Gentile's assistant and pupil, Jacopo abruptly fled the artist's employ and the city of Florence. Jacopo probably had learned that young Bernardo came from an influential family of Florentine citizens who had close ties to local justices.[17] In medieval and Renaissance Florence, being verbally shamed and physically beaten, and by a visiting Venetian no less, constituted a public humiliation that could tarnish a family name.[18] To redeem that name, Bernardo's family might commit an act of retribution against Jacopo, potentially a violent one, the threat of which perhaps prompted Jacopo's departure.[19]

Political events that had been set in motion several years earlier offered Jacopo an unusual route of escape. In 1406, Pisa and its shipbuilding yards had fallen to Florentine forces, and in 1421 the Republic of Florence had spent 100,000 gold florins to purchase from Genoa both Livorno and Porto Pisano, among the most important seaports in Italy, and thereby gained access to the Mediterranean via the Ligurian Sea.[20] By rapidly constructing a fleet of state merchant galleys, Florence quickly rose to become a maritime power and a substantial employer of sailors.[21] Whether Jacopo intended to seek favor with the Florentine government, quench his wanderlust by visiting exotic ports of the Mediterranean, or simply slip as far away as possible, in the summer of 1423 Gentile's loyal assistant set sail as a hired seaman, probably destined for the Levant.[22]

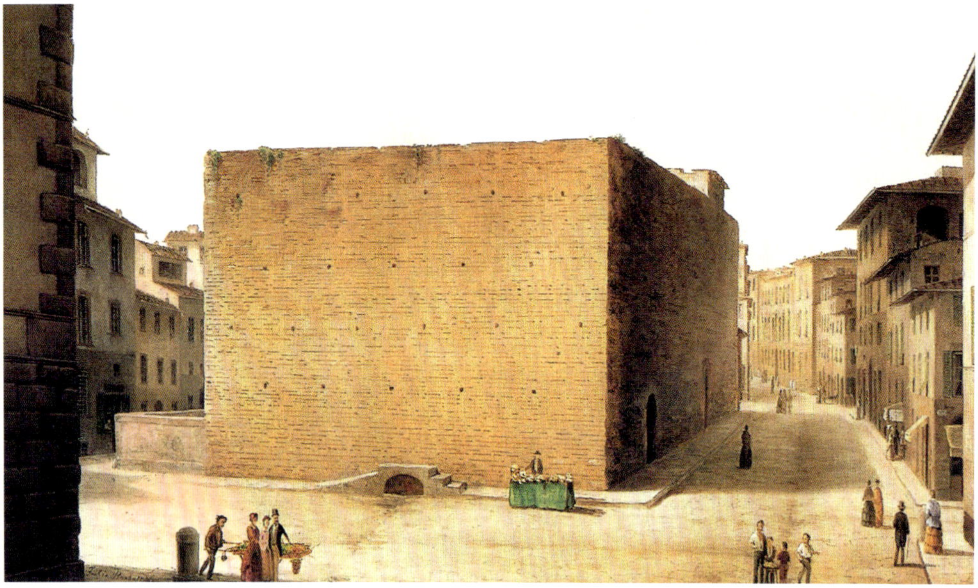

FIGURE 8 Fabio Borbottoni, *Le Stinche Prison Seen from Via Ghibellina*, ca. 1860. Oil on canvas, 43 × 56 cm. Palazzo dell'Ente Cassa di Risparmio, Florence. Giovanni Villani (d. 1348), a well-known chronicler of Florence, Benvenuto Cellini (1500–1571), the famous Florentine sculptor, and Niccolò Machiavelli (1469–1527), the so-called father of modern political science, also served time at Le Stinche prison, once located where the Teatro Verdi stands today.

A short time later, on September 2, 1423, when Jacopo was already at sea, Bernardo's father, Silvestro son of Tommaso, a notary of the Florentine parish of Santa Trinità, officially brought charges against the Venetian.[23] In court with Jacopo absent, Bernardo testified that Jacopo had attacked him with a wooden bat, maliciously and without cause, and had used the bat to bash Bernardo on the left arm, though not hard enough to draw blood.[24] Jacopo and Bernardo's fair fight was thus transformed into an armed assault against a Florentine innocent, a fabrication that would have served to vindicate Bernardo and help expunge his family's name. Judge Romano de Benveduti, a friend of Bernardo's father, proceeded to convict Jacopo *in absentia* and fine him the substantial sum of 450 lire of small florins (a currency specific to Florence), with a penalty of a quarter more if Jacopo neglected to pay the fine within the month.[25]

It would be over a year, however, before Jacopo returned to Florence. When he did, he was arrested. On October 24, 1424, a few days after his merchant ship docked at port, "Jacopo of Venice," the former painting assistant turned galley hand, was captured, informed of his fines, and thrown into Florence's infamous jail, Le Stinche (meaning "crest of a hill").[26] A Florentine court document of 1425 described Jacopo as poor and unable to pay his fines—and indeed, Le Stinche principally incarcerated debtors.[27] Although Jacopo's native city of Venice lay 160 miles to the north, he was a *forestiero* (foreigner) in Florence, rather than a Florentine citizen whose social network of family and friends might support his cause or influence his release.

Jacopo remained confined in jail for weeks and then months.[28] Le Stinche was among the first purpose-built prisons in Europe, an enormous, depressing brick trapezoid without windows or even a kitchen (fig. 8).[29] Meals were provided to each inmate by family and friends, and in their absence by lay friars.[30] Like most prisoners, Jacopo would have lived in a common ward with little space for recreation, virtually no reading materials, and minimal opportunities for any exercise or labor.[31] If Gentile da Fabriano had endeavored to help Jacopo, perhaps by marshaling assistance from Palla Strozzi (1372–1462), the richest man in Florence in 1427 and Gentile's former patron, Gentile's efforts had no noticeable effect.[32] Jacopo could do little but await a new trial. He had strayed far from painting and his circumstances seemed bleak: he was in his early thirties, with little or no money, in a squalid foreign prison serving a sentence he did not deserve, for how long he did not know.

The Tinsmith

In Venice on April 11, 1424, when Jacopo was probably still aboard a merchant galley and before he was arrested, Jacopo's father, Nicoletto Bellini, drew up his last will and testament. To execute and enact the document, he commissioned the notary Lorenzo Buscarino.[33] Notaries in medieval and early modern Venice, as in many localities across Europe, functioned as minor judges who both drafted and assured the legality of testaments, contracts, and other documents for clients ranging from noblemen and men of letters to the illiterate.[34] One of Nicoletto Bellini's main concerns in his newly drawn-up will was to ensure that his son Jacopo would repay him a sizable loan that he had earlier borrowed. The will stated that if Jacopo neglected to repay his father by the time of Nicoletto's death, then the loan, the exact amount of which was unspecified, would be subtracted from Jacopo's inheritance. It is unclear, however, whether this loan was directly related to Jacopo's recent legal troubles.

Jacopo's father was by no means rich. Nicoletto Bellini was a *batistagno* (literally "tin beater"), or tinsmith. He skillfully hammered, soldered, and burnished thin sheets of tin into small household items, such as bowls, mugs, pans, basins, and storage vessels, and he repaired tinware.[35] From at least the last decade of the fourteenth century onward, he lived in the Venetian parish of San Salvador near the Rialto, in Venice's commercial heart, probably on the Calle dei Stagneri (the alleyway of the tinsmiths, fig. 9).[36]

Nicoletto's first wife, Giovannina, or Zanina in Venetian dialect, was Jacopo Bellini's mother. Almost nothing is known about her—neither her place of origin, nor her maiden name, nor her year of death, except that it was before 1424.[37] Nicoletto and Zanina had two children, Elena (d. after 1443) and Jacopo, whose birth order is unknown. Elena would become the mother of Leonardo Bellini (ca. 1424–d. after 1484), a famous miniaturist whom Jacopo would train in the profession.[38] Jacopo himself seems to have been born in ca. 1393, or perhaps a few years earlier, but not much later, because by 1412 he was already documented as Gentile da Fabriano's assistant.[39] At some point, Nicoletto had also adopted a daughter named Menegà (d. after 1424), who would have a daughter named Alixeta (d. after 1424), but the

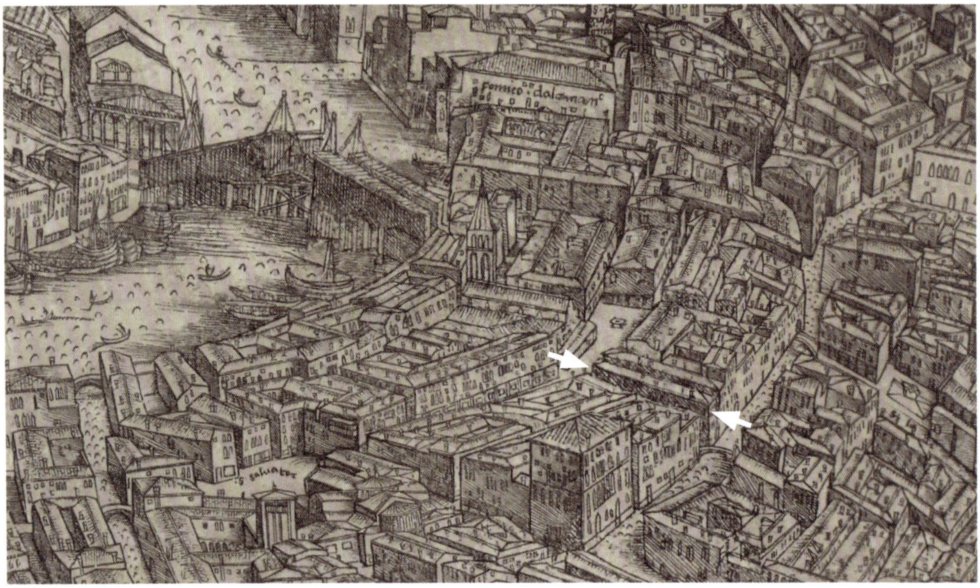

FIGURE 9 Jacopo de' Barbari, *View of Venice* (detail of San Salvador and Rialto area), 1500. Woodcut print, 132.7 × 277.5 cm. Minneapolis Institute of the Arts. Arrows indicate the Calle dei Stagneri, or "alleyway of the tinsmiths," probable home to Nicoletto Bellini.

circumstances of the adoption, as well as what became of Menega and Alixeta, are unknown.[40]

Like many Venetians in the late Middle Ages, Nicoletto Bellini had formed strong ties to his local parish church, the Church of San Salvador.[41] Indeed, it was there that the guild of tinsmiths, to which Nicoletto belonged by law, maintained an altar dedicated to the guild's patron saint, John the Evangelist.[42] In his will, Nicoletto also bequeathed a ducat each to two *scuole piccole* (small confraternities) that met in San Salvador: the Scuola di San Leonardo (Confraternity of Saint Leonard), which was concerned with the welfare of prisoners, and the Scuola di San Teodoro (Confraternity of Saint Theodore), which would become a *scuola grande* in 1552.[43] San Salvador is presumably where Nicoletto's children were baptized, but this cannot be confirmed because the church did not keep baptism records before 1564.[44]

Unusually for a tinsmith, and perhaps indicative of the social aspirations Nicoletto modeled in his household, in ca. 1390 he was admitted into an exclusive lay confraternity, called the Scuola di Santa Maria della Valverde and better known as the Scuola di Santa Maria della Misericordia (Confraternity of the Madonna of Mercy), which was run by upwardly mobile non-noble Venetians.[45] Founded in 1261, the *scuola* functioned by the turn of the fifteenth century as a philanthropic institution that participated in various prominent religious ceremonies and civic processions.[46] It was one of four prosperous *scuole dei battuti* (schools of the beaten, because of earlier rituals of self-flagellation) that came to be known as *scuole grandi* (great confraternities), each with an average membership of between 500 and 600, and at times more.[47] The *scuole grandi* would come to play a central role in the lives of the Bellini family of artists, not least by supplying them with numerous important commissions.

While the Scuola della Misericordia itself was elite, Nicoletto was not among its elite members. From 1393 to 1394, he served as its *nonzolo*, which was a housekeeper and errand boy who was required to perform all requested tasks for the managerial board (*banca*) or be expelled from the post and perhaps the confraternity itself.[48] It was a job for the poorest members. Still, membership in the prestigious institution would have provided Nicoletto with networking opportunities, the promise of a well-attended funeral, and the possibility of various social services, including healthcare, poor relief, and housing assistance, if needed.[49] As the years progressed, Nicoletto never ascended to a higher position within the *scuola* and was never elected to the managerial board's lowest post of *degano* (deacon).[50] As a tinsmith, he might have reached a glass ceiling—or perhaps he was just not well liked.

Nevertheless, over the course of his life, Nicoletto accumulated a comfortable level of wealth, as indicated by the various legacies he bequeathed in his will.[51] For instance, Nicoletto left 10 ducats toward the dowry of his granddaughter Caterina (d. after 1424), and the inheritances of Elena and Jacopo included a payment of 24 ducats each (Jacopo's share being reduced by his outstanding loan if not repaid).[52] However, this sum of 48 ducats apparently equaled or approximated the dowry brought into the marriage by Jacopo and Elena's deceased mother, Zanina, and was thus legally owed to her biological children.[53]

By the early 1420s, Nicoletto's household in San Salvador had largely dispersed. His wife, Zanina, had died. His daughter, Elena, had married an oarmaker named Paolo (d. by 1443) and begun a family of her own, which included her daughter, Caterina, and son, the future miniaturist Leonardo.[54] And Nicoletto's own son, Jacopo, who according to Venetian custom would have been expected to follow Nicoletto into the family business of tinsmithing, had chosen instead to leave Venice with the itinerant artist Gentile da Fabriano, who was recorded in the city by 1408.[55] With his wife deceased, his daughter married off, and his son far from home, Nicoletto decided to remarry.

A New Family

Franceschina Vendramin was probably more than 20 years younger than Nicoletto Bellini when, sometime before the spring of 1424, she became his second wife.[56] Franceschina's name appears only in her husband Nicoletto's will and in no other known document or source.[57] Her near absence from the historical record, however, is not surprising: most non-nobles of the Middle Ages and Renaissance led lives that went largely unrecorded, and a dowry receipt, tax record, or last will and testament might be the sole surviving evidence of their existence.

Franceschina had a younger sister named Samaritana (d. after 1509), who drew up a will in 1509 when she was probably in her nineties.[58] Franceschina also had a brother, Giovanni Vendramin (d. by 1509), who at some point had a daughter named Marina (d. after 1509).[59] These members of the Vendramin family—Franceschina, Samaritana, Giovanni, and Marina—are not identified as patricians in any existing documents. Nor are they listed among the well-known branch of the Vendramin family who became ennobled for their patriotic actions during Venice's war of Chioggia against the Genoese (1378–81).[60] Thus, Franceschina, even with her distinguished Vendramin surname, was almost certainly a non-noble, as common sense would dictate, since a young Venetian noblewoman was unlikely to marry an old tinsmith.[61]

Nevertheless, Franceschina must have been dear to her husband Nicoletto, if the elaborate care he took in planning for her future welfare is any indication. In the event of his death, Nicoletto declared in his will, Franceschina was "to receive the major share."[62] He named four executors to his estate: Franceschina; Paolo, his daughter Elena's husband; Pietro Musolino, presumably a friend; and "the painter Jacopo Bellini," his only son at the time.[63] If any executor were to "vexatiously trouble" Franceschina, Nicoletto's will stated that she would be made "the sole executor irrespective of the stage of the transaction."[64] And if Nicoletto's son Jacopo or daughter Elena tried to sue Nicoletto's estate to recover the dowry of their deceased mother, Zanina, they would be cut off from all inheritance left to them by Nicoletto.[65] Nicoletto's foremost concerns thus appear to have been twofold—to ensure that the loan earlier extended to Jacopo would, if not repaid, be deducted from Jacopo's inheritance, and that Franceschina would receive her full legacy without interference.

Giovanni Bellini was born to Franceschina and Nicoletto sometime after Nicoletto's will of April 11, 1424, and almost certainly before September 13, 1426.[66] The reason for the former date is that legitimate sons legally had to be identified in wills, even if a father's intention was to disinherit them.[67] Since Giovanni was not named in Nicoletto's 1424 will, he must not yet have been born. The reason for placing Giovanni Bellini's birth before September 13, 1426, is that 14 years later, on September 13, 1440, Giovanni agreed independently, meaning without the countersignature of magistrates, to a document called a *divisio,* or a charter of division, for which action he legally had to be at least 12, as Venetian law clearly stated, and almost certainly had to be at least 14, as indicated by another Venetian law declaring the male age of majority to be 14.[68] This range of dates for Giovanni's birth—after April 11, 1424, and before September 13, 1426—accords closely with the earliest written identification of Giovanni's birth year by Giorgio Vasari. In his *Lives of the Artists* (1550) he stated that Giovanni, who died on November 28 or the morning of November 29 in 1516, had died at the age of 90; thus Vasari located the artist's birth between November 28, 1425, and November 29, 1426.[69]

The above-mentioned 1440 *divisio* also confirms that Giovanni was legitimately born. The *divisio* states that it was enacted by "Giovanni Bellini and Jacopo Bellini, brothers and sons of the deceased ser Nicolò [Nicoletto]"—indeed, the two were half-brothers, separated in age by over 30 years.[70] When a father died in fifteenth-century Venice, his legitimate sons automatically entered into a fraternal partnership that collectively owned their father's estate. Illegitimate sons had no such rights of inheritance and did not enter into fraternal partnerships.[71] Therefore, only legitimate sons might have need of a *divisio* to dissolve their fraternal partnership (the Bellini *divisio* is further discussed in Chapters 2 and 3).

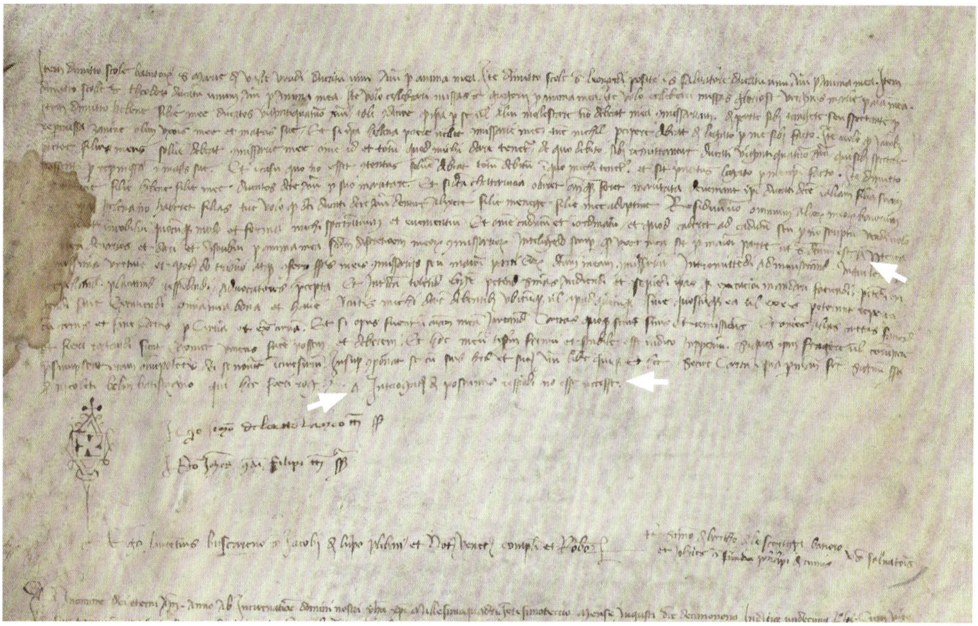

FIGURE 10 Will of Nicoletto Bellini (detail), April 11, 1424. Archivio di Stato di Venezia, Venice. The insertion point in the main document text refers to the usual position of the clause added at the end, which states that Nicoletto expected no further children to be born (*Interogatus de postumis respondit non esse necesse*).

Some evidence suggests that Giovanni Bellini was born after the death of his father, Nicoletto. The primary clue is a short revision made to Nicoletto Bellini's will by the notary Buscarino. At some point after writing the will's main text, Buscarino appended the statement that Nicoletto, when asked about the possibility of having posthumous children, responded that it was not necessary, meaning that no children were expected (fig. 10).[72] Buscarino added an insertion mark in the main text of the will to identify the place where this statement would conventionally have appeared and should initially have been written.

Buscarino's emendation needs to be understood in the context of fifteenth-century Venetian law, which granted legitimate children specific and nearly inalienable rights of inheritance over their father's property. These rights had to be taken into account in their father's will, even if a father's intention was to disinherit his child. If a will disregarded or overlooked these rights, it would be voided.[73] Thus, the birth of a legitimate child would annul a father's will, unless the will had specifically made provisions for the child's birth or was later modified by a codicil to include the child.[74] Venetian notaries were usually careful to ask testators, when pertinent, about the possibility of *postumi*, that is, children who might be born to a pregnant mother after the father's death, because if proper provisions had not been made, the father's last will would become a *testamentum ruptum*, or a voided testament.[75]

In Nicoletto Bellini's only known will, however, Buscarino did not initially record whether Nicoletto had anticipated the birth of another child. A notary typically visited a testator (who might be on his or her deathbed) at the testator's home, wrote notes to document the testator's wishes, and then used those notes to draw up a final will that would remain in the notary's register for safekeeping. Nicoletto's will stated that his motives for drawing it up were to put his affairs in order and not die intestate, rather than that he was ill or his body infirm, or that death seemed imminent, reasons that were perhaps more likely to prompt a notary to inquire about the possibility of a posthumous child. In any event, Buscarino did not initially include in the main text of Nicoletto's will whether Nicoletto expected the birth of another child.[76]

At some later point, however, Buscarino made an addition to Nicoletto's will that stated it was not necessary to plan for a posthumous child, meaning that no child was expected. This short addition, however, was curiously prophetic. Because months later, Giovanni would indeed be born and his birth would annul his father's will since it was not provided for therein. Thus, Nicoletto appears to have died intestate. The 1440 *divisio* between his two legitimate sons, Giovanni and Jacopo, also suggests that Nicoletto died intestate, because their *fraterna* had automatically been formed upon Nicoletto's death to control their father's assets, rather than those assets having been distributed according to the provisions of Nicoletto's will, which presumably had been voided.

The question, then, is: How did Buscarino come to write this uncannily predictive emendation to Nicoletto's will? Was it pure coincidence that the only addition to the will was a short statement preempting a future event that would indeed happen? Perhaps the most plausible answer is that the later addition to the will was not curiously prescient at all; rather, Buscarino possibly returned to emend the will *after* Giovanni Bellini's birth, and thus his emendation was a response to the birth itself. In this scenario, Buscarino would have realized his mistake—of neglecting to ask Nicoletto whether a child was to be expected—only after Nicoletto had died and Giovanni had been born posthumously. Buscarino would then have returned to the will to "correct" it. For Buscarino, adding the statement that "no posthumous children are expected" would not only have covered up his earlier error, but would also, perhaps, have absolved him from possible censure by a judge, because Nicoletto, despite having commissioned Buscarino to draw up his will, and despite Nicoletto's own specified wishes to the contrary, nonetheless appears to have died intestate. Moreover, had Nicoletto been alive when Giovanni was born, he could have made a new will or attached a codicil to the old one, assuming he was in good enough health and remembered to do so. Furthermore, Nicoletto's 1424 will is the last known document in which Nicoletto was recorded as being alive. In a document of July 23, 1429, he is described as already deceased, though it does not state for how long.[77] Thus, it seems quite possible that Giovanni, born between the summer of 1424 and September 13, 1426, was born posthumously, that is, after the death of his father, Nicoletto.

Albeit scant, the evidence suggests that Franceschina also died when Giovanni was very young, perhaps even during his birth.[78] First, she disappears from all known recorded history, which by itself, as already mentioned, was not uncommon for the period. Second, in

1440, Giovanni was recorded as living in the Venetian parish of San Geminiano, presumably with his half-brother, Jacopo Bellini, and not in San Salvador, where his parents Nicoletto and Franceschina had lived.[79] Finally, Giovanni and his family entirely accepted his communal (rather than biological) identity as Jacopo Bellini's son, which certainly would not have occurred had Franceschina lived to raise Giovanni.[80]

As either a baby or boy, then, Giovanni apparently became an orphan. Many decades later and toward the end of his long life, he would lose his wife and his only child to illness, and he would die without close family.[81] We now know that Giovanni Bellini's earliest years were also full of loss, and the question, which perhaps had no clear answer at the time, was: Who would step forward to raise the child?

2 The Bellini Family Workshop

In Florence, Jacopo Bellini remained in prison. Winter passed and spring arrived with the new year of 1425, which the Florentines celebrated on March 25 as the Feast of the Annunciation of the Virgin.[1] Then on Easter Sunday, April 8, Jacopo was escorted out of Le Stinche. Incarcerated for nearly six months, he exited bareheaded and carrying a torch. He found himself in a penitential procession, with trumpets blaring before him, marching alongside other inmates toward the Baptistery of San Giovanni across from Florence's cathedral.[2]

A few months earlier, in a notarized agreement dated November 28, 1424, Jacopo had reconciled with young Bernardo.[3] Jacopo admitted to wrongdoing and consented to pay Bernardo 25 florins of gold, an enormous sum for a painter's assistant who might earn only 12 or 15 ducats a year. (The gold florin weighed slightly less than the Venetian ducat.)[4] Bernardo, in turn, agreed to forgive his grievance against Jacopo in perpetuity.

Yet Jacopo was still not a free man. There remained the large fines he owed to Florence—the 450 lire of small florins and a quarter more. For over a century, however, Le Stinche had struggled with overcrowding. Numerous debtors like Jacopo were too poor to pay their fines and became a burden on the state. Thus, a statute of 1322 declared that all prisoners who had committed minor infractions and had subsequently made amends with their accusers were eligible, after serving a sentence of six months, to be released from their debts and prison.[5] Those who had successfully petitioned the Signoria of Florence were required, on either Christmas, Easter, or the feast day of Florence's patron saint, Saint John the Baptist (June 24), to process in line toward Florence's Baptistery of San Giovanni as part of a final act of penance before being set free.[6]

Between Jacopo's release on Easter Sunday, 1425, and early 1429, his whereabouts are not recorded. Perhaps he returned to work for Gentile da Fabriano, who was in Florence finishing a polyptych for a member of the Quaratesi family (figs 11–13).[7] Gentile would install the work in May 1425, on the high altar of San Niccolò sopr'Arno, which is a brisk ten-minute walk across the Ponte Vecchio from the baptistery of San Giovanni, where Jacopo was released.[8]

If Jacopo continued to assist Gentile, he would likely have accompanied the artist to Siena in the summer of 1425 to help execute a now-destroyed polyptych, the *Virgin and Child with Saints John the Baptist, Peter, Paul, and Christopher*, for the Sienese notaries' guild.[9] In August 1425, he might have traveled with Gentile to the small city of Orvieto in Umbria to assist with a fresco of the *Virgin and Child* in the north aisle of the cathedral, and later returned with Gentile to Siena to finish the polyptych for the notaries' guild.[10] Then, together, they might have headed to Rome. By January 1427, Gentile was working on a fresco cycle commissioned by Pope Martin V (1369–1431) for the Basilica of San Giovanni in Laterano.[11] It was in Rome, sometime between August 2 and October 14, 1427, that Gentile da Fabriano died.[12] He left no will, and his niece was named his heir.[13] Both Gentile's daughter, who was baptized in Brescia in 1416, and Gentile's wife, if indeed he had one (for there is no mention of her in extant documents), appear to have predeceased him.[14]

At some point during these years, Jacopo would likely have received word that his father Nicoletto had died. He must also have learned of the birth of his half-brother Giovanni and perhaps of the death of Giovanni's mother. Upon receiving this news, either while still in jail or not long after his release, Jacopo had several compelling reasons to leave Gentile's employ—if that is indeed what happened—and return to Venice.

One reason was the matter of Jacopo's inheritance. Described as "very poor" in the Florentine court document releasing him from prison, Jacopo now stood to inherit a portion of his father's patrimony—a larger amount, evidently, than his father had intended, given that Nicoletto had apparently died intestate.[15] As mentioned in Chapter 1, when the *paterfamilias* or male head of a Venetian household died, his legitimate sons (unless already emancipated) automatically formed a *fraterna compagnia* or fraternal partnership that owned the entirety of their father's estate, unless the father had willed it otherwise.[16] Each son possessed an equal share of the partnership.[17] The idea behind the *fraterna* was to keep intact family businesses, which were the backbone of Venice's economy and might otherwise break up upon the patriarch's death. Thus, after Nicoletto died, Jacopo and Giovanni Bellini were placed together in a fraternal partnership, bonded both in blood and in business.

Another reason for Jacopo to return to Venice was that, upon the death of his father, he finally became emancipated, a legal status that enabled him to establish his own workshop. In early Renaissance Venice, and in certain other territories whose legal system was based on Roman law, emancipation from one's father did not occur at a specific age, but when a father died or executed a charter of emancipation (*carta emancipationis*) to free one or more of his sons.[18] Hence, a man might be 60 years old and remain unemancipated.[19] We can be sure that Nicoletto had not previously emancipated Jacopo, because emancipated sons were excluded from fraternal partnerships.[20]

After Nicoletto died, Jacopo became a *homo sui iuris*, in possession of full legal rights, and a *paterfamilias* or patriarch of his own family under the law.[21] Prior to his emancipation,

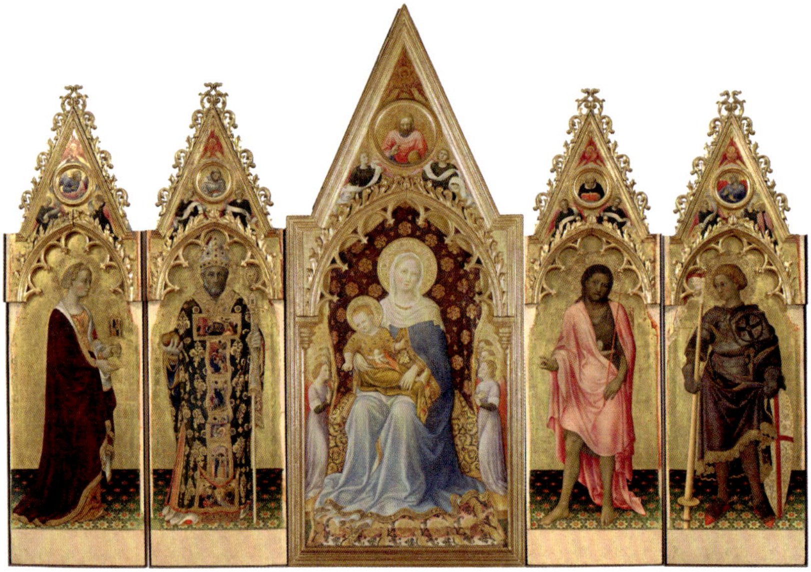

FIGURE 11 Reconstruction of Gentile da Fabriano's now dispersed Quaratesi Altarpiece, 1425. Tempera on panel. Left compartments: *Mary Magdalene,* and *Saint Nicholas of Bari*; right compartments: *Saint John the Baptist,* and *Saint George,* each 197 × 57 cm (including frame). Galleria degli Uffizi, Florence. Central panel: *The Virgin and Child,* 220.5 × 85 cm (including frame). National Gallery, London (on loan from her Majesty the Queen)

had Jacopo desired to marry or establish a workshop in Venice, he would have required Nicoletto's approval at every step, since unemancipated sons could not legally enter into contracts without their father's consent.[22] The sculptor Andrea Riccio (1470–1532), for instance, labored unemancipated for many years in a Paduan workshop overseen by his father, Ambrogio, a goldsmith.[23] Of course, father and son had to be on reasonably good terms and agree to the expensive endeavor of establishing a new workshop, which might not have been the case with Nicoletto and Jacopo. In any event, Nicoletto's death empowered Jacopo to start his own family, sign his own contracts, and found his own business, which as a native-born Venetian citizen (*cittadino originario*) he now had every legal right to do.[24]

Indeed, if Jacopo's plan had been to return to Venice and establish an artist's workshop, then he probably also needed to marry. Jacopo's inheritance would contribute toward running his household, but a good marriage—meaning, in this context, a marriage in which the wife brought a sizeable dowry—would provide Jacopo with additional capital for establishing a workshop and nurturing a business through the lean years that it could take to succeed.[25] In Renaissance Venice, the dowry—in general terms, a daughter's portion of her father's patrimony—theoretically always remained hers. In marriage, it became the wife's share of her husband's estate that might be returned to her if the husband died or if there was a separation.[26] Dowries enabled many and perhaps most men in medieval and Renaissance Venice to start businesses and families, endeavors that were otherwise frequently cost-prohibitive.[27] Marriage at this juncture was a sensible strategy for Jacopo, for it would mean not only receiving a dowry, but also having a wife to care for his half-brother, the orphaned Giovanni.

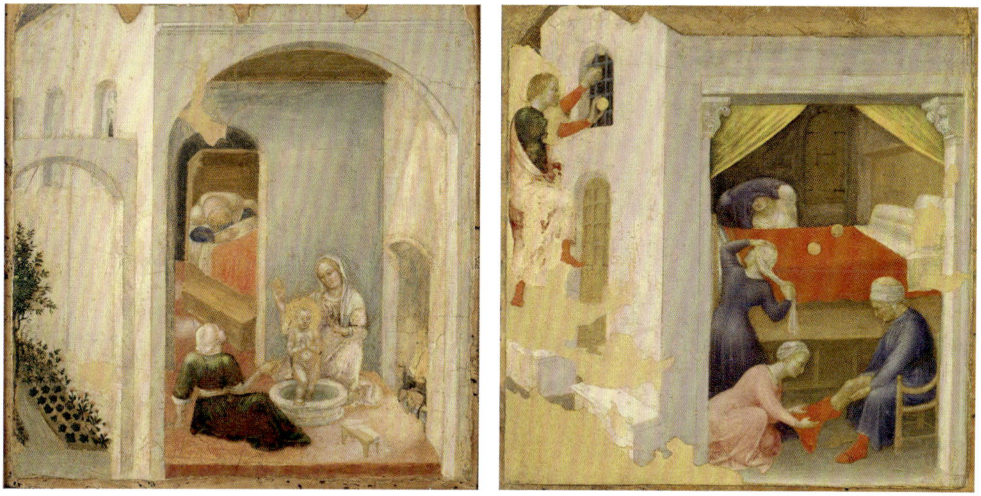

FIGURES 12 & 13 Gentile da Fabriano, *The Birth of Saint Nicholas* (*left*) and *The Gift of Saint Nicholas* (*right*) 1425. Both tempera on panel, 30 × 62 cm. From *The Stories of Saint Nicholas of Bari* predella of the Quaratesi Altarpiece (see fig. 11), Pinacoteca Vaticana, Rome. These panels are loosely comparable to the *Birth of Virgin* predella of the Brescia Altarpiece (see fig. 49).

The Bellini in 1429

The will of Jacopo Bellini's only recorded wife, Anna Rinversi, drawn up on February 6, 1429, a few years after Giovanni's birth, offers us a hazy snapshot of the Bellini family just prior to the end of the decade.[28] The will indicates that Jacopo did indeed return to Venice and that he married Anna, the daughter of a deceased Venetian silk broker (*sanser*) named Branca Rinversi (d. before 1429), whose father was from Lucca.[29] As an adolescent, Jacopo might have met the Rinversi family in Venice as early as ca. 1408, perhaps while he was assisting Gentile da Fabriano on paintings for two wealthy non-noble Lucchese families, also in the silk industry, named the Amadi and the Sandei.[30] By 1429, Jacopo had received the dowry Anna brought to their union, a sizable amount totaling 250 ducats, which was apparently enough for Jacopo to establish the Bellini workshop.[31]

Anna had drawn up her will in early 1429 because she was pregnant. Death during childbirth was so prevalent in fifteenth-century Venice that women customarily drew up their will during their first pregnancy specifically to bequeath their dowry should they not survive the perils of labor.[32] Anna would eventually give birth to four children that we know of: Gentile, Nicolosia, Nicolò, and Leonello (whose existence can be determined by his dowry receipt from 1466, published in this book for the first time, fig. 14).[33] The children's birth order is unknown, but it seems likely that Leonello—probably named after Leonello d'Este (1407–1450), the eventual Marchese of Ferrara, whom Jacopo would visit in ca. 1440–41—was born during or after that sojourn.[34]

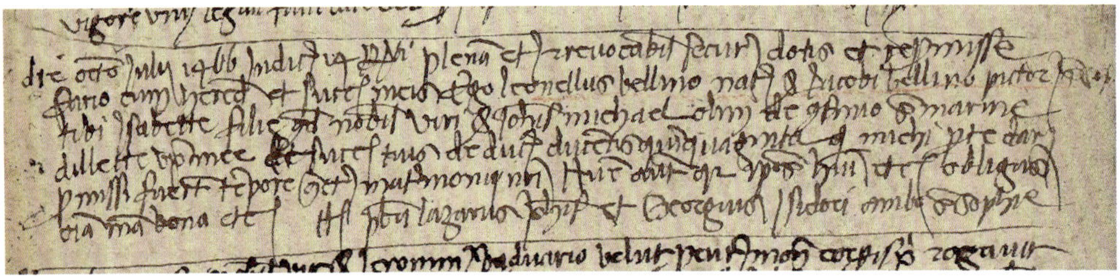

FIGURE 14 Leonello Bellini's dowry receipt, July 8, 1466. Archivio di Stato di Venezia, Venice. This previously unpublished document reveals a new member of the Bellini family, "Leonello Bellini son of ser Jacopo Bellini, painter."

In February 1429, there were seemingly only three members of the Bellini household: Jacopo, the pregnant Anna, and the child Giovanni, then no older than age four. They lived in the Venetian parish of San Geminiano, steps away from the Basilica of San Marco (fig. 15). Until Giovanni came of age, Jacopo would legally control their fraternal partnership and owe to it the money he had borrowed from his father, Nicoletto, against his inheritance.[35] Moreover, it is likely that Jacopo was made Giovanni's guardian (*tutore*), as Jacopo was seemingly the best candidate and perhaps the only viable one in the Bellini family, being as he was in the prime of his life, trained to operate a painter's workshop, and recently married with funds for supporting a household.[36]

Giovanni also maintained relations with his biological mother's side of the family. Through them, it appears, he would eventually meet his future wife, Ginevra Bocheta (d. ca. 1489), whom he probably married in the late 1450s or early 1460s.[37] Giovanni's maternal aunt, Samaritana, was married to Giobbe Dominici (d. by 1462), a merchant trader in Constantinople.[38] Giobbe's mother was Lucia Bocheta (d. after 1457), who lived in the parish of San Luca and referred to herself as a noblewoman in her will of 1457.[39] I would speculate that Lucia's brother, Alvise, was the father of Giovanni Bellini's wife, Ginevra.[40] This biological link has yet to be proven, however, but if it is indeed the case, then Giobbe Dominici and Ginevra Bocheta would have been first cousins, and it would thus suggest that Giovanni met his wife, Ginevra, through his uncle Giobbe.[41] Sadly for Samaritana, her husband Giobbe apparently died in 1459, and his and Samaritana's only son, also named Giovanni, died in an Ottoman prison in 1463.[42] Giobbe and Samaritana also had a daughter, Lucrezia, who must have died prior to Samaritana's will of 1509, because it does not mention a daughter.[43] At some point after her husband's and her son's deaths, it seems that Samaritana's nephew, Giovanni Bellini, took her in, and he must have continued to care for her, because she declared in her will that Giovanni "with love and kindness, treated me, always, as a mother."[44]

It was therefore only through tragedy and luck, along with a series of contingent and accidental events, that Giovanni Bellini was set on the path to becoming the most celebrated painter of early Renaissance Venice. Had his father Nicoletto lived, Giovanni would likely have trained as a tinsmith. Had his mother Franceschina lived, she would have raised him,

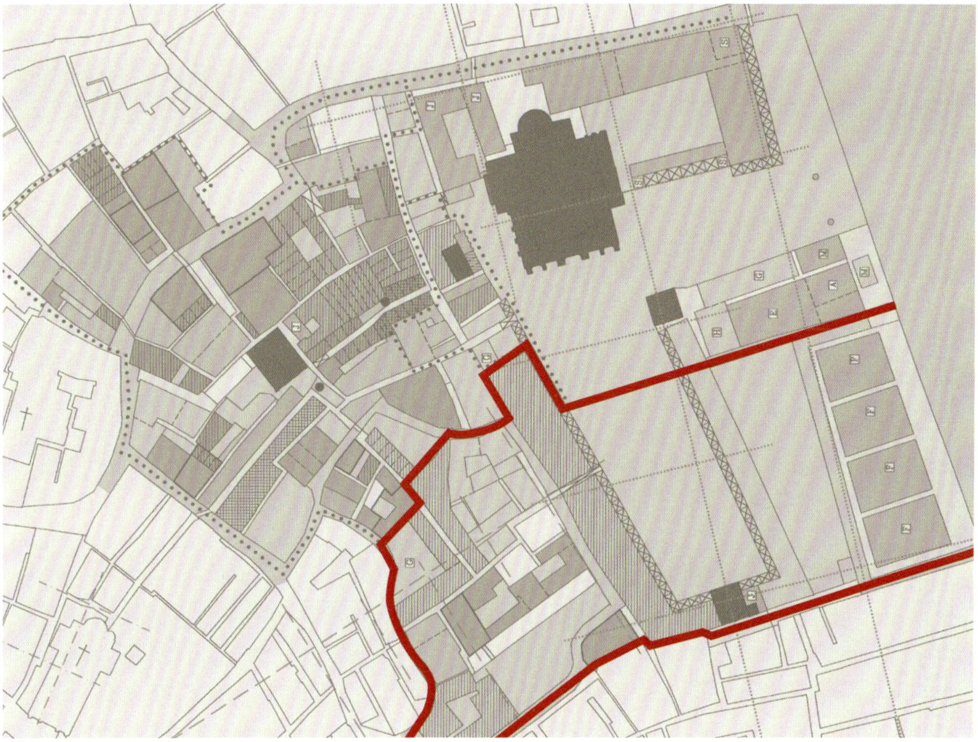

FIGURE 15 Map showing the parish of San Geminiano (outlined area) in the period 1300–60, from Wladimiro Dorigo, *Venezia romanica. La formazione della città medioevale fino all'età gotica,* Istituto Veneto di Scienze Lettere ed Arti, Venice, 2003. Giovanni Bellini grew up in the parish of San Geminiano, steps away from the Basilica of San Marco and the Ducal Palace.

and his pathway to art would have been far from certain. The death of both of his parents, however, led Giovanni to his half-brother Jacopo, who would care for Giovanni, raise him as a son, and teach him "with all diligence," as Vasari wrote, "the principles of design" and the art of painting.[45] Jacopo would come to call Giovanni his son, and Giovanni would come to describe himself as Jacopo's son. Thus it was as Jacopo Bellini's son that the artist became known, in Venice and throughout Italy. Contemporary writers and biographers such as the diarist Marin Sanudo (1466–1536) and Giorgio Vasari were evidently unaware of the two artists' biological relationship.[46] Written history has therefore described Jacopo and Giovanni as father and son. In the eyes of the law, however, they were not: Giovanni was neither legally bound to Jacopo, nor entitled to an inheritance from him, nor in need of emancipation from him. Yet in the perception of Venetian society and in the lived experience of Jacopo and Giovanni, the relationship between the two appears to have been nearly indistinguishable from that of father and son.

3 Letters, Numbers, and Art

Venice nurtured Giovanni Bellini with a unique visual aesthetic. The city floats on the Upper Adriatic and extends across some hundred small islands connected by bridges and linked by canals. When natural light illuminates Venice and reflects on the undulating seawater coursing through it, its building façades and paved streets, or *calli*, become iridescent, gleaming at dawn, glimmering at dusk, and sparkling in moonlight, with colors that are more opalescent in summer and muted in winter (figs 16 and 17).[1] To a perceptive child with an artistic mind, the floating metropolis would provide an expansive education in the variable effects of light. It can hardly be a coincidence that Giovanni Bellini, born and raised in Venice, became one of the greatest observers of light in the Western artistic tradition.[2]

Giovanni grew up as a member of Jacopo's hardworking non-noble Venetian family in the parish of San Geminiano. Piazza San Marco was Giovanni's playground, along with the Piazzetta and Campanile. His childhood parish church, the Church of San Geminiano (now destroyed), faced the Basilica of San Marco directly across the piazza (fig. 18).[3] His exact address is unknown, but it must have been little more than a stone's throw from San Marco, Venice's most important church, which is adjacent to the Ducal Palace, Venice's center of government.[4] The basilica's mosaics of saints and seraphs and its coffered vaults would later provide Giovanni with artistic inspiration and models for pictorial quotation.[5]

Venice's Byzantine and Gothic styles, respectively defined by San Marco and the Ducal Palace, along with local architectural variants, saturated Giovanni's youth and provided human-made exemplars complementing the city's natural beauty. As capital of the Venetian Republic, Venice ruled over a far-flung maritime empire, and, as a principal entrepôt for trade between East and West, Venice became arguably the wealthiest city in the late-medieval Western world.[6] Centuries of prosperity resulted in widespread municipal construction that projected Venice's sovereignty, honored its Christian God and saints, and declared its inhabitants' wealth and status. These monumental Byzantine

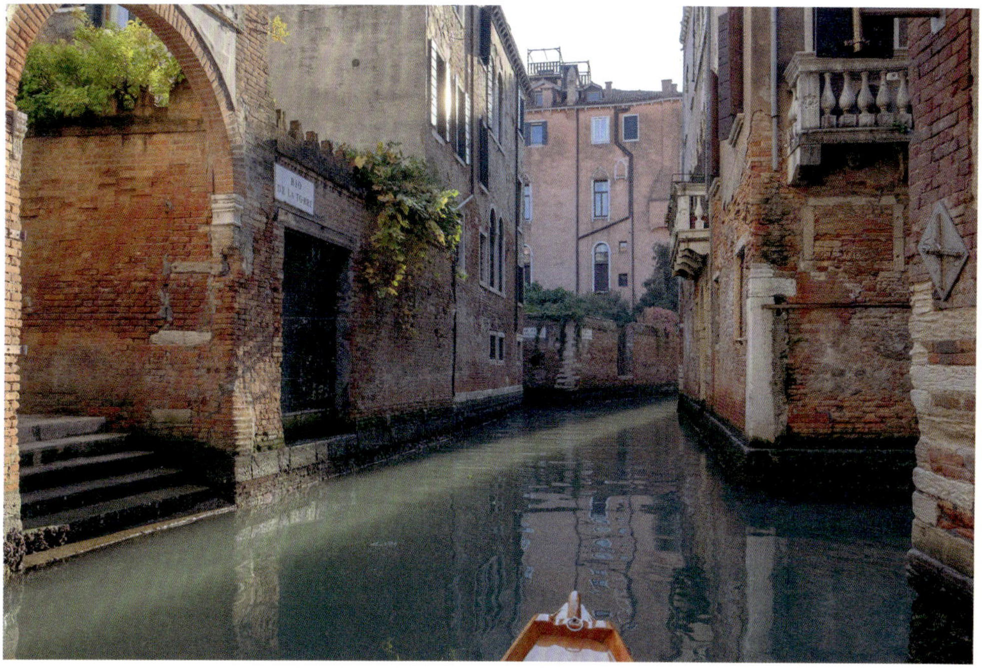

FIGURE 16 Sunrise on the Rio de la Torre, Venice. Photograph by Steven Varni

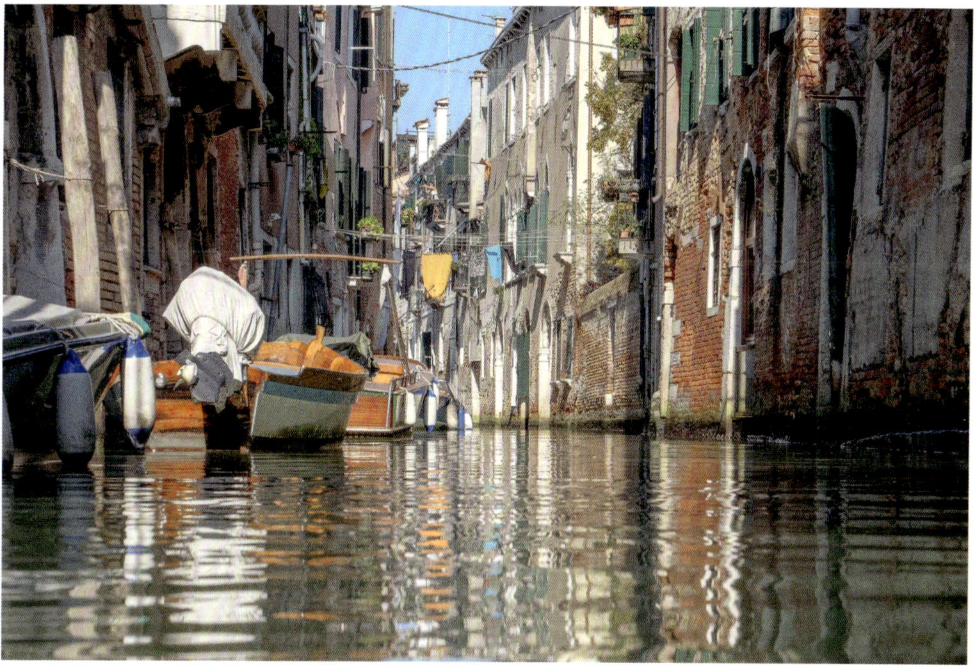

FIGURE 17 An opalescent canal, Venice. Photograph by Steven Varni

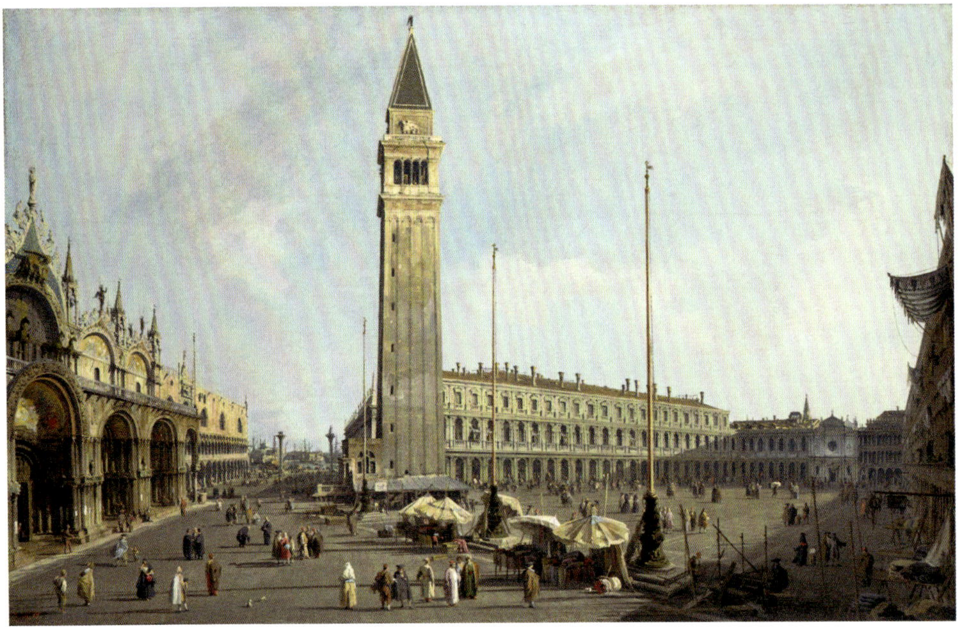

FIGURE 18 Canaletto, *The Square of Saint Mark's and the Piazzetta, Venice*, ca. 1731. Oil on canvas, 67 × 103 cm. Wadsworth Atheneum Museum of Art, Hartford, CT. The Church of San Geminiano is the white building on the right.

and Gothic forms, commissioned by the Signoria, the clergy, and Venice's elite citizens, became models for many of the buildings and architectural structures that would appear in Giovanni's paintings.

Letters and Numbers

Giovanni almost certainly was literate, although there is only one known letter that bears his signature. Written on July 2, 1504, in an elegant *mercantesca* script to Isabella d'Este (1474–1539), the Marchesa of Mantua, the letter asks forgiveness for the artist's long delay in delivering a painting (fig. 19).[7] There is a question regarding whether Giovanni wrote the letter himself, since some artists, such as Titian (d. 1576), did not always write their own letters when corresponding with royalty.[8] The body of Giovanni's letter and its signature appear to be by the same hand, however, which is not necessarily the case in Titian's letters.[9] Had Giovanni dictated the missive to a scribe or a humanist friend, then he likely would still have signed the letter himself, which perhaps suggests that Giovanni did indeed write the letter to Isabella in its entirety.[10] Yet Giovanni's refined signature here is strikingly different from his less sophisticated signature that appears at the bottom of a contract in the account books of the Scuola Grande di San Marco, dated April 24, 1470, to acknowledge acceptance of a commission for the *scuola* that Giovanni would, uncharacteristically, never complete (fig. 20).[11] The differences in penmanship between the two signatures are perhaps

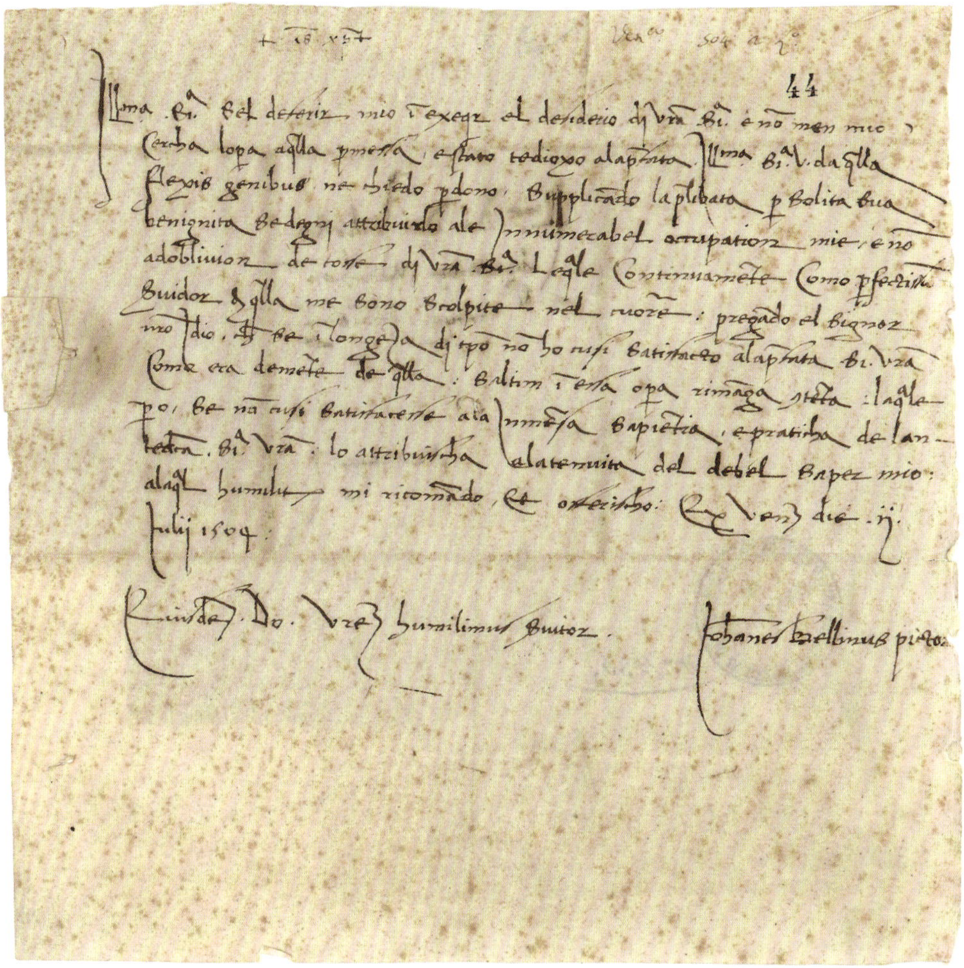

FIGURE 19 Letter from Giovanni Bellini to Isabella d'Este, July 2, 1504. Archivio di Stato di Mantova, Mantua. The only known letter bearing Giovanni's signature, although it is unclear whether it was written by the artist or a notary.

attributable to the etiquette of each document. Unlike the account book, the letter required an elegant script befitting Mantuan decorum and the language of courtly contrition.[12] Moreover, signatures can change significantly over time, as Michelangelo's did.[13]

Mercantesca is a script that Giovanni would have learned in school. Presumably, the artist received a formal education befitting his social status and economic position as a non-noble Venetian citizen from a poor-to-middle-income upwardly mobile family who was expected to become a businessman, merchant, or workshop master. The new humanistic education, or *studia humanitatis* (studies of humanity), that was then revolutionizing schools in Italy—and would soon spread across Europe—was almost certainly out of Giovanni's socioeconomic reach.[14] Initially intended for the sons of rich nobles and elite non-nobles, the humanist curriculum arrived in Venice in the early fifteenth century by way of private

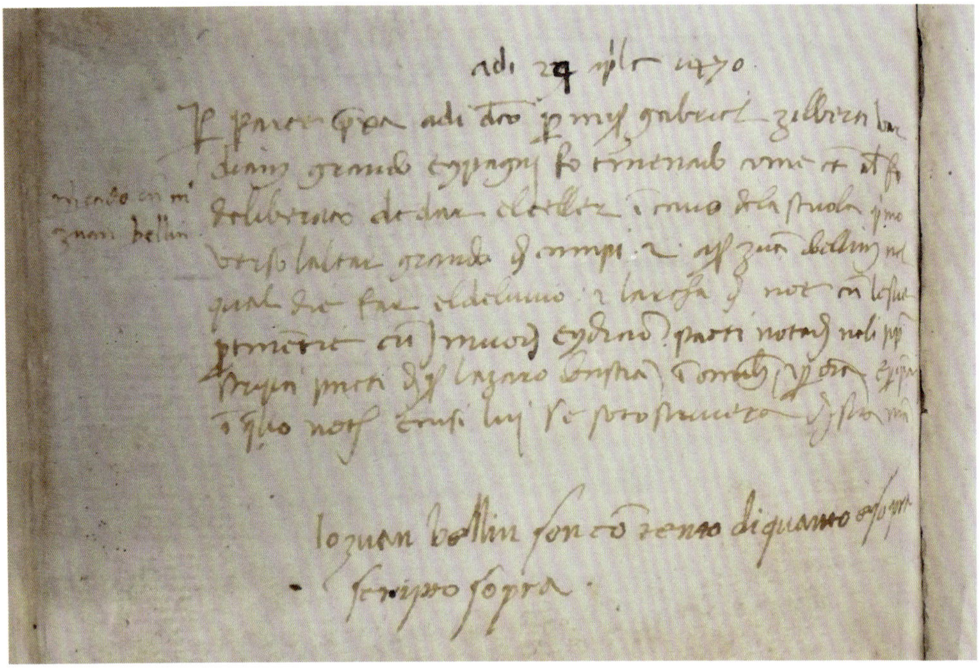

FIGURE 20 Document in which Giovanni accepts a commission at the Scuola Grande di San Marco (detail showing artist's signature), April 24, 1470. Archivio di Stato di Venezia, Venice

tutors, who instructed students to read a classical canon in Latin and sometimes Greek, and in conjunction study grammar, rhetoric, writing, poetry, history, and moral philosophy.[15]

Instead, if Giovanni was indeed provided with formal instruction, he probably received a vernacular education designed for the sons of merchants and tradesmen and usually taught by a private master at a cooperative school, as no state or church schools yet existed in Venice.[16] The lessons emphasized mathematics and focused on practical knowledge applicable to mercantile and daily Christian life.[17] Giovanni would have studied *abbaco*, a commercial algebra introduced in Italy by Leonardo Fibonacci (ca. 1170–ca. 1250) in his *Liber abaci* (1202).[18] This course of study included Hindu-Arabic numeration, basic operations, counting and reckoning with the fingers, monetary units, weights and measures, fractions and decimals, simple geometry, and usually double-entry bookkeeping, all of which provided the future shopkeeper with tools for solving everyday problems.

Giovanni's other academic focus would have been the study of Italian within a religious and moral context. Likely textbooks would include the *Fior di virtù* (*Flower of Virtue*), a compilation of stories teaching the virtues and vices, and the *Epistole e Evangeli* (*Epistles and Gospels*), a book of scripture learned as daily lessons.[19] He would also have read *volgarizzazione* (free translations) of Latin texts, and especially hagiographies, such as *Vite dei Santi Padri* (*Lives of the Holy Fathers*) by Domenico Cavalca (ca. 1270–1342), a translation of *Vitae Patrum* (*Lives of the Fathers*), which was about the Desert Fathers and Mothers—hermits of the Church in Egypt—with the addition of other saints.[20] In addition, Giovanni would have read *Leggendario dei santi* (*Legends of the Saints*), a mid-fourteenth-century Italian translation of the thirteenth-century *Legenda aurea* (*Golden Legend*) by Jacobus de Voragine (ca. 1230–1298), whose imagery Giovanni would later draw upon in his paintings.[21] Sometimes basic Latin grammar was included in the vernacular course of study, but it was not a requirement. As for writing, Giovanni probably did not learn *rotunda,* the Italian version of Gothic script, but rather *mercantesca* as mentioned, a script commonly used for ledgers, accounting, and writing letters, as seen in his correspondence to Isabella d'Este.[22]

Drawing and Painting

Giovanni's formal education in the arts began, of course, with Jacopo. After their father died, the Bellini family business was no longer tinsmithing but painting. Jacopo established his family workshop in San Geminiano sometime between 1425 and 1429, and it was here that he taught Giovanni to be an artist. A century later, Vasari would write that "Jacopo himself had taught them [Giovanni and Gentile] with great diligence the principles of design" and that both eventually surpassed him.[23]

Jacopo's effort in this regard was not entirely selfless. Workshop masters needed well-trained assistants, preferably their legitimate sons, who did not require salaries. According to Venetian law, only legitimate sons were legally entitled to inherit their father's workshop and patrimony, which was viewed as compensation for their free and sometimes lifelong labor.[24] Yet despite Jacopo's having raised and even described Giovanni as his own son, he remained his legitimately born brother in the eyes of the law. Thus, the law held that Giovanni, when he came of age, would be Jacopo's equal partner in their father's legacy and the Bellini family business. Until that time, however, and in broad terms, Giovanni's childhood appears to have been nearly indistinguishable from those of Jacopo's three sons, Gentile, Nicolò, and Leonello, of whom only Gentile would become a professional painter.[25]

It was undoubtedly formative to Giovanni's early career that, for most of his childhood, he witnessed Jacopo as a struggling artist rather than a flourishing success. When Jacopo returned from Florence, or perhaps Rome, to his birthplace of Venice in the late 1420s to establish a painting workshop, he would have been altogether mistaken if he had imagined that he would be embraced by the city's wealthiest patrons and showered with commissions by virtue of having been Gentile da Fabriano's assistant and leading protégé. While it was true that Gentile da Fabriano, who had died in 1427, had profoundly influenced Venetian painting, after he departed the city, probably in late 1413, the arts in Venice continued to develop in his absence.[26] When Jacopo returned some 15 years later, Venice laid claim to many of the finest late Gothic painters in Italy.

Jacopo found himself in competition with Jacobello del Fiore (fl. 1400–1439), a more senior master who had probably worked alongside Gentile da Fabriano in decorating the Great Council Hall of the Ducal Palace in ca. 1412.[27] In the interim, Jacobello had developed a lavishly decorative mixed-media style, often ornamented with gilded *pastiglia* (pastework)

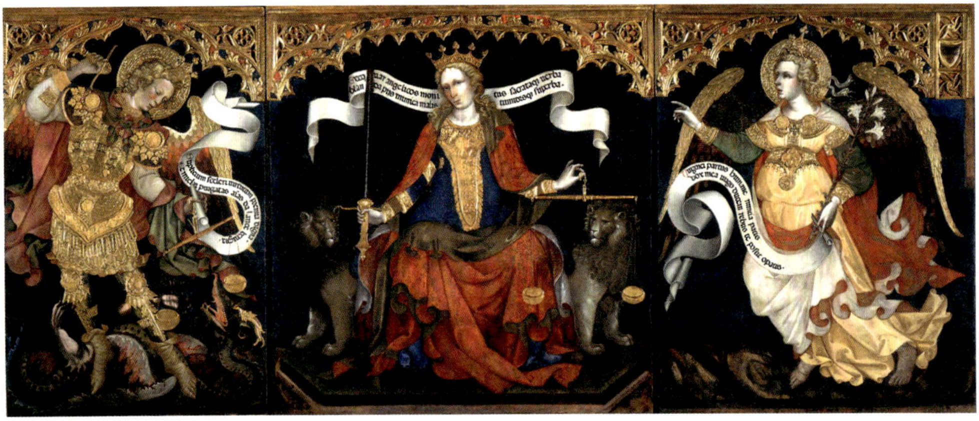

FIGURE 21 Jacobello del Fiore, *Justice Enthroned between the Archangels Gabriel and Michael (The Triptych of Justice)*, ca. 1421. Tempera and gilded pastework on panel, 208 × 490 cm. Gallerie dell'Accademia, Venice

relief, that is perhaps most magnificently expressed in his *Justice Enthroned between the Archangels Gabriel and Michael* (ca. 1421, fig. 21).[28] There was also Michele Giambono (fl. 1420–1462), arguably Venice's leading painter in the 1430s, whose late Gothic style was marked by an idealism in depicting divine figures, a naturalism in depicting animals and nature, and a lavish ornamentalism, typically characterized by the sumptuous portrayal of undulating brocaded or damasked fabrics that were often intricately creased like crumpled paper unfurled (fig. 22).[29] Later, Jacopo and Giambono would, to some extent, become collaborators.[30] Finally, there were Giovanni d'Alemagna (d. 1450) and Antonio Vivarini (d. 1476/84), whose beloved altarpieces, which depicted full-length saints standing on plinths, molded by naturalist light sources, and housed in elaborately carved and gilded Gothic frames, nearly monopolized the Venetian altarpiece market during the 1440s (fig. 23).[31]

To distinguish himself in this competitive environment, Jacopo implemented an array of long-term business and artistic strategies, strategies that Giovanni would learn in his youth and later apply.[32] For instance, Jacopo began to advertise himself through his signatures and inscriptions.[33] Later, Giovanni would create, refine, and standardize his own signature in incised Roman imperial capitals, which would become one of the first and most effective uses of branding in Western art.[34] Jacopo cultivated helpful relationships with humanists, such as Ulisse degli Aleotti (d. 1488), who might assist in the construction of inscriptions or praise him in poetry, and with other artists, such as Giambono and Donato Bragadin (d. 1473), who might subcontract work to Jacopo or with whom he might share commissions.[35] As an independent painter, Giovanni would nurture similar types of relationships with famous humanists of his day.[36]

Beginning in ca. 1430, and undoubtedly driven in large part by the need to innovate in light of Venice's competitive artistic marketplace, Jacopo executed two sketchbooks of drawings that would come to serve Giovanni as visual points of departure for many of his own early paintings.[37] These 192 pages of multipurpose drawings, which functioned as the

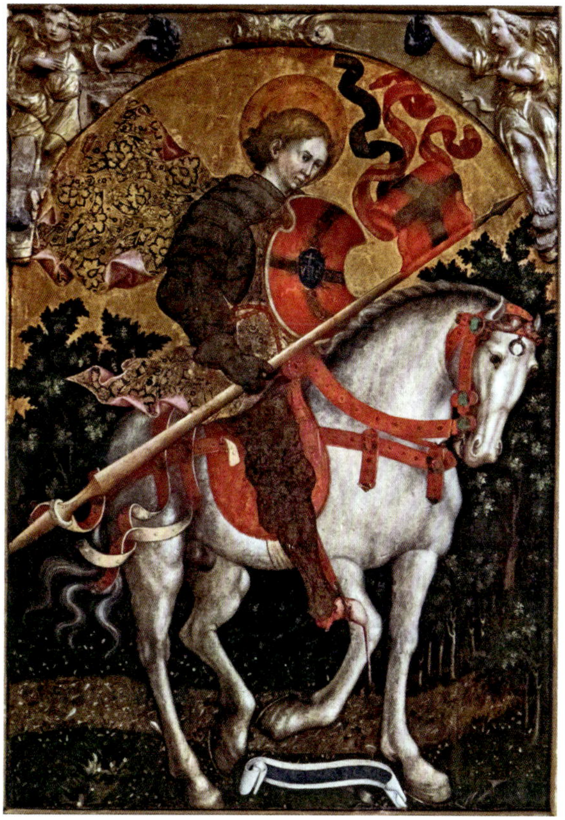

FIGURE 22 Michele Giambono, *Saint Chrysogonus on Horseback*, ca. 1450. Panel, 199 × 134 cm. Church of San Trovaso, Venice

early Bellini workshop's experimental laboratory, comprise the Renaissance's two most celebrated drawing notebooks, one begun earlier on vellum and now in Paris, the other begun later on paper and now in London.[38] A number of sheets illustrate how Jacopo drew after the work of other celebrated artists, including Altichiero (d. ca. 1390) and Donatello (ca. 1386–1466), presumably to master and assimilate their artistic skills and even to improve upon their compositions (see figs 91 and 92).[39] Jacopo collected various pictorial motifs in his notebooks, some of which derived from fourteenth-century model books, but most he composed himself. In some drawings, Jacopo became an antiquarian, recording ancient scripts and classical imagery and depicting fantastical renderings of classical subjects that would prove to be decades ahead of their time.[40] A number of compositions were highly finished, especially several of the drawings on vellum, and might have been used as showpieces for future patrons. Others were clearly intended to explore new pictorial subjects or altarpiece designs; indeed, his pioneering drawings of imagined Renaissance altarpieces preceded the earliest known Renaissance altarpiece in Venice by many years (see figs 89 and 90).[41] Many of the earlier Paris drawings seem to have been intended to help Jacopo learn to construct images in mathematically precise linear perspective—a pictorial

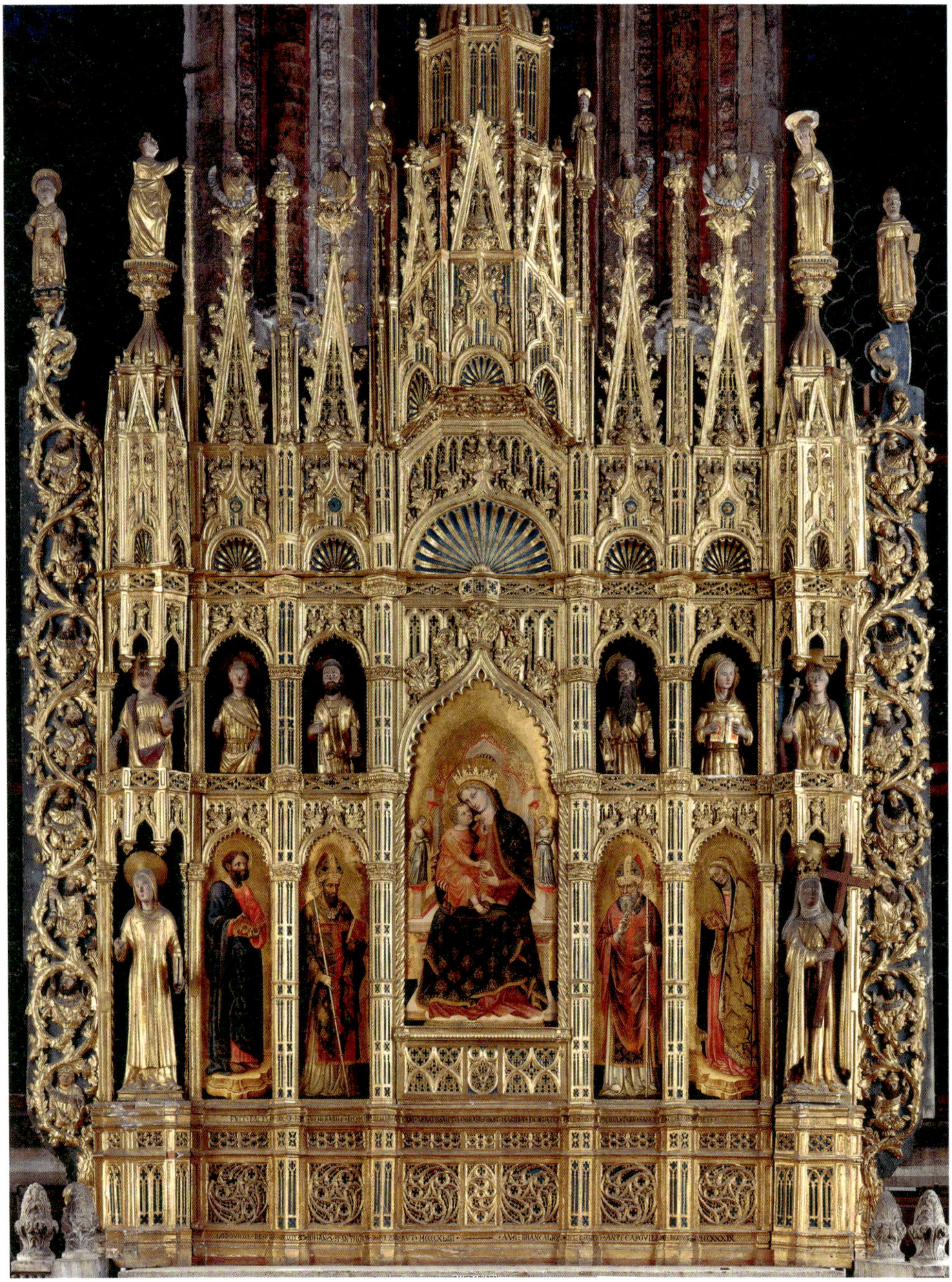

FIGURE 23 Giovanni d'Alemagna and Antonio Vivarini, *Madonna of the Rosary*, 1443. Panels, 600 × 320 cm. Chapel of San Tarasio, Church of San Zaccaria, Venice

innovation discovered in central Italy, employed by artists beginning in the 1420s, and that no other Venetian painter of Jacopo's generation had mastered.[42] Learning this groundbreaking advance in the arts for rendering complex cityscapes, landscapes, and other subjects would eventually help set apart the Bellini workshop in Venice.

Success for Jacopo, however, would only come later. As a boy and teenager, Giovanni would instead have witnessed that, despite Jacopo's wellspring of artistic ideas and business strategies, he apparently found limited work in Venice itself during the 1430s and into the 1440s and was thus forced to become peripatetic.[43] When he was old enough, Giovanni would have been expected to travel with Jacopo as his assistant, just as Jacopo had traveled with Gentile da Fabriano a generation earlier. In these years, Jacopo executed paintings either in or destined for Padua, Verona, Ferrara, Bologna, Brescia, and probably other cities.[44] Panel paintings might be shipped, while frescoes, of course, had to be executed on site.[45] Even at age 10 or 11, Giovanni might have assisted Jacopo on his monumental but now-destroyed fresco of the *Crucifixion* for the cathedral in Verona in 1436.[46] Venetian boys called *garzoni* could begin their apprenticeships in painting workshops as young as eight.[47]

Crucial to Giovanni's artistic formation, then, were these unrecorded years as Jacopo's apprentice. He would have spent long hours with Jacopo, the two perhaps journeying overland and by boat with their supplies, working together from morning to dark for months on end. Jacopo would also have spent long hours teaching Giovanni the craft of painting on walls, panels, and linen. He would have taught Giovanni how to prepare each surface for the paint, how to prepare gesso and glues, how to grind and steep pigments, how to gild and burnish, and how to manipulate the many materials of their craft.[48] At some point, Jacopo must have recognized Giovanni's developing talents. Years later, when Giovanni was already a successful independent artist, he willingly and loyally returned to help Jacopo on projects, such as the lost Gattamelata Altarpiece of 1460, which Jacopo inscribed as executed by himself and his two sons, Gentile and Giovanni Bellini, thus demonstrating that Jacopo thought of Giovanni as a son.[49]

Around 1440, Jacopo was called to the court of Ferrara, and Giovanni, about age 15, probably accompanied him. Jacopo, perhaps recalling when he and Gentile da Fabriano had departed Venice for the court of Brescia in 1413 to remain there for some six years, began making arrangements for his workshop in Venice, as if he might similarly remain in Ferrara for an extended period. He drew up a contract with Donato Bragadin, an agreement which—for unknown reasons—was never finalized with signatures, but which would have entered the two artists into a five-year business agreement to split profits from commissions received in Venice, but not beyond the lagoon.[50] Jacopo apparently anticipated that, during his absence while in Ferrara, his Venice workshop might continue to accept orders that Donato would execute. To enter into the business agreement, however, Jacopo needed to be legally independent, and this appears to be the reason he dissolved his fraternal partnership with Giovanni.[51] Thus, the 1440 *divisio* drawn up between Jacopo and Giovanni to end their fraternal partnership seems to have been a legal formality. Indeed, the document itself lacks

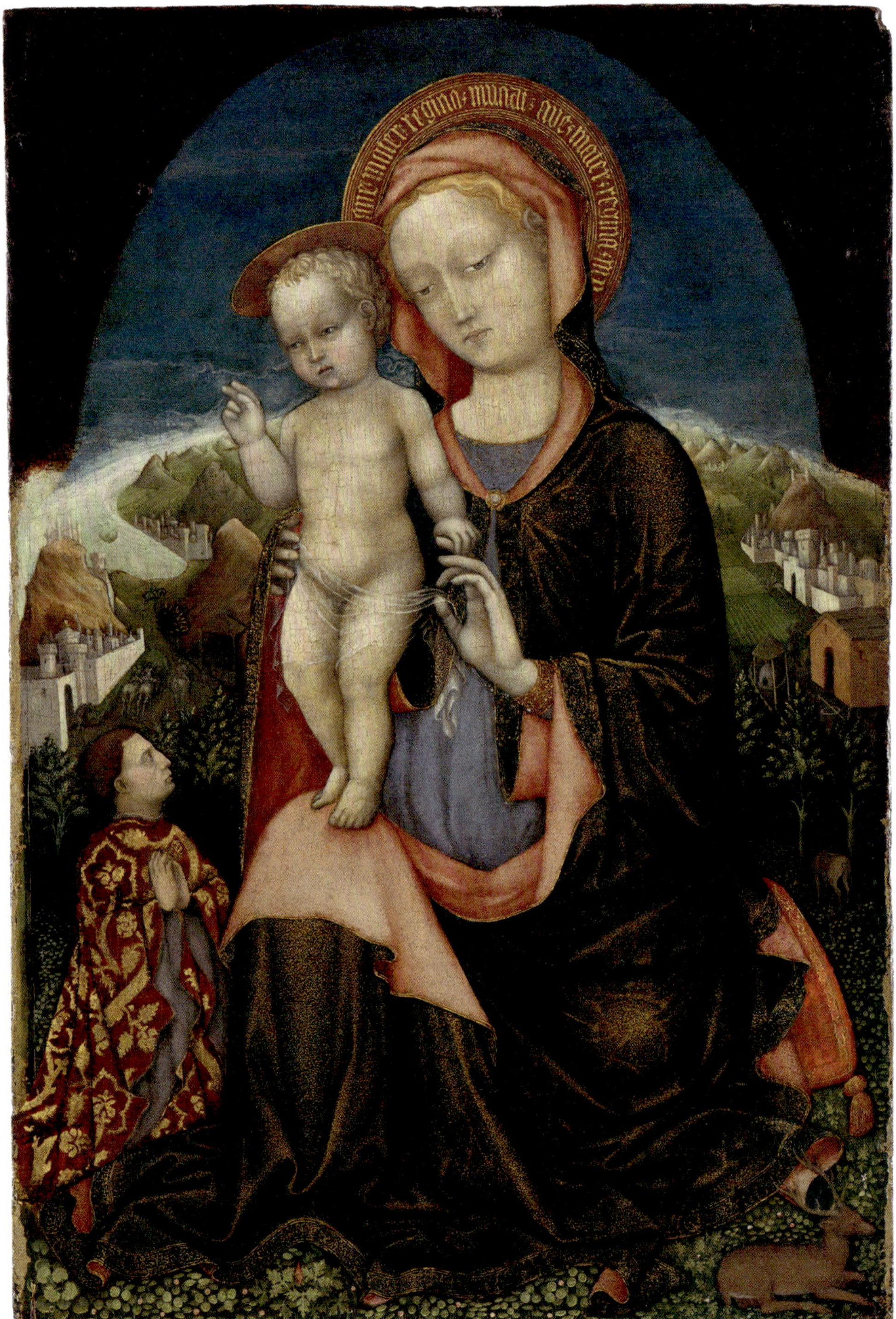

FIGURE 24 Jacopo Bellini, *The Virgin and Child with Donor* [Leonello d'Este?], ca. 1440. Tempera on panel, 60 × 40 cm. Musée du Louvre, Paris

any specifics about their separation, such as which brother would retain what property, which is normally described in divisions, thus supporting the idea that it was executed out of legal compliance rather than the two brothers' desire to go their separate ways, which, of course, did not occur.

As it turned out, however, Jacopo's sojourn in Ferrara was rather short, probably less than a year, since we know that he was elected *degano* of Venice's Scuola Grande di San Giovanni Evangelista in March 1441, which suggests that he had returned home by that time.[52] The single work linked to his visit to Ferrara is the *Virgin and Child with Donor*, which includes a kneeling figure often identified as Leonello d'Este (ca. 1440, fig. 24), who would become marchese upon the death of his father, Niccolò III d'Este (1383–1441).[53] Although it cannot be known for certain, it seems probable that the artist named his son Leonello after Leonello d'Este, especially since Leonello is a rather uncommon name in Venice. Through this show of respect, Jacopo may have hoped for the continued patronage of the d'Este family.

In sum, while Giovanni's formal education in school would have been typical, his education in art was singular. Indeed, it is hard to imagine a better education in painting and the realities of executing an artistic commission in Renaissance Italy. Giovanni's seemingly unceasing and lifelong work ethic, as well as his constant drive to achieve mastery over every artistic genre, might be viewed as an outgrowth of experiencing and empathizing with Jacopo's long struggles to find work.

Possibly the most durable artistic lesson that Jacopo taught to Giovanni, however, was Jacopo's wide-ranging looking. From viewing works executed in linear perspective, Jacopo sought to duplicate the technique. From studying Altichiero, Jacopo attempted to update the fourteenth-century master. Classical, medieval, and contemporary works of art all inspired Jacopo. Giovanni, perhaps less interested in the antique than Jacopo, became acutely aware of recent and innovative works of art executed in and around Venice. And from the beginning, as we shall see, Giovanni was fastidious in selecting which compositions or motifs would serve as models for constructing his own paintings.

4 The First Painting

The *Coronation of the Virgin* (ca. 1441–42) in the Pinacoteca Nazionale in Ferrara is with little doubt Giovanni Bellini's earliest known work of art, identified here for the first time (fig. 25).[1] Donated to the museum in 1977, with its earlier provenance unknown, the painting has received little scholarly attention.[2] It has never before been attributed to Giovanni, presumably because it lacks his well-known autograph style—which, as we shall see, had yet to develop.[3] The painting's overall spirit and use of motifs inspired directly from Jacopo Bellini's drawings, its deployment of artistic ideas drawn from works of art local to Giovanni, the fact that Giovanni would later expand upon several pictorial ideas in the *Coronation*, and the work's authentic signature, "*Iohannes Belinus me fecit*" ("Giovanni Bellini made me", fig. 26), all forcefully establish his authorship.[4] The Ferrara *Coronation* is a great treasure, both as a window into Giovanni's earliest artistic approach and as a rare example of an adolescent painting executed by an Italian Renaissance master.[5]

The *Coronation* illustrates the festivities and multitude of attendees celebrating Christ's crowning of Mary as the Queen of Heaven. It is a scene from the apocryphal story of the Virgin's death, popularized by its inclusion in Jacobus de Voragine's widely read medieval collection of hagiographies, *Legenda aurea* (*Golden Legend*).[6] In three-quarter view, Christ as Salvator Mundi holds the golden orb in one hand and with the other places a golden crown on the Virgin's bowed head, the pair's flowing garments partially concealing the plush cushions upon which they sit. Hovering above them and flanked by a chorus of angels is God the Father, over whom the small bust of a bearded Old Testament prophet emerges from a cloud, bearing a scroll with the artist's signature. The central group is surrounded by a highly elaborate and fanciful throne of stone and wood, conceived as if it were the multi-tiered façade of a Gothic cathedral and decorated with niched saints and colored inlays. At the top of the painting, four floating roundels each contain a portrait bust of a father of the Church, and at the bottom, two diminutive musical angels play *lire da braccia*.

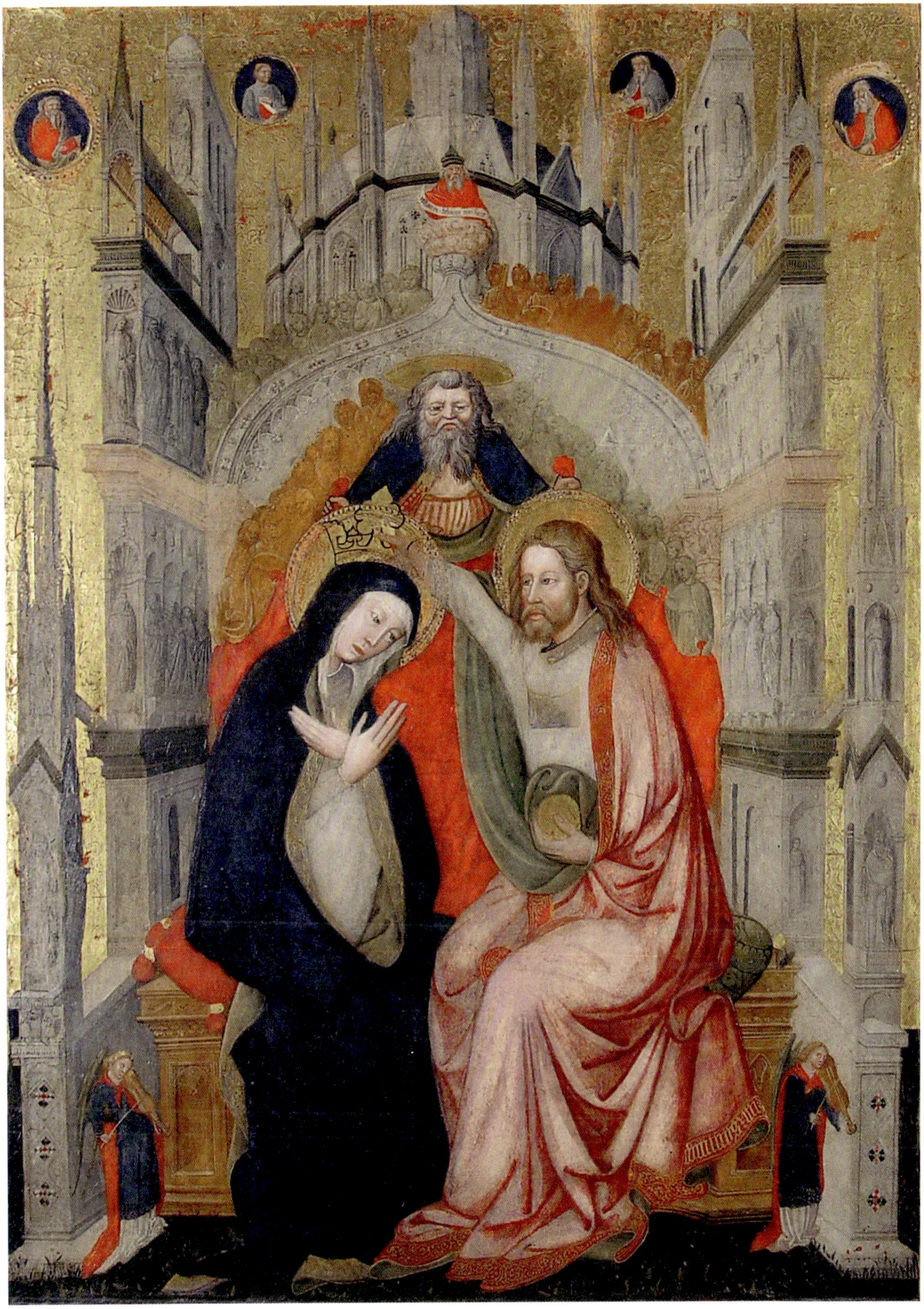

FIGURE 25 Giovanni Bellini, *The Coronation of the Virgin*, ca. 1441–42. Tempera on panel, 98 × 72 cm. Pinacoteca Nazionale, Ferrara

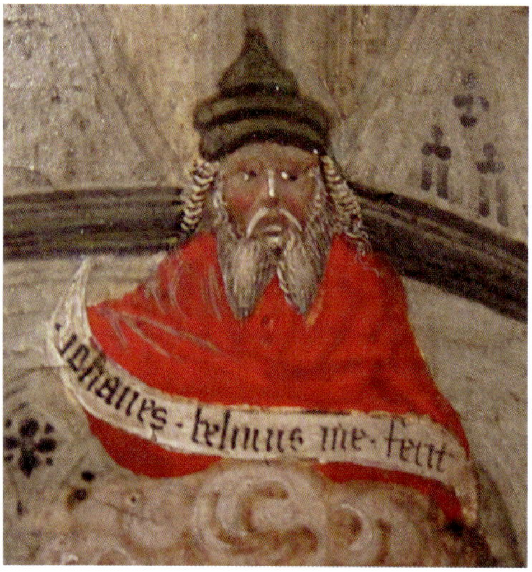

FIGURE 26 Detail of fig. 25, showing Giovanni's signature

The work was heavily abraded and restored in the central part depicting Christ and the Virgin. Radiography has determined that the signature is coeval with the painting and thus authentic.[7]

Giovanni probably executed the *Coronation* at age 15 or 16, since, as discussed below, the painting likely dates from ca. 1441–42. As would perhaps be expected from an adolescent artist educated in a fifteenth-century family workshop, much of the Ferrara *Coronation* seems derivative. Nevertheless, other aspects of the painting register not only Giovanni's inventiveness and early brilliance in culling from a broad range of sources, but also perhaps a certain aspirational audaciousness.

Artistic Sources

The primary inspiration informing the *Coronation*—as is the case for much of Giovanni's early work—was the art of Jacopo Bellini. The picture's spirit derives from several drawings of the 1430s in Jacopo's Paris sketchbook, especially those depicting unique perspectival constructions of fanciful architecture, with miniature figures, idiosyncratic ornamentation, and typically a central vanishing point, such as Jacopo's *Departure for the Hunt* (ca. 1435–40, fig. 27).[8] Jacopo's *Death of the Virgin* (ca. 1435–40) appears to have been a direct inspiration as well (fig. 28). The line of niched saints and the ogee arch in Giovanni's painting recall Jacopo's line of mourners and barrel vault; and Jacopo's highly eccentric open-air barrel-vaulted balcony (similar to that known in Venetian dialect as *liagò* or *diagò*), which recedes sharply toward the vanishing point, must have been the direct source for the two analogous balconies in the *Coronation* (figs 29 and 30).[9] Jacopo seems to have enjoyed drawing these fanciful, often ribbed, barrel-vaulted passageways, which can also be seen in his *Judgment of Solomon* (ca. 1435–40, fig. 31), and apparently Giovanni, in this moment of his adolescence, appreciated them as well.[10]

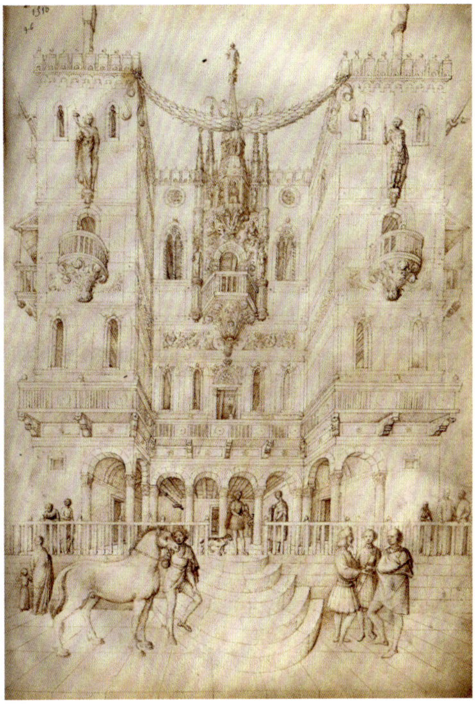

FIGURE 27 Jacopo Bellini, *Departure for the Hunt*, ca. 1435–40. Vellum, 38 × 26 cm. Cabinet des dessins, Musée du Louvre, Paris

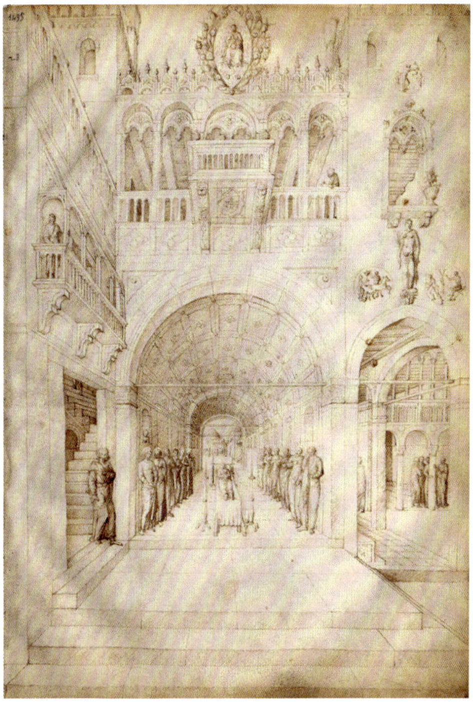

FIGURE 28 Jacopo Bellini, *The Death of the Virgin*, ca. 1435–40. Vellum, 38 × 26 cm. Cabinet des dessins, Musée du Louvre, Paris

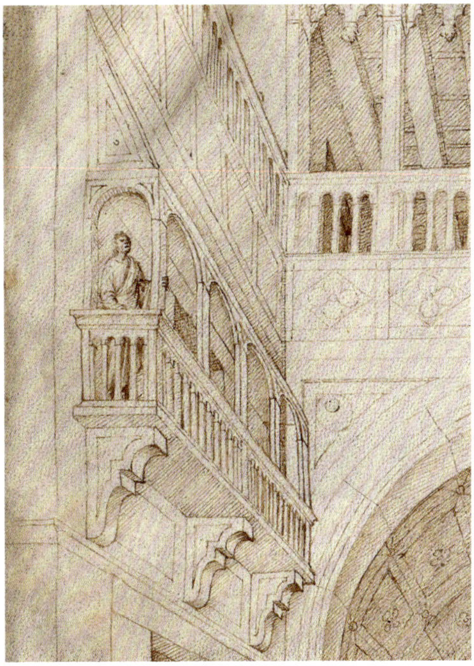

FIGURE 29 Detail of fig. 28

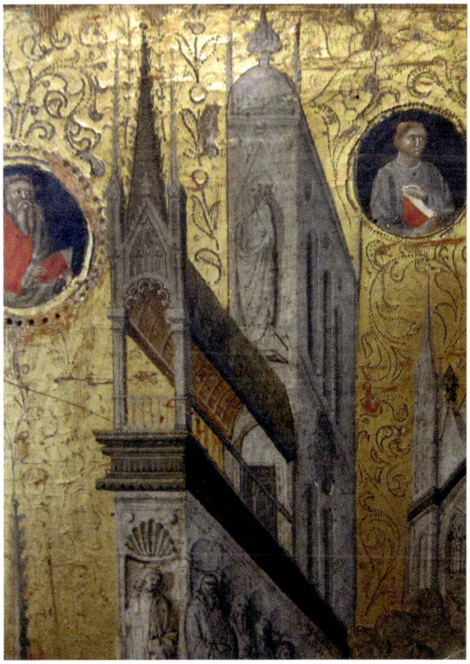

FIGURE 30 Detail of fig. 25

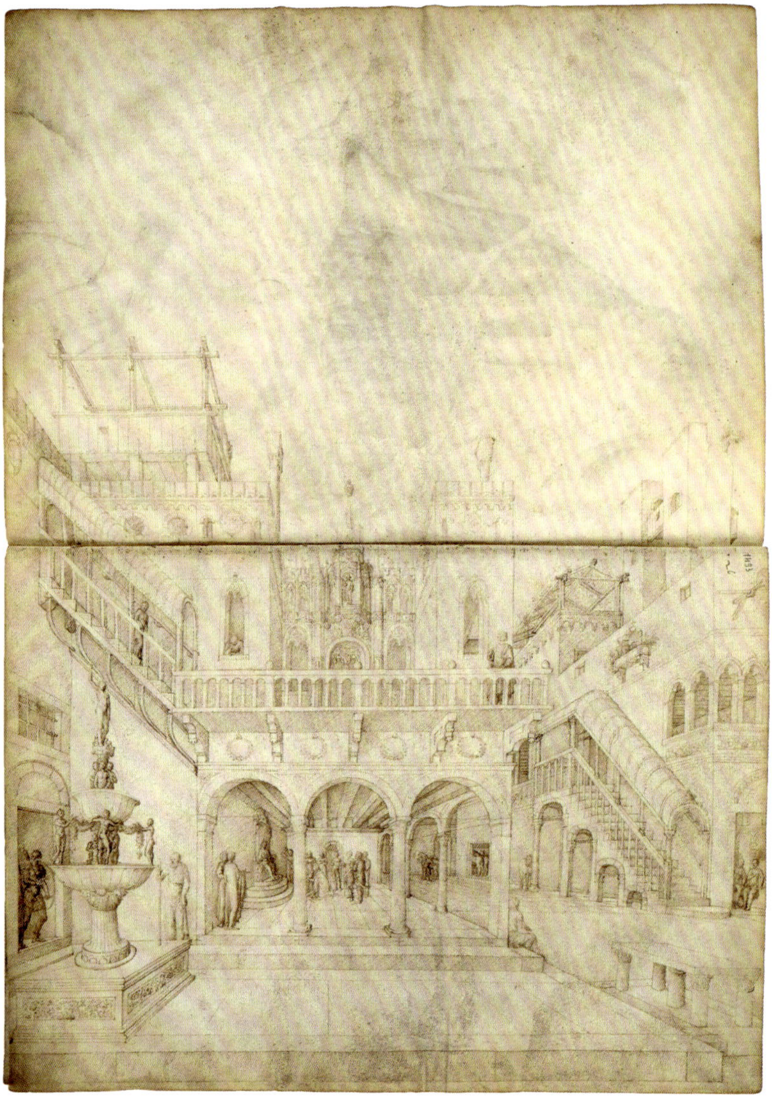

FIGURE 31 Jacopo Bellini, *The Judgment of Solomon*, ca. 1435–40. Vellum, 52 × 38 cm. Cabinet des dessins, Musée du Louvre, Paris

This is not an exhaustive list of Jacopo's drawings that provided the architectural ideas and individual motifs seen in the *Coronation*. For instance, the decorative scheme of saints in niches is a frequent motif in Jacopo's architectural fantasies, as are portrait medallions; both appear in Jacopo's *Christ among the Doctors* (ca. 1440–45, fig. 32).[11] Note also that Giovanni seems to have nearly duplicated Jacopo's distinctive Madonna type, seen in such works as Jacopo's *Virgin and Child with Donor* (ca. 1440, see fig. 24) and his *Madonna and Child* (ca. 1440s, fig 33), both of which have the heavy-lidded eyes, long nose, and pursed mouth of the Virgin in the *Coronation* (fig. 34).[12]

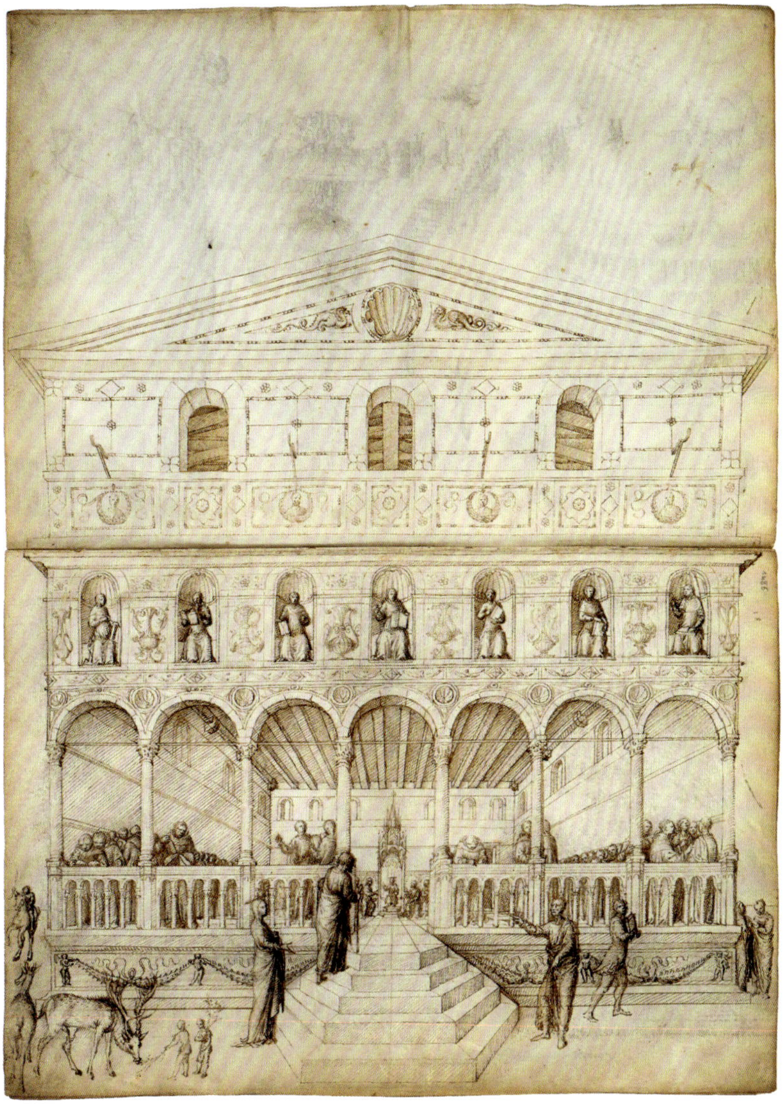

FIGURE 32 Jacopo Bellini, *Christ among the Doctors,* ca. 1440–45. Vellum, 52 × 38 cm. Cabinet des dessins, Musée du Louvre, Paris

The general composition of the central group, however, along with the small musical angels, apparently derives not from Jacopo but from his teacher, Gentile da Fabriano, either from his *Coronation of the Virgin with Saints* (Valle Romita Polyptych) (ca. 1410, fig. 35) or a similar work, one perhaps closer to Venice that is now lost.[13] Jacopo, who is documented as already working for Gentile da Fabriano by 1412, could have assisted on the Valle Romita Polyptych and retained a sketch of the painting. It is also possible that, during one of Jacopo's many itinerant commissions, he had occasion to visit the Valle Romita Polyptych, then located in a Franciscan hermitage on the outskirts of Fabriano, and perhaps took along

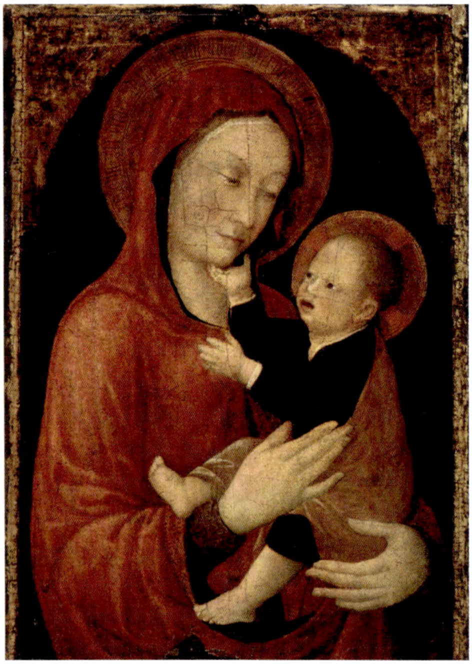

FIGURE 33 Jacopo Bellini, *The Madonna and Child*, ca. 1440s. Panel, 71 × 52 cm. Gallerie dell'Accademia, Venice

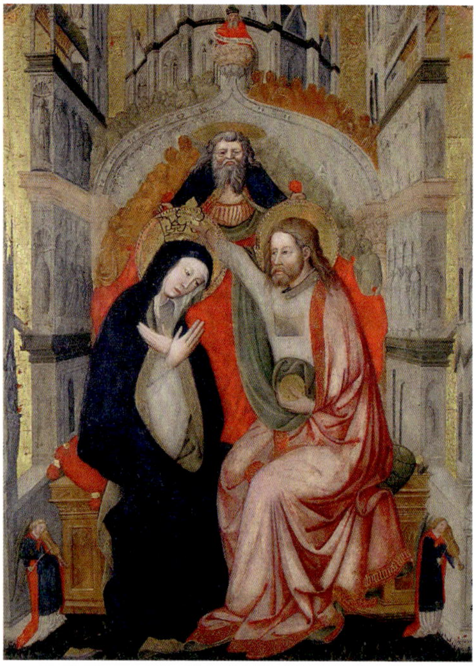

FIGURE 34 Detail of fig. 25

FIGURE 35 Gentile da Fabriano, *The Coronation of the Virgin with Saints* (Valle Romita Polyptych) (detail of central panel), ca. 1410. Tempera on panel, 280 × 250 cm. Pinacoteca di Brera, Milan

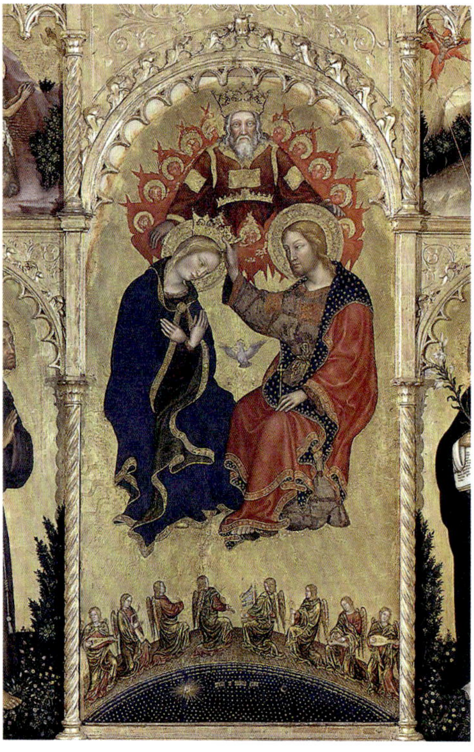

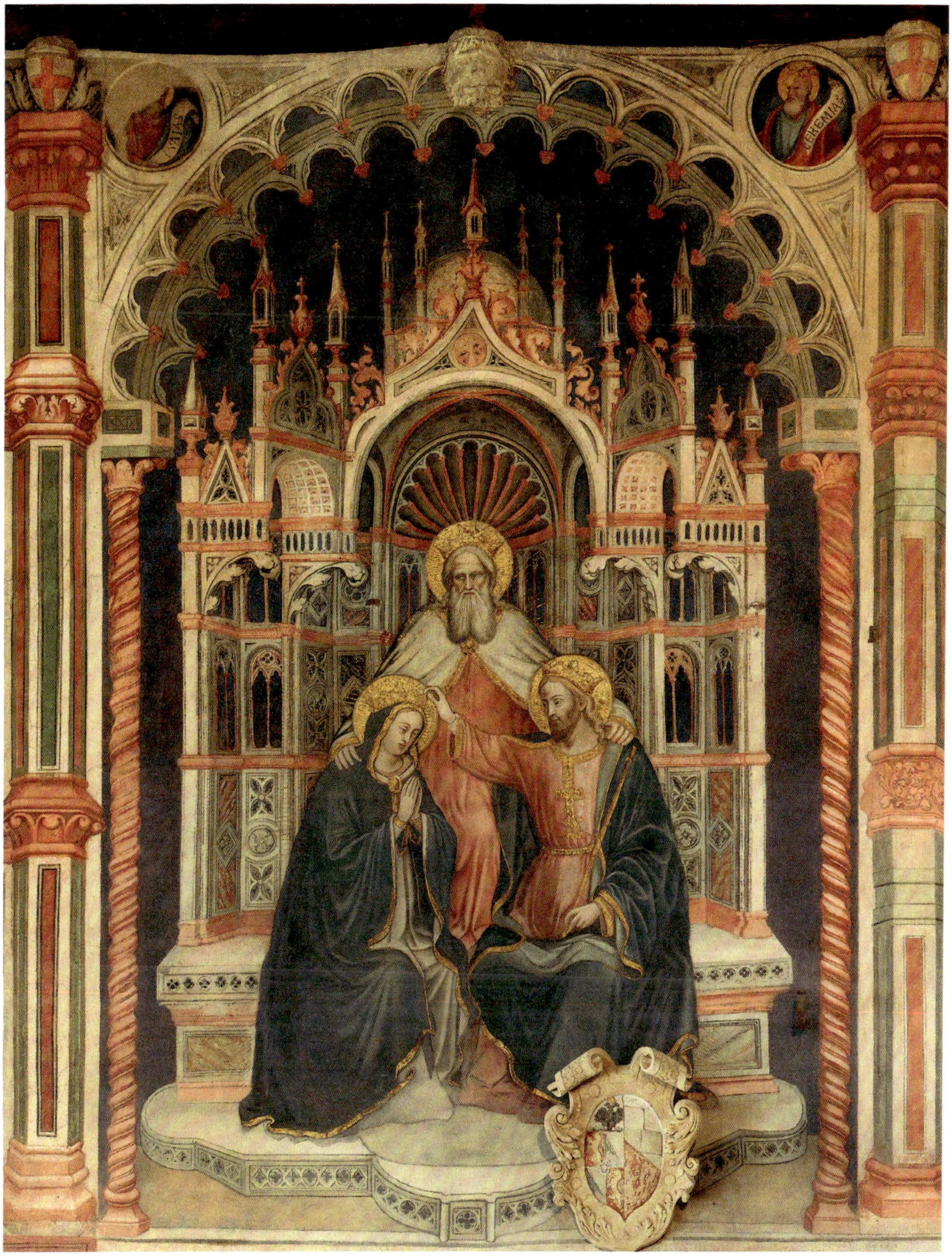

FIGURE 36 Nicolò Miretto, *The Coronation of the Virgin*, ca. 1435–40. Fresco. Palazzo della Ragione, Padua

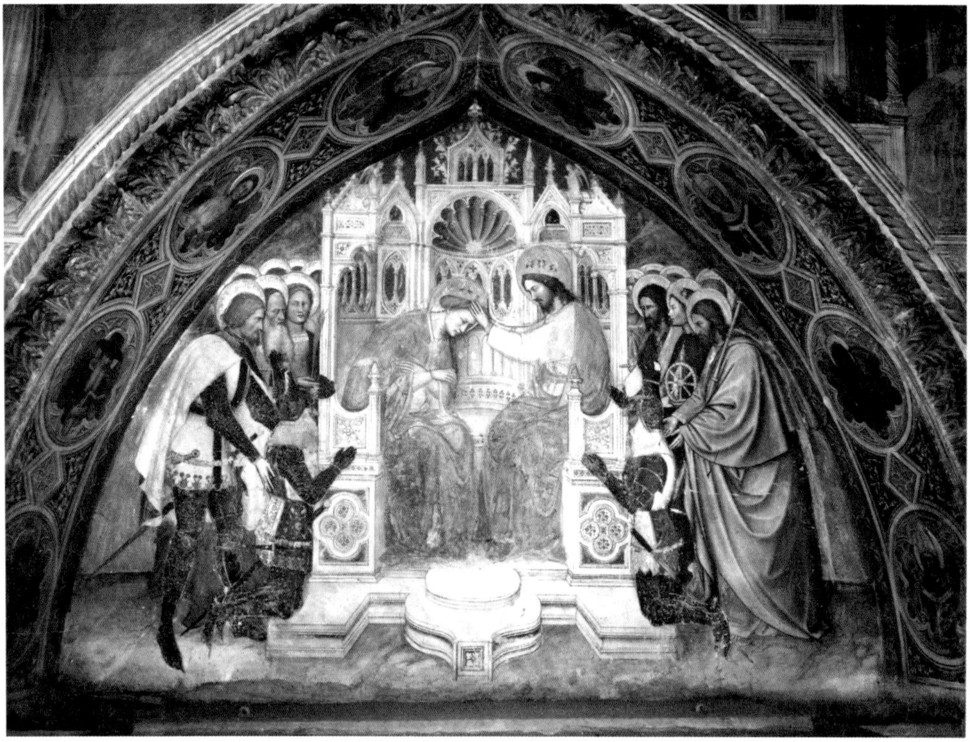

FIGURE 37 Altichiero, *The Coronation of the Virgin*, ca. 1360–70. Fresco. Formerly in the Church of the Eremitani, Padua (destroyed in 1944)

his young assistant, Giovanni.[14] Gentile da Fabriano's depiction of the Virgin and her robes, her crowning by Christ, the figure of God the Father surrounded by seraphim, and the angels playing *lire da braccia* each to some extent find analogues in the Ferrara painting (see fig. 34).

A fresco of the *Coronation of the Virgin* (ca. 1435–40) in the Palazzo della Ragione in Padua, probably executed by an accomplished and now largely forgotten artist named Nicolò Miretto (d. after 1448), must also have provided Giovanni with an important model that he studied firsthand (fig. 36).[15] After February 1420, when the Palazzo della Ragione and its famous frescoes by Giotto (d. 1337) were destroyed by fire, Venice, as ruler over Padua, financed the palazzo's reconstruction and redecoration. Miretto and other artists were tasked to convey Venice's hegemony, as well as other themes, and their resulting fresco cycle became regionally famous.[16] The tiered and complex architecture of Miretto's *Coronation*, the background pinnacles and dome recalling Venice's San Marco, and the two Old Testament prophets depicted in roundels, among other details, seem to have inspired the Ferrara painting. In executing his *Coronation*, Miretto apparently relied on Altichiero's *Coronation* (ca. 1360–70, destroyed in 1944, fig. 37) in the nearby Church of the Eremitani in Padua.[17]

Most fascinating, however, is how architectural elements from the Porta della Carta inspired young Giovanni (figs 38 and 39). Constructed from 1438 to 1442 by Bartolomeo Bon (fl. 1421–1464), the greatest Venetian architect-sculptor of the period, the Porta della Carta

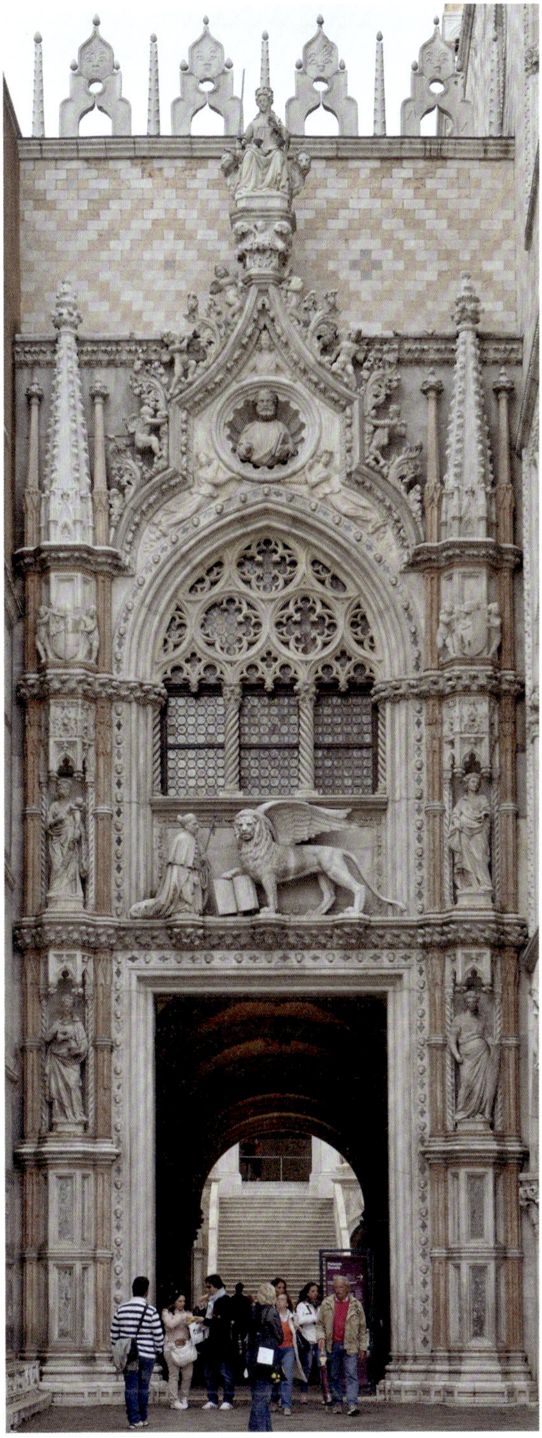

FIGURE 38 Bartolomeo Bon, Porta della Carta, 1438–42. Istrian stone, Carrara marble, red Verona marble, Greek marble. Ducal Palace, Venice.

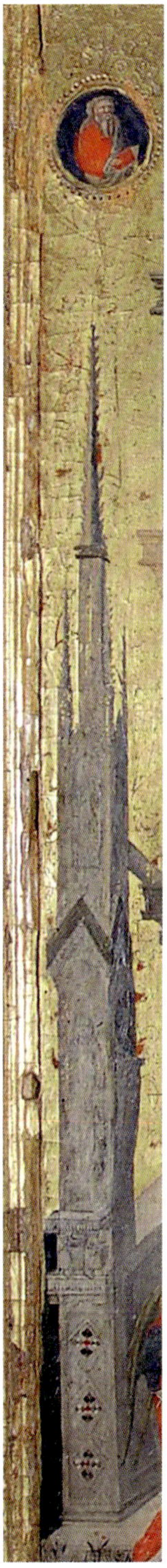

FIGURE 39 Detail of fig. 25

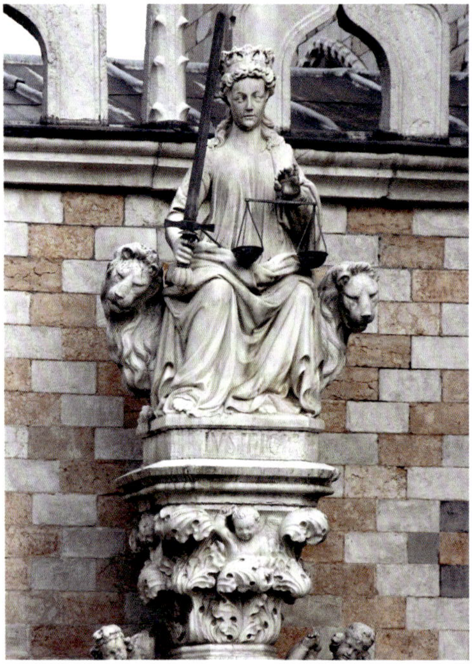

FIGURE 40 Detail of fig. 38, showing *Justice*

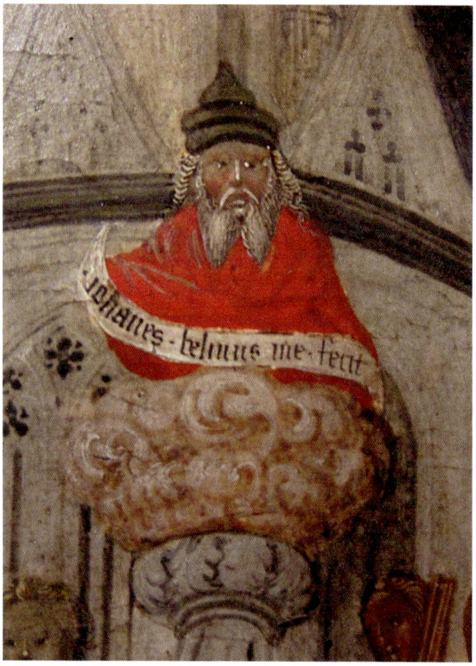

FIGURE 41 Detail of fig. 25

was the stunning and monumental new entrance to the Ducal Palace, situated next to San Marco and across the piazza from Giovanni's childhood parish church, the Church of San Geminiano.[18] Giovanni must have witnessed it being built. Like Miretto's *Coronation* in the Palazzo della Ragione, the architecture of the Porta della Carta is segmented into tiers, two of which house saints in niches much as do the tiers in Giovanni's painting. The towers with crocketed pinnacles of the Porta become buttresses topped by pinnacles and crockets in Giovanni's work. Additionally, Giovanni transforms the crowning figure of *Justice* atop a putto and cloud, with her name inscribed below, into an Old Testament prophet emerging from a cloud, with a scroll bearing Giovanni's signature (figs 40 and 41).[19] Bon's Porta della Carta must have been near completion or already completed when Giovanni extracted pictorial ideas from it to execute the Ferrara *Coronation*. As we shall continue to see, Giovanni typically responded almost immediately to the work of other artists, and a date of 1441–42 therefore seems plausible for the Ferrara *Coronation*.

In his earliest known painting, then, Giovanni appears to have selected his models from works of art that may be grouped into two broad categories. The first would include works of art by Jacopo, namely his drawings and paintings, as well as works registering Jacopo's own artistic inheritance, from Gentile da Fabriano and even Altichiero by way of Miretto. The second, however, would include more recently created works of art within Giovanni's ambit that the artist himself observed and appreciated: in this case the Porta della Carta and the frescoes of the Palazzo della Ragione, both of which were commanding respect even before their completion.

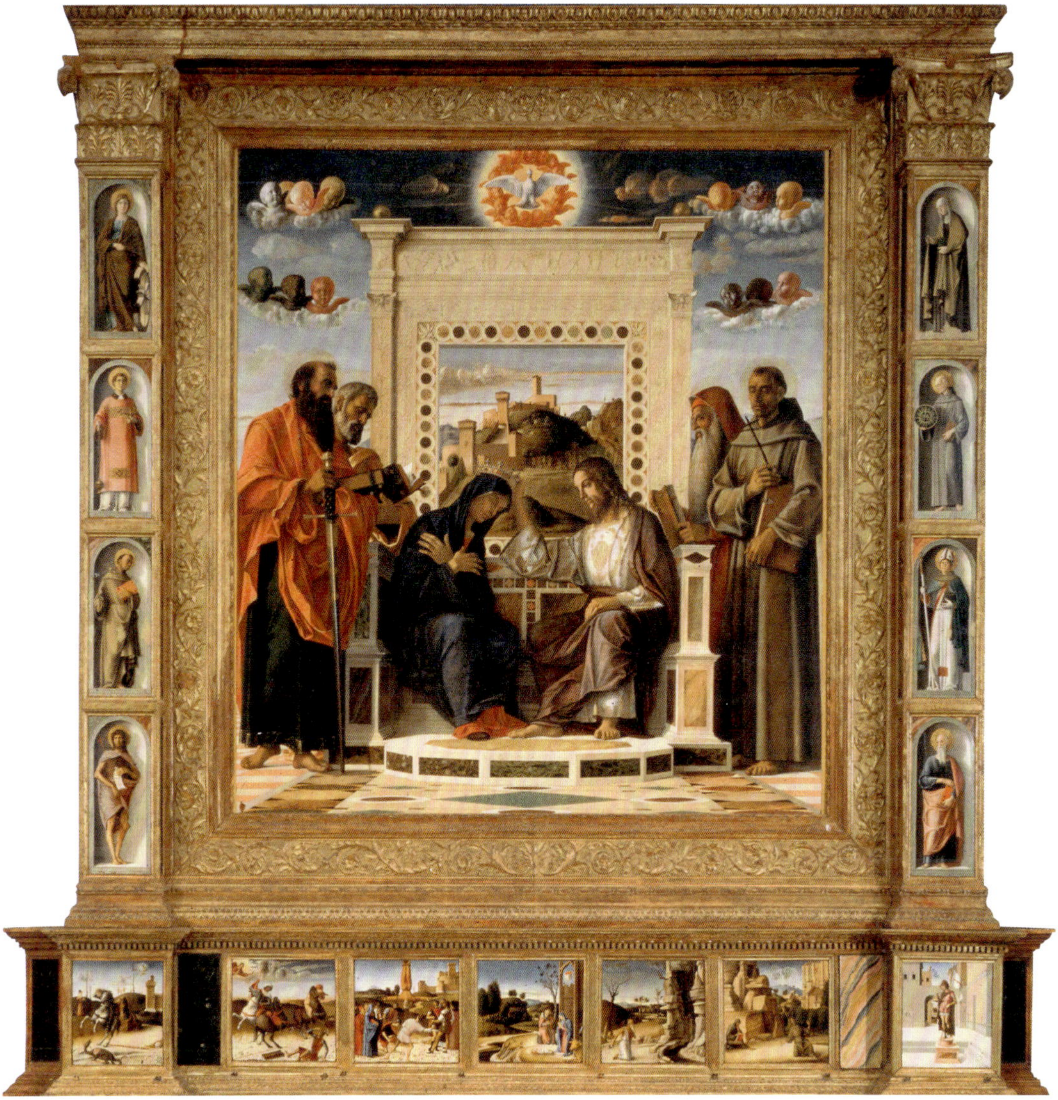

FIGURE 42 Giovanni Bellini, *The Coronation of the Virgin* (Pesaro Altarpiece), ca. 1474. Oil on panel, 262 × 240 cm. Museo Civico, Pesaro

In addition to indicating Giovanni's aesthetic tastes through his choice of models, the Ferrara *Coronation* also displays his own artistic interests. For instance, Giovanni purposely juxtaposed objects composed of different materials in the *Coronation*: stone and marble inlays contrast with wood, plush cushions, and flowing fabrics. This strong interest in contrasting materials, an interest that would be lifelong for Giovanni, does not appear to have derived from Jacopo, whose own drawings and extant paintings rarely explore and only occasionally depict such contrasts—although a few examples may be found, such as in Jacopo's portrayal of a gossamer veil that is sometimes set against the Virgin's face or the body of the Christ Child (see fig. 24), or of an inlaid wooden lectern in his Brescia *Annunciation* (see fig. 45).[20] In the Ferrara *Coronation*, however, it appears that one of Giovanni's *concetti*, or guiding artistic ideas, was to create a pleasing variation for the eye by placing objects of different materials side-by-side with one another, despite his youthful limitations in visually rendering these materials.

Toward the end of his life, when Giovanni was at the height of his painterly skills, he told his friend, the poet and humanist Pietro Bembo, that he did not appreciate patrons who would "limit his brush" because he preferred "to wander [*vagare*] according to his will in paintings" so that they might "satisfy whoever admires them."[21] Since *vagare* suggests a physical wandering, this quotation is often taken to mean Giovanni's approach to executing landscapes, but the eye might equally wander over surfaces and textures of differing materials, taking pleasure in their depictions and collocations in order to experience a visual delight.[22]

Remarkably, Giovanni displayed the same interest in juxtaposing materials when executing the same pictorial subject some 30 years later in his brilliant Pesaro Altarpiece (ca. 1474, fig. 42).[23] Given that the Ferrara *Coronation* was executed in a Gothic style when Giovanni was still an adolescent and that the Pesaro Altarpiece is an entirely Renaissance work executed by an accomplished artist of nearly 50 years old, one might expect little similarity between these paintings. Perhaps startlingly, however, the two works are indeed visually related: in the geometric marble inlays and rectilinear bases of their thrones; in the emphasis Giovanni placed on the contrasting materials of wood and stone; in the careful positioning of the usual blue and red colors of the Madonna and her pillow; in the saints in niches of the framing architecture; and in the splash of red paint, placed near the apex of the vertical axis, that portrays the seraphim surrounding the Holy Spirit and the robe of the Old Testament prophet.[24] It is tempting to see the Pesaro Altarpiece as the maturation of an artistic sensibility that, to some extent, was already in place in Giovanni's youthful Ferrara *Coronation*.

Another of Giovanni's experiments in the Ferrara *Coronation*, although of less enduring interest to the artist than his juxtaposition of materials, was his use of a painting's vertical axis to inflect color contrasts: thus the groups of angels to either side of God the Father and the Old Testament prophet are executed in two contrasting colors. Giovanni's model may have been the blue and red seraphim separated by a central throne in a painting of the *Coronation of the Virgin* (1438, fig. 43) attributed by some scholars to Ercole del Fiore, who served as a witness to Giovanni and Jacopo Bellini's 1440 *divisio*.[25] Years later, Giovanni

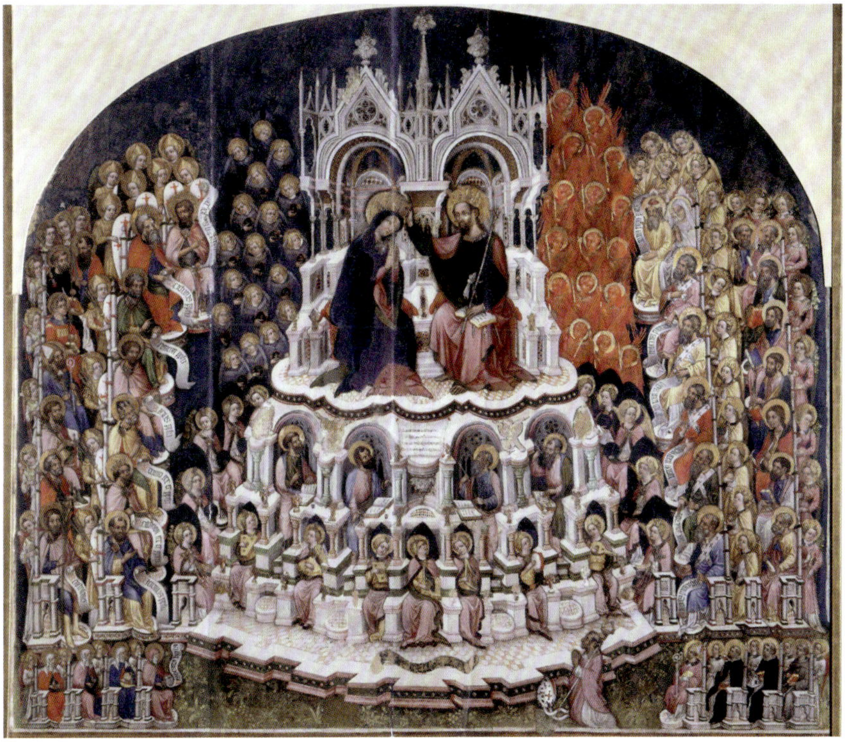

FIGURE 43 Attributed to Ercole del Fiore, *The Coronation of the Virgin*, 1438. Tempera on panel, 283 × 303 cm. Gallerie dell'Accademia, Venice

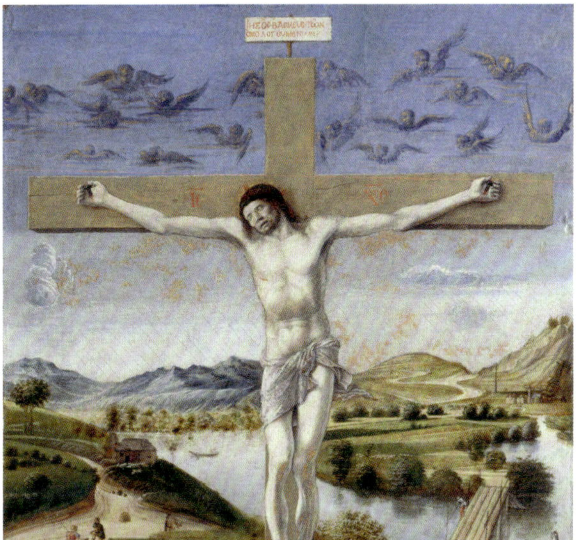

FIGURE 44 Giovanni Bellini, *The Crucifixion with the Virgin and Saint John the Evangelist* (detail), ca. 1457. Tempera on panel, 54 × 30 cm. Museo Correr, Venice

would explore a similar pictorial strategy in his *Crucifixion with the Virgin and Saint John the Evangelist* (ca. 1457, fig. 44), by executing the background landscape behind the crucifix in two tones, one cooler and bluer, the other warmer with earth tones, on either side of Christ's cross.[26] This two-tone splitting along the central vertical axis was a clever visual experiment, but perhaps not an emotionally or spiritually grounded one, which may be why Giovanni rarely employed the strategy later in his career.

A Rare Example

A basic question one may ask about the Ferrara *Coronation* is: why does it exist at all, given that children and adolescents in the Italian Renaissance almost never executed paintings? Paintings were luxury items, created with expensive materials—the blues might derive from lapis lazuli mined in Afghanistan, and the gold leaf was real gold. A single painting might sell for more than an artist earned in an entire year. Hence, very few childhood works were executed during the Renaissance. Why is the Ferrara *Coronation* one of these very few?

One possible answer is that Giovanni might have executed the painting for himself and without an outside commission. At about the age of 16, Giovanni found himself in an immensely unusual social, legal, and economic position for a young Renaissance artist-in-training. He was legally emancipated, since his father Nicoletto had died, and, under the previously discussed *divisio*, he would have inherited his share of his father's patrimony. Unlike nearly all other Italian Renaissance masters—although with a handful of exceptions (notably Raphael, also because of the death of his father)—Giovanni came into an early inheritance in his adolescence, one that he had every legal right to spend.[27] Moreover, Giovanni probably had no significant expenses, since he presumably continued to live with Jacopo and work for him as an assistant following the 1440 *divisio*.[28] Thus it seems possible that, with the *Coronation*, Giovanni chose to produce his own rather large work of art (38.6 × 28.3 in. / 98 × 72 cm); his costs were the materials, and he would provide the labor. The painting might have been executed as a practice piece, a showpiece, or for some other combination of reasons. Indeed, perhaps the most famous painting by an adolescent in the entire fifteenth century, Michelangelo's *Torment of Saint Anthony* (ca. 1487–88) was also seemingly executed for the artist himself without having been commissioned.[29]

It is also possible, although less probable, that there had been a patron willing to hire Giovanni during the artist's adolescence. However, few commissioned artists in the early 1440s would have signed their name across the center of a painting. In those years, an artist, as a lowly artisan or craftsman lucky to get work, typically would sign his name, if at all, discreetly at the bottom, perhaps in the corner.[30] That the Ferrara *Coronation* is signed in the center and above God the Father may suggest a certain adolescent boldness in its artist, and it seems questionable whether a Venetian patron at that early date would have accepted such an audacious signature in a commissioned work, which perhaps further suggests that Giovanni executed it for himself.

The iconography of the painting may also demonstrate an aspirational brashness and youthful daring on the part of its artist. The Coronation of the Virgin was among the most complicated pictorial subjects in early fifteenth-century Italy. It required a sophisticated compositional balancing, the integration of dozens of figures placed carefully within convoluted architecture, and the dramatic evocation of the Virgin and Christ as the central group of the composition, sometimes accompanied by God the Father and the Holy Spirit. Many if not most of the greatest artists of Northern Italy during the late Middle Ages and early Renaissance undertook the complex subject: Guariento di Arpo (d. by 1370), Paolo Veneziano (d. by 1362), Altichiero, and Gentile da Fabriano among others. Thus, in his adolescence, Giovanni dared to aim high, and the Ferrara *Coronation* may be read as announcing his youthful temerity, perhaps before the artist's painterly skills could match his bold aspirations.

The Ferrara *Coronation of the Virgin* marked a significant step in Giovanni's artistic development and allowed him to experiment with a number of visual ideas to which he would later return. His picture filters the late Gothic fascination with architectural forms through Jacopo's endeavors to master linear perspective.[31] Yet perhaps the most surprising quality of this early painting is not the extent to which the young artist emulated Jacopo's work, but rather how, as an adolescent, Giovanni had already become an extraordinarily keen and discerning observer of a wide-ranging array of drawings, paintings, and sculpture executed in and around Venice. Through his careful selection of motifs, and their alteration and seamless integration into his composition of the *Coronation*, Giovanni established an approach to constructing art that he would continue to develop. Scholars frequently mention that Giovanni, throughout his career, continually sought to assimilate the artistic innovations of his contemporaries.[32] Remarkably it appears that, by about the age of 16, Giovanni had already begun to employ this very strategy.

5 Flashes of Brilliance

If one accepts that Giovanni Bellini executed the signed Ferrara *Coronation*, then a strong case can be made for his authorship of the five predella panels of Jacopo Bellini's *Annunciation* Altarpiece in Brescia (1443–44, fig. 45). The reasons for ascribing the predella to Giovanni are discussed below, along with what these panels might teach us about Giovanni's artistic approach and development around the age of 18. It should be noted, however, that this new attribution has not yet been debated or established in art historical circles.

The Bellini workshop executed the Brescia *Annunciation* Altarpiece apparently in Venice, during the latter part of 1443, and sent it to the Servite Church of Sant'Alessandro in Brescia, where it remains today.[1] A seventeenth-century transcription of a now-lost account book records that in January 1444, two friars from Sant'Alessandro apparently went to collect the *Annunciation* from Vicenza, about halfway between Venice and Brescia, and that its shipping costs from Vicenza were paid on February 1, 1444.[2] It has been hypothesized that Jacopo was asked by the patron to execute a free variant of a now-lost *Annunciation* panel by Fra Angelico (ca. 1395–1455), which was based on the fresco at Santissima Annunziata in Florence, the Servites' mother church. Indeed, the Brescia Altarpiece resembles other such loose "copies," each of which includes a main field depicting the Annunciation and a predella portraying various scenes from the life of the Virgin.[3]

While Jacopo executed the main panels of the Brescia *Annunciation*, scholars have generally agreed that the predella panels are not in Jacopo's hand and have often attributed them ambiguously to "Jacopo's workshop."[4] Indeed, they bear remarkable stylistic parallels to the Ferrara *Coronation* (see fig. 25). Take, for example, the image of the high priest in the predella panel depicting the *Presentation of the Virgin* (fig. 46). The musical angels' distinctive blue robes and floor-length red capes in the Ferrara *Coronation* similarly clothe the high priest (fig. 47). The Old Testament prophet from the Ferrara *Coronation* and the high priest, both with French fork beards, display the same idiosyncratic accent: single strands of

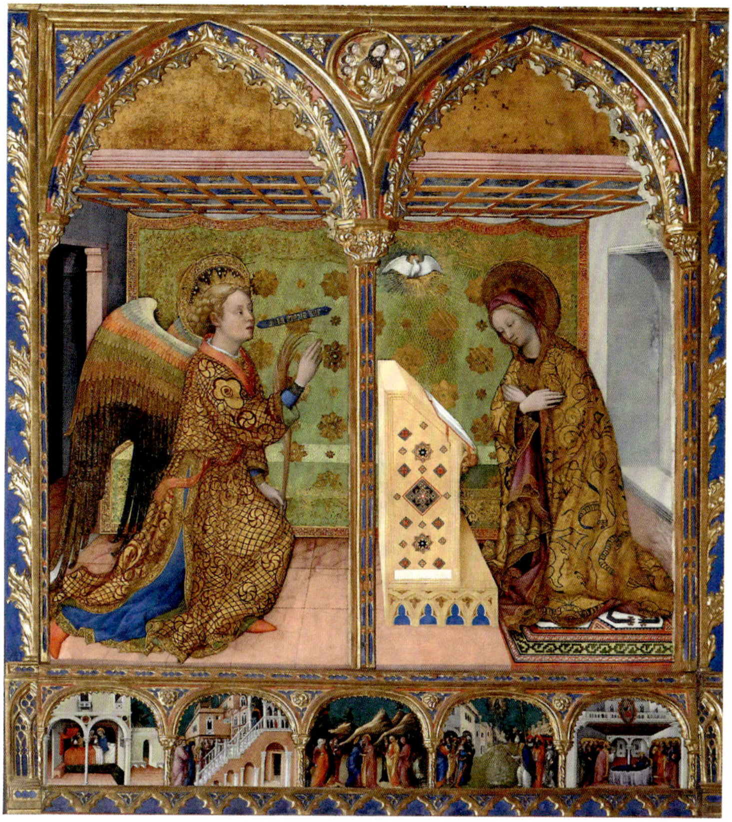

FIGURE 45 Jacopo and Giovanni Bellini, *The Annunciation* (Brescia Altarpiece), 1443–44. Tempera on panel, 298 × 196 cm. Church of Sant'Alessandro, Brescia

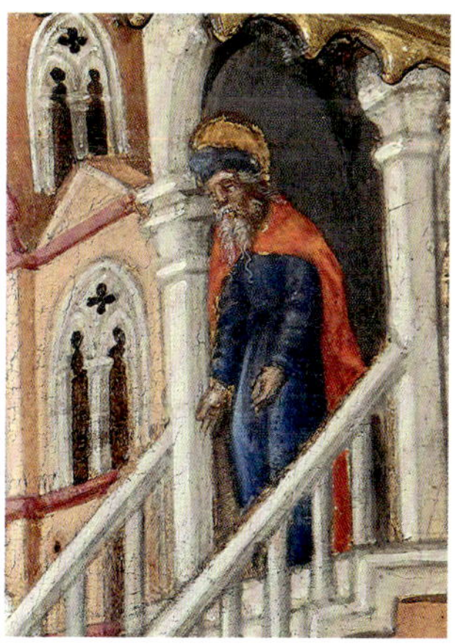

FIGURE 46 Giovanni Bellini, *The Presentation of the Virgin* (detail of fig. 45), predella panel of the Brescia Altarpiece

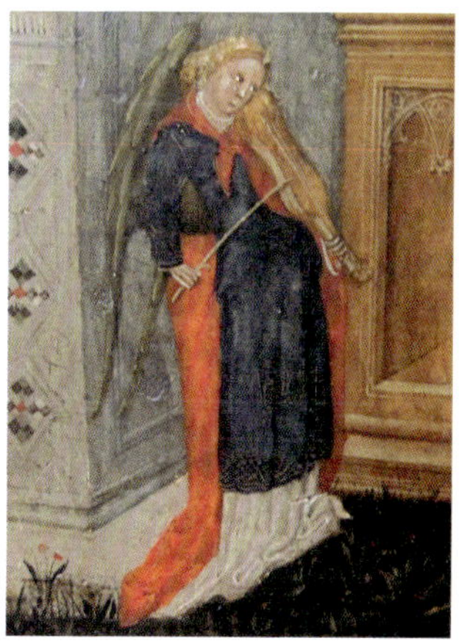

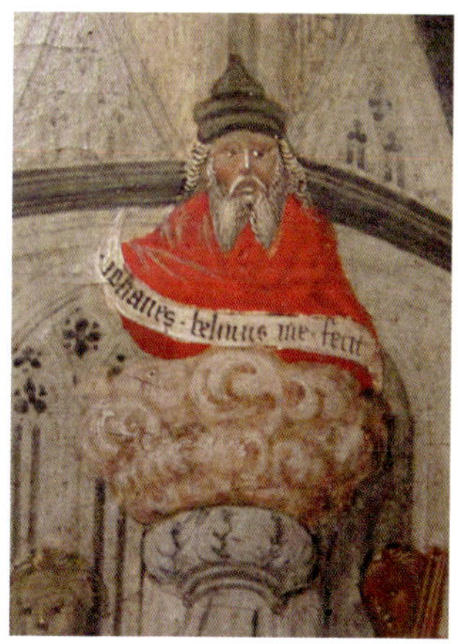

FIGURES 47 & 48 Giovanni Bellini, *The Coronation of the Virgin* (details of fig. 25)

unkempt hair that delicately curl downward, from the *peyot* (sidelocks) of the prophet and the beard of the high priest (fig. 48). Small quatrefoil windows, among other elements, link the images. This narrow example highlights only a handful of the stylistic connections between the Ferrara *Coronation* and the predella panels of Jacopo Bellini's *Annunciation* Altarpiece in Brescia.

In the early 1440s, Giovanni must have been Jacopo's foremost assistant in the Bellini workshop. Gentile, born between 1429 and ca. 1435, might also have been a young assistant by then, but his development into an independent artist was slow, and his first paintings date to the early 1460s.[5] The first works of Leonardo Bellini, who had signed a two-year contract in 1443 to assist Jacopo, were manuscript illuminations that began to appear in the mid-1450s.[6] In any event, Giovanni was surely the most talented artist in the workshop, and it seems safe to assume that, as he matured, he would have been assigned more substantial responsibilities and the execution of small works, such as a series of predella panels. In 1443, Giovanni was about 18, certainly old enough to have executed the predella panels. In addition, the 1443 date for the Brescia predella accords stylistically with what one might expect from Giovanni in the year or so following his presumed execution of the Ferrara *Coronation*: namely, that in late adolescence he was developing his artistic skills in steps rather than great leaps. Thus a range of evidence—the stylistic similarities between the Ferrara *Coronation* and the *Annunciation* predella, the latter's 1443 year of execution, and Giovanni's presence and position in Jacopo's workshop—strongly supports Giovanni's authorship of the panels, identified here for the first time, and it seems likely that Giovanni executed the entire predella, as there is a stylistic uniformity running through the five small pictures.

The Birth of the Virgin

Viewed through two arches of a loggia, Anne sits in bed holding her infant daughter, Mary, and is attended by two women and a child (fig. 49). To the left of the bedchamber, an arched doorway reveals a partially visible room, and to the right, a patio with two low benches ends in a crenellated wall with an archway and garden area beyond. An upper story above the loggia features a small balcony between two rectangular windows decorated with inlays. Like the main panel of Jacopo's altarpiece, the composition is executed using linear perspective, with its vanishing point located on the chamber's central column, although above the capital rather than below it.

Giovanni's point of departure appears to have been a lost work probably by Altichiero, which is apparently recorded to some extent in an unattributed painting executed in ca. 1400–10 and now in Strasbourg (fig. 50).[7] Both pictures owe much to Giotto's early fourteenth-century fresco of the same subject in the Scrovegni Chapel, Padua (fig. 51). As discussed in Chapter 4, Altichiero and Gentile da Fabriano were the two primary artistic models for Jacopo, so it is perhaps telling that young Giovanni would also look to

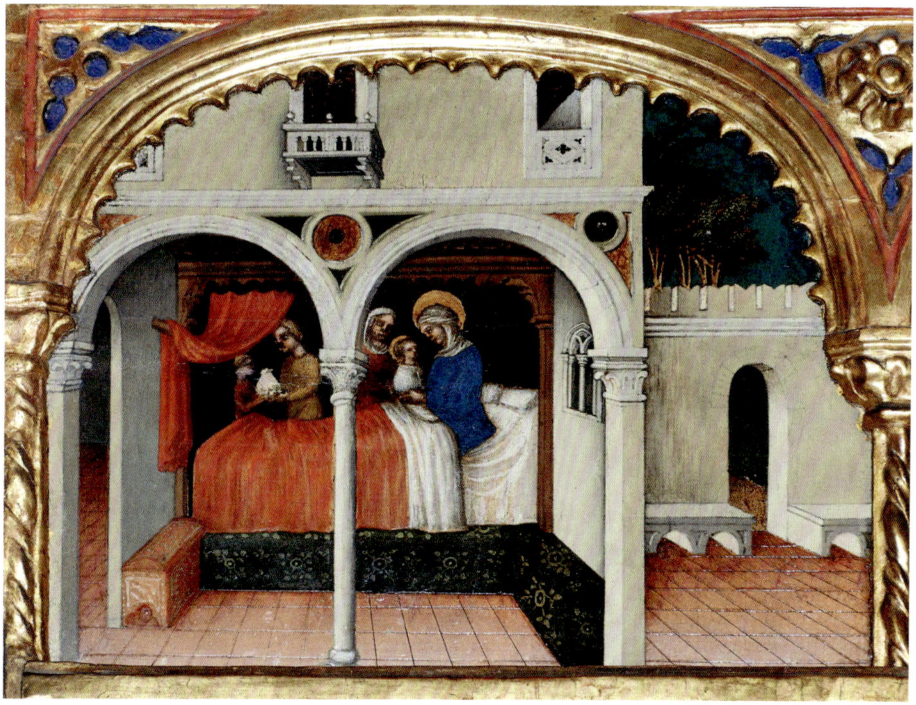

FIGURE 49 Giovanni Bellini, *The Birth of the Virgin* (detail of fig. 45), predella panel of the Brescia Altarpiece

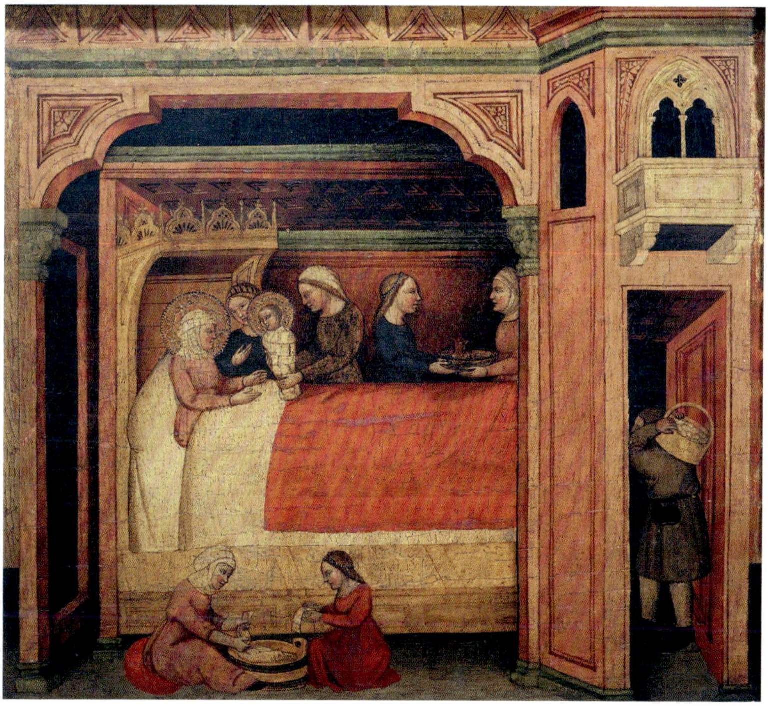

FIGURE 50 Anonymous (after Altichiero?), *The Birth of the Virgin*, ca. 1400–10. Oil on panel, 54.4 × 61.5 cm. Musée des Beaux-Arts, Strasbourg

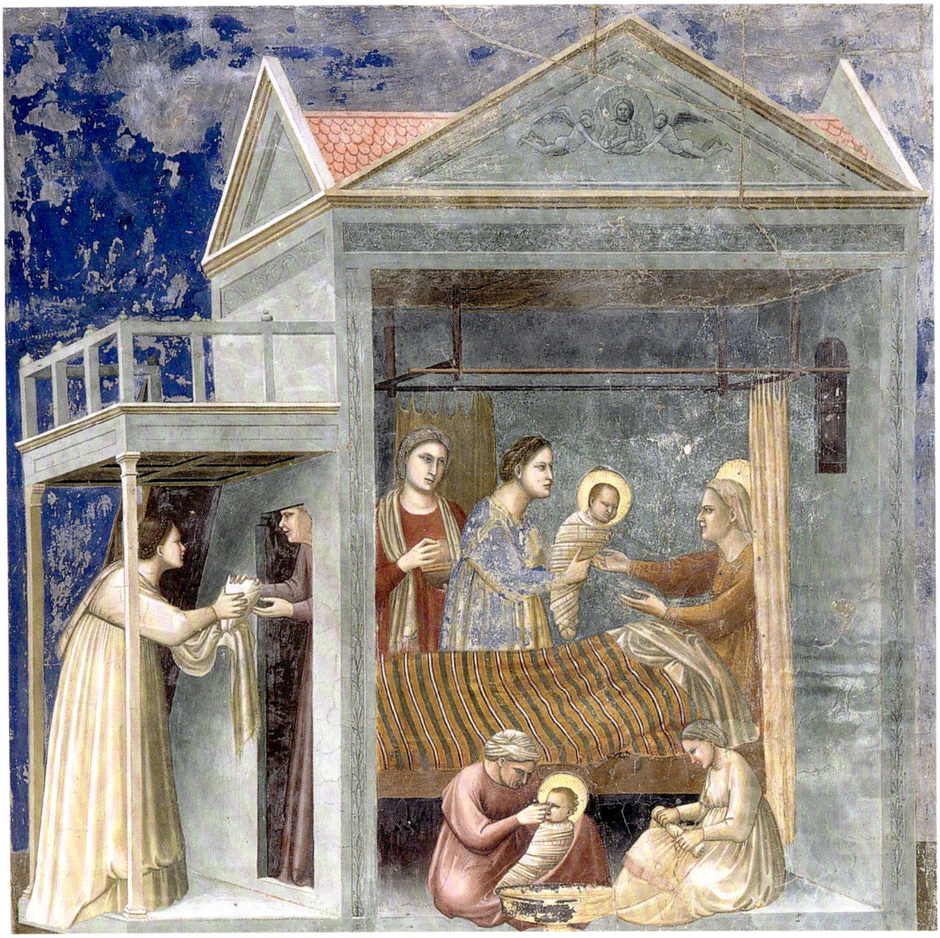

FIGURE 51 Giotto di Bondone, *The Birth of the Virgin*, ca. 1305. Fresco, 200 × 185 cm. Scrovegni Chapel, Padua

Altichiero for inspiration. Altichiero probably inspired Giovanni's depiction of the architectural space, with an open entranceway on the left and a wall with a window on the right, Anne seated in bed with attendants beyond, and perhaps even the balcony. Giovanni also borrowed several motifs from Jacopo's sketchbooks, such as the bull's-eye medallions set in marble spandrels that are similarly placed in several of Jacopo's Paris drawings (see fig. 89).[8]

A number of extraordinary features of this small predella panel reveal aspects of Giovanni's early aesthetic sensibilities. The first was his choice *not* to fill the entire composition with Anne's bedroom, as he might have. Instead, he created a number of distinct spaces and ornamented planes for the viewer to explore. The eye moves down from the balconied façade, around the bed area, through the inner doorway, then perhaps out onto the patio, and toward the unseen garden and its trees, whose leaves are gently rustling—away from Anne and the Virgin, perhaps by divine force (Giovanni would return to this idea in his *Saint Francis in the Desert*, ca. 1476–78, see fig. 3).[9] In the *Birth of the Virgin*, Giovanni therefore created his first known image through which the observer has little choice but to wander, which recalls Giovanni's artistic strategy of wandering as he is painting, mentioned in Chapter 4.[10]

Another feature of this panel is Giovanni's remarkable attention to the depiction of light. Notice his representation of glare off the second-story window, which might be the earliest depiction of sunlight on glass in Italian Renaissance art.[11] Indeed, it is reminiscent of the sun glinting off the palazzo shutters in the photograph in Chapter 3 (see fig. 16). Here, Giovanni shows himself as extremely sharp-eyed and able to bring his observations of nature into his art. It is also remarkable that in this panel, Giovanni created a single, coherent light source, positioned outside the frame on the upper left, to illuminate both interior and exterior spaces, from the arches and columns of the loggia to the tiled patio that recedes toward the darkness of the garden. This light casts only minimal shadows, however, such as where the *cassone* (marriage chest) meets the floor or where the bedroom wall slightly darkens the patio flooring. In some areas of the composition the light seems imperfectly rendered, for there are no shadows from the columns onto the terrazzo flooring or from the small balcony onto the building's façade.

Constructing a single light source to model objects and unify the composition constituted a new step for the Bellini workshop. Jacopo's sketchbooks, for all their innovation, demonstrate little interest in exploring the effects of illumination. This is surprising, especially given that the predella panel depicting the *Nativity* in Gentile da Fabriano's Strozzi Altarpiece (1423, fig 52), on which Jacopo surely assisted, was a notable early example of an Italian painting representing consistent lighting effects emanating from a source (the Christ Child) depicted within the painting itself.[12] The Brescia panels reveal Giovanni's emergent sensibilities and developing skills in the portrayal of light, although the artist was still far from the master of light that he would eventually become.

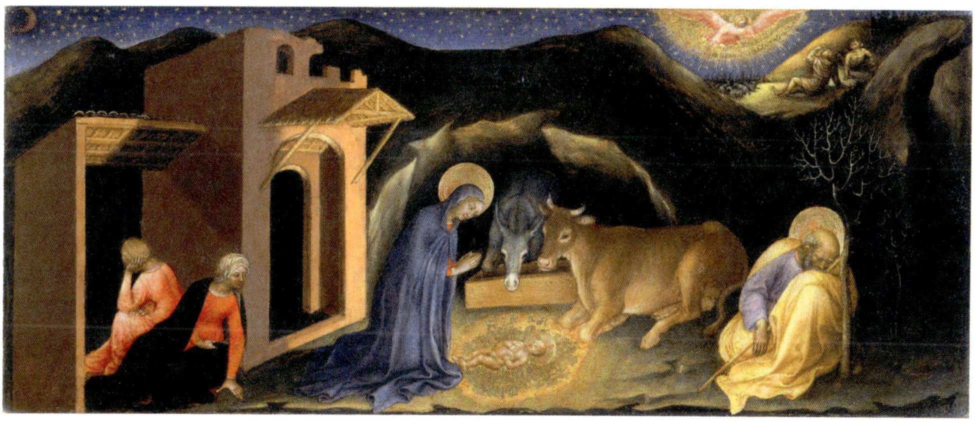

FIGURE 52 Gentile da Fabriano, *The Nativity*, predella panel of the Strozzi Altarpiece, 1423. Tempera, gold, and silver on panel. Galleria degli Uffizi, Florence

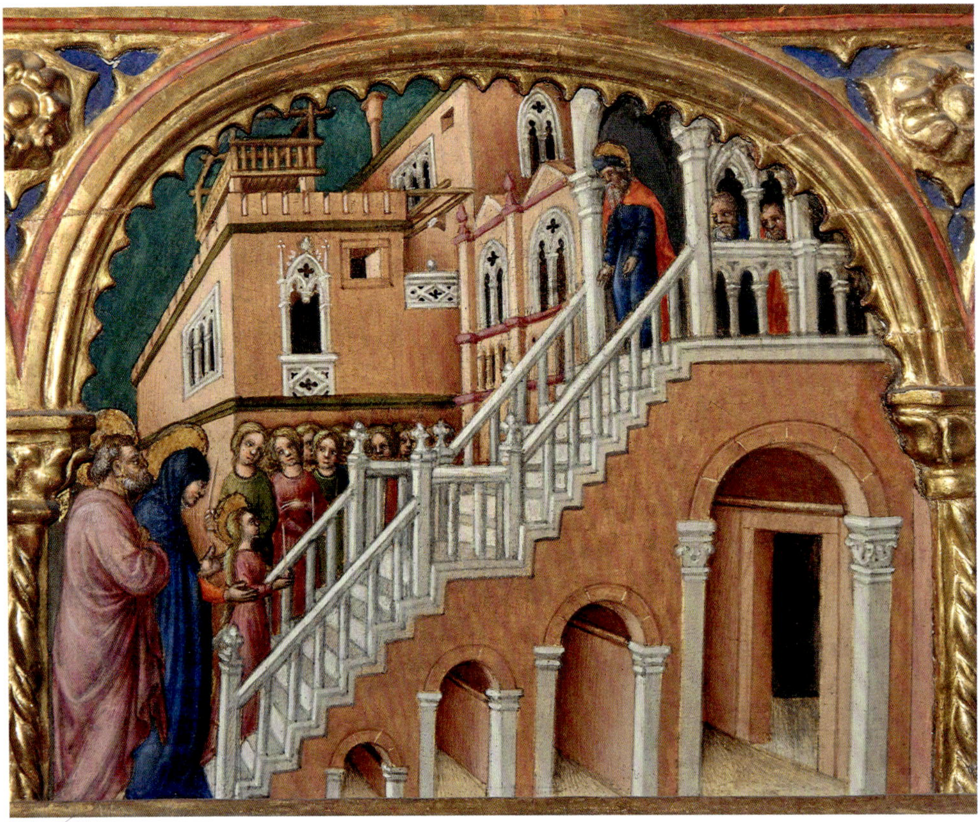

FIGURE 53 Giovanni Bellini, *The Presentation of the Virgin* (detail of fig. 45), predella panel of the Brescia Altarpiece

Giovanni's use of linear perspective is also clearly in development. He competently united the loggia scene and outdoor patio in one-point geometric perspective, but neglected to execute the upper balcony and its corbels according to his established vanishing point on the loggia's central column, which would have required the balcony to be rendered in extreme foreshortening, perhaps a difficult endeavor for the young artist (although he might have easily replicated a foreshortened balcony from one of Jacopo's drawings, see fig. 28).[13] Giovanni's balcony, with its own distinct vanishing point, located near the nape of Anne's neck, compromises the composition's perspectival coherency; it is an inconsistency that Jacopo was unlikely to make in the early 1440s, further implying Giovanni's sole authorship of the predella panels.

The Presentation of the Virgin

The scene is from the *Legenda aurea*, which itself relied on an apocryphal gospel of St. James (fig. 53). When the Virgin Mary was three years old, her parents, Joachim and Anne, took her to the Lord's Temple to be raised with the other virgins by the high priest.[14] Without assistance from her parents, Mary climbed the temple's 15 steps, which, we are told, correspond

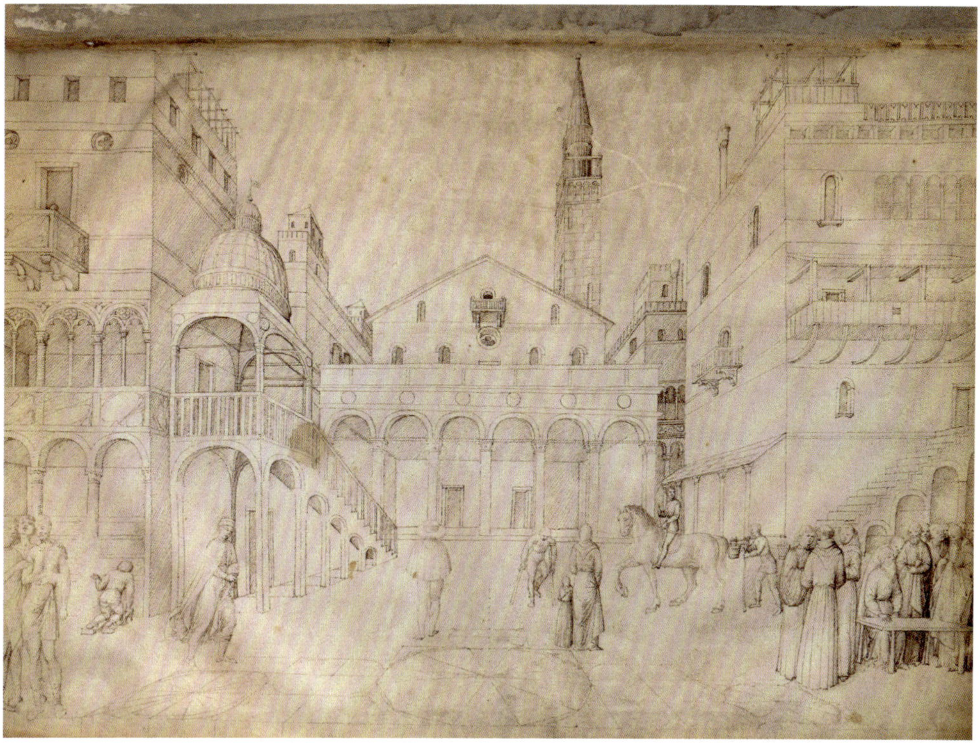

FIGURE 54 Jacopo Bellini, *Urban Square with Church Façade*, ca. 1440–45. Vellum, 26 × 38 cm. Cabinet des dessins, Musée du Louvre, Paris

to the 15 Gradual Psalms (120–34).[15] Giovanni set his *Presentation* in architecture resembling the exterior of a Venetian palazzo adorned with Gothic windows, a bell-shaped Venetian chimney, and a viewing loggia (an early *altana*, or Venetian terrace). At the base of the temple's staircase, Anne, standing beside Joachim, steadies her small daughter Mary, who carries a ceremonial candle and ascends the stairs to the high priest, while the temple virgins, also bearing candles, look on. Again, Giotto's fresco of the *Presentation of the Virgin* in the Scrovegni Chapel was important in establishing the conventional Northern Italian treatment of the subject.

Giovanni unified the image using both a single light source, placed outside and above the picture frame to the left, and linear perspective, with the vanishing point positioned above Joachim's head. The unique staircase (which is built upon a series of four architecturally unlikely arches), viewing loggia, and chimney appear in a drawing in Jacopo's Paris sketchbook (ca. 1440–45, fig. 54).[16] Jacopo drew the idiosyncratic staircase, with or without an *altana*, on a number of other sheets, such as his *Judgment of Solomon*, which Giovanni had previously used as a model for his Ferrara *Coronation* (see fig. 31).[17] Jacopo's later drawing of the *Presentation of the Virgin* from the 1460s, with Joachim and Anne at the base of a staircase parallel to the picture plane, the Virgin in the midst of her ascent, and an *altana* on the background rooftop, seems to "update" Giovanni's predella with monumental forms, suggesting how Jacopo might also have been inspired by Giovanni (fig. 55).[18]

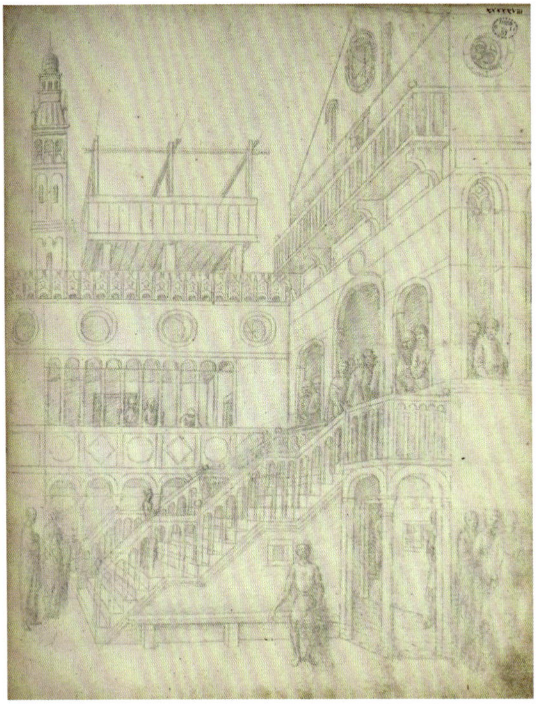

FIGURE 55 Jacopo Bellini, *The Presentation of the Virgin in the Temple*, early 1460s. Paper, 41.5 × 33.6 cm. Department of Prints and Drawings, British Museum, London

The Visitation

As described in the Gospel of Luke (1:39–56), Mary visited her cousin Elisabeth when they were both pregnant, Mary with Christ, and Elisabeth with John the Baptist (fig. 56).[19] The *Visitation* depicts the earliest known landscape by Giovanni Bellini, who would become one of the greatest painters of landscape in the Renaissance. Here, he artfully balanced the composition, with two groups of four onlookers framing the Virgin and Elisabeth, who embrace in the center, and a winding stream on the right counterbalanced by a single tree and a small boy on the left. The painting has a tenderness not found in Jacopo's work, especially in how Giovanni executed the small boy, reminiscent of the musical angels in the Ferrara *Coronation* in its sensitivity. The boy gazes toward his mother, who holds the child's hand in a way that seems intended to prevent him from running off.

To help construct the image, Giovanni once again borrowed and refined motifs found in the work of Jacopo and Altichiero. The mother with the small boy, and perhaps the greeting between Mary and Elisabeth, appear to derive from Altichiero's *Crucifixion* scene for the Chapel of San Giacomo in Padua (ca. 1376–79, fig. 57).[20] The small wooden bridge that crosses a winding stream to the right of Giovanni's picture may have been inspired by Jacopo's similar stream crossed by a similar bridge toward the middle of the sheet in

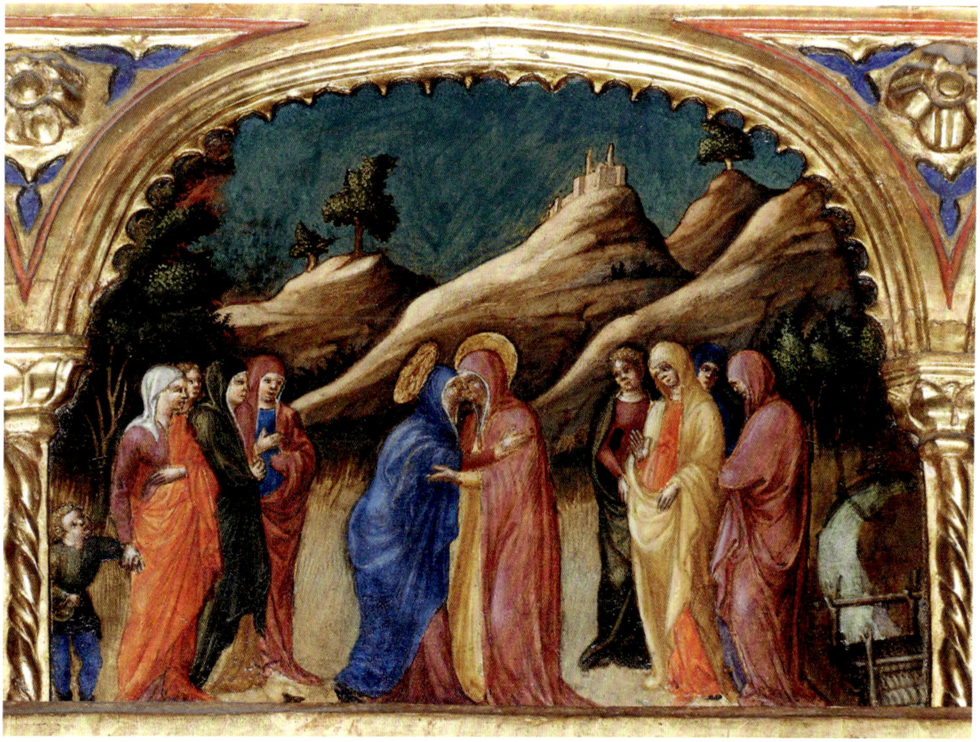

FIGURE 56 Giovanni Bellini, *The Visitation* (detail of fig. 45), predella panel of the Brescia Altarpiece

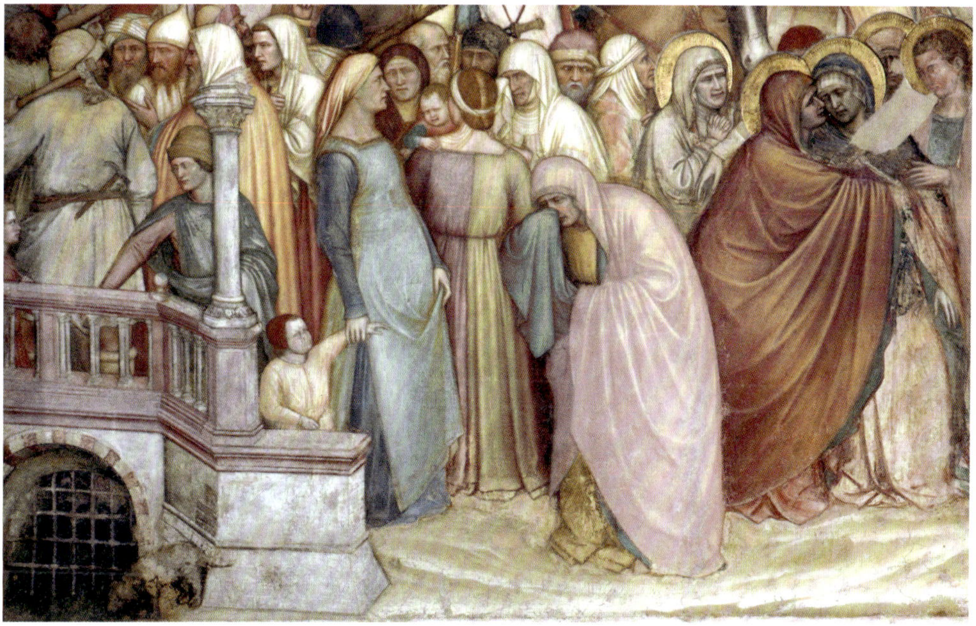

FIGURE 57 Altichiero, *The Crucifixion* (detail), ca. 1376–79. Fresco, 240 × 840 cm. Chapel of San Felice (formerly of San Giacomo), Basilica of Sant'Antonio di Padova, Padua

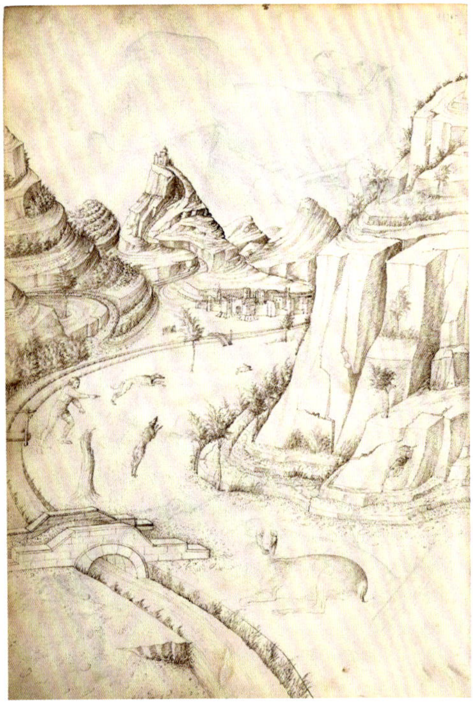

FIGURE 58 Jacopo Bellini, *The Stigmatization of Saint Francis*, ca. 1440–45. Vellum, 38 × 26 cm. Cabinet des dessins, Musée du Louvre, Paris

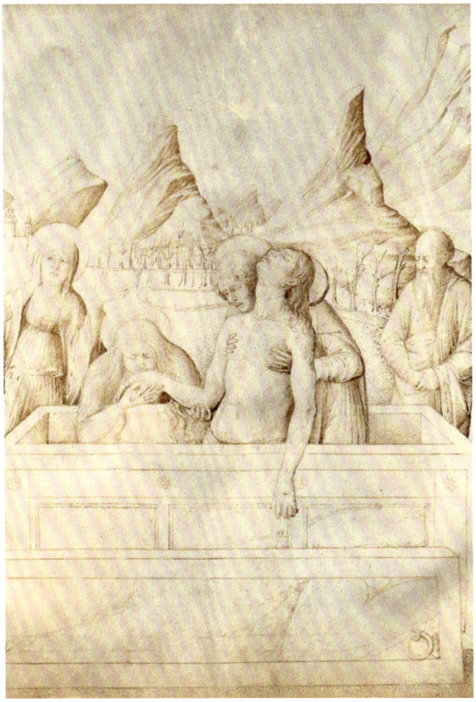

FIGURE 59 Jacopo Bellini, *The Lamentation/Entombment of Christ* (detail), ca. 1430. Vellum, 38 × 26 cm. Cabinet des dessins, Musée du Louvre, Paris

his Paris drawing, the *Stigmatization of Saint Francis* (ca. 1440–45, fig. 58).[21] Giovanni's overlapping background mountains, pinnacled with one or two robust trees or a fortress, are common motifs in Jacopo's sketchbooks. However, Giovanni's hills seem like swirls of ice cream melting in the sun, while Jacopo's generally appear more angular and faceted, although some may still have served as models for Giovanni (ca. 1435, fig. 59).[22] Again, Giovanni was careful to unite the image with a single source of light, the sun, and to depict the sunlit side of the mountains, hilltop trees, and fortress all gradually falling into shadow.

The Miracle of the Snow

The miracle purportedly occurred one summer in fourth-century Rome under the reign of Pope Liberius (r. 352–66). On August 5, the Virgin caused snow to fall on the summit of the Esquiline hill, thus indicating the building site for the Church of Santa Maria Maggiore.[23] In Giovanni's painting, snow falls from the heavenly Virgin, who is set within an aureole of golden rays (fig. 60). Below, Pope Liberius swings his hoe onto a patch of snow, breaking ground on the site of the future church, as cardinals and townspeople watch. Beyond the snowfall, a long street, flanked by buildings, recedes toward distant trees and mountains crowned with fortresses to a central vanishing point. The composition appears to have been

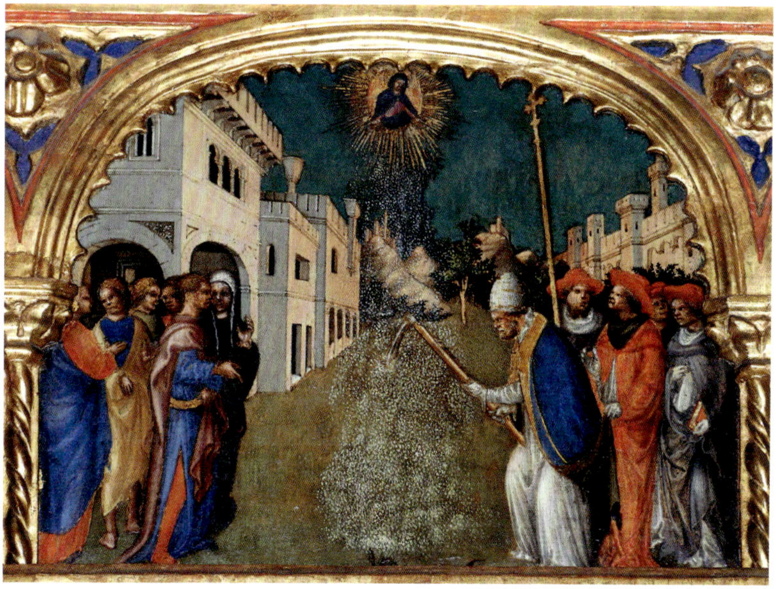

FIGURE 60 Giovanni Bellini, *The Miracle of the Snow* (detail of fig. 45), predella panel of the Brescia Altarpiece

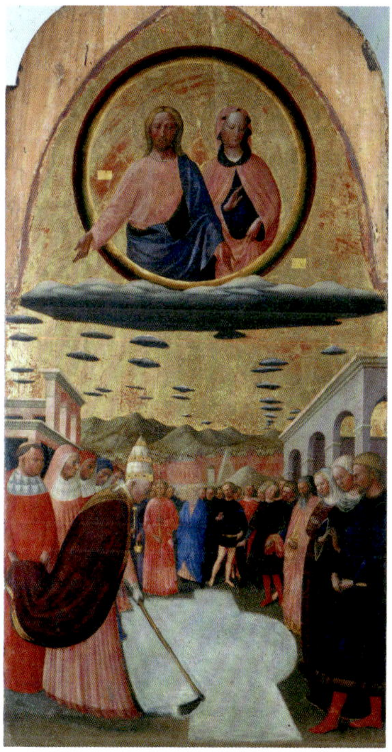

FIGURE 61 Masolino, *The Founding of Santa Maria Maggiore*, ca. 1428–32. Tempera and gold leaf on panel, 144 × 76 cm. Museo Nazionale di Capodimonte, Naples

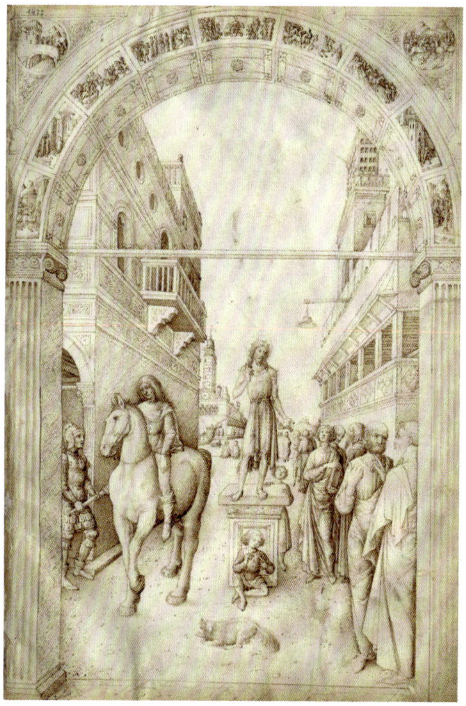

FIGURE 62 Jacopo Bellini, *Saint John the Baptist Preaching in a Harbor City*, ca. 1440. Vellum, 38 × 26 cm. Cabinet des dessins, Musée du Louvre, Paris

based on a painting of the same subject by Masolino (ca. 1383–ca. 1436), part of the so-called Colonna Altarpiece at Santa Maria Maggiore in Rome that is now dispersed (ca. 1428–32, fig. 61), but it seems doubtful that Giovanni would have seen Masolino's work in person.[24] Giovanni's composition also perhaps relies on Jacopo's drawing of *Saint John the Baptist Preaching in a Harbor City* in the Paris sketchbook (ca. 1440, fig. 62), with its architectural façades positioned on orthogonal lines that define a centralized street and converge toward a distant hill topped by a citadel, but no specific motifs appear to have been inspired by Jacopo's work.[25]

Two further aspects of this predella panel deserve brief mention: the care with which Giovanni individualized each figure and the delicacy of his brush. Giovanni attentively fashioned distinct clothing for each person, from the pope wearing blue and gold and a papal tiara, to the cardinals in their red hats and red or gray copes, to the onlookers variously garbed in reds, blues, blacks, and golds. Giovanni's brush is remarkably adept at placing fine details, such as the index finger of an onlooker pointing downward, or white highlights on the pope's sleeve, both perhaps executed with a single paintbrush hair.

The Death of the Virgin

The Virgin's dormition and ascendance to heaven are described in the *Legenda aurea*, which followed apocryphal writings that included Pseudo-John the Evangelist's *Liber de Dormitione Mariae*.[26] By the twelfth century, the standard Byzantine iconography depicted the Virgin lying on a bier, parallel to the picture plane, and surrounded by apostles. Peter is usually pictured in liturgical garbs delivering the last rites, while John is elderly and often found kneeling to comfort the Virgin as he did during the Crucifixion. Christ hovers above, surrounded by a mandorla and holding a swaddled infant representing the Virgin's soul.[27]

Giovanni embellished this traditional iconography with architecture, a consistent light source, and linear perspective (fig. 63). He echoed Jacopo's *Annunciation* panels above by positioning the vanishing point near the capital of the central column and by representing a latticework ceiling, a tiled floor, and a colonnade of two round arches (although not Gothic) supported by Corinthian columns. Giovanni's point of departure might have been Jacopo's Paris drawing the *Judgment of Solomon,* with its boxlike interior, wooden ceiling supporting an overhead balcony, and colonnade with a flattened foreground area (ca. 1435–40, fig. 64).[28] The line of onlookers peering at the Virgin and the overhead mandorla of a seated God the Father presumably derive from Jacopo's Paris drawing of the same subject (see fig. 28).[29] Again, Giovanni registered his own pictorial interests in illumination and materials. Light from the upper left illuminates the walls and interior of the rightmost round arch. And he took care to render white marble architecture, a wooden ceiling and wooden arms of the bier, terracotta flooring, marble inlays in the spandrels of the colonnade, and various colored fabrics worn by the Virgin and apostles.

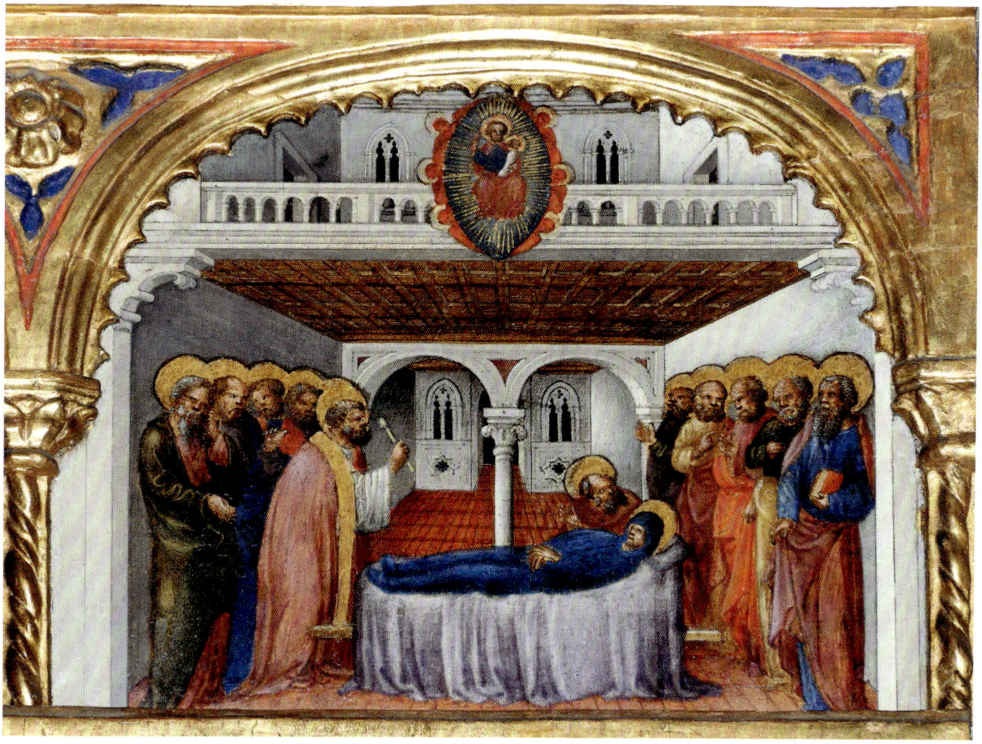

FIGURE 63 Giovanni Bellini, *The Death of the Virgin* (detail of fig. 45), predella panel of the Brescia Altarpiece

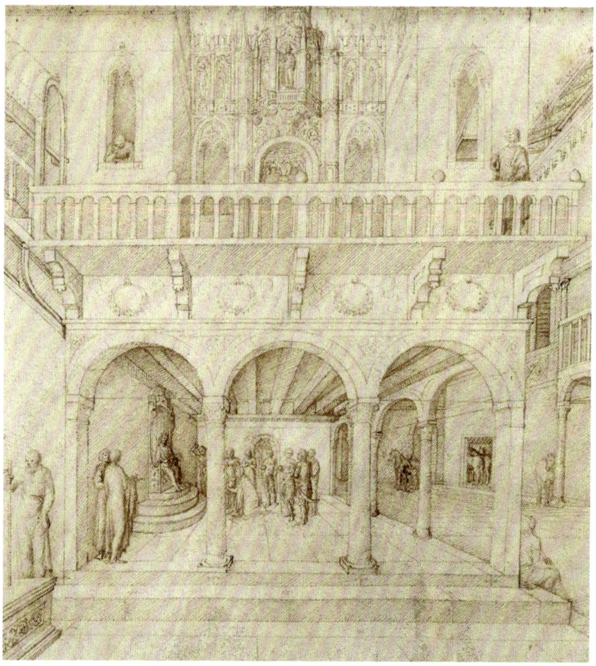

FIGURE 64 Jacopo Bellini, *The Judgment of Solomon* (detail), ca. 1435–40. Vellum. Cabinet des dessins, Musée du Louvre, Paris

Visual Empathy

The five predella panels of the Brescia *Annunciation* reveal a crisp aesthetic sensibility by a young artist burgeoning with ideas and developing toward maturity. I would suggest that Giovanni's pictorial strategies in executing the Ferrara *Coronation* are continued here, such as his practice of utilizing compositions and motifs from Jacopo and Altichiero, his juxtaposition of different materials, and his more complex use of linear perspective. Little has been written about Giovanni's masterful use of perspective in mature works such as his *Saint Francis in the Desert* at the Frick, but its beginnings—and missteps—can be traced to the Ferrara *Coronation* and these small predella panels.[30]

The panels also suggest Giovanni's adolescent sensibilities. If the artist seemed rather audacious in his choice of subject and the placement of his signature in his Ferrara *Coronation*, then in this predella, under Jacopo's watchful eye, Giovanni reveals a purer sense of his creativity, one conveyed in small and sometimes tender observations. These include his depiction of the sun's glare on the window shutters in *Birth of the Virgin*, the mother holding the hand of her child who perhaps wants to be elsewhere in the *Visitation*, and Anne steadying her daughter Mary as she ascends the staircase in *Presentation of the Virgin*. As mentioned, a similar quality also appears in the sweet depiction of the two small angels in Giovanni's Ferrara *Coronation*. It is arguably this visualized empathy, as it might be described, that helped Giovanni develop into perhaps the most sensitive painter of the Virgin and Child in the Renaissance. In his hands the Christ child plays, sleeps, or appears physically childlike, and the Virgin is loving, pensive, or even wistful, perhaps reflecting on her role and intuiting the difficulties and sacrifice that lie ahead (fig. 65).[31] The knowledge that Giovanni was raised without a biological mother makes his later images of mother and child even more emotionally transfixing.[32]

As we have seen, Jacopo's drawings and paintings exhibit no similar quality of tenderness. Although Jacopo may depict various actions and gestures of minor characters apart from the main subject, at no time does he approach such an observant rendering of detail or emotion. This is another pictorial quality that distinguishes Giovanni's early art from Jacopo's known paintings, along with Giovanni's close attention to light. Indeed, Giovanni's dynamic interest in depicting the quality and effects of light, which would soon lead him to study the work of Northern European artists, will eventually help revolutionize Venetian art and lay the foundations for the treatment of light by Giorgione (d. 1510), Titian, and other sixteenth-century Venetian painters.[33] This explosion of interest in depicting light and shadow that would transform Venetian painting began, in some sense, with Giovanni in these five small predella panels of the Brescia altarpiece.[34]

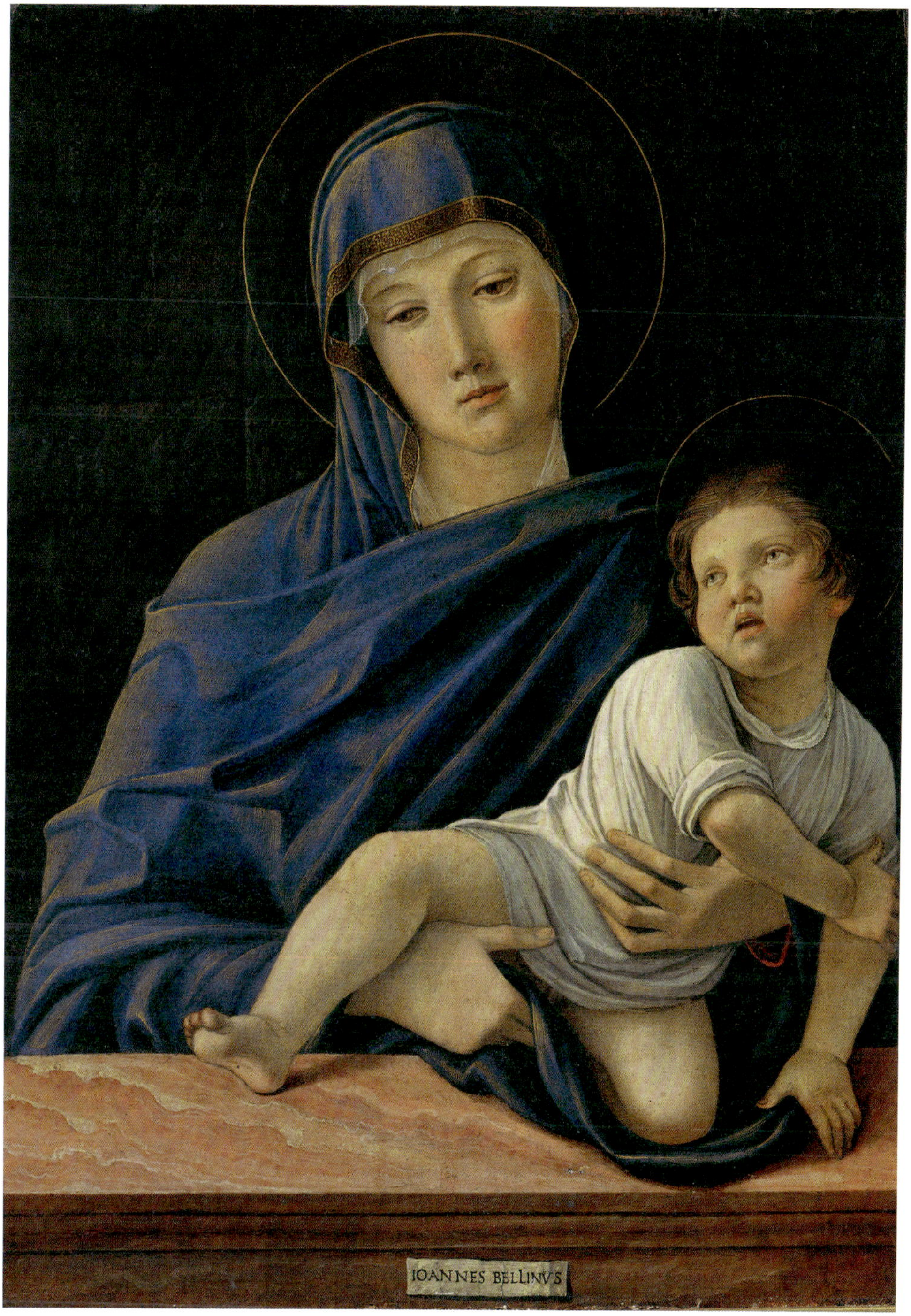

FIGURE 65 Giovanni Bellini, *The Virgin and Child* (Lochis Madonna), ca. 1476. Tempera on panel, 47.4 × 33.8 cm. Accademia Carrara, Bergamo

6 Lessons for Jacopo's Assistant

It is unfortunate that nearly all Jacopo's paintings from 1444 to 1450 no longer exist, and therefore it is impossible to assess Giovanni's possible contributions to them. The conspicuous absence of known works by Giovanni during this interval may be attributed to the fact that he was not yet an independent artist. (The Ferrara *Coronation*, as discussed in Chapter 4, was likely a unique occurrence.) During the 1440s, Giovanni must have primarily functioned as Jacopo's assistant, along with Leonardo Bellini and, when he was old enough, Gentile Bellini, neither of whom produced securely attributable paintings until the mid-1450s or later.[1]

As we have seen, in fifteenth-century Venice it was common for a young artist within a family workshop to serve many years as an assistant before embarking on a fully independent career. For instance, the painter Alvise Vivarini (ca. 1442/53–1503/05) was probably about 30 when he commenced his independent career in ca. 1476 in the workshop of his father, Antonio.[2] The sculptor Antonio Lombardo (ca. 1458–1516) executed his first documented independent commission in 1500–04, apparently in his forties: "His earlier career," wrote Sarah Blake McHam, "which probably spanned about 15 years, had been spent in the family workshop collaborating on commissions awarded [to] his father, Pietro."[3] If a family workshop was regularly receiving commissions, there was often no pressing need for sons to seek early independence. Thus, Gentile Bellini probably began his independent career in his early thirties after collaborating with Jacopo for many years.[4] Indeed, Jacopo himself served as Gentile da Fabriano's assistant from at least 1412 and did not become an independent painter until the late 1420s, when he was probably in his mid-thirties. If Giovanni commenced his independent career in ca. 1450 at about age 25, he would have been precocious relative to when many Venetian artists began executing commissions on their own.

Yet by the age of about 18, Giovanni can be thought of as having proved himself an observant young artist who, if indeed he had executed the predella for Jacopo's Brescia *Annunciation* (1443–44, see fig. 45), was already sensitive to the effects of light and capable of

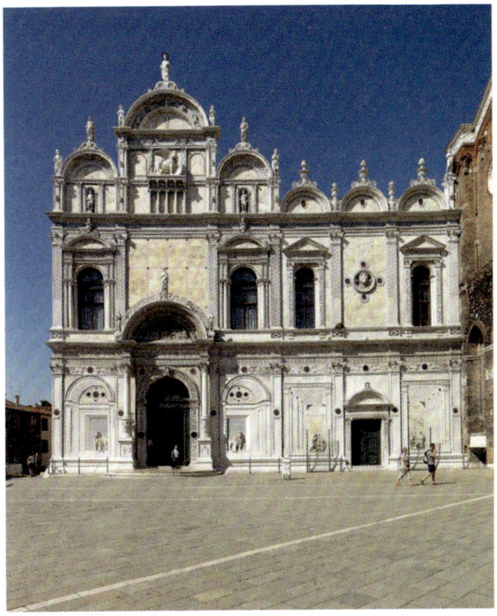

FIGURE 66 Pietro, Tullio, and Antonio Lombardo, Giovanni Buora, and Mauro Codussi, Façade of the Scuola Grande di San Marco, Venice, 1488–ca. 1495

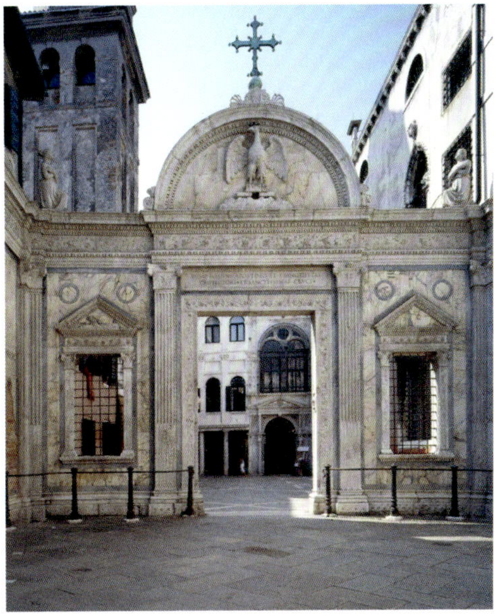

FIGURE 67 Pietro Lombardo, Marble Screen at the Scuola Grande di San Giovanni Evangelista, Venice, 1478–81

completing small-scale narrative compositions on an important ecclesiastical commission. Perhaps surprisingly, it appears that this is the only firmly attributable predella that Giovanni would execute for Jacopo, although it is possible that he might also have helped produce the predella for Jacopo's now-lost Gattamelata Altarpiece of 1460.[5]

Soon after Jacopo and Giovanni Bellini completed the Brescia Altarpiece, a change occurred in Jacopo's patronage that would help transform the Bellini workshop from a struggling *bottega* into one of the most successful workshops in Northern Italy. As early as October 1444, Venice's Scuola Grande di San Marco (the Great Confraternity of Saint Mark) selected Jacopo to decorate the *albergo* (boardroom) of its new meeting house (fig. 66). This was a watershed commission for the Bellini family, one that would help establish their workshop's reputation as narrative specialists and soon lead to another large commission: the decoration of the *sala capitolare* (chapter hall) of the Scuola Grande di San Giovanni Evangelista (Saint John the Evangelist) with some 17 or so narrative paintings (fig. 67).[6] These two *scuola grande* cycles constituted years of income for Jacopo—and in a difficult Venetian market that was dominated to a significant extent by the partnership of Giovanni d'Alemagna and Antonio Vivarini, whose beloved ornate late Gothic altarpieces arguably made them the leading Venetian atelier of the 1440s (see fig. 23).[7] The *scuole* cycles offered Jacopo an opportunity to become Venice's foremost narrative painter, and, after the death of Giovanni d'Alemagna in 1450, led to the Bellini becoming the leading painters in Venice until the beginning of the following century.[8] The Scuola Grande di San Marco and the Scuola Grande di San Giovanni Evangelista would largely monopolize Jacopo's artistic production for the next eight years or so.[9] From the early 1450s, the Scuola Grande di Santa Maria della Carità (Saint Mary of Charity) also commissioned work from Jacopo.[10] Curiously, the Scuola Grande di Santa Maria della Misericordia (Saint Mary of Mercy), to which Jacopo's father had belonged, does not appear to have ordered pictures from the artist.

The paintings of the *albergo* cycle of the Scuola Grande di San Marco were destroyed by a fire in 1485 and thus cannot be explored in this study. There is, however, evidence relating to Giovanni's professional development connected to the cycle to consider. During his childhood and young adulthood, Giovanni witnessed Jacopo slowly advance from struggling artist to perhaps the most famous painter in Venice. Jacopo's success depended on his strategic approach to both the creation and the commerce of painting (see Chapter 3). As an assistant, Giovanni would have helped Jacopo undertake the actions that resulted in the landmark Scuola Grande di San Marco commission, and this formative experience would lay foundations for his own strategic approach to art.

The *Albergo* Commission for the Scuola Grande di San Marco

By the early fifteenth century, the *scuole grandi*, which were all-male lay confraternities administered by non-noble Venetian citizens, had become the wealthiest private corporate institutions in Venice (fig. 68).[11] Their financial capital grew exponentially when members, especially those without heirs, began bequeathing possessions and property to their own *scuola*.[12] Having largely outgrown their modest meeting rooms, these *scuole* sought to accommodate their extensive administrative and procession-related activities by building lavish new meeting houses, or by enlarging current meeting spaces, thereby projecting their members' expanding influence across the socioeconomic fabric of Venice.

New meeting halls required interior decoration. Soon after April 25, 1438, when the Scuola Grande di San Marco moved into their new meeting house adjacent to the Church of Santi Giovanni e Paolo, construction began on ornamental ceilings for both the *albergo* and the *sala capitolare*.[13] On October 4, 1444, the governing board and elite members of the *scuola* voted unanimously to decorate the *albergo* with painted scenes that presumably would depict the life of Saint Mark, the patron saint of Venice after whom the *scuola* was named.[14] This decision continued a burgeoning tradition of decorating *scuola grande* interiors with narrative scenes that had begun by April 6, 1421, when the Scuola Grande di San Giovanni Evangelista voted to decorate its main meeting hall with narrative paintings depicting scenes from the Old and New Testaments.[15]

Given the swiftness with which the Scuola Grande di San Marco had built its new meeting house and decorated its interior ceilings, it seems likely that the painted decoration of the *albergo* commenced soon after the unanimous vote in the autumn of 1444.[16] The specific pictorial subjects of the completed narrative works remain unknown, however, because the next mention of the cycle in the historical record occurs only after the meeting house was consumed by fire on the night of March 31, 1485, and then later rebuilt.[17]

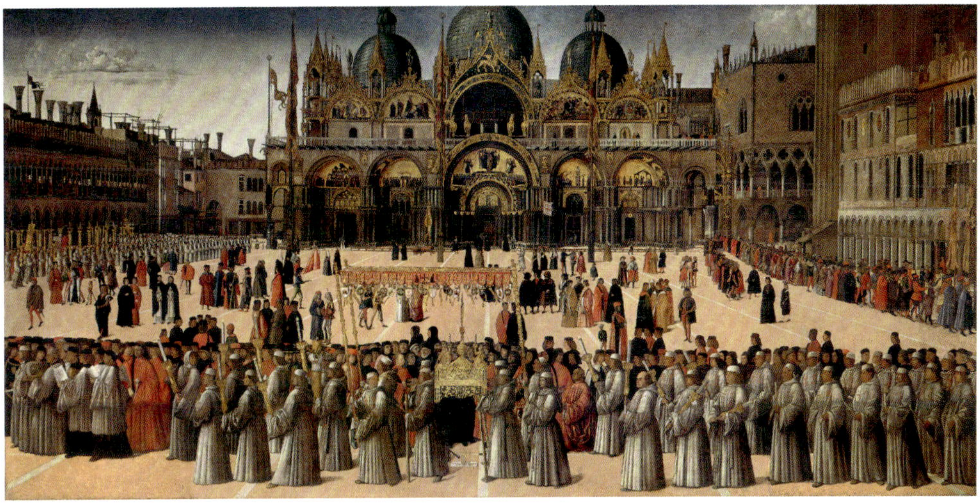

FIGURE 68 Gentile Bellini, *Procession in Piazza San Marco*, 1496. Oil on canvas, 373 × 745 cm. Gallerie dell'Accademia, Venice

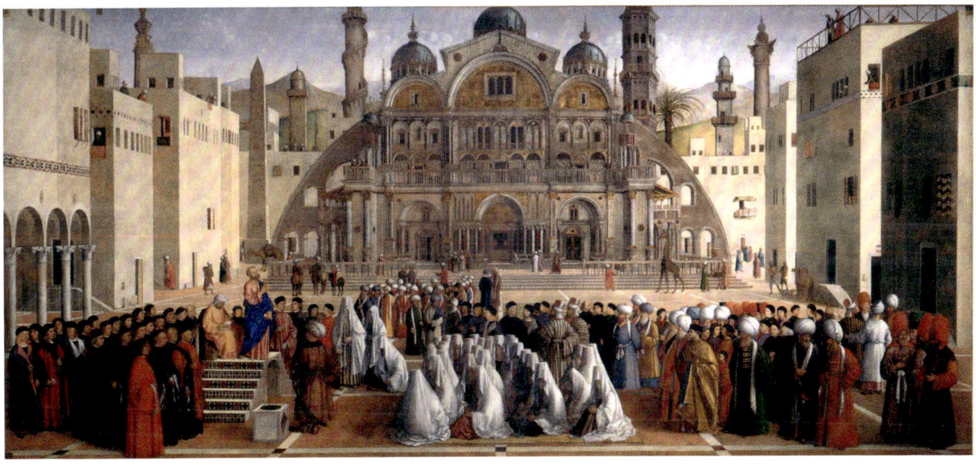

FIGURE 69 Gentile Bellini and Giovanni Bellini, *Saint Mark Preaching in Alexandria*, 1504–07. Oil on canvas, 347 × 770 cm. Pinacoteca di Brera, Milan. This is the first work of the campaign that replaced Jacopo Bellini's earlier paintings in the *albergo* of the Scuola Grande di San Marco, which were burned in a fire of 1485.

On July 15, 1492, Gentile Bellini, acting also on behalf of Giovanni Bellini, offered to replace his father Jacopo Bellini's "earlier paintings" that had adorned the *albergo* and had been "burnt in the fire" (fig. 69).[18] Jacopo and his workshop probably executed all of the original pictorial decorations of the *albergo*—he is the only artist associated with the cycle in the primary sources, and Gentile's later offer to replace the burned narratives implies Jacopo's primary responsibility for the room.[19]

The decoration of this *albergo* must have been one of the most sought-after painting commissions in mid-fifteenth-century Venice. It was a multi-year undertaking at an elite Venetian institution requiring at least a half-dozen monumental paintings, if not more, as it appears that the *albergo*'s original dimensions corresponded to those of the rebuilt *albergo* after the fire, which was decorated by seven paintings, each about 11 ft (3.3 m) high and the two largest over 25 ft (7.6 m) wide.[20]

Winning the Commission

Giovanni would have been about 19 when he witnessed Jacopo—rather than the workshops of Giambono, the Vivarini, or artists outside Venice—secure the Scuola Grande di San Marco commission. One factor in Jacopo's success that Giovanni would have registered was Jacopo's connection to the past. Prior to the 1440s, large-scale narrative painting cycles had been commissioned only occasionally in Venice. The most prestigious of these was the campaign of history paintings decorating the Great Council Hall of Venice's Ducal Palace, which were begun in the mid-to-late fourteenth century and completed in the first decades of the fifteenth century.[21] For that campaign, the Signoria had primarily commissioned non-Venetian artists, beginning in ca. 1369 with Guariento di Arpo and continuing in ca. 1410 with Gentile da Fabriano, who was followed by Pisanello (d. ca. 1455), although Jacobello del Fiore and other locals might also have contributed to the decoration.[22] That Jacopo had assisted Gentile da Fabriano, perhaps on the Great Council Hall frescoes themselves in ca. 1410–13, must have elevated Jacopo's local reputation, especially as a narrative specialist.[23] Some 30 years later, this legacy would have made Jacopo a compelling candidate to execute large-scale narratives for the Scuola Grande di San Marco, a *cittadino* (citizen) organization that frequently emulated Venice's government of nobles.[24] Later, in 1474, after Jacopo's death, this same lineage to Gentile da Fabriano also surely contributed to Jacopo's son Gentile Bellini receiving the important lifelong commission to restore and repaint the same narrative cycle in the Great Council Hall of the Ducal Palace.[25]

Another element in Jacopo's winning the commission must have been what we today call "good press." Several of Jacopo's humanist contacts praised him in literary works, again elevating his regional fame. For instance, Giovanni Fontana (ca. 1390–ca. 1455), a Venetian-born physician educated in Padua who wrote at least 18 texts on subjects as diverse as sand clocks, measurement methods, hydraulics, and war machines, dedicated to Jacopo a now-lost treatise on the pictorial arts, written prior to 1440, which discussed atmospheric perspective, among other topics.[26] A Milanese humanist named Angelo Decembrio (b. ca. 1415), resident at the Ferrarese court during the 1430s and 1440s when Jacopo had visited, recorded a painting contest between "Pisanello and Bellini, the finest painters of our time."[27] Jacopo and Pisanello purportedly competed over who could paint the best portrait of Leonello d'Este. The Venetian humanist poet Ulisse degli Aleotti extolled Jacopo's victory over Pisanello in two commemorative sonnets in which he employed a well-worn trope to describe Jacopo as a "second Phidias," who was among the most renowned artists of Antiquity, and likened Jacopo both to Apelles, the famous portraitist of Alexander the Great, and to Polykleitos, the great Greek sculptor of the fifth century BCE.[28]

Yet perhaps the most crucial factor in the Bellini workshop's winning the *albergo* commission was that Jacopo, arguably to a greater extent than any other Northern Italian artist of that period prior to Mantegna, had endeavored to position himself at the forefront of narrative innovation. Numerous drawings datable to the 1430s and early 1440s in Jacopo's Paris sketchbook demonstrate his artistic experimentation in narrative composition, with special attention given to landscapes, architecture, and figural studies. In many of these drawings, Jacopo incorporated and expanded upon the work of other leading artists. For instance, he sought out and studied the paintings of Altichiero, the late trecento's most celebrated narrative painter, seemingly in an attempt to both learn from and "update" Altichiero's art (see Conclusions and Attributions, figs 91 and 92). Jacopo went so far as to make drawings after Altichiero's narrative frescoes in the Chapel of San Giacomo in the Basilica of Sant'Antonio (ca. 1376–79) and the adjacent oratory of San Giorgio (1379–84) in Padua, and in the *sala grande* of the Palazzo Scaligeri in Verona (ca. 1364–70, called the Palazzo del Podestà during Jacopo's time, and mostly destroyed today).[29] Judging by the number and range of these drawings after Altichiero, Jacopo's study program was an extensive, multi-year process of autodidacticism and experimentation.[30]

Moreover, Jacopo had, apparently by the early 1440s, unlocked the secrets of drawing in linear perspective. As Gentile da Fabriano's assistant in Florence in the 1420s, it is likely that Jacopo had viewed artistic works executed in linear perspective.[31] In Venice in the 1430s, Jacopo endeavored to teach himself the mechanics of this pictorial innovation. Experimental drawings in his Paris sketchbook datable to these years register the artist's struggle to render this new visual system accurately, for example, in *An Architectural Setting with the Presentation of Our Lady* (fig. 70).[32] Jacopo clearly understood that the orthogonals met at a vanishing point on the horizon line, but for a long time he "eyeballed" or estimated the placement of transversal lines that ran parallel to the picture plane and receded into the distance, evidently uncertain how to space them according to geometrically derived principles (figs 71 and 72). In their 1990 monograph on Jacopo's drawings, Degenhart and Schmidt described Jacopo's divergence from the systemized deployment of perspective as the "arbitrariness of [Jacopo's] early perspectival experiments."[33] In his other drawings from the 1430s, Jacopo followed neither a methodological process for accurately constructing perspective nor aspects of Leon Battista Alberti's (1404–1472) other suggested procedures,

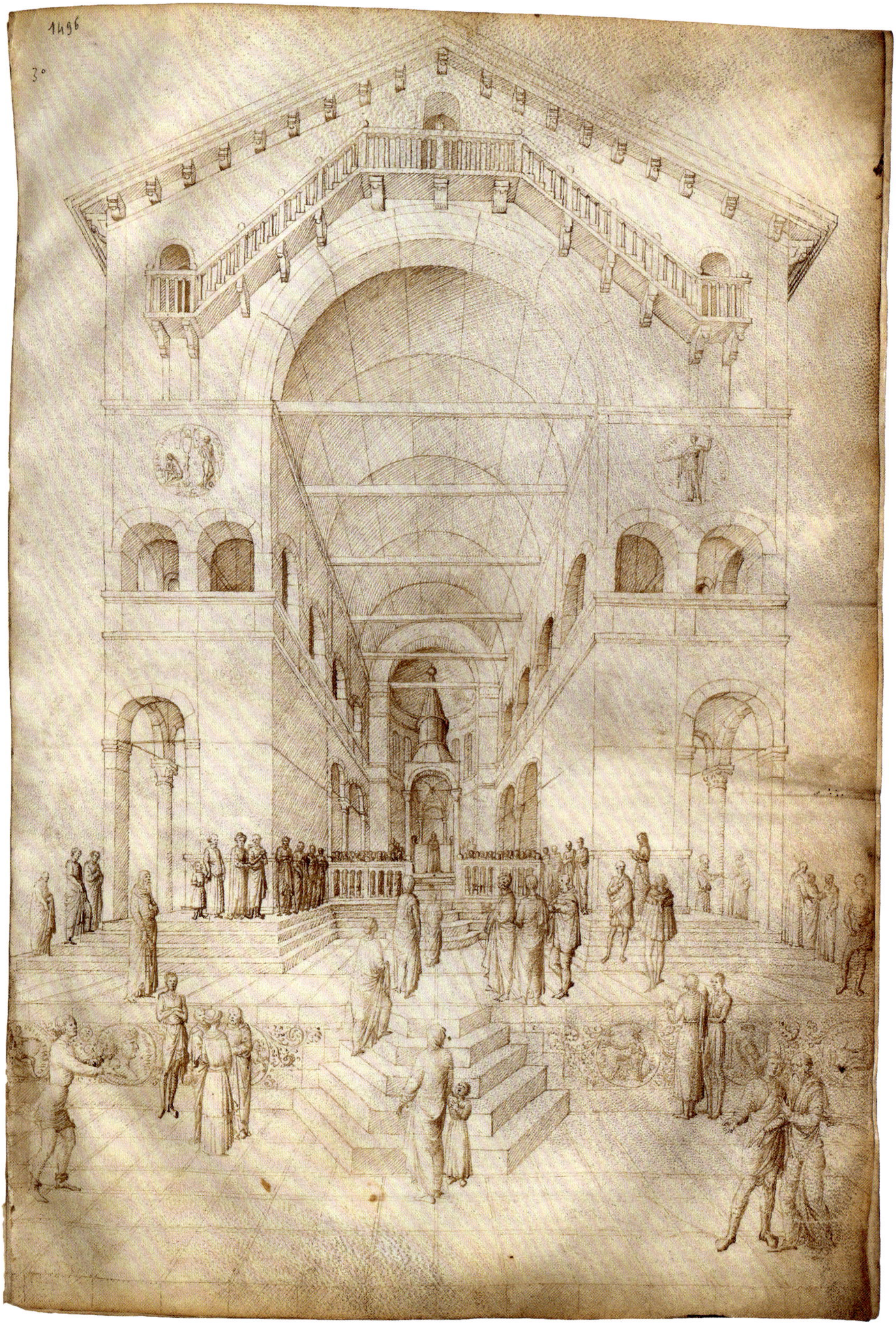

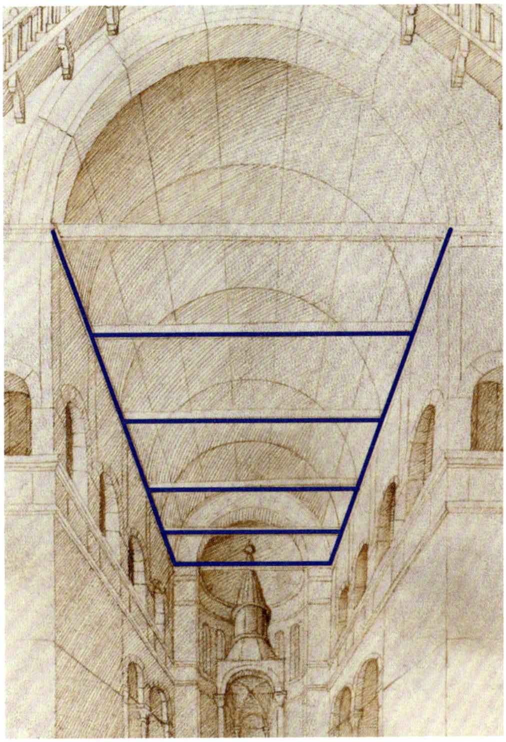

FIGURE 71 The transversal lines highlight Jacopo's efforts to master linear perspective. Illustration by Elisabetta Fava.

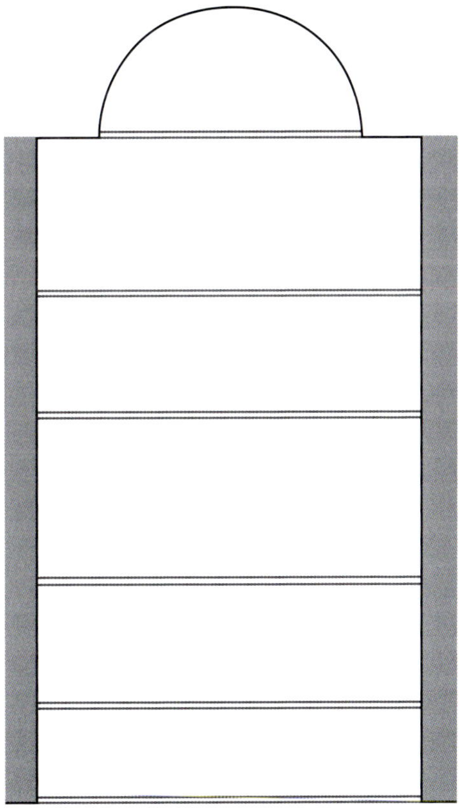

FIGURE 72 The imagined building in a cross-section view from above, demonstrating how Jacopo's transverse beams would have been unevenly spaced in reality. Illustration by Elisabetta Fava.

FIGURE 70 (OPPOSITE PAGE) Jacopo Bellini, *An Architectural Setting with the Presentation of Our Lady*, ca. 1435–40. Vellum, 38 × 26 cm. Cabinet des dessins, Musée du Louvre, Paris

such as that people should be drawn three *braccia* high ("the average height of a man's body") with the tops of their heads directly at the horizon line.[34]

Drawings datable to the early 1440s, however, show that Jacopo had finally solved the problem of spacing the transversals to achieve a mathematically consistent perspectival image. The turning point might have come during his visit to the court of Ferrara in ca. 1440–41, a stay that possibly coincided with that of Alberti himself.[35] If Jacopo had not met Alberti personally, he might nonetheless have examined a copy of Alberti's manuscript *De pictura* at the d'Este court.[36] Several of Jacopo's drawings from the early 1440s demonstrate his knowledge of Alberti's method as codified in *De pictura*. For instance, in his drawing *Urban Square with Church Façade*, Jacopo seems to have strictly incorporated Alberti's method of constructing foreground figures that are three *braccia* high (see fig. 54).[37]

Thus, throughout the 1430s, as demonstrated in his Paris sketchbook drawings, Jacopo strove in his middle age to master various artistic innovations, including drawing in linear perspective. In his sketchbooks (discussed in Chapter 3), he also devised new compositions for conventional religious iconographies, and he collected various pictorial motifs, some of which derived from trecento model books, and most of which he sketched himself. To a great extent, Jacopo's sketchbooks were like a fifteenth-century sandbox, where he experimented in reinventing his art and distinguishing himself from other local Venetian painters.

In late 1444, when the Scuola Grande di San Marco voted to decorate its *albergo* with narrative paintings, Jacopo was arguably the most innovative narrative specialist in Venice—at least on the parchment of his Paris sketchbook. His experimental drawings constituted a new type of art that we would now call an early Renaissance style, drawings that might be exhibited to prospective patrons and that reflected a style similar to what Donatello had brought to Padua in 1443. Indeed, at that moment, Jacopo might have been the only person in Venice who knew how to execute paintings in linear perspective, having already demonstrated the innovation in his Brescia Altarpiece of 1443–44 (see fig. 45). That few, if any, of Jacopo's Venetian competitors showed great interest in mastering the art of drawing in linear perspective may indeed be because of the rarity of commissions for large-scale narrative cycles in Venice prior to those of the *scuole*.[38] Thus, after years of study and experimentation, Jacopo moved beyond the late Gothic style of his master, Gentile da Fabriano, and distinguished his art from the work of his Venetian contemporaries, such as Giovanni d'Alemagna, the Vivarini, and Giambono. Both the Scuola Grande di San Giovanni Evangelista and the Scuola Grande di San Marco would continue to turn to the Bellini workshop for many of their narrative needs, and other Venetian commissions would follow. Jacopo's days traveling the mainland to seek work or execute commissions had largely come to an end.

Giovanni not only witnessed Jacopo's ceaseless attempts at incorporating pictorial advances to distinguish his work from that of local competitors, but he had also been preparing himself to help Jacopo execute important commissions, such as the painting campaign for the Scuola Grande di San Marco. Under Jacopo's guidance, Giovanni had experimented in linear perspective in the small-scale works of the Brescia *Annunciation* predella, while also studying Jacopo's sketchbooks and the work of Altichiero. He had been observing, and presumably sketching, important contemporary works of art in and around Venice. So many of Giovanni's later skills as an artist seem to have derived from Jacopo's example, such as Giovanni's ability to manage a workshop, train younger artists, and establish advantageous relationships with humanists. Yet perhaps Jacopo's most important lesson was to teach Giovanni how to absorb the innovations of other artists into his own artistic style. Throughout his life, Giovanni was able to incorporate the exceptional ideas and pictorial techniques of local, regional, and even international artists into his own work, as will be further discussed in the Conclusion. By adapting and employing Jacopo's workshop strategies to his own circumstances, Giovanni continued to keep his work fresh and relevant throughout his long career.

7 A Small Masterpiece

At first glance, Giovanni Bellini's *Saint Jerome in the Wilderness* (ca. 1450) may appear neither particularly accomplished nor innovative (see fig. 79).[1] The picture was executed in egg tempera on panel, and its patron and original location are unknown.[2] Nevertheless, a case can be made that it is a highly significant painting in the history of art. The work is not only the first stylistic blossoming in what would be an extraordinary career, but also perhaps the first example of an influential pictorial type that would become tremendously popular in Venice: a small meditational painting for private devotion and aesthetic enjoyment intended for the home (or perhaps a monastic setting). Indeed, it is the conceptual model for important later works by Giovanni, such as his subsequent paintings of Saint Jerome and his *Saint Francis in the Desert* (ca. 1476–78, see fig. 3), which has been called a "meditational *poesia*" that, in turn, set the stage for the mythological *poesie* by Giorgione and Titian.[3] This chapter focuses on the creative processes that led Giovanni to execute the Birmingham *Saint Jerome*, a painting that gives voice to the sensitive observations of a young man who would soon become the leading artist of Venice.

During the second half of the 1440s, all evidence suggests that Giovanni continued to act as Jacopo Bellini's assistant. As discussed in Chapter 5, Giovanni had (arguably) executed the predella panels for Jacopo's 1443–44 Brescia Altarpiece (see fig. 45), and as seen in Chapter 6, as early as October 1444, Giovanni must also have assisted Jacopo on the prestigious campaign of paintings for the Scuola Grande di San Marco, a multi-year project destroyed by fire in 1485. Because of this destruction, there are very few known works by the Bellini workshop during this period, either by Jacopo, Giovanni, Gentile, or Leonardo, further suggesting that the now-lost campaign for the *scuola* had largely monopolized their time.

In the late 1440s, however, Giovanni appears to have assisted on at least two additional projects overseen by Jacopo. The first was the design for a mosaic depicting the *Visitation*, one of four scenes from the life of the Virgin that decorates the Mascoli Chapel in the

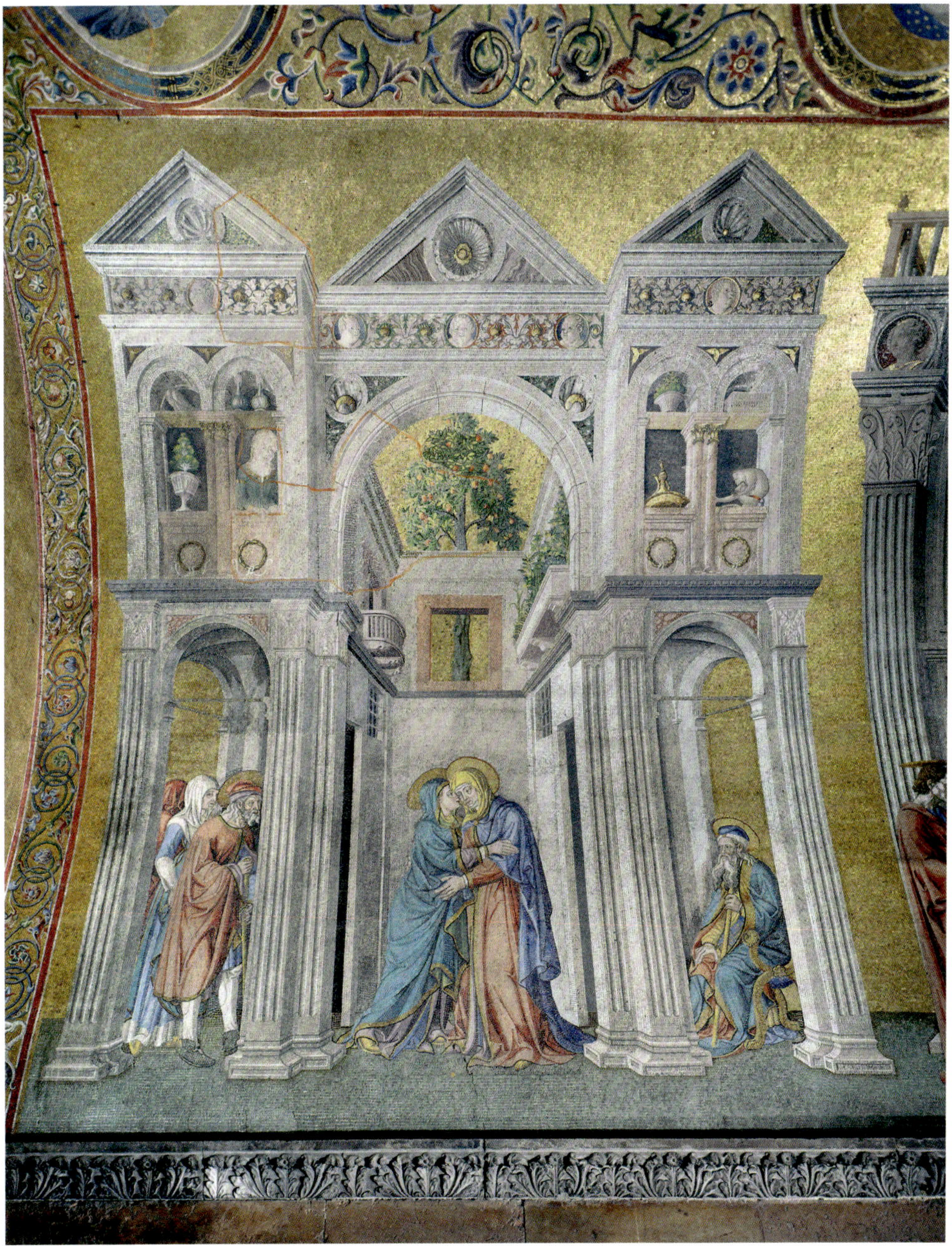

FIGURE 73 Jacopo and Giovanni Bellini, *The Visitation*, ca. 1449. Mosaic. Mascoli Chapel, Basilica of San Marco, Venice

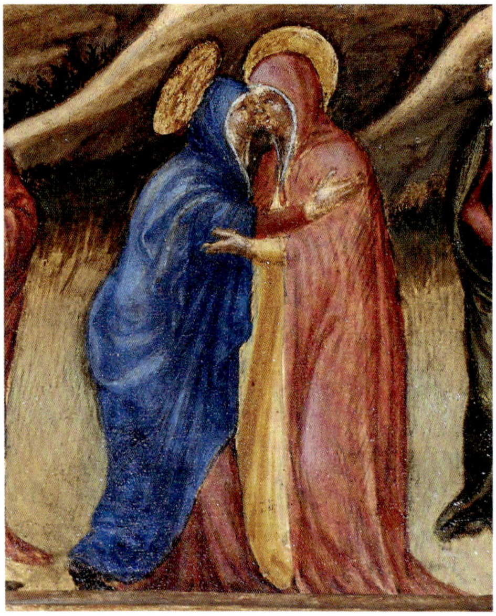

FIGURE 74 Giovanni Bellini, *The Visitation* (detail of fig. 45)

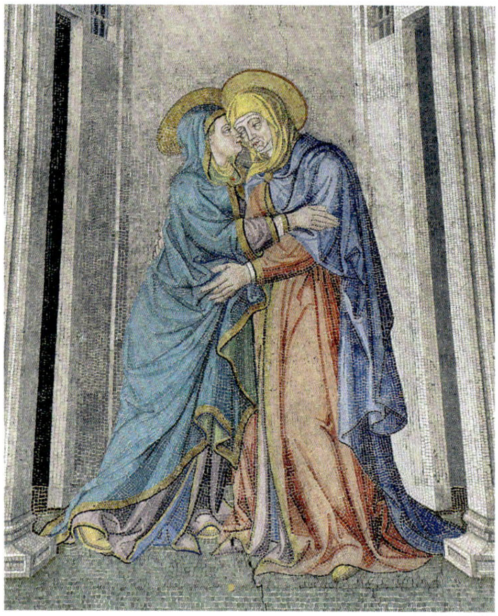

FIGURE 75 Detail of fig. 73

Basilica of San Marco in Venice (fig. 73).[4] For over a century, scholars have debated the attributions of the mosaics, likely to have been commissioned by Doge Francesco Foscari (1373–1457).[5] According to two contemporary sources, by 1449 work was already underway on the mosaics for the *cappella nova* (new chapel), as it was known until its ownership was transferred to the Scuola dei Mascoli in 1618.[6] The general consensus is that Giambono designed the two mosaics on the left wall, which are indeed signed *"Michael zambono venetus fecit"* ("Michele Giambono of Venice made [this]"). The design of the *Visitation* on the right wall is generally credited to Jacopo Bellini, while it is unclear who designed the fourth mosaic representing the *Death of the Virgin*; candidates have included Jacopo Bellini, Mantegna, and Andrea del Castagno (1419–1457), among others.[7]

Some evidence suggests that Giovanni helped Jacopo design the Mascoli Chapel's *Visitation*, although this ascription is made cautiously, as the skill and artistic interpretation of the mosaicist, who was often an unknown artist in Renaissance Venice, can distance the final mosaic from its designing artist and make attributions difficult.[8] Nonetheless, the two main figures of the Mascoli *Visitation*, those of the pregnant Virgin greeting her pregnant cousin Elisabeth, to some extent recall the same two figures depicted several years earlier in the *Visitation* predella of the Brescia *Annunciation*, ascribed here to Giovanni for the first time (see Chapter 5). If responsible for designing the figures of the Virgin and Elisabeth in the Mascoli *Visitation*, Giovanni would likely have employed the Brescia *Visitation* as his point of departure, and indeed, the two female figures of the Mascoli *Visitation* seem refined, with Mary's halo, which was awkwardly rendered in the Brescia painting, pleasingly intersecting with Elisabeth's halo to create a partial figure eight (figs 74 and 75).

Also, Giovanni is the most likely candidate to have devised the "portal motif" for the Mascoli *Visitation*: the square second-story window behind Mary and Elisabeth, trimmed by a reddish-orange perimeter, through which the trunk of a distant tree is viewed (fig. 76). The conceit is to transform a dead middle-ground space into one of aesthetic interest by rendering a portal, that is, a hole or window in an opaque surface through which the background landscape is revealed. No precise antecedent for this pictorial strategy is to be found in Jacopo's Paris sketchbook—the most similar is perhaps Jacopo's depiction of a background arcade framing distant mountains in his *Flagellation of Christ* (fig. 77).[9] In other drawings, Jacopo experiments with the architectural framing of the main scene itself or with barrel vaults through which the background is visible.[10] Giovanni would continue to develop the portal motif in later works such as his Birmingham *Saint Jerome* (see fig. 79), his 1452–53 *Assembly of the Order of the Crescent* (see Conclusions and Attributions, fig 93), and, perhaps most famously, his Pesaro Altarpiece (see fig. 42). The motif would continue to be used by other artists in Giovanni's circle, such as Vittore Carpaccio (ca. 1465–1525/26) in his *Preparation of Christ's Tomb* (ca. 1505, Gemäldegalerie, Berlin).[11]

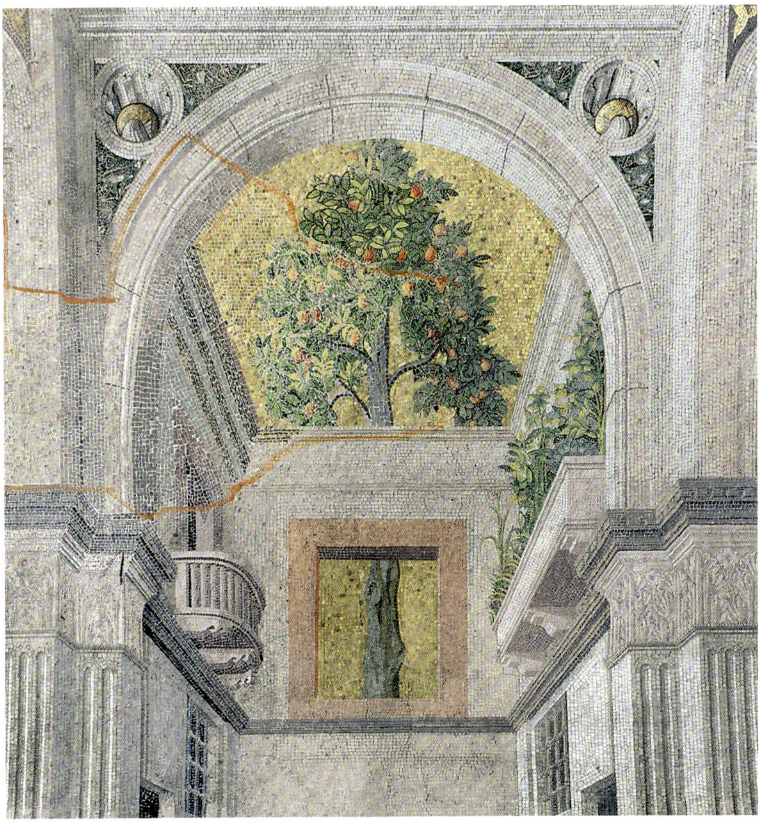

FIGURE 76 Detail of fig. 73, showing portal motif

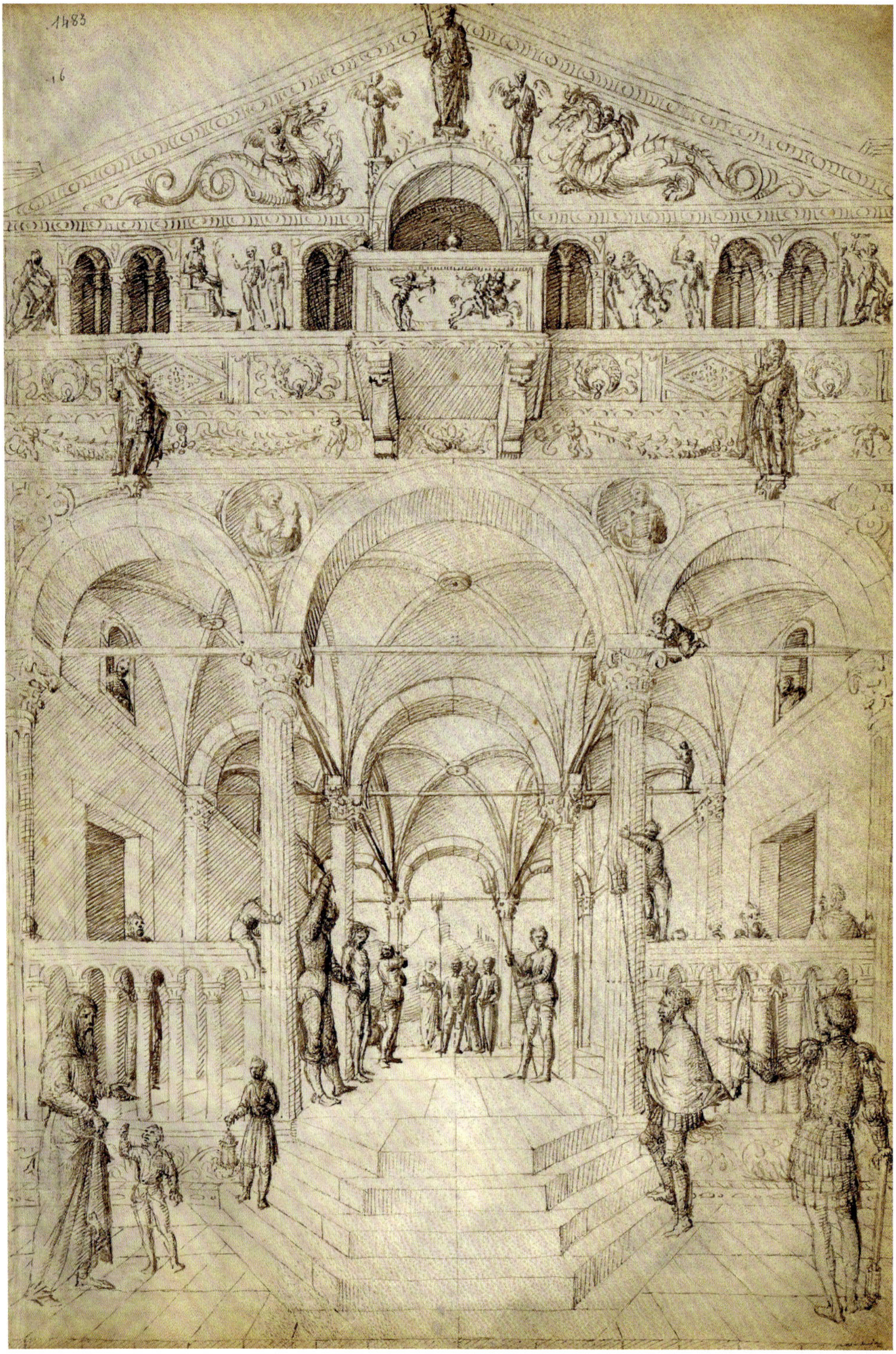

FIGURE 77 Jacopo Bellini, *The Flagellation of Christ*, ca. 1440–45. Vellum, 38 × 26 cm. Cabinet des dessins, Musée du Louvre, Paris

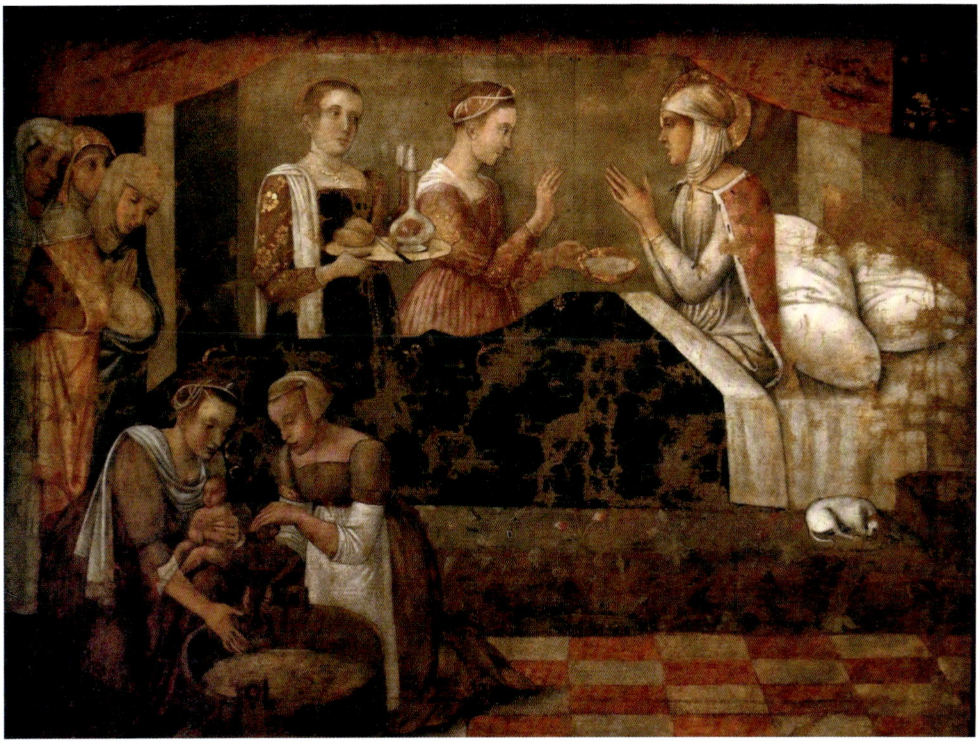

FIGURE 78 Attributed to Giovanni Bellini, *The Birth of the Virgin*, ca. 1452–53. Tempera on canvas, 112 × 152 cm. Galleria Sabauda, Turin

The portal motif adds a sense of depth to the painted image by creating additional areas and surfaces for the viewer to explore. When well executed, the motif offers an unexpected pleasure as the viewer's eyes move around and then through the portal, journeying past a wall or surface that would normally block exploration of the background. Whether or not invented by Giovanni, the portal motif seems related to the approach that the artist later described to Pietro Bembo (see p. 60) wherein he preferred freedom for his brush "to wander according to his will" in order to create aesthetic satisfaction for the viewer, in this case by providing paths for the observer's eye also to wander.[12]

The Scuola di San Giovanni Evangelista Cycle

The second of Jacopo Bellini's projects to which Giovanni contributed during this time was a cycle of around 17 New Testament scenes decorating the *sala capitolare* (chapter hall) of the Scuola Grande di San Giovanni Evangelista, as mentioned in Chapter 6.[13] This must have been another multi-year campaign, perhaps begun in the late 1440s and finished ca. 1453, probably concluding before Jacopo served as a *degano* for the *scuola* in March 1454, because it is doubtful that the *scuola* would have assigned him a position with such significant responsibilities, and bestowed the honor on him, had he not already completed the paintings.[14]

Of the assumed scenes in the cycle, nine are currently known, and Giovanni probably executed two of these: the *Birth of the Virgin* (fig. 78) and the *Annunciation*, both now in the Galleria Sabauda in Turin and both datable to ca. 1452–53.[15] Since *Young Bellini* ends its study in 1450, these works are not treated in depth here, but it is interesting to note that Jacopo assigned Giovanni the subject of the Birth of the Virgin, which as we have seen he had already executed for the Brescia *Annunciation* predella (see fig. 49). Although the works differ hugely in scale, there are similarities between them, including the mille-fleur textiles used in the decoration of the bedstead.[16] Giovanni also appears to have contributed background elements to one or more of the other seven known paintings, for which Jacopo appears to be primarily responsible.[17]

The Birmingham *Saint Jerome*

Saint Jerome (ca. 347–420), one of the four great Doctors of the Latin Church, received his education in Rome, became an ascetic in the Syrian desert, and entered the priesthood in Antioch. He later translated the Bible into Latin (the Vulgate), which would become Western Europe's definitive edition for over 1,000 years.[18] Jerome was among the most frequently illustrated saints of the Italian Renaissance, and his depiction in the *deserto* (wilderness) became one of the most popular pictorial subjects in Northern Italy (fig. 79).[19] Giovanni's main biographical sources for Jerome's life would have been the *Vite dei Santi Padri* by Domenico Cavalca and the *Legenda aurea* (*Golden Legend*), a widely read hagiography written by the thirteenth-century Dominican priest Jacobus de Voragine, who in turn relied on earlier *Vitae Hieronimi* (Lives of Jerome), such as the ninth-century *Plerosque nimirum*.[20] The *Legenda aurea* quotes a letter in which Jerome described himself as a hermit in the "vast solitude" of the wilderness: "My fleshless bones, hardly holding together, scraped against the bare ground . . . all the company I had was scorpions and wild beasts."[21] Years later in Bethlehem, we are told, a wandering lion limped into Jerome's monastery and "showed him his wounded foot . . . torn by thorns," which Jerome ordered the brothers to dress (an episode perhaps deriving from the folktale of "Androcles and the Lion" attributed to Aesop, ca. 620–564 BCE).[22] The lion, viewed by Jerome as a spiritual messenger of God, stayed and was duly assigned a daily chore: "to lead the [monastery's] ass out to pasture and watch over her safety."[23]

A passage relating to Jerome's name in the *Legenda aurea* might also have inspired Giovanni's innovative rendition: "Jerome (Hieronymus in Latin) comes from *gerar*, holy, and *nemus*, a grove—hence a holy grove."[24] Giovanni seems to illustrate Jerome within a spiritual landscape, truly to some extent a holy grove (though with few trees), infused with a light that may be read as numinous. It is a conceit with few, if any, precedents in Venice and Northern Italy, although some earlier images had sought to represent sacred light as early as ca. 1400, such as those depicting the Adoration of Christ in which the holy radiance of the Christ Child illuminates the grotto, in accordance with Saint Bridget's vision.[25] An example of

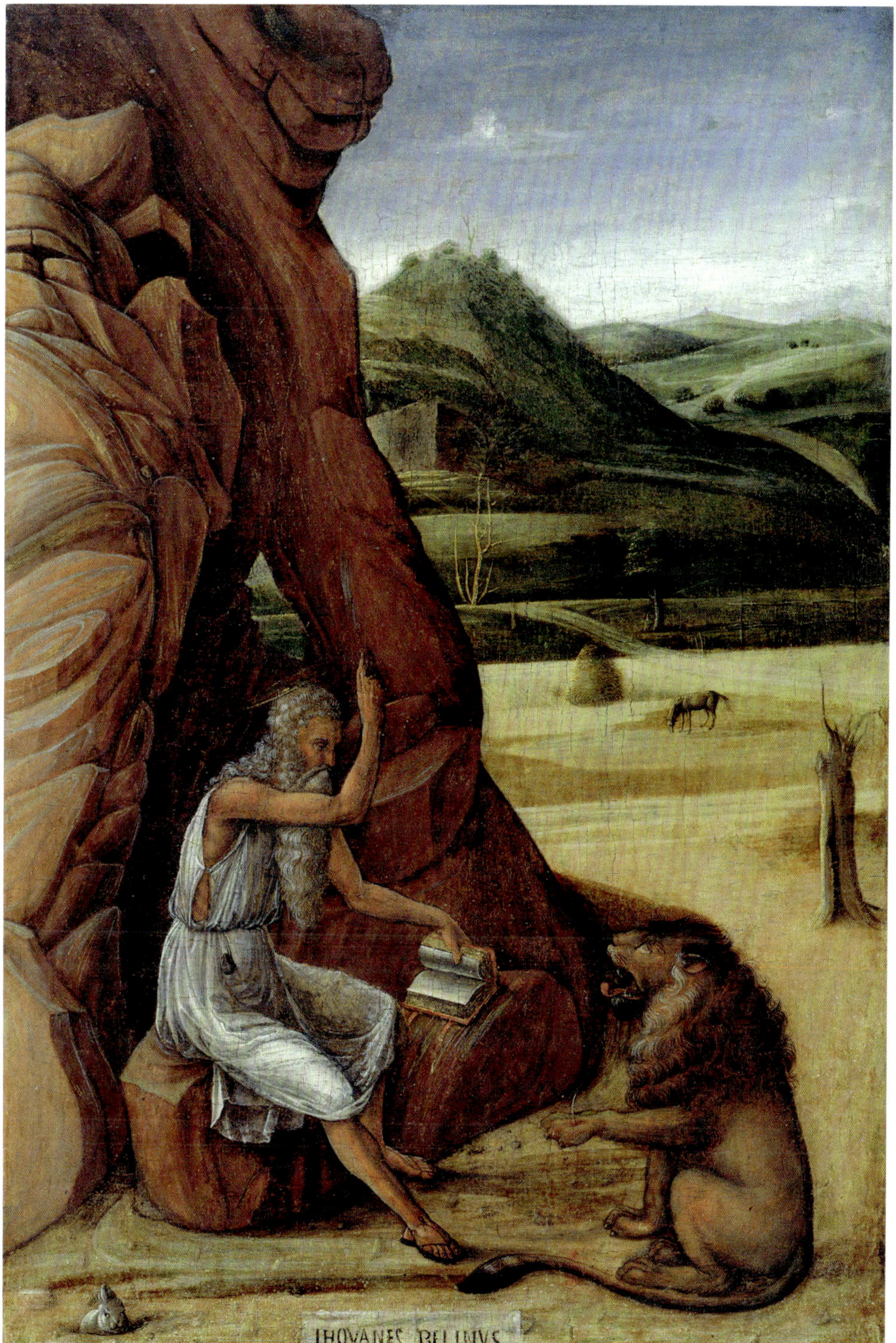

FIGURE 79 Giovanni Bellini, *Saint Jerome in the Wilderness*, ca. 1450. Tempera on panel, 44 × 22.9 cm. Barber Institute of the Fine Arts, Birmingham

this type is Gentile da Fabriano's *Nativity* predella in the Strozzi Altarpiece (1423), on which Jacopo Bellini almost certainly assisted (see fig. 52).

At this early moment in his career, Giovanni was already treating the fall of light across the composition as its own pictorial element. The light in his *Saint Jerome* illuminates the landscape, models figures and objects, and casts shadows. Giovanni used delicate parallel hatching in the underdrawing to distinguish areas of light and shade.[26] It remains unknown how the young artist developed his first serious interest in the close observation of light, but it probably did not stem from the work of Jacopo. It is instructive to compare Giovanni's *Saint Jerome* with Jacopo's rendering of the same saint from about the same time (ca. 1450, fig. 80). In his treatment of light, here and elsewhere, Jacopo tended to model individual objects as if each one was isolated, and there is little sense, in Jacopo's extant paintings or his sketchbooks, that he strove to illuminate his scenes with a consistent light source. In contrast, Giovanni was decisively interested in rendering a logical and consistent luminosity, beginning with the Brescia predella panels of ca. 1443–44 and continuing with *Saint Jerome* in ca. 1450.

Giovanni appropriated compositional elements and motifs for the *Saint Jerome* from Jacopo as well as other artists, refining and integrating those elements into his own artistic vision (as he did in the Ferrara *Coronation* and the Brescia *Annunciation* predella). Giovanni's point of departure was likely Jacopo's Paris drawing of *Saint Jerome Reading in the Wilderness* (fig. 81).[27] For Jacopo, the text of the *Legenda aurea* becomes an island wilderness hazardous to men, with corpses strewn across the shore, and real and fanciful beasts that present no danger to Jerome, who reads tranquilly upon a rocky ledge, his discarded clogs suggesting holy ground, with his bare feet stretched beside an unthreatening lion and sleeping lioness. Jacopo's landscape juxtaposes the solitary saint with a lost pagan antiquity, signified by a distant pedestalled classical statue set in opposition to a ruined column near Jerome, and with the far-off bustle of civilization, as ships traverse a body of water toward mountainside towns.[28] For Giovanni, however, Jacopo's beasts, corpses, and artifacts of a failed civilization, while perhaps appealing to the intellect, would have detracted from the visualization of the sacred and were therefore omitted.

Giovanni's overall composition, however, appears to have derived directly from Mantegna's fresco of the *Calling of Saints James and John* for the Ovetari Chapel, Church of the Eremitani, Padua, likely completed by the spring of 1450 (fig. 82).[29] The German scholars Degenhart and Schmitt wrote that the Birmingham *Saint Jerome* "does not yet reflect Mantegna's influence on the young Giovanni Bellini."[30] This opinion may largely be true of the style, but it is not true of the composition. Standing before a towering outcrop, the white-robed Christ in Mantegna's fresco transforms into a seated and white-robed Jerome in Giovanni's painting; the crouching Saint James with hands clasped in prayer and gazing fixedly on Jesus becomes a seated lion with outstretched paw imploring Jerome to remove its thorn. In each work, the rocky tower forms a proscenium that gives way to a receding landscape on the right, with a nearby tree, water that Giovanni transmutes into flowing

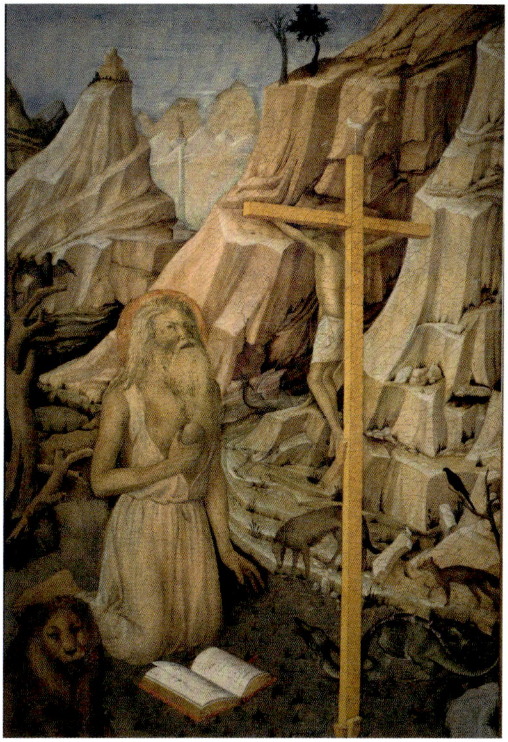

FIGURE 80 Jacopo Bellini, *Penitent Saint Jerome*, ca. 1450. Tempera on panel, 96 × 64 cm. Museo di Castelvecchio, Verona

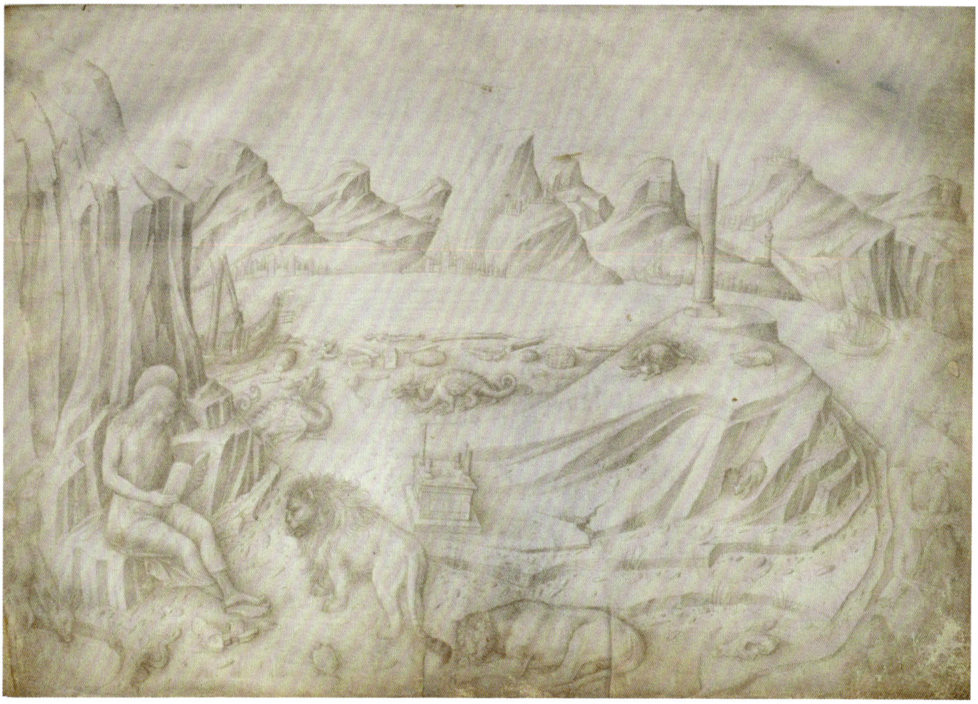

FIGURE 81 Jacopo Bellini, *Saint Jerome Reading in the Wilderness*, ca. 1445. Vellum, 26 × 38 cm. Cabinet des dessins, Musée du Louvre, Paris

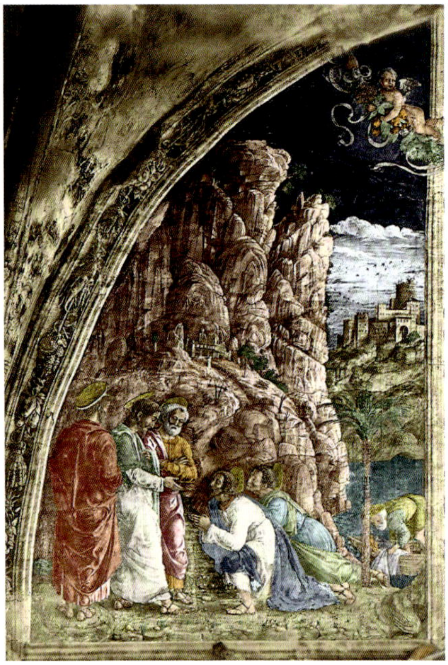

FIGURE 82 Andrea Mantegna, *Calling of Saints James and John*, 1450. Fresco, Ovetari Chapel, Church of the Eremitani, Padua (colorized black-and-white photo)

golden fields, and a distant hill and fortress. Thus, the much-discussed artistic dialogue between Giovanni and Mantegna, who would marry Jacopo Bellini's daughter, Nicolosia, in ca. 1453, appears to have begun with the Birmingham *Saint Jerome*. Their creative interchange continued through the 1450s and slowed after 1459 or 1460, when Mantegna departed nearby Padua to become court painter to Marchese Ludovico Gonzaga of Mantua (1412–1478).[31] As previously noted, when Giovanni responded in his paintings to the innovative ideas of other artists, rather than borrowing a motif from Jacopo's sketchbooks, he generally did so contemporaneously, a strategy that kept his art fresh. Hence his *Saint Jerome* was most likely executed at the same time as or soon after Mantegna's 1450 *Calling of Saints James and John*.[32]

As already mentioned, Giovanni incorporated the portal motif from the Mascoli *Visitation* into his image of Saint Jerome, and he also borrowed and refined individual motifs from Jacopo's drawings. Thus, as noted by Crowe and Cavalcaselle in the nineteenth century, the image of the lion derives from folio 72v of Jacopo's Paris sketchbook (fig. 83).[33] The tree stump resembles those in a different drawing of *Saint Jerome in the Wilderness* by Jacopo on folio 22v of the Paris sketchbook (fig. 84).[34] Even Giovanni's signature, "IHOVANES BELINVS," accepted as autograph by many but not all scholars, appears to derive from Jacopo.[35] It was executed in crudely drawn rustic capitals that are very different from his later Roman majuscules, with a single "L" in his family name, and an unusual Latin spelling of his Christian name that would not be repeated in his oeuvre. The signature is closely comparable with Jacopo's signature on the Tadini *Virgin and Child* (ca. 1450, Galleria Tadini, Lovere): "IACHOBVS BELINVS," which suggests that Giovanni used Jacopo's signature as a model for its form, its spelling of the Bellini surname, and its inclusion of the "H" in the

Christian name (figs 85–87).[36] If Giovanni's signature is indeed autograph, then it may be understood as an early experiment toward the more standard signature the artist would develop later in the decade.[37]

The Birmingham *Saint Jerome* also inaugurates a technique Giovanni would continue to develop brilliantly: visualizing the sweep and pivotal events of a saint's life by conflating the subject's various biographical episodes into a single narrative image. Jerome, seated on a ledge beside his cave in Chalcis, with one hand holds open a book that recalls his scholarly pursuits and later translation of the Bible in Rome and Antioch. With his other hand he gesticulates skyward, as if blessing or indoctrinating the infirm lion, an episode set in Bethlehem. An ass, perhaps alluding to the one eventually put under the lion's protection, grazes in the background pasture that recedes into distant hills. With beautiful economy, Giovanni integrates multiple incidents and pregnant motifs drawn from Jerome's life into a dramatic and spiritual whole. Jerome is presented by the artist not only as the subject of the work but also as a constituent feature of its divine landscape. The artist's most famous example of this approach is, of course, the Frick's *Saint Francis in the Desert* (see fig. 3).

As viewers of Giovanni's *Saint Jerome*, we are invited to meditate on the saint, not least by contemplating the carefully placed motifs that recall various moments of his life. We might also meditate on the journey of its artist to create the work. Giovanni was abandoned

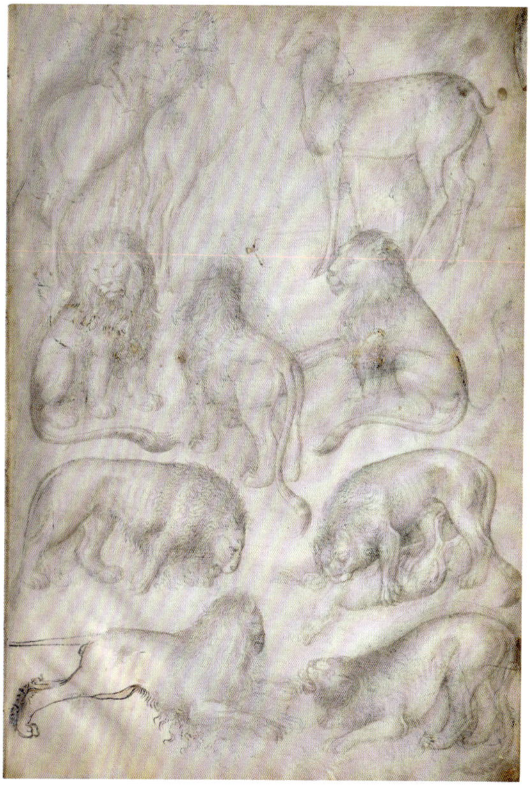

FIGURE 83 Jacopo Bellini, *Seven Lions and Three Stags*, ca. 1450. Vellum, 38 × 26 cm. Cabinet des dessins, Musée du Louvre, Paris

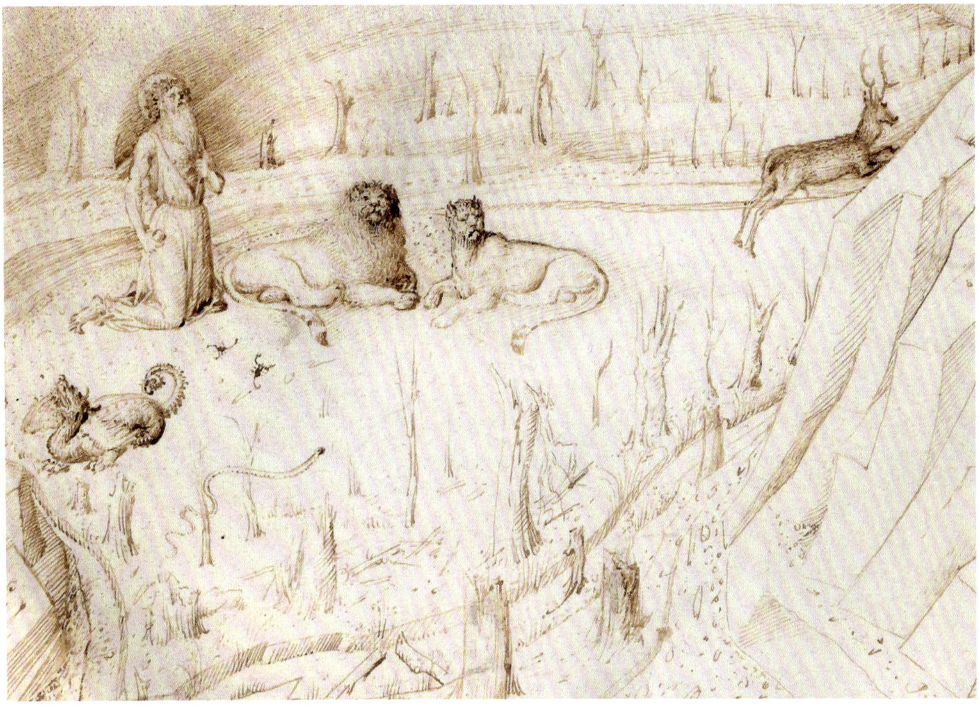

FIGURE 84 Jacopo Bellini, *Saint Jerome in the Wilderness*, ca. 1440. Vellum, 26 × 38 cm. Cabinet des dessins, Musée du Louvre, Paris

with the death of his parents, an infant in a vast wilderness. He found a home with his older half-brother, Jacopo, who would raise him as a son and teach him how to paint. As a boy perhaps attending vernacular school, Giovanni was likely assigned to read the *Legenda aurea* and the story of Saint Jerome. One might imagine Giovanni in Venice, or visiting Padua, his own sketchbook in hand, drawing works of art that he admired, including the fresco of the *Calling of Saints James and John* in the Ovetari Chapel by Mantegna, who would become both a friend and a relative. The Birmingham *Saint Jerome*, then, represents not only a saint's journey, but also that of the young artist who had achieved creative self-expression in his first important work.

The Birmingham *Saint Jerome* is the turning point of Giovanni's youth. The painting represents the culmination of the skills and artistic approaches Giovanni had learned since childhood (fig. 88). To some extent, medieval traditions and the late Gothic style continued to remain strong in Jacopo's workshop. The *Saint Jerome*, however, marks the moment of Giovanni's artistic emancipation from Jacopo and the beginning of his own artistic voice. With this work, Giovanni set the stage in fifteenth-century Venice for a new kind of consumer demand: small narrative paintings intended for personal viewing in a domestic setting. It was the beginning of a new type of mediational art in early Renaissance Venice.

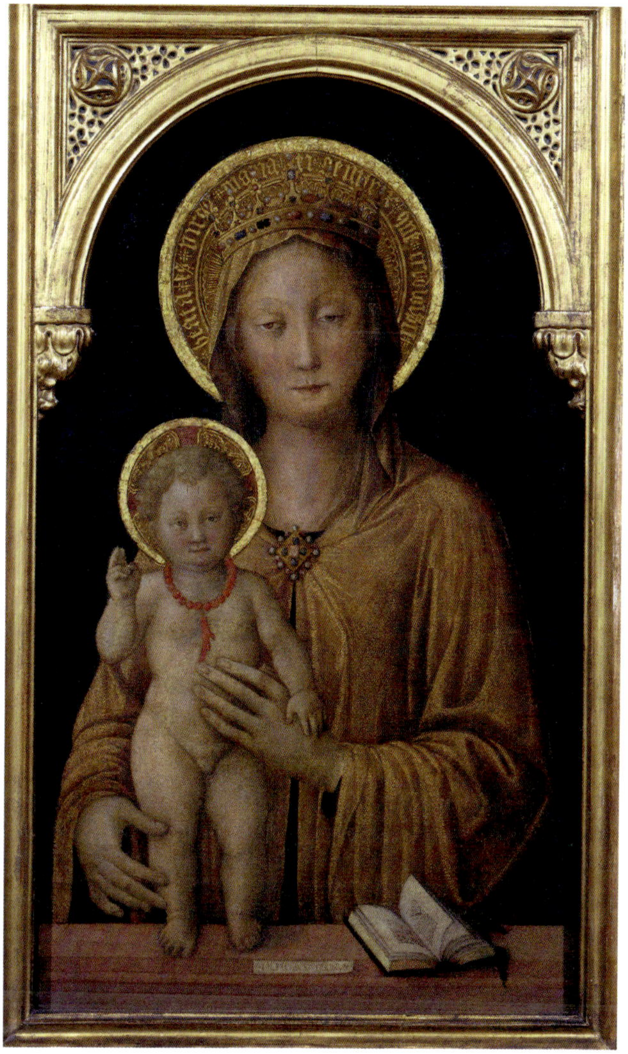

FIGURE 85 Jacopo Bellini, *The Virgin and Child*, ca. 1450. Tempera on panel, 98 × 58 cm. Galleria Tadini, Lovere

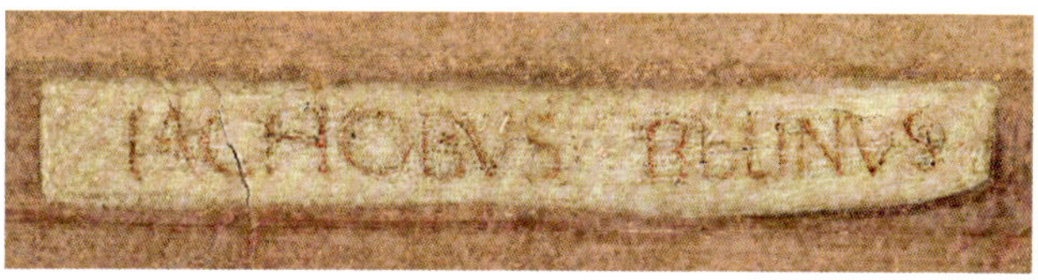

FIGURE 86 Detail of fig. 85, showing signature

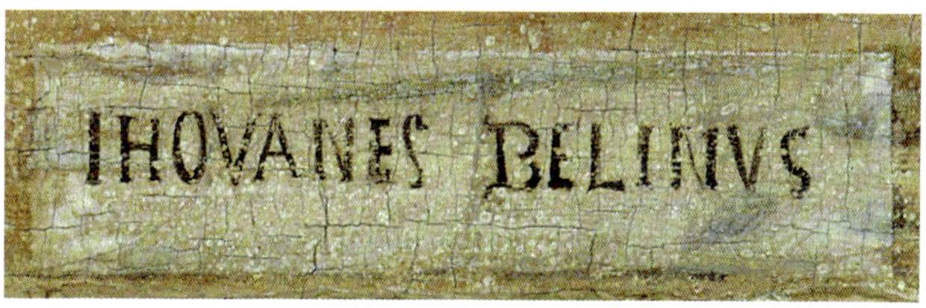

FIGURE 87 Detail fig. 79, showing signature

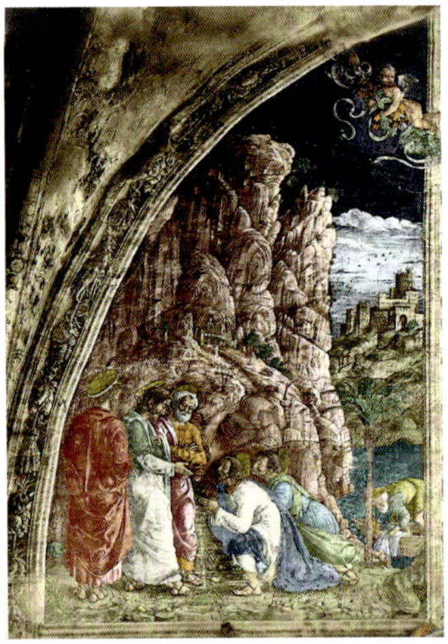

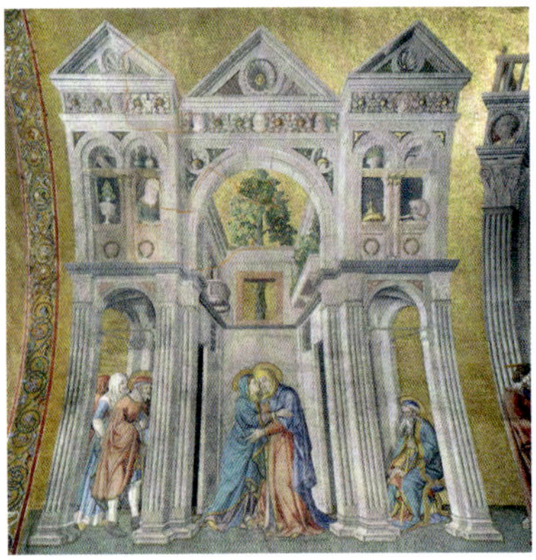

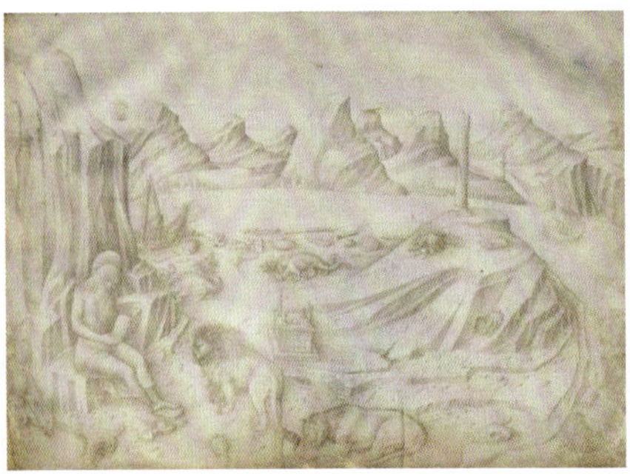

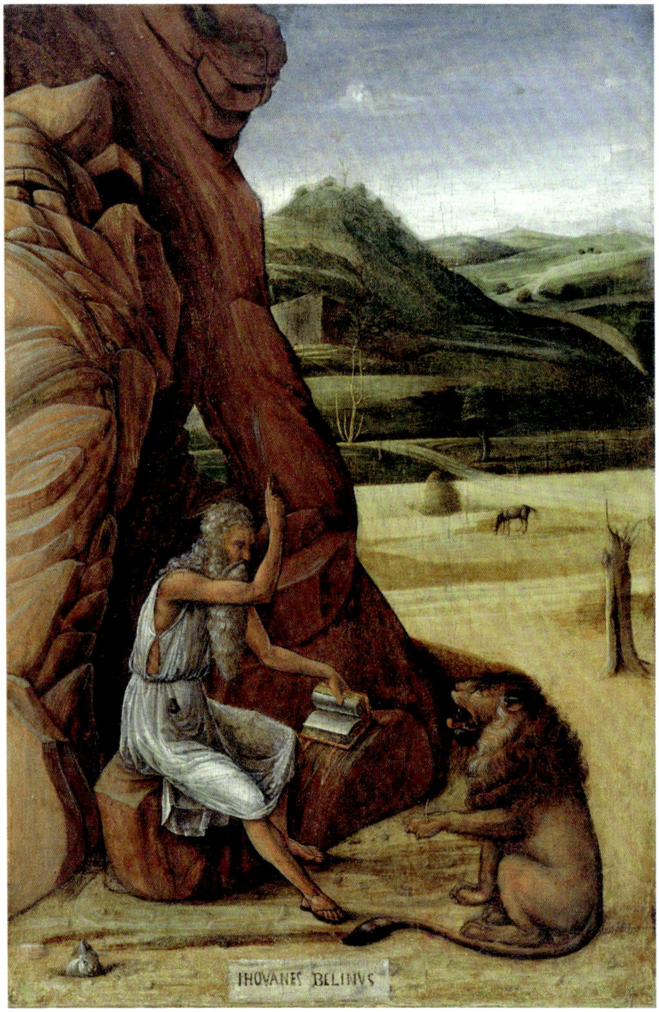
IHOVANES BELINVS

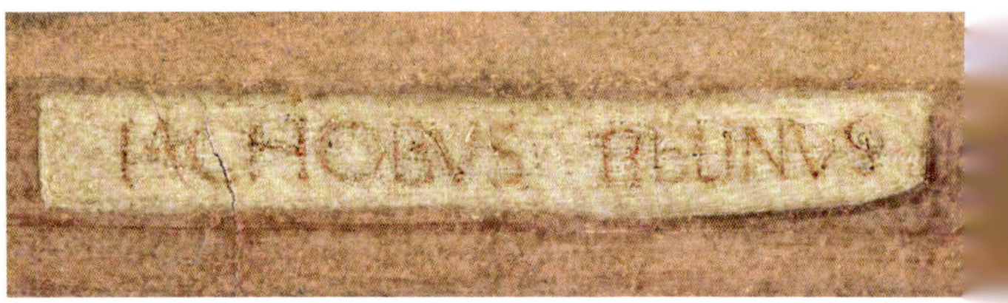
IACHOBVS BELINVS

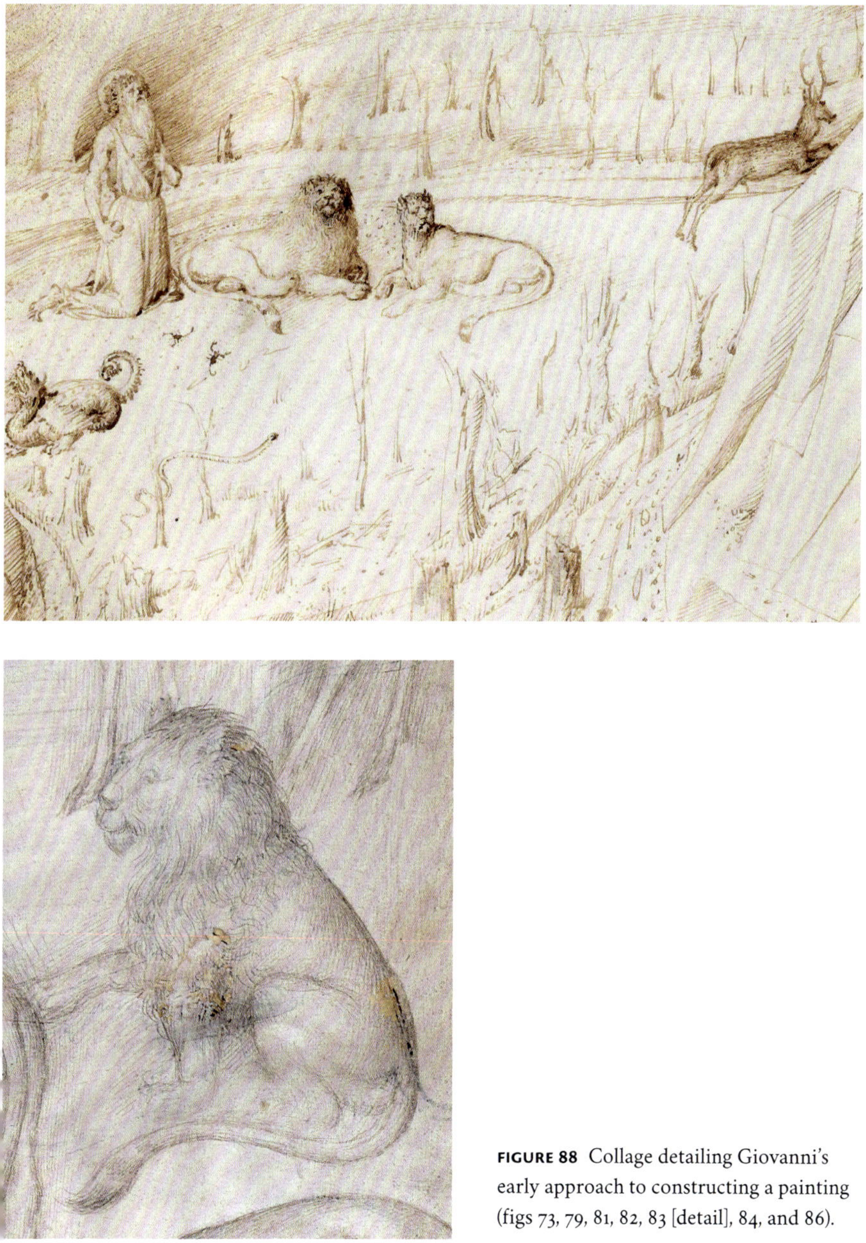

FIGURE 88 Collage detailing Giovanni's early approach to constructing a painting (figs 73, 79, 81, 82, 83 [detail], 84, and 86).

Conclusions and Attributions

As a young artist composing paintings in Jacopo Bellini's workshop, Giovanni paid imaginative attention to the literary sources describing his subject and precociously explored the diffusion and effects of light.[1] Yet the representational strategy most characteristic of Giovanni's early practice was perhaps his creative integration of compositional ideas and specific motifs from the work of other artists into his own conceptual framework. As Giovanni developed into mid-career, he depended less on other artists' work and more on his own invention. Increasingly he turned to his earlier compositions as points of departure or to reuse motifs.[2] While Giovanni's youthful process of integration diminished in importance, an essential aspect of his early approach nonetheless remained intrinsic to his art. Even in old age, he continued to be inspired by the work of contemporaries and to absorb their pictorial innovations.[3]

For medieval and Renaissance painters, especially those at the beginning of their careers, the assimilation of motifs and pictorial ideas from other artists was hardly new. Indeed, it is closely related to the advice offered to young artists by the painter Cennino Cennini (ca. 1370–ca. 1440) in his *Il libro dell'arte*, the so-called *Craftsman's Handbook* (ca. 1390):

> [E]ndeavor to copy and draw after as few masters as possible . . . take pains and pleasure in constantly copying the best things which you can find done by the hand of great masters . . . [and] select the best one every time, and the one who has the greatest reputation. And, as you go on from day to day, it will be against nature if you do not get some grasp of his style and of his spirit. . . . Then you will find, if nature has granted you any imagination at all, that you will eventually acquire a style individual to yourself, and it cannot help being good.[4]

Jacopo Bellini might have known Cennini's text firsthand: a manuscript copy of it was made at Le Stinche in ca. 1437, the decade following Jacopo's incarceration in the prison.[5]

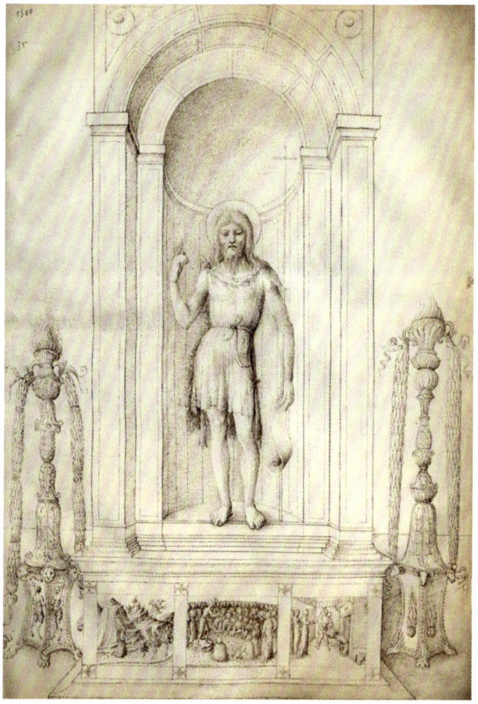

FIGURE 89 Jacopo Bellini, *Saint John the Baptist Standing in a Niche*, ca. 1438. Vellum, 38 × 26 cm. Cabinet des dessins, Musée du Louvre, Paris

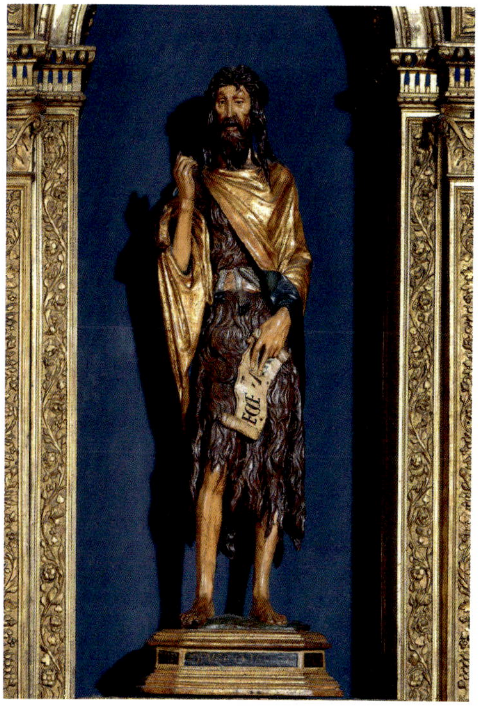

FIGURE 90 Donatello, *Saint John the Baptist*, 1438. Painted wood, height 141 cm. Chapel of San Giovanni Battista, Church of Santa Maria Gloriosa dei Frari, Venice

Whether or not he was familiar with Cennini's text, Jacopo presumably would have received similar instructional advice from Gentile da Fabriano during his long apprenticeship. In any event, several of the earlier compositions in Jacopo's Paris sketchbook were drawn after the work of "great masters," and especially after frescoes in Padua and Verona by the late trecento artist Altichiero, as discussed below.

Thus, it seems likely that Jacopo employed the strategies of drawing after and integration to help train Giovanni. According to the 1471 will of Jacopo's wife, Anna Rinversi, the Bellini workshop owned "works in gesso, in marble, and in relief," perhaps to study or for use in a painting.[6] Moreover, Jacopo apparently taught the same methods to Gentile Bellini, who employed a similar approach in his first independent paintings. For instance, Gentile's earliest known monumental work, the organ doors in the Basilica of San Marco (1464), borrowed and integrated motifs from Jacopo's drawings, paintings by Mantegna, and other local sources.[7]

There were crucial differences, however, in how the young Giovanni and the mature Jacopo each approached the execution of a work of art—differences that might aid in the attribution of certain paintings. In the sketchbooks he presumably kept, Giovanni apparently included drawings of recently executed works of art that pleased him.[8]

Jacopo occasionally did the same, as when he drew Donatello's statue of *Saint John the Baptist* in the Church of Santa Maria dei Frari, which had been placed on the altar in 1438 (figs 89 and 90).[9] However, Jacopo's process of drawing after, as evinced by his extant works of art, was of a different nature from Giovanni's approach. Jacopo's main objective does not appear to have been to appropriate compositions and motifs for later integration into his own paintings. Rather, in many of his drawing-after sketches, Jacopo endeavored to update the earlier work of an artist into more modern pictorial terms, or challenge himself to equal an artist's mastery in the execution of a subject or a series of motifs.[10] Thus, Jacopo transformed Donatello's sculpture of *Saint John the Baptist* into an imagined Renaissance altarpiece.[11] Another example is Jacopo's Paris drawing of the *Adoration of the Magi* (ca. 1435–40), which "updates" Altichiero's fresco of the same subject in Padua (ca. 1379–84) by employing linear perspective and a greater spatial depth in both architecture and background (figs 91 and 92).[12] Jacopo excavated Altichiero's cliffs to create a passageway from which the procession emerges, and he transformed the humble stable into a cavernous structure depicted in one-point perspective that recedes toward the mountainous background.[13] In this and other examples in his drawings, Jacopo endeavored to bring the trecento compositions of Altichiero into the early quattrocento world of scientific perspective.

In contrast, Giovanni appears instead to have observed and absorbed the visual ideas of other artists and then both refined and expanded upon those ideas in his own paintings—paintings that in fact often portrayed a different subject or iconography. A typical example of this is his innovative Birmingham *Saint Jerome* (ca. 1450, see fig. 79), which, as discussed in Chapter 7, elaborated on the overall composition of Mantegna's fresco of the *Calling of Saints James and John* in the Ovetari Chapel in Padua (1450, see fig. 82), employed ideas and motifs from Jacopo's drawings, visually interpreted aspects of Jerome's hagiography in the *Legenda aurea*, and sought to depict an identifiable and consistent source of light, the last of which was a concern largely absent from Jacopo's work.

Miniatures for the *Passion of Saint Maurice*

The differences in approach between the young Giovanni and the mature Jacopo strongly suggest that the four famous Marcello manuscript illuminations (1453, figs 93–96), the authorship of which has been a burning question for art historians for decades, should be assigned to Giovanni. In 1449, a Venetian general named Jacopo Antonio Marcello (1398–d. by 1465) was admitted into René I, Duke of Anjou's (1409–1480) chivalric Order of the Crescent, and afterward Marcello commissioned a manuscript of the *Passion of Saint Maurice* that he sent as a diplomatic gift to the duke on June 1, 1453.[14] Some scholars have attributed its four full-page illuminations to Mantegna, others to Jacopo Bellini.[15] In 1960, Giles Robertson was the first to ascribe these miniatures to Giovanni, largely due to their telltale depiction of "pervading light." In 2008, Luciano Bellosi supported the attribution on stylistic grounds.[16] Few scholars have agreed, however, in part because Giovanni's birthdate shifted towards

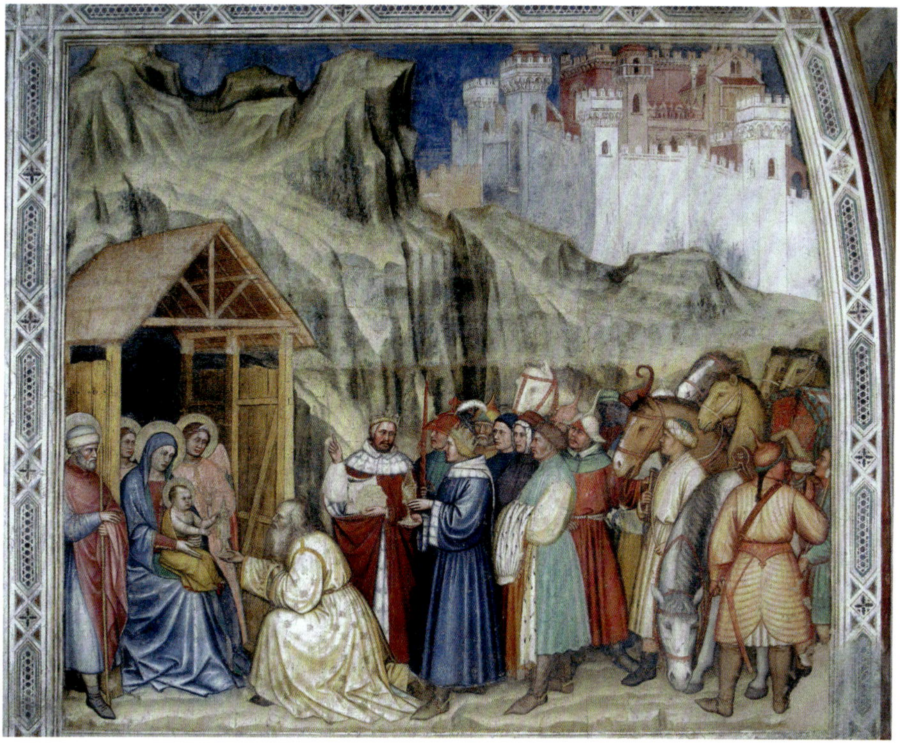

FIGURE 91 Altichiero, *The Adoration of the Magi*, ca. 1379–84. Fresco, Oratory of San Giorgio, Padua

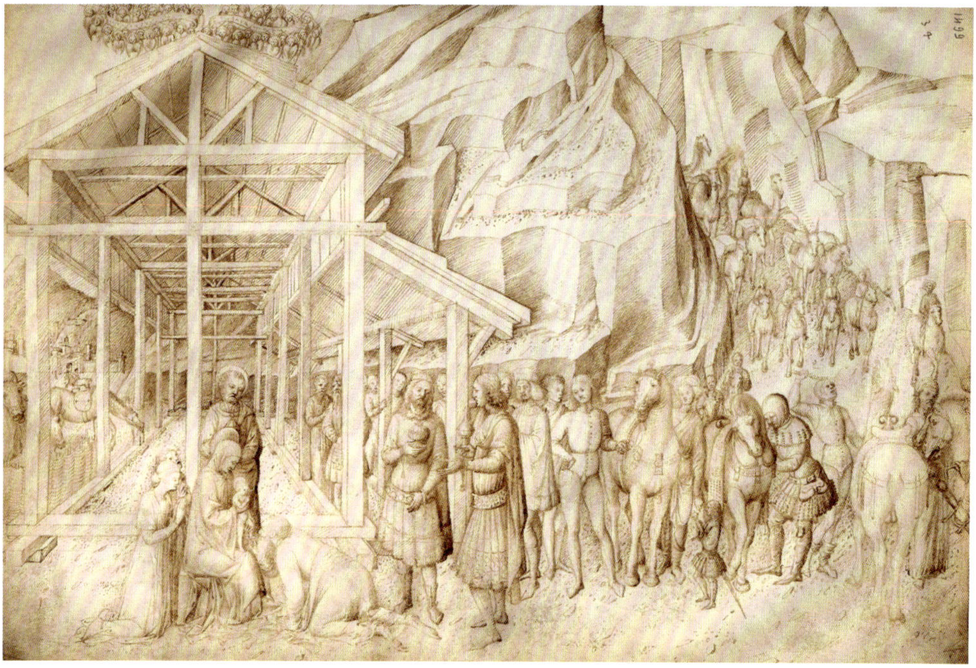

FIGURE 92 Jacopo Bellini, *The Adoration of the Magi*, ca. 1435–40. Vellum, 26 × 38 cm. Cabinet des dessins, Musée du Louvre, Paris

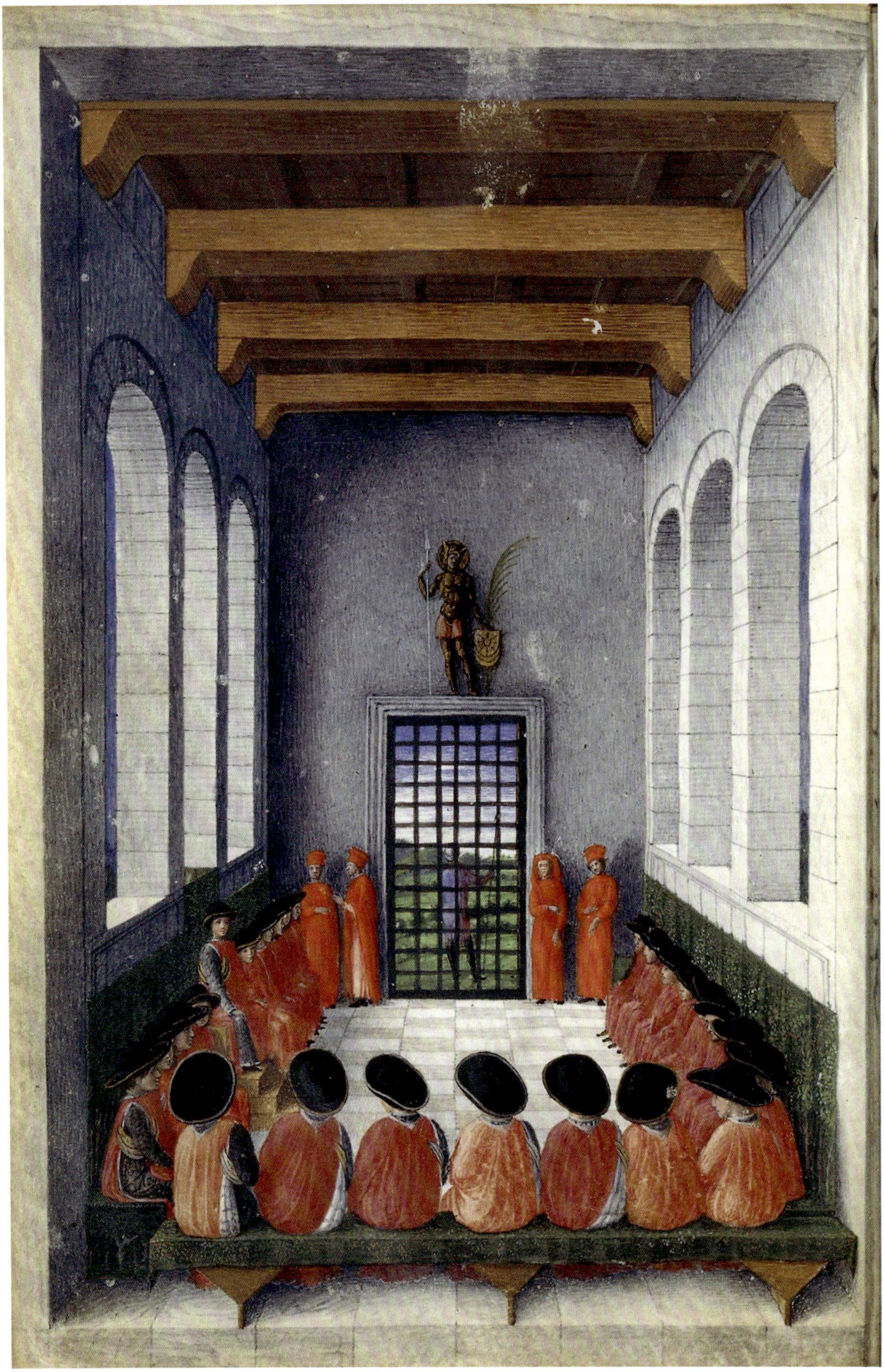

FIGURE 93 Giovanni Bellini, *Assembly of the Order of the Crescent,* 1453. Miniature from Jacopo Antonio Marcello's *Passion of Saint Maurice* manuscript. Tempera, gum, or glue on vellum, 18.7 × 14 cm. Bibliothèque de l'Arsenal, Paris

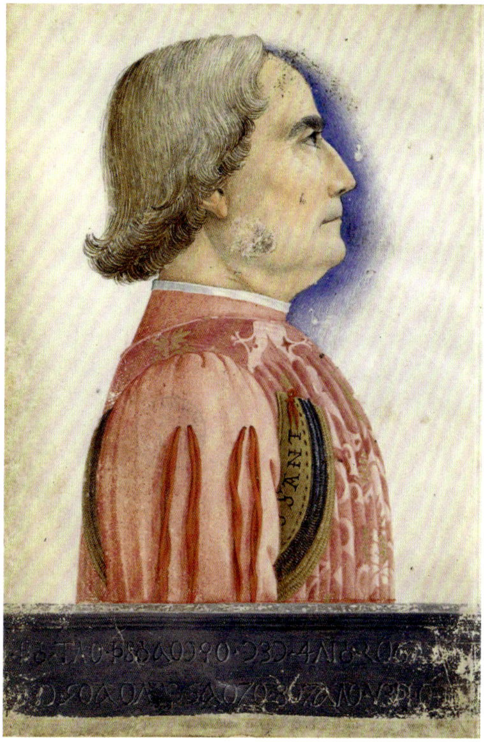

FIGURE 94 Giovanni Bellini, *Jacopo Antonio Marcello*, 1453. Miniature from Jacopo Antonio Marcello's *Passion of Saint Maurice* manuscript. Tempera, gum, or glue on vellum, 18.7 × 14 cm. Bibliothèque de l'Arsenal, Paris

FIGURE 95 Giovanni Bellini, *Allegory of Venice*, 1453. Miniature from Jacopo Antonio Marcello's *Passion of Saint Maurice* manuscript. Tempera, gum, or glue on vellum, 18.7 × 14 cm. Bibliothèque de l'Arsenal, Paris

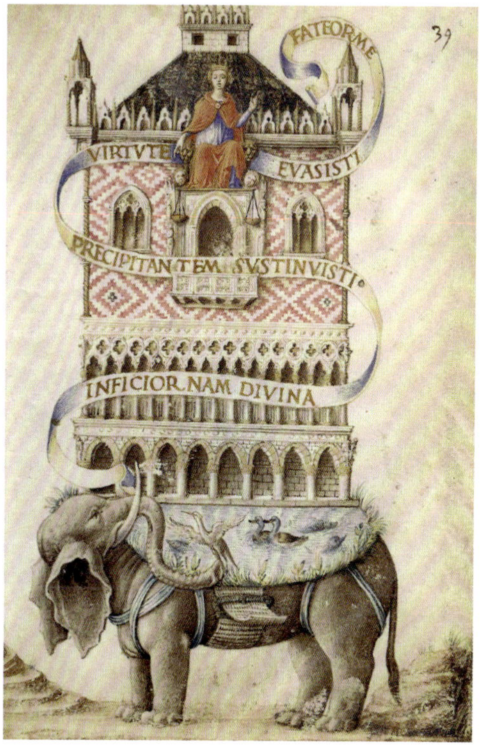

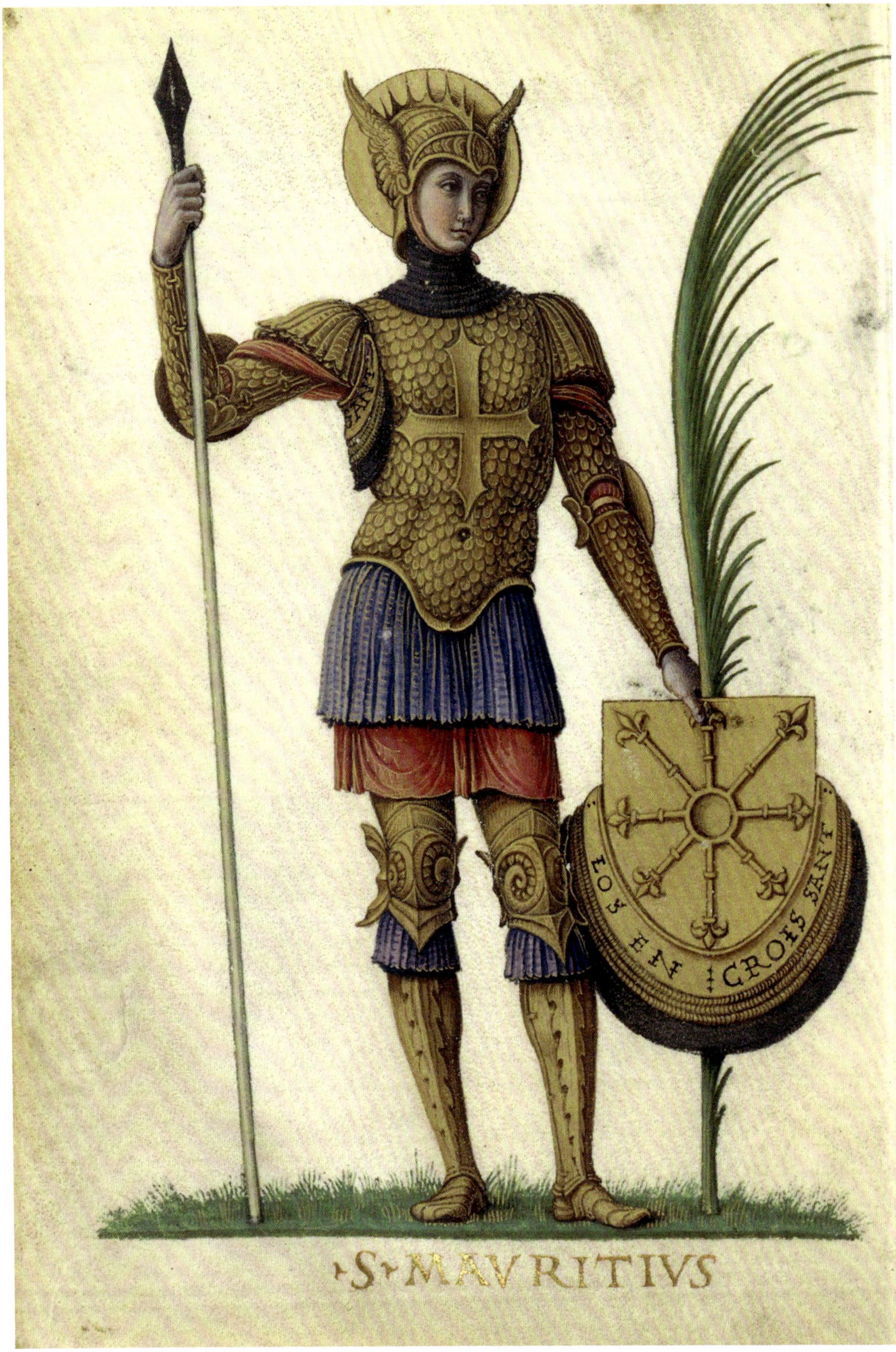

FIGURE 96 Giovanni Bellini, *Saint Maurice*, 1453. Miniature from Jacopo Antonio Marcello's *Passion of Saint Maurice* manuscript. Tempera, gum, or glue on vellum, 18.7 × 14 cm. Bibliothèque de l'Arsenal, Paris

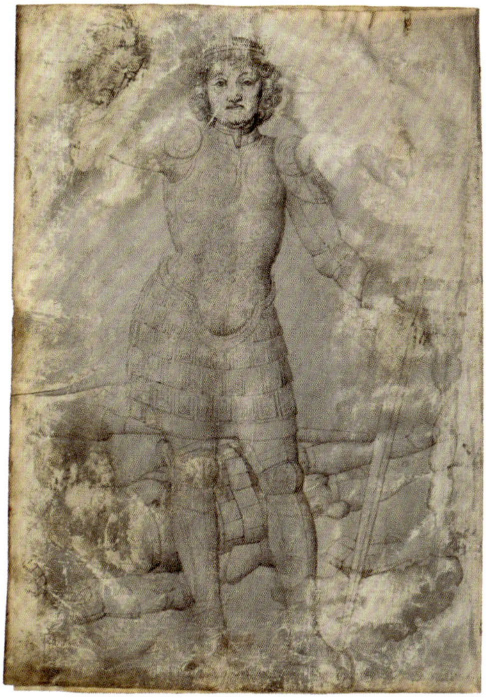

FIGURE 97 Jacopo Bellini, *King David Conquering Goliath*, ca. 1450. Vellum, 38 × 26 cm. Cabinet des dessins, Musée du Louvre, Paris

the late 1430s in recent decades, which would make the artist too young to have executed the illuminations in 1452 or 1453.

We know, however, that Giovanni was an illuminator. He is documented in 1474 as executing a miniature in the humanist poet Raffaele Zovenzoni's (1434–ca. 1485) *Istrias*.[17] In contrast, no evidence suggests that Jacopo ever illuminated manuscripts. Moreover, scholars have often observed that, especially in his early paintings, Giovanni employed techniques drawn from manuscript illumination, such as the use of gilded highlights.[18] Giovanni's early artistic process also strongly supports the attribution of the Marcello miniatures to the young artist. Take, for instance, the Marcello illumination that illustrates Saint Maurice (fig. 96). The stance, gesture, and overall figure of Maurice were undoubtedly inspired by Jacopo's Paris drawing of *King David Conquering Goliath* (ca. 1450, fig. 97).[19] David's raised and bent right arm clutching the decapitated giant's head becomes Maurice's holding a long spear, and David's lowered left arm grasping a sword becomes Maurice's steadying a shield and palm branch. The most telling evidence that Giovanni adapted Jacopo's drawing, however, appears in the midsection (figs 98 and 99). Maurice, like David, distinctly shifts his right hip, which creates a jog in his waist that seems to crease his cuirass on both sides; and the unusual u-shaped cut of the cuirass as well as the placement of David's navel have been transferred to Maurice.

To construct Maurice's armor, Giovanni also adapted at least two other drawings of fanciful soldiers from Jacopo's Paris sketchbook (figs 100 and 101).[20] The saint's eccentric headgear, with winged ears and spiny scales over the scalp, derives from the winged ears

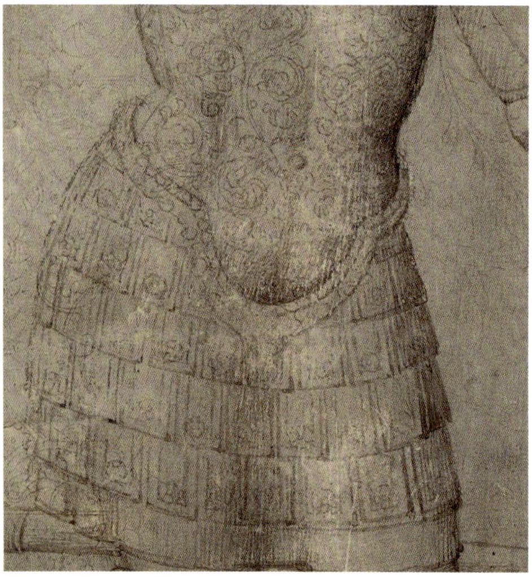

FIGURE 98 Detail of fig. 97

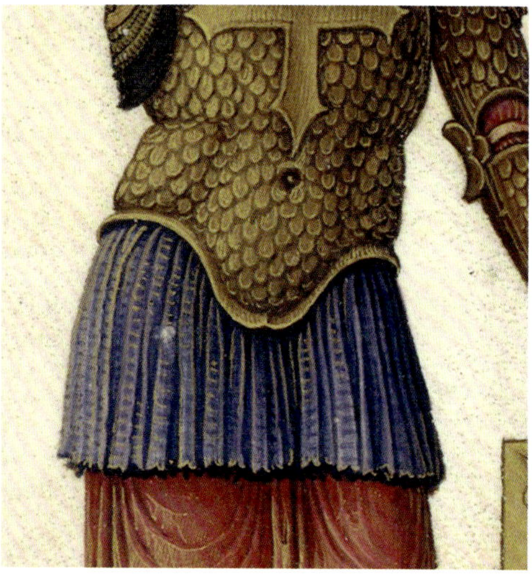

FIGURE 99 Detail of fig. 96

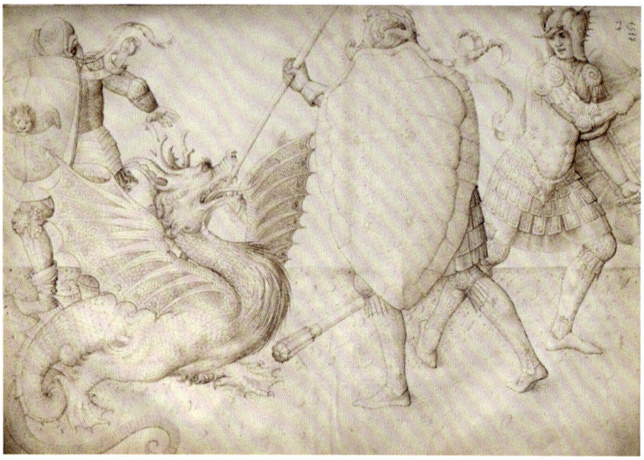

FIGURE 100 Jacopo Bellini, *Warriors Combat a Dragon,* ca. 1430. Vellum, 26 × 38 cm. Cabinet des dessins, Musée du Louvre, Paris

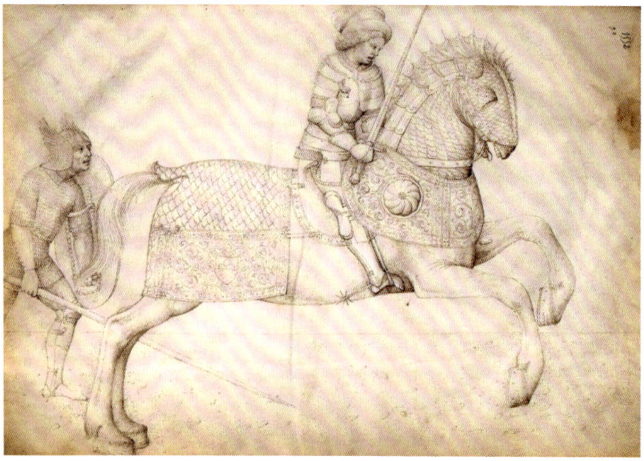

FIGURE 101 Jacopo Bellini, *Galloping Horseman and Warrior on Foot,* ca. 1440. Vellum, 26 × 38 cm. Cabinet des dessins, Musée du Louvre, Paris

of one of Jacopo's fictive soldiers and the spiny headgear of the other (figs 102–04). The distinctive mollusk whorls and ray fins decorating the spaulders that cover the shoulders of the right-most soldier in fig. 100, and the couter that protects his elbow, become the spiral and wings on Maurice's poleyns that shield the saint's knees.

There is no question that Maurice emerged from the pages of Jacopo's Paris sketchbook, and in the exact manner consistent with Giovanni's artistic approach during this period, namely, by borrowing, refining, and integrating motifs from the work of other artists, most of all Jacopo. No evidence suggests this was Jacopo's approach to painting, especially when he was about 60 years old.[21] Thus, Giles Robertson seems to have been correct when he attributed the Marcello manuscript illuminations to Giovanni, noting that "Both Jacopo and Gentile Bellini seem, as far as our limited knowledge of them extends, to be out of the question here on qualitative grounds."[22] Furthermore, the face of Maurice is executed with Giovanni's idiosyncratic sweetness, a quality absent from Jacopo's work (see p. 78), and the virtuosity of the illuminations suggests the authorship of neither Gentile nor Leonardo Bellini, who, in 1453, had yet to commence their independent careers. Only Giovanni Bellini, who was about 27 years old when the manuscript was sent to René d'Anjou in 1453, could have produced these high-quality illuminations by employing the defining artistic approach of his early years.

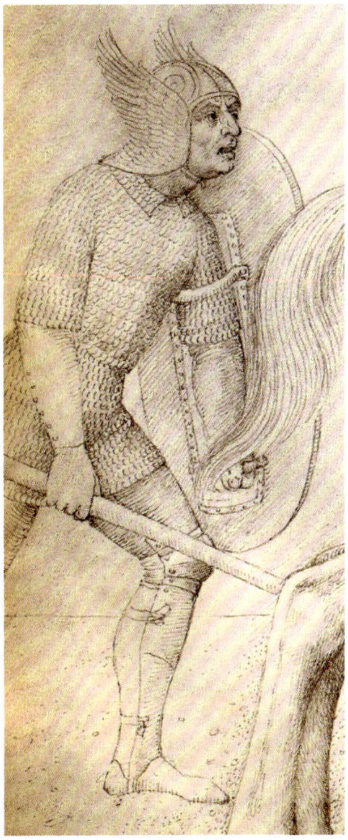

FIGURE 102 Detail of fig. 101

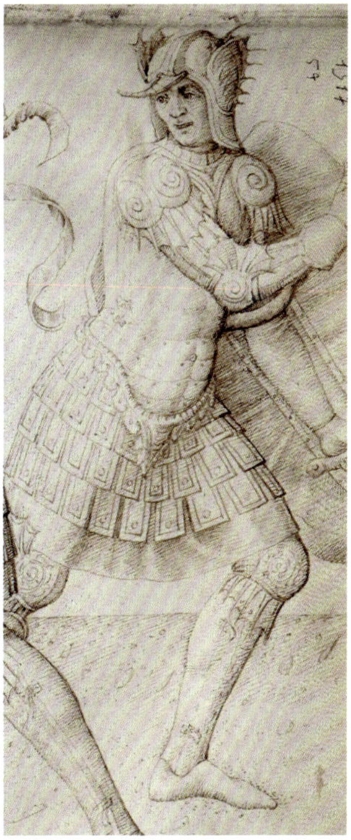

FIGURE 103 Detail of fig. 100

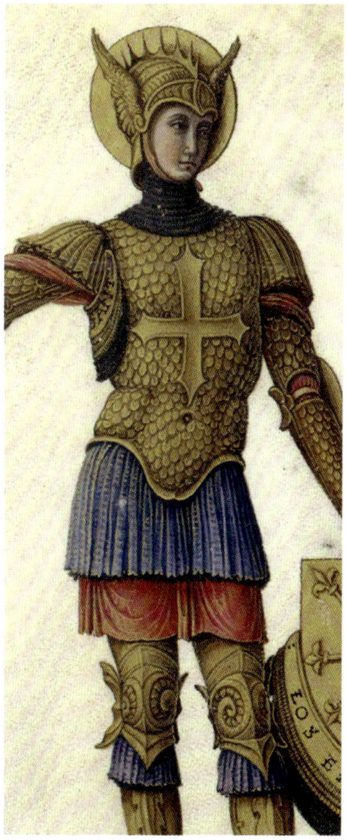

FIGURE 104 Detail of fig. 96

For the art historian seeking to date Giovanni's first paintings, and to distinguish them from Jacopo's own work, three observations may be made. The first is that Giovanni employed this process of integration, and Jacopo, at least in his securely attributed extant paintings, apparently did not. The second is that Giovanni, beginning with the Brescia predella panels, endeavored to portray a consistent source of light, while Jacopo rarely if ever sought to unify his paintings or drawings in this way. The third is that Giovanni seems to have infused his paintings with ideas from recently executed works of art, or, in the case of certain Netherlandish influences, from works that had recently arrived in Venice and that he had presumably viewed for the first time. Only in his very first paintings, it would seem, did Giovanni use frescoes from the trecento or early quattrocento as models. Giovanni's preference for responding to recently completed or still-in-progress works of art can help in dating his early paintings, which were often, though not in every case, executed soon after the execution of the works of art upon which they relied. Thus, the Ferrara *Coronation* (see fig. 25), which depended on motifs from Bartolomeo Bon's Porta della Carta (completed in ca. 1442, see fig. 38), may be dated to ca. 1441–42, and Giovanni's Birmingham *Saint Jerome* (see fig. 79), which used Mantegna's *Calling of Saints James and John* (1450, see fig. 82) as a compositional model, may be dated to ca. 1450.

The Correr *Crucifixion*

An example of Giovanni's more mature process of reinterpreting and integrating the pictorial ideas of other artists is his *Crucifixion with the Virgin and Saint John the Evangelist* (ca. 1457, fig. 105), completed when the artist was in his early thirties. Giovanni's first known painting to have been strongly inspired by Northern European art, the Correr *Crucifixion* features perhaps the most accomplished landscape by the artist prior to his *Agony in the Garden* (ca. 1459, National Gallery, London).[23] The crucified Christ, set in front of a blue sky scattered with tiny cloud-like cherubim, is flanked by the grieving figures of the Virgin Mary and Saint John the Evangelist. These figures, like the image of the Savior, appear to be illuminated from the far left and cast no shadows on the plateau, which may therefore be read as a spiritual space. Behind them, a horizontal rocky ledge separates the foreground from a marvelously realized, slowly receding rural landscape, thinly populated by horses, soldiers, and other figures. One's eye meanders down its winding paths, around its sculpted earthen mounds, and, most spectacularly, along its shimmering river that bends under a footbridge from a distant hamlet on the right toward a mountain range at the horizon on the left. For Renaissance viewers, the sacrifice of Christ set against a vista representing this world must have conveyed the comforting possibility of their own salvation in the next one. Both epigraphic and x-ray analysis suggest that the crude Greek red lettering of the *titulus*, which translates to "Jesus, King of the Confessors," is a later addition, perhaps from the sixteenth century.[24]

It has long been recognized that both the central group and the angels derive from a drawing of the Crucifixion in Jacopo's Paris sketchbook (fig. 106).[25] In many of Jacopo's other

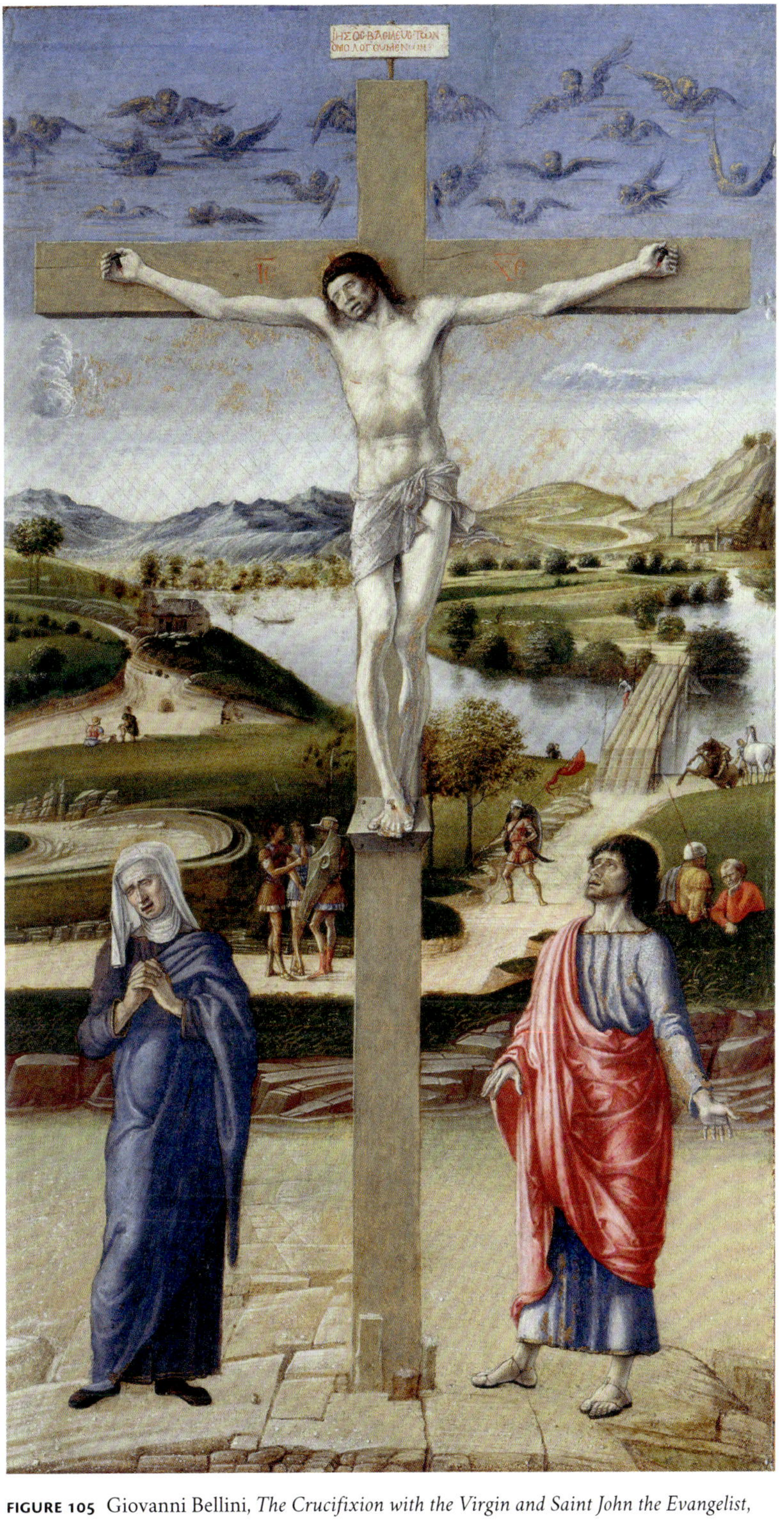

FIGURE 105 Giovanni Bellini, *The Crucifixion with the Virgin and Saint John the Evangelist*, ca. 1457. Tempera on panel, 54 × 30 cm. Museo Correr, Venice

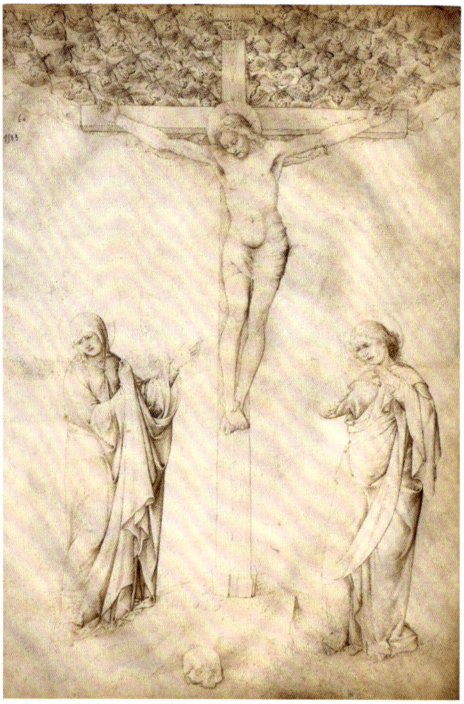

FIGURE 106 Jacopo Bellini, *The Crucifixion with the Virgin and Saint John*, ca. 1435–40. Vellum, 38 × 26 cm. Cabinet des dessins, Musée du Louvre, Paris

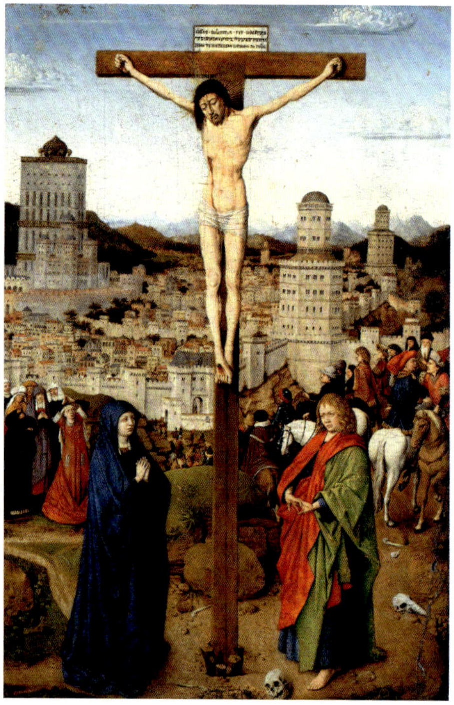

FIGURE 107 Anonymous (after Jan van Eyck?), *The Crucifixion*, ca. 1450. Oil on panel, 46 × 31 cm. Galleria Giorgio Franchetti alla Ca' d'Oro, Venice

drawings, he delighted in inserting figures engaged in various conversations and activities, an approach Giovanni followed in the *Crucifixion* with moderation.[26] Giovanni's motif of three soldiers talking, for instance, recalls a similarly arranged trio on folio 42 of the Paris sketchbook, and that of the rearing horse whose rider's face is hidden recurs on folios 37, 69, and 75.[27] It is interesting to note that in this painting, Giovanni has begun to reuse motifs from his own work. The thin band of rocks directly behind the bottom of the cross is a smaller-scale, free-form replication of part of the plateau in his *Transfiguration of Christ* (ca. 1455, see fig. 2).[28]

Although Jacopo executed landscapes with curving landforms and bending rivers with bridges, Giovanni's topography seems to depend on the Northern European vistas depicted in Netherlandish art.[29] Crucifixions based on Eyckian models were known in the Veneto by the 1450s, and some—such as that now in the Ca' d'Oro, Venice (ca. 1450, fig. 107), which was executed in oils and almost certainly by a Netherlandish follower of Jan van Eyck (d. 1441)—contrasted the idle indifference of various figures in the middle ground with the sorrow of the Virgin and John the Evangelist; thus they likely provided both thematic and compositional models for Giovanni.[30] But the principal source for Giovanni's landscape appears to have been a now-dispersed polyptych on linen by the Haarlem-born artist Dieric Bouts (ca. 1415–1475) that scholars have convincingly argued

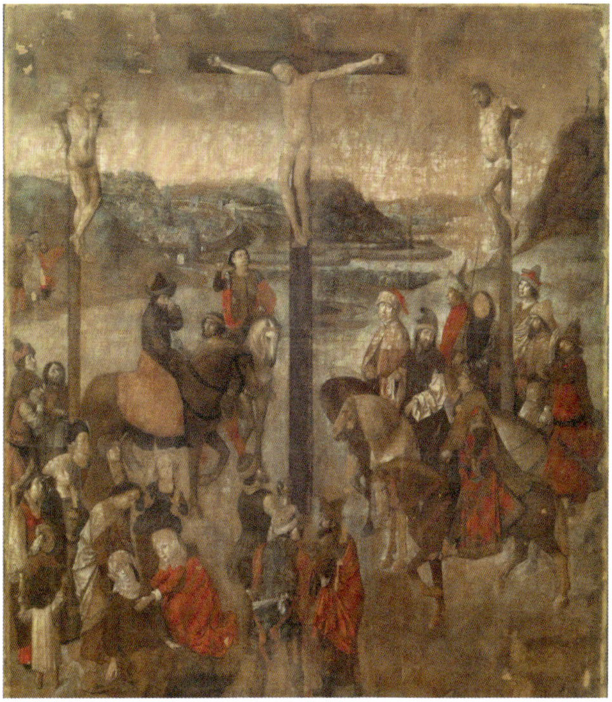

FIGURE 108 Dieric Bouts the Elder, *The Crucifixion*, ca. 1450–55. Tempera on linen, 181.5 × 153.5 cm. Royal Museums of Fine Arts, Brussels

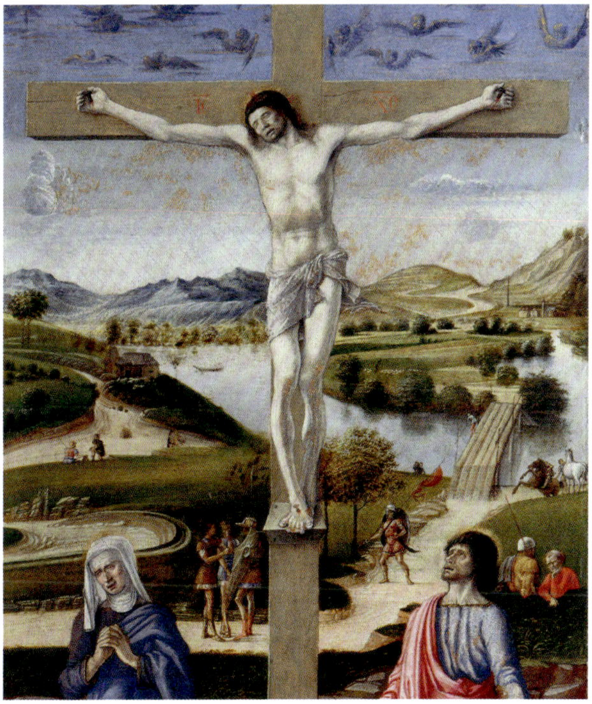

FIGURE 109 Detail of fig. 105

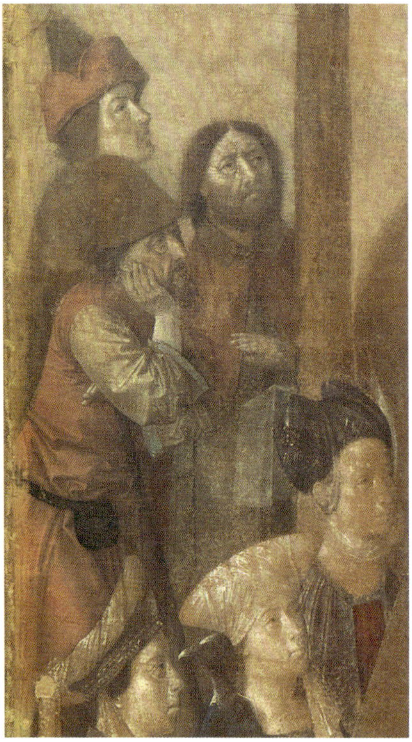

FIGURE 110 Detail of fig. 108

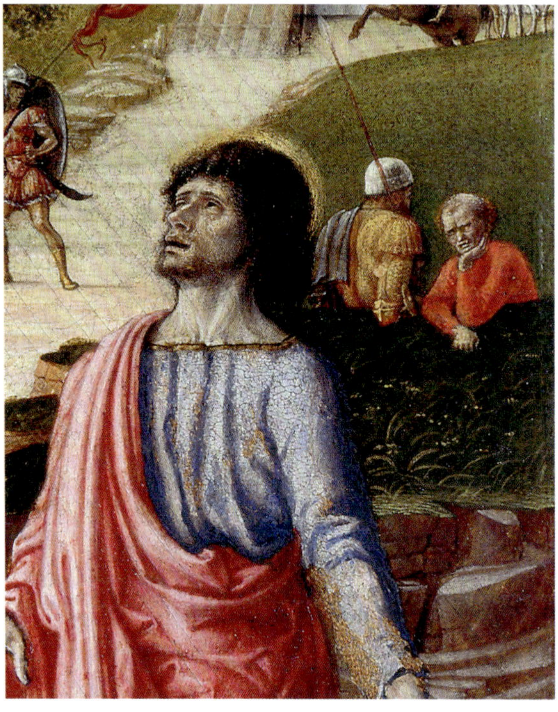

FIGURE 111 Detail of fig. 105

was shipped to Venice, perhaps as an altarpiece for a Venetian church, as early as ca. 1450.[31] The central image of the polyptych seems to have been Bouts's deeply abraded *Crucifixion* (ca. 1450–55, fig. 108), which features a broad river, presumably once reflective, with clusters of trees dispersed along its bank, winding toward the hills of the horizon.[32] The position of Christ in Giovanni's *Crucifixion* is close to his position in Bouts's depiction, with the Savior's head slightly forward and his hands partially clenched (fig. 109).[33] Both *Crucifixions* also share the unusual motif of a man with his hand to his cheek, on the left margin in the Bouts and on the right in Giovanni's work (figs 110 and 111).[34]

The Correr *Crucifixion* is thus one of many examples of Giovanni's process of creatively incorporating pictorial ideas by other artists into his own work. As Giovanni matured, his procedure of integrating individual compositions and specific motifs developed into a more general practice of observing and absorbing the stylistic or conceptual elements of vanguard works. In this way, Giovanni was able to assimilate an extraordinary range of innovations into his art, arguably to an extent unsurpassed by other artists in the Renaissance. For instance, in middle age Giovanni became one of the first Italian artists to master the use of oils as revolutionized by Netherlandish painters, and in old age, Giovanni learned from his former students, Giorgione and Titian, to explore new artistic subjects, such as classical allegories and the female nude.[35] Many scholars believe that Giovanni's keen awareness of pictorial experiments by his contemporaries was a defining characteristic of his own artistic approach, one that allowed his art to progress with the times and remain relevant.[36] It is remarkable to consider, then, that Giovanni's lifelong ability to infuse his pictures with fresh ideas is traceable to the artistic approach he employed as an adolescent in the Ferrara *Coronation*.

The revisionist history presented in this book has sought to expand our understanding of Giovanni's early activity and provide a new foundation for future studies of the artist. The transformative evidence pushing Giovanni's date of birth back to 1424–26 has opened up a previously unknown phase in the artist's life that allows paintings from the 1440s to be ascribed to him, while leaving open the possibility that other works from this period will be attributed to the artist in the future.[37] Indeed, the dating and even perhaps the interpretation of a number of Giovanni's later paintings, especially those currently assigned to the 1450s and 1460s, may need reappraisal, along with his artistic relationship with Mantegna, who was not older than Giovanni, as is generally believed, but rather a few years younger.[38] These possible re-datings and shifts in the direction of pictorial influence may lead to a broader reassessment of the central role Giovanni played in the stylistic development of early Renaissance art in Northern Italy.[39]

Appendix A

The New Genealogy

"We should never forget that the birth of Giovanni Bellini is one of the most ideological dates in the entire history of Italian art."
— Giovanni Agosti, 1993[1]

When was Giovanni Bellini born? Was Giovanni older or younger than Gentile Bellini? Was Giovanni born legitimately? Scholars have yet to arrive at a consensus regarding the answers to these three questions, which have been debated since the nineteenth century. Nonetheless, the questions remain central, because the correct identification of Giovanni's birth year would help establish a chronology for the artist's early works that in turn would support a critical reassessment of Giovanni's early career.

To these three longstanding questions may be added a fourth: was Giovanni older or younger than Andrea Mantegna, the other leading artist of early Renaissance Northern Italy? In ca. 1453, Mantegna married Jacopo Bellini's daughter, Nicolosia, bringing Giovanni and Mantegna into close family contact.[2] Yet the extent to which either artist exerted creative influence on the other, or whether the two mutually benefited from a sharing of pictorial ideas, has not been firmly established. Thus, the important factor is not so much Giovanni and Mantegna's relative ages, but rather the chronology of their early works of art. How scholars answer this question and reconstruct these chronologies has significant implications for our understanding of the stylistic development of early Renaissance art in Northern Italy.

This appendix presents an updated and truncated version of my biographical research on Giovanni Bellini published in 2013 that underlies this book.[3] On November 29, 1516, the Venetian diarist Marin Sanudo wrote, "We learned this morning of the death of Giovanni Bellini, the great painter, who died at the age of . . .."[4] His ellipsis leaves a gap that historians have endeavored to fill for more than five centuries. In 1550, the Tuscan artist and historian Giorgio Vasari was the first to publish an indication of Giovanni Bellini's birth year, writing in his *Lives* that the artist had died at the age of 90 (on November 28 or 29, 1516).[5] Vasari thus located Giovanni's birth in late 1425 or 1426, which was widely accepted by biographers for the subsequent three centuries. Then, in 1894, the Italian scholar Pietro Paoletti rediscovered and published the first will of Anna Rinversi, who was Jacopo Bellini's wife and ostensibly Giovanni Bellini's mother.[6] In this will, drawn up on February 6, 1429, Anna indicated that she was currently pregnant but did not yet have children, therefore implying that Giovanni, if he was indeed her son, was born after that date.[7]

The rediscovery of Anna's will prompted most Bellini scholars to dismiss Vasari's dating of Giovanni's birth year as 1425–26 and instead relocate his birth to 1429 or later. Yet in the first monograph on Giovanni Bellini, published in 1899, the English painter, critic, and scholar Roger Fry alternatively suggested that perhaps "Giovanni was not Anna's son at all; for in a later will, made in 1471, she left everything to 'Gentile et Nicolao'"—Anna and Jacopo Bellini's sons, as Anna herself described them—with no mention of Giovanni.[8] A half-century later, in 1949, the Italian art historian Giuseppe Fiocco accepted Fry's suggestion that Giovanni was not Anna's son and, believing that the artist had been legitimate, argued that Giovanni was either Jacopo's offspring from a previous marriage or Jacopo's legitimated son from a previous liaison.[9] Consequently, Fiocco returned Giovanni's birthdate to ca. 1425, thus in loose agreement with Vasari.[10] Some scholars, such as the influential art historian Roberto Longhi, concurred with Fiocco's reasoning, but most continued to place Giovanni's birth as occurring after Anna's 1429 will.[11]

In the last several decades, a group of international Bellini specialists has shifted Giovanni's birthdate to much later, to after ca. 1435 and perhaps closer to 1440.[12] They argue that Giovanni began his independent career no earlier than the mid-1450s or 1460, and by subtracting 20 years from that range, they situate the artist's birth in the second half of the 1430s.[13] Many of these scholars also believe that Giovanni was strongly influenced by Mantegna, who was born in ca. 1431 or slightly earlier, and thus they argue that Mantegna must have been Giovanni's elder by at least several years.[14] Finally, if Giovanni had indeed been born in ca. 1440, then he would have been in his mid-seventies when executing later works such as the *Feast of the Gods* (1514, National Gallery of Art, Washington, DC), which is an age that seems more likely to some scholars rather than the artist being in his late eighties had he been born ca. 1425–26.

Following this group of Bellini specialists, some museum curators have recently accepted a later birth year and chronology of works for Giovanni. At the time of this writing, the Barber Institute indicates on their website that Giovanni's *Saint Jerome in the Wilderness* (see fig. 79) was executed "about 1460."[15] Giovanni Bellini's biography page on the website of the National Gallery, London, places his birth "about 1435."[16] However, the website of the National Gallery of Art, Washington, DC, gives "ca. 1430/35," the two dates reflecting the two main differences of opinion in Bellini scholarship today regarding Giovanni's birth.[17] Vasari's suggested birth-year range of 1425–26 has largely been dismissed.

The second longstanding question concerning Giovanni's birth is whether he was older or younger than his brother Gentile Bellini, an artist principally known for his large-scale narrative paintings and a celebrated trip to Istanbul in 1479–80, where he apparently executed the well-known portrait of Sultan Mehmet II (1480, fig. 112).[18] Beginning in 1503,

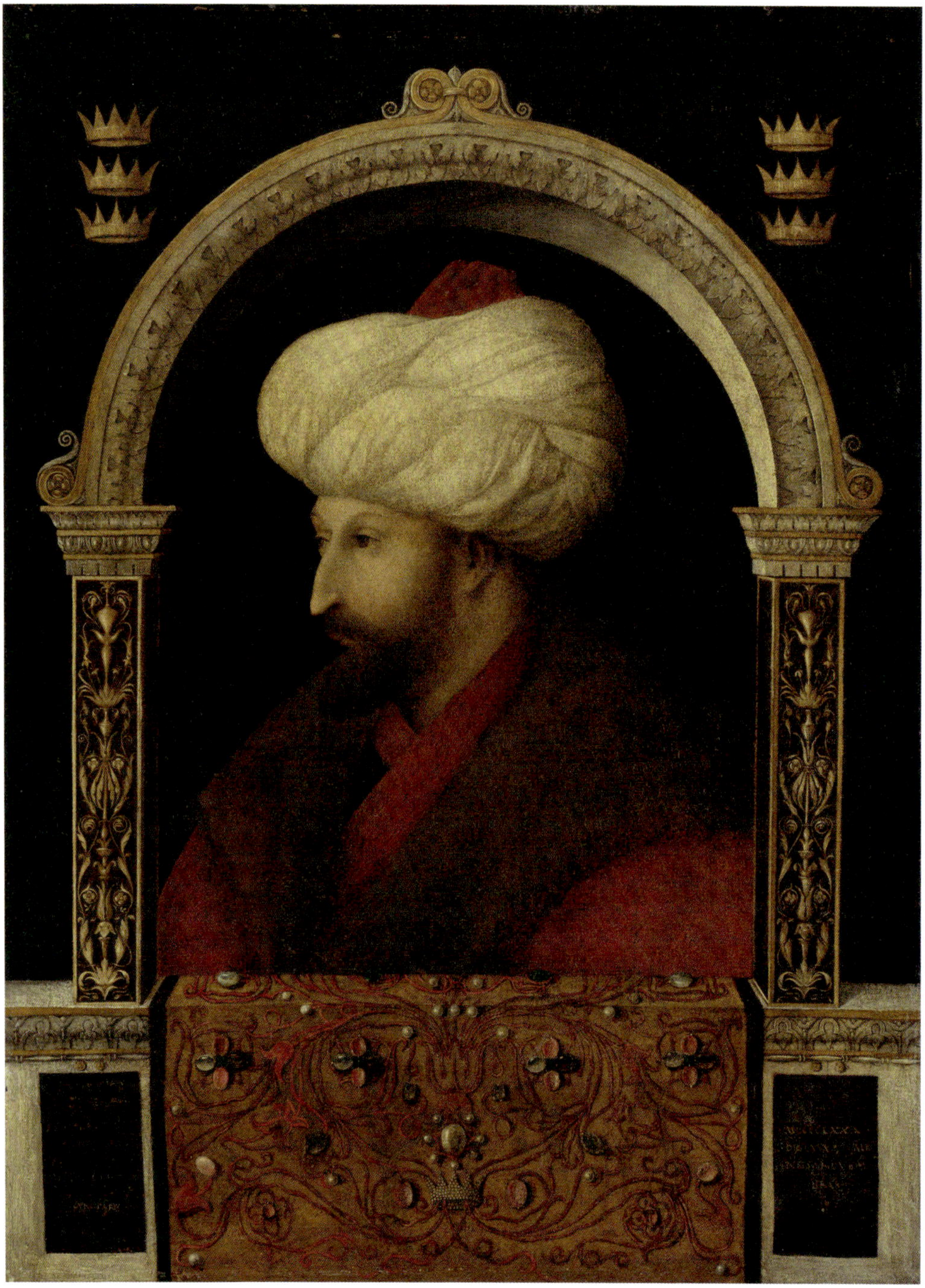

FIGURE 112 Gentile Bellini, *Sultan Mehmet II*, 1480. Oil (19th-century repaint) on canvas, perhaps transferred from wood, 69.9 × 52.1 cm. National Gallery, London

when both Giovanni and Gentile were still alive, the Augustinian friar Jacopo Filippo Foresti (1434–1520) wrote in his regularly updated encyclopedic text, *Supplementum chronicarum*, that Gentile was the younger brother (*Gentilis minimus frater*).[19] In 1550, Vasari also stated that Gentile was younger (*più di lui giovane*), and in the second, expanded version of the *Lives* of 1568, he wrote that the Venetian Senate decided not to send Giovanni to Sultan Mehmet's court in Istanbul (in 1479) because Giovanni was too old for the journey and they did not want to deprive their city of so great a man; hence, they sent Gentile instead.[20] While the story may be spurious, it seems clear that Vasari believed that Giovanni was older than Gentile.

However, it seems that Vasari had made an error concerning Gentile Bellini's date of birth. In both versions of the *Lives*, he stated that Gentile was nearly 80 when he died in 1501, but Gentile in fact died in 1507.[21] This mistake, perhaps typographical, caused the Bellini family biography in the *Lives* to be internally inconsistent: Vasari explicitly declared that Giovanni was older than Gentile, while at the same time indicating that Giovanni and Gentile were born in 1425/6 and ca. 1421, respectively, which would have made Gentile the elder of the two.

Most historians during the next several centuries, including the painter and biographer Carlo Ridolfi (1594–1658) in his influential *Le maraviglie dell'arte* (*The Marvels of Art*) of 1648, repeated Vasari's error by incorrectly placing Gentile's birth in 1421, when he must have been born in 1429 or later (Gentile being Anna Rinversi's son and born after her first will of 1429).[22] These historians chose to disregard Vasari's statement that Giovanni was the elder, and they were perhaps unaware of Foresti's identical declaration in the *Supplementum chronicarum*. Thus, in an annotated publication of Vasari's *Lives* written between 1832 and 1838, the editor Giovanni Masselli noted that "Gentile was the elder, being himself born in 1421 and Giovanni born in 1426."[23]

In 1834, the art historian Giannantonio Moschini identified Vasari's mistake. Moschini had learned from the then-unpublished diaries of Sanudo that Gentile was buried in Venice on February 23, 1507, within days of his death.[24] Thus, following Vasari, Moschini wrote that Giovanni was "born in Venice in the year 1426" and, revising Vasari, wrote that Gentile, "if it is true that he completed his life in his eightieth year, would have been born in the year 1427, and his brother Giovanni would have been the firstborn."[25]

Thus, Giovanni was once again identified as Gentile's older brother, but other conflicting evidence soon surfaced. By 1800, scholars had discovered an unpublished manuscript by the Venetian humanist Francesco Negri (1452–ca. 1523), probably written in the early 1490s, that briefly mentioned Giovanni and Gentile and stated that Gentile was firstborn (*maior natu*).[26] In 1871, the influential art historians Joseph Archer Crowe and Giovanni Battista Cavalcaselle identified Gentile as "the elder" by citing Negri's statement "contradicting Vasari, who makes Giovanni the eldest of the two brothers."[27] Since the late nineteenth century, despite Vasari's and Foresti's assertions to the contrary, most Bellini scholars have followed Crowe and Cavalcaselle in identifying Gentile as being older than

Giovanni. Moreover, well into the twentieth century, Gentile's birth year was often given as ca. 1429 and Giovanni's as ca. 1430—both were presumed to have been born after Anna's 1429 will, with Gentile born first.

The third longstanding question regarding Giovanni Bellini's birth is whether Giovanni was born legitimate, that is, to legally married parents.[28] Since Bellini scholars have always accepted that Giovanni was Jacopo Bellini's biological son, the question posed by Fry and others is whether Giovanni's omission from Anna Rinversi's 1471 will meant that Giovanni was not her son and was perhaps born out of wedlock. The fact that Giovanni was documented in 1459 as living in the Venetian parish of San Lio, and thus apart from Jacopo Bellini's household in the nearby parish of San Geminiano, while Gentile continued to live with Jacopo and would eventually inherit Jacopo's home-workshop, has further suggested to some scholars that Giovanni was indeed born illegitimate.[29] However, other prominent Bellini specialists, such as Giles Robertson and Rona Goffen, have argued that Giovanni was more likely born legitimate, since no documentation or direct evidence suggests otherwise.[30] Robertson further proposed that Giovanni "had already received his portion of the estate under Jacopo's will, which has not come to light," and he speculated that if Giovanni had truly been born illegitimate, then such a "gossipy detail" would likely have been recorded by Vasari or Ridolfi.[31]

The lack of consensus regarding the answers to these questions has led to uncertainty in reconstructing an early biography for Giovanni and a chronology of his works. Yet one statement regarding the artist's beginnings has always seemed definite: Giovanni Bellini was Jacopo Bellini's biological son. As discussed below, however, this bedrock "truth" is instead an assumption, one that in many respects is responsible for the centuries-old confusion over Giovanni's origins, and one, there is evidence to suggest, that is wrong.

My Answers to the Longstanding Questions

The research supporting this book (first published in 2013 in a *Renaissance Quarterly* article titled "Giovanni Bellini: Birth, Parentage, and Independence") provides comprehensive answers to the above-mentioned questions surrounding Giovanni's birth.[32] The article analyzed legal documents in accordance with the civil code of fifteenth-century Venice to demonstrate that Jacopo Bellini was not the biological father of Giovanni Bellini but rather his biological half-brother. These documents indicate that Jacopo and Giovanni were both born to a tinsmith named Nicoletto Bellini but to different mothers, who were Nicoletto's first and second wives, Zanina and Franceschina. It can be shown that Nicoletto Bellini died when his son Giovanni was four years old or younger (see Chapter 1 for a discussion of Giovanni's birth possibly occurring after Nicoletto's death). Franceschina, it appears, also died when Giovanni was very young, perhaps even during childbirth. Thereafter, all evidence suggests that Giovanni's much older half-brother, Jacopo Bellini, raised Giovanni as his son, the two separated in age by over 30 years.

Giovanni's birth year may also be determined as falling within a range of dates. As discussed in Chapter 1 and again below, it appears that he was born between mid-1424 and September 13, 1426. Giovanni would therefore have been a few years *older* than Mantegna.[33] Giovanni would also have been older than Gentile Bellini, who was born in 1429 or later and raised as Giovanni's brother, although biologically he would have been Giovanni's nephew. When Giovanni died on November 28 or 29, 1516, he would have been between the ages of 90 and 92 years old—as such Giorgio Vasari's assertion that Giovanni had died at the age of 90, which some scholars perhaps imagined was a trope for "very old," turns out to have been either correct or close to it.[34]

The archival evidence recording Giovanni and Jacopo as biological brothers is a legal document called a *divisio* (charter of division). It was drawn up on September 13, 1440, by the Venetian notary Vittore Pomino to separate the property of two brothers, Giovanni and Jacopo Bellini, sons of the deceased Nicoletto Bellini, who were residing in the Venetian parish of San Geminiano.[35] When this document was first published by Paoletti in 1929, it was understandably misinterpreted to mean that Jacopo Bellini not only had a son named Giovanni, the famous painter, but also a brother named Giovanni, the individual named in the *divisio*, to whom scholars would refer as "Giovanni Bellini il Vecchio" or "Giovanni Bellini the Elder," to distinguish him from Jacopo's son Giovanni.[36] As we shall see, however, this interpretation appears to have been incorrect; the Giovanni Bellini identified as Jacopo's brother in the *divisio* is with little doubt the famous artist Giovanni Bellini.

As a result of the publication of the *divisio* in 1929, art historians have sought to confirm the independent existence of the so-called "Giovanni Bellini il Vecchio."[37] No documents or other credible evidence, however, indicate that this hypothesized individual ever existed. For an examination of the step-by-step creation of this apparently fictional character as an early Renaissance artist with his own biography and corpus of works, see Appendix B (pp. 136–45).

In actuality, the 1440 *divisio* recording that Jacopo and Giovanni Bellini were brothers was a very common notarial instrument which, as its first line states, was executed on behalf of legitimately born brothers: "The division to occur between the brothers is declared lawful, et cetera."[38] When a father died in fifteenth-century Venice, his legitimately born unemancipated sons were immediately thrust into a *fraterna compagnia* (fraternal partnership) that owned the entirety of the father's estate, unless the father had willed some part of it otherwise.[39] Fraternal partnerships, the most common form of business association among craftsmen and merchants in medieval and Renaissance Venice, bound legitimate brothers together both legally and financially, which helped ensure that family businesses would remain intact rather than be dissolved upon the death of the patriarch.[40]

A more complex form of a *fraterna compagnia* might include other legitimate male family members, such as the one that Marco Polo, the famous Venetian traveler, shared with several of his close male relatives.[41] In general, however, if one of the brothers did not wish to remain in the fraternal partnership—for instance, if he desired his portion of the inheritance or intended to enter into a different business association apart from his brothers—then, in amicable separations, only a notary was required to draw up a *divisio*, which would assign to each brother an equal portion of the fraternal partnership and grant to each legal independence from his brothers.[42]

On September 13, 1440, the legitimately born brothers Jacopo and Giovanni Bellini terminated their fraternal partnership. Eleven days later, on September 24, 1440, Jacopo Bellini engaged a different notary to draft a contract between himself and the painter Donato Bragadin to enter into a five-year business partnership.[43] For unknown reasons, Jacopo's partnership with Bragadin was never finalized; the contract lacks witnesses and was crossed out in the notary's register.[44] Nonetheless, it provides a plausible reason for Jacopo and Giovanni's *divisio* of 11 days earlier: Jacopo needed to end the fraternal partnership with Giovanni before entering into a business partnership with another party.[45]

Indeed, the 1440 *divisio* itself offers evidence that it was drafted as a formality rather than to divide meticulously the communal property between two working adults. In general, divisions between two or more adult brothers were careful to itemize the shared property held by the fraternal partnership and to state important details such as whether the partnership included or excluded the dowries of the brothers' wives. A typical *divisio* would then specify which brother retained ownership over which properties or monies.[46] For instance, in the *divisio* between Luca and Vito Bono, drawn up by the same notary, Vittore Pomino, a few months before the *divisio* between Giovanni and Jacopo, the Bono brothers were described as *varotarii* (furriers) who had employed their wives' dowries in their business and who agreed to separate such that Luca would retain a shop near the Rialto while Vito would receive 39 ducats in exchange.[47] However, the Bellini *divisio* neither describes the profession of the two Bellini brothers, nor stipulates which one would receive ownership of the workshop or other property, nor enumerates any particulars whatsoever, such as whether the dowry of Jacopo's wife had been included in the partnership.[48] Rather, it was written in standardized, unspecific language, as if purely a formality.[49]

To agree independently to the *divisio*, Giovanni Bellini was legally required to be over the age of 12, as Venetian law states, and almost certainly required to be over the age of 14, as stated by a different Venetian law declaring the male age of majority to be 14.[50] Thus, Giovanni must have been born before September 13, 1428, 12 years before the date of the *divisio*, and almost certainly before September 13, 1426, 14 years prior to the *divisio*. These dates are also supported by the fact that Giovanni's father, Nicoletto, died sometime before July 23, 1429, as discussed below.[51]

The 1440 *divisio* also establishes that both Jacopo and Giovanni were *legitimate* sons of Nicoletto Bellini, because illegitimate sons did not enter into fraternal partnerships and had no such rights of inheritance.[52] This fact is important because 16 years earlier, on April 11, 1424, Giovanni and Jacopo's father, Nicoletto Bellini, had a notary draw up his will that named Nicoletto's legitimate son Jacopo as an heir, but that did not mention Giovanni.[53] In medieval and Renaissance Venice, fathers were legally required to identify their legitimate sons in their wills, even if their intent was to disinherit them.[54] Otherwise, the will could be overturned.[55] The omission of Giovanni from Nicoletto's 1424 will indicates that he had not yet been born (a conclusion also supported by the notary's unusual addition to the will, discussed in Chapter 1). Therefore, Giovanni Bellini must have been born after April 11, 1424, the date of Nicoletto's will, yet almost certainly before September 13, 1426, 14 years prior to the date of the 1440 *divisio*.

Nicoletto Bellini's will is the last known record of Nicoletto being alive. He died sometime prior to July 23, 1429, for on that date Jacopo Bellini engaged a notary to draw up a *carta securitatis et manifestacionis repromisse* in which he acknowledged receiving his wife Anna's dowry of 250 ducats and was described as "Jacopo Bellini, a painter residing in the parish of San Geminiano and son of the deceased ser Nicoletto Bellini."[56] Thus, Giovanni Bellini was no more than four years old, and he might even have still been in his mother Franceschina's womb, when his and Jacopo's father died. The existing evidence also suggests that Franceschina herself died when Giovanni was very young, perhaps during or soon after his birth. After Nicoletto's 1424 will, no known documents mention her; by 1440, Giovanni was living in the parish of San Geminiano, presumably with Jacopo, and not in the parish of San Salvador, where Nicoletto and Franceschina's home had been; and had Franceschina lived to raise Giovanni, then it seems unlikely that he would later have become known as Jacopo Bellini's son.[57]

I propose that the Giovanni Bellini named in the *divisio* was the same person as the famous painter Giovanni Bellini. For, as I wrote in my earlier article on Giovanni's birth:

> if they were not the same, then there were two boys named Giovanni Bellini, both under the age of 16 in 1440, both living in the Venetian parish of San Geminiano, both lineal descendants of Nicolò Bellini and both closely connected to, and likely residing in, Jacopo Bellini's household, one becoming a renowned painter, and the other, Jacopo's half-brother, leaving not a single conclusive trace of his existence except for the *divisio* of 1440.[58]

To this one might add that there exists no evidence—not a single document, signature, or inscription—demonstrating that there was a *second* Giovanni Bellini directly related to Jacopo Bellini (on this point, see also Appendix B). Furthermore, the Giovanni Bellini named in the *divisio* was born between 1424 and 1426, almost precisely as indicated by Vasari for the famous painter; he was orphaned, having lost his father and apparently his mother soon thereafter; and he was between the ages of 14 and 16 when recorded as living in San Geminiano, presumably with Jacopo and therefore being raised by him. Thus, vital details from the early life of the Giovanni Bellini named in the *divisio* align with those of Giovanni Bellini, the famous artist. Moreover, once it is understood that Jacopo's half-brother, Giovanni Bellini, was in fact the famous painter whom Jacopo raised as a son, then the centuries-old questions surrounding Giovanni's early biography become straightforward to answer.

Whether Jacopo, after the deaths of his father Nicoletto, and his stepmother, Franceschina, legally adopted Giovanni or simply raised him as his own son is unknown.[59] In either event, Giovanni would have been emancipated upon Nicoletto's death, for in Venetian law an adopted son remained outside the paternal authority of the adoptive father.[60] Fathers as patriarchs of the family held sovereign rights over their legitimate male descendants along the male line, and therefore had the right to their unemancipated sons' movable property, the usufruct from their sons' inherited immovable property, and the income from their sons' labor.[61] Legitimately born sons remained legal dependents of their fathers until they were emancipated—which in Venice did not occur when the sons reached a certain age or were married, but only upon the death of the father or through a legal act of emancipation (or in rare cases by adoption).[62] The death of the father thus liberated the son, making him a *homo sui iuris*, possessed with full legal rights, and a *paterfamilias* (patriarch of his own family) under the law.[63]

Recall that in 1459, Giovanni, then in his mid-thirties, resided in the Venetian parish of San Lio rather than in Jacopo's household in San Geminiano.[64] Some scholars have wondered how he was legally able to live apart from Jacopo.[65] Giovanni, however, had been emancipated upon his father Nicoletto's death, and therefore, when he came of age, had the right to establish his own household and become patriarch of his own family. In contrast, Gentile continued to reside with his father, Jacopo, almost certainly under paternal authority (*in patris potestate*), as no charter of emancipation has been located for Gentile.[66] Only upon Jacopo's death in 1470/71 would Gentile have become emancipated, after which he continued to live in San Geminiano, apparently in his father's home workshop, for the duration of his life.[67]

It is now also understandable why, in her 1471 will, Jacopo Bellini's wife, Anna Rinversi, bequeathed her estate to her sons Gentile and Nicolò without naming Giovanni.[68] Giovanni was not Anna's biological son but her brother-in-law, and thus she was not legally required to bequeath him anything. In fact, Anna named none of her affinal relatives in her will, neither her sister-in-law Elena nor her nephew-by-marriage Leonardo, whom she and Jacopo had helped raise from about six or eight years old.[69]

The most significant challenges to this revised genealogy come from the many primary sources that describe Giovanni Bellini as Jacopo's son or Gentile's brother. These sources began to appear in 1459, when the artist, at about age 35, witnessed a testament as "Giovanni, son of master Jacopo Bellini."[70] Later examples include Giovanni's 1485 *securitatis carta*, in which he acknowledged receipt of his wife's dowry, naming him as "Giovanni, son of the deceased Jacopo"; a contract he witnessed in 1487 naming him as "Giovanni Bellini, painter, son of the deceased master Jacopo"; Jacopo Bellini's signing of the Gattamelata Altarpiece of 1460 as a work by himself and his sons Gentile and Giovanni; and Gentile's February 18, 1507, will, in which he referred to Giovanni as "my dearest brother."[71] Moreover, both contemporary and later observers, including Foresti, Negri, Sanudo, and Vasari, among others, described Giovanni as Jacopo's son or Gentile's brother.[72]

While it is possible that Jacopo adopted Giovanni—notaries in legal documents often referred to adopted sons simply as sons, making it impossible to determine whether a child was adopted or biological—the more likely scenario is that Jacopo simply raised Giovanni, from such a young age and in such a manner that Giovanni was accepted by his family and the community as Jacopo's son without the formality of a legal adoption.[73] As most historians of the period know well, written or inscribed personal names in fifteenth-century Northern Italy, like elsewhere in Western Europe, did not necessarily convey biological fact. They might project how a person was known, or desired to be known, by the community.[74] For example, Jacopo Bellini's nephew was the well-known miniaturist Leonardo Bellini, but "Bellini" was not the last name of Leonardo's father, Paolo; it was rather a surname that Leonardo assumed.[75] Another example is a Renaissance artist named Vittore, son of Matteo, who decided to call himself Vittore Belliniano after working with Giovanni Bellini for many years, and he was so named in his own will and even that of his mother.[76] There was often a fluidity to names during this period, in which most Venetians did not have surnames and most births were not officially recorded. This fluidity might extend to legal documents, where notaries were apparently given a degree of latitude when identifying individuals—if the identification itself did not, of course, conflict with the legal purpose of the document.

After his father, Nicoletto, died, the young Giovanni became regarded as Jacopo's son by the Bellini family, the local community, and eventually, the writers of the period. Thus, in 1459, at about age 35, Giovanni witnessed a will, which typically required identifying oneself by naming one's father, and signed it as Jacopo's son, which had been Giovanni's identity for over 30 years and perhaps from infancy. Later, when Giovanni acknowledged receipt of his wife's dowry or witnessed other contracts, the notaries described him as Jacopo's son, again recording the identity under which he had lived for many decades, an identity that had no direct bearing on the legal function of these documents. In the *divisio*, however, Giovanni needed to be identified as Nicoletto's son because he and Jacopo were legally separating from their *fraterna compagnia* as brothers, and the purpose of the document specifically required Giovanni to indicate his biological lineage. Perhaps the only other standard legal document that might have offered a clue to Giovanni's biological identity would have been Jacopo Bellini's will, because Giovanni did not have the same legal rights as Jacopo's biological children. An example of such a testamentary identification occurred when the Venetian artist Jacobello del Fiore named "my adopted son Ercole" in his October 2, 1439, will, but in other documents, including as a witness to the Bellini *divisio*, Ercole typically signed his name as "Ercole, son of Jacobello del Fiore."[77] Yet it seems doubtful that Jacopo ever drew up his will. For had Jacopo's will existed, then Jacopo presumably would have bequeathed the contents of his workshop and his drawing notebooks to either Gentile or Giovanni or some combination of the two. Instead, Jacopo's widow, Anna Rinversi, in her own last will, bequeathed these items to Gentile as if she had owned them. This suggests, although it does not prove, that Jacopo had died intestate and that the ownership of the contents of his workshop had perhaps been in question.[78]

That Giovanni was accepted by his own family as Jacopo's son was reflected in Jacopo's inscription on the lost Gattamelata Altarpiece that named Giovanni as his son.[79] That Gentile accepted Giovanni as a brother is recorded in Gentile's last testament of February 18, 1507 (he was reported buried five days later), in which Gentile referred to Giovanni as his "dearest brother."[80] As the two had grown up as brothers, and were known as brothers far and wide throughout their lives, it is difficult to imagine that, on his deathbed, Gentile would have set aside some 75 years of shared experience to privilege their biological relationship by calling Giovanni "my dearest uncle."[81] Contemporary and slightly later observers, including Foresti, Negri, Sanudo, Vasari, and others, had no reason to question whether Giovanni was Jacopo's biological son—and none ever suggested that Giovanni was adopted or illegitimate or not Jacopo's son, even though Giovanni must have been one of these by virtue of his not being mentioned in Anna's last will. Instead, contemporary observers simply recorded Giovanni's well-established communal and social identity as Jacopo's son. It is only through the close study of Bellini-related legal documents that we can determine Giovanni's true lineage.

An Archival Discovery

In 2014, the last will of Samaritana Dominici, almost certainly Giovanni Bellini's maternal aunt, was identified and published in its entirety.[82] The will, drawn up by a notary on January 19, 1509, reveals that Samaritana had the maiden name Vendramin, and, it can therefore be assumed, so did her sister (Giovanni's mother) Franceschina.[83] Neither Franceschina nor Samaritana can be located in the well-documented Vendramin line of patricians, however, and thus they must have come from a non-noble branch of the family—which is hardly surprising, given Franceschina's marriage to Nicoletto, a tinsmith who was probably in his fifties at the time of their union.[84]

In her will, Samaritana bequeathed her entire estate to her nephew Giovanni, declaring that he "with love and kindness, treated me, always, as a mother."[85] This might suggest that Giovanni's mother, Franceschina, had indeed died young, and that Samaritana became to some extent a mother figure for Giovanni. More likely, however, Samaritana was referring to the fact that after her husband, Giobbe, died, probably in August or September 1459 and evidently by 1462, and her only son died, in 1463, it appears that Giovanni took Samaritana into his home and cared for her during the ensuing decades, thus treating her with the same "love and kindness" as he might have treated his own mother.[86] Giovanni was between 82 and 84 years old when Samaritana drew up her will in 1509—old enough for Samaritana to stipulate that, should he predecease her, her estate would instead be left to her niece Marina.[87] When trying to assess Samaritana's age, it is important to bear in mind that Samaritana must have been Franceschina's younger sister, although by how many years is unknown, and that Franceschina might have married Giovanni's father when she was between the ages of 13 and 15, which was the preferred age range for patrician brides during this period, although the Bellini were not nobles.[88] Thus, Samaritana may have been only a few years older than Giovanni, and presumably between her late eighties and mid-nineties when she drew up her will, although she might have been older. There is a common misconception, even among scholars, that very few people lived into old age during the Renaissance, yet demographic data from the sixteenth century onward indicate that a significant number of Venetians lived well into their nineties and some past one hundred.[89]

The rediscovery of Samaritana's will provides new information about the maternal side of Giovanni Bellini's family (see Bellini Family Tree, pp. 6–7). It appears that Giovanni met his future wife, Ginevra Bocheta, through his extended maternal family. Giovanni's aunt Samaritana was married to Giobbe Dominici, whose mother was Lucia Bocheta and whose maternal uncle was Lucia's brother, Alvise Bocheta.[90] Bocheta was a very rare surname in Venice. Previously, I had speculated that Alvise Bocheta was Ginevra Bocheta's father.[91] However, it has not been possible to prove this relationship, especially since sections of the Venetian archives have been closed at the time of writing because of COVID-19. Alvise Bocheta and Francesco Bocheta, the latter of whom may be identified as Ginevra's brother, were both members of the Scuola Grande di San Marco. On July 6, 1466, they both cast favorable votes to commission three to five paintings to decorate the Scuola's *sala capitolare*. The vote passed and ten days later, on July 16, Jacopo Bellini was hired to execute two of the paintings. On December 15 of the same year, Gentile Bellini was also hired to execute two paintings. Presumably, the Bocheta family was helping to support their extended Bellini family. Also, Giovanni and Ginevra named their only son Alvise, perhaps after the boy's maternal grandfather, although Alvise was a common Venetian name. If Alvise Bocheta was indeed Ginevra Bocheta's father, then Ginevra would have been a first cousin to Giobbe Dominici, who was Giovanni Bellini's uncle by marriage.

Scholars' Reactions to the New Genealogy

My proposed new genealogy for Giovanni was first published in 2013, and art historians' responses have been mixed. Some have found the arguments persuasive. Others have disagreed with the conclusions of my research, especially that Giovanni was born between 1424 and 1426. Still others have remained uncommitted, perhaps awaiting additional research, which to some extent is provided by this book.[92]

The last group includes several scholars who published on Giovanni after my 2013 article. A 2015 book of essays titled *Examining Giovanni Bellini: An Art "More Human and More Divine,"* edited by Carolyn C. Wilson, did not include serious discussion of the new Bellini genealogy.[93] However, most of these essays derived from a Renaissance Society of America conference held in 2010 and subsequently underwent a lengthy publication process. In her review of the book in *Renaissance Quarterly* in 2017, Andrea Bayer, the Metropolitan Museum of Art's deputy director for collections and administration, noted that "the rather long lapse of time between the conference in 2010 and the appearance of the book has led to some missed opportunities . . . . Daniel Maze's complex and debated article on Giovanni's birth and family relations . . . could not be addressed."[94] Augusto Gentili, a well-known expert on Renaissance Venetian painting, wrote in an essay in *Bellini e i Belliniani. Dall'Accademia dei Concordi di Rovigo* (2017) that the new genealogy was being "tenaciously ignored, by accident or on purpose, especially among Italians."[95] Gentili himself championed the new research, declaring that it had "definitively cleared up" the problem of Giovanni's parentage and controversial birth year.[96] In her review of the 2018–19 *Mantegna and Bellini* exhibition in London and Berlin in *CAA Reviews,* the American scholar and Renaissance Venetian art specialist Debra Pincus wrote that "Maze's new dating proposal is not addressed in the exhibition," even though it "makes a persuasive case for Giovanni and Jacopo being sons of the same father but different mothers," and the placement of Giovanni's birthdate in the mid-twenties "would put Mantegna, considered to have been born around 1431, almost a contemporary of Bellini."[97]

Those who explicitly disagree with my new genealogy fall into two groups. The first group has rejected my research with a few cursory words, claiming, for example, that "A birth year in the mid to late 1420s is incompatible with Giovanni Bellini's chronology."[98] Similarly, the essays in both *Giovanni Bellini: La nascita della pittura devozionale umanistica; Gli studi* (2014) and *Padua and Venice* (2017) either omitted discussion of the new genealogy or dismissed it with a few words in a footnote.[99] An article by David Alan Brown and Anna Pizzati in which they published Samaritana's will simply rejected the possibility that Giovanni was born in the mid-1420s by saying, "Since Samaritana would have to have been appreciably older for Giovanni to treat her like a mother, her will of 1509 almost certainly excludes Vasari's date of 1426" for Giovanni's birth.[100] A number of scholars have since cited Brown and Pizzati's unproven hypothesis—that Samaritana's will demonstrates that Giovanni was "almost certainly" not born in 1426—to "dismantle" the new genealogy for Giovanni, as one scholar wrote.[101] I believe that my detailed arguments in this book address all of the concerns raised in these comments.

The second group of scholars who disagree with my genealogy/chronology provide more detailed criticisms. These include scholars who have argued that Jacopo Bellini had a brother who was distinct from the famous painter Giovanni Bellini, and who has been called "Giovanni Bellini il Vecchio" or "Giovanni di Nicolò Bellini." For instance, in a recent 2019 collection of essays on Giovanni titled *Giovanni Bellini ". . . il migliore nella pittura,"* one scholar dismissed the new genealogy, as he did in an earlier essay, on the grounds that he believes that "Giovanni Bellini il Vecchio" was a real individual.[102] Appendix B establishes with little doubt that this person is a fiction.

Finally, Johannes Grave is one of the few scholars to have responded at length to the new genealogy.[103] In his monographic study *Giovanni Bellini: The Art of Contemplation* (2018), Grave disagreed with it by arguing that: Giovanni was described as Jacopo's son "in many contemporary sources" including legal documents; Samaritana's will suggests that Giovanni was born later than the 1420s; and Jacopo Bellini used the word "*natus*" in his inscription on the Gattamelata Altarpiece to describe both Gentile and Giovanni as his sons, which "emphasizes biological descent," according to Grave, instead of using the word "*filius*," which might include adoptive sons.[104]

My responses to Grave's first and second objections are discussed in detail above. The third objection concerns the inscription on the lost Gattamelata Altarpiece that was published by Fra Valerio Polidoro in 1590 as "*Iacobi Bellini Veneti Patris, ac Gentilis, & Ioannis Natorum opus. MCCCCIX*". (The Roman numeral "I" should probably be read as an "L," indicating the year as 1460.[105]) The term "*natorum*" (the genitive masculine or neuter plural declension of "natus"), however, may mean "sons'" or "children's," without necessarily indicating a biological rather than adoptive relationship.[106] For instance, the most famous adoptee in the Roman world, Augustus Caesar, Julius Caesar's biological great-nephew, was described by Ovid as Julius Caesar's son using the word "*natus*" (*natus suus*).[107] Since Jacopo Bellini almost certainly did not know Latin, he probably requested a Latin translation of the altarpiece inscription from a humanist friend who perhaps selected the word "*natorum*," a somewhat more elevated term than "*filiorum*."[108] Moreover, since one might infer that the purpose of the inscription was to advertise the Bellini workshop to a Paduan audience as a father and two sons, any possible distinction between "*natus*" and "*filius*" might not have concerned Jacopo.

In sum, the arguments provided in *Young Bellini* have addressed the major criticisms of the new genealogy that scholars have offered thus far. This book presents a rich range of both documentary and visual evidence that supports Giovanni Bellini's new genealogy and chronology.

Appendix B

Creating Another Giovanni Bellini

The construction of the fictional "Giovanni Bellini il Vecchio" as an artist with his own corpus of paintings may be broken down into three stages, and, as we shall see, with each successive stage building on the shaky foundations of the previous to create an elaborate house of cards.

Many men living in Renaissance Italy were named Giovanni Bellini. The surname "Bellini" and its variants were quite common, and Giovanni was a popular Christian name because of John the Baptist and John the Evangelist.[1] There was even another painter in fifteenth-century Northern Italy called Giovanni Bellini. A will drawn up in February 1470 in Rovereto, a town approximately 85 miles northwest of Venice, was witnessed by a painter named Giovanni Pietro Bellini, the son of Stefano of Venice (fig. 113).[2] The historian Gian Maria Varanini, who first cited this document in 1990, was unable to locate additional information about Giovanni Pietro Bellini or link him to the "well-known dynasty of Venetian artists."[3]

Other documented individuals in Renaissance Italy also bearing the name Giovanni Bellini include Zohanne Bellino, a conveyor of goods through Ferrarese territory in 1436 (fig. 114);[4] Johannes Bellino, a priest of the Venetian Church of San Giovanni in Bragora, documented between 1441 and 1444;[5] Zuane Belin, the father of one Zuane Batista, who entered the Venetian Scuola Grande di San Marco in 1493;[6] Johannes Belinus, a painter active at the cathedral of Milan between 1534 and 1543;[7] Zovano de Belin da Modena, a painter who witnessed wills in Venice in 1541 and 1542;[8] and Giovanni Bellini, the deceased husband of a certain Maria from the Venetian parish of San Stae (an abbreviation of Sant'Eustachio), who had her will drawn up on December 18, 1554.[9]

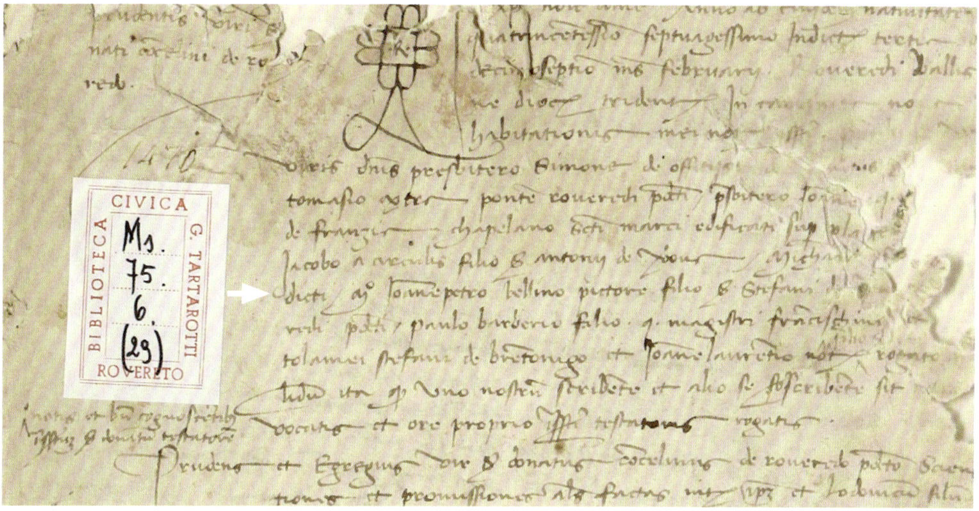

FIGURE 113 Giovanni Pietro Bellini, son of Stefano, witnesses a will, Biblioteca Civica Tartarotti di Rovereto. Another painter named Giovanni Bellini documented in Rovereto in February 1470.

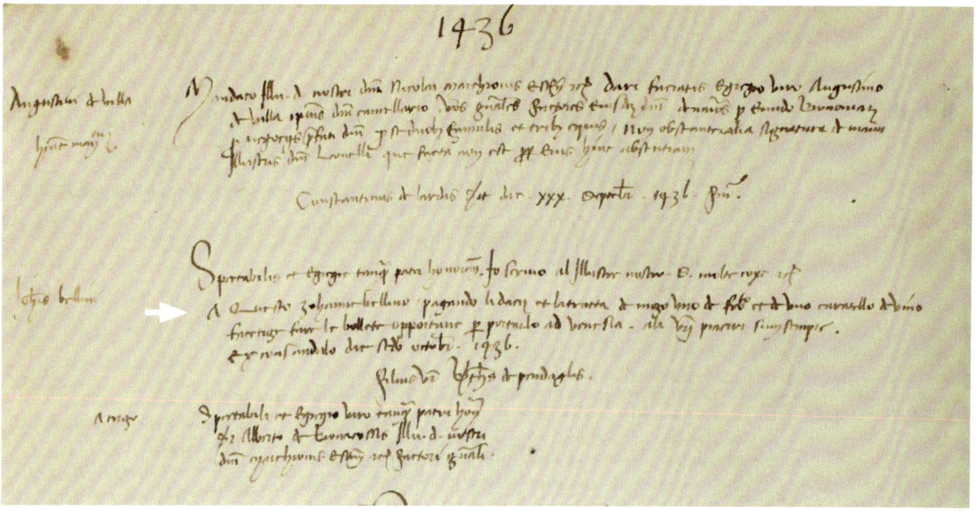

FIGURE 114 Payment to Zohanne Bellino, October 2, 1436. Archivio di Stato di Modena. This 1436 payment in Ferrara to a "Zohanne Bellino" for conveying wheat and wine to Venice records one of the many men named "Giovanni Bellini" who lived in Italy during the fifteenth century.

Giovanni Bellini Ferrarese

In 1621, the Ferrarese writer Marc'Antonio Guarini (1570–1638) stated in his *Compendio historico . . . di Ferrara* (1621) that there was an artist named Giovanni Bellini who had been buried in Ferrara. This report, however, is problematic on several counts, and it seems likely that the figure was, wittingly or unwittingly, Guarini's invention. Guarini first mentions Giovanni Bellini when discussing the Church of San Nicolò in Ferrara, which had been rebuilt in 1475:

> The Bellini were buried for a time in this church, among whom there was that most celebrated painter Giovanni Bellini, who merited for his great worth to be mentioned by the poet Ludovico Ariosto, in the thirty-third canto of his poem [Orlando Furioso, 1516], in which he says.
>
> And those, who were in our day, or are now,
> Leandro [Leonardo], Andrea Mantegna, Giovanni Bellini.[10]

This entry, taken alone, suggests that Guarini was referring to the famous Venetian painter Giovanni Bellini. He described him as "that most celebrated painter" and he quoted Ariosto's poem naming the Venetian. It is known, however, that Giovanni was buried in 1516 in Venice, next to the Church of Santi Giovanni e Paolo and along the external wall of the Scuola di Sant'Orsola, as were many of his family members.[11] It would seem that Guarini was simply mistaken in his belief that the famous Giovanni Bellini had been buried in Ferrara. Later in the text, however, Guarini returned to Giovanni Bellini when discussing the Church of San Vitale (now demolished):

> Also buried in this church are the Codi, one of whom was Benedetto, who became an excellent painter, and was a pupil of Giovanni Bellini Ferrarese, described by me in the Church of San Nicolò, I said Ferrarese to distinguish him from Giovanni Bellini the Venetian.[12]

In this light, Guarini's "most celebrated painter Giovanni Bellini" buried in San Nicolò was not the Venetian, but rather a painter with the same name from Ferrara. Guarini therefore seems to assert that "Giovanni Bellini Ferrarese" was the artist Ariosto had named in *Orlando Furioso* and was the teacher of the painter Benedetto Coda (d. before 1544). Yet there are no known sources prior to Guarini writing in 1621 that describe a painter named Giovanni Bellini from Ferrara or buried in Ferrara. And needless to say, Ariosto was referring to the Venetian Giovanni Bellini and not to an otherwise unknown Ferrarese artist, while Vasari stated in his *Lives* that "Benedetto Coda of Ferrara" was a student of the famous Giovanni Bellini.[13] Hence, later scholars writing about Benedetto Coda have dismissed Guarini's account.[14] One wonders whether Guarini, in describing "Giovanni Bellini Ferrarese," was simply confused, or dishonestly sought to promote Ferrara, or, perhaps during the printing of his book, realized his earlier misstatement, that Giovanni Bellini was buried in San Nicolò, and attempted to correct it by inventing a second Giovanni Bellini of Ferrarese origin.

Whichever the case, it is important to note that Guarini neither cited documents nor mentioned dates concerning "Giovanni Bellini Ferrarese." Nonetheless, some later scholars will claim without evidence that this artist was indeed "documented," or active in Ferrara in ca. 1450, or buried in the Church of San Nicolò in ca. 1460 (see below for further discussion).

For nearly a century after the publication of Guarini's 1621 text, there was no further discussion in the literature of a "Giovanni Bellini Ferrarese." Then, in a manuscript begun by 1704 and published posthumously in 1844–46 as *Vite de' pittori e scultori ferraresi*, the Ferrarese poet and critic Girolamo Baruffaldi (1675–1755) noted Guarini's error. Baruffaldi wrote that Guarini described a Giovanni Bellini from Ferrara and "attributes to him that praise from Ariosto . . . in his *Furioso*," yet the praise, according to the authors Borghini, Vasari, Ridolfi, and Fornari, is "appropriate to the Venetian Bellini."[15] Baruffaldi also wrote that he was unable to discuss "the school of Giovanni Bellini Ferrarese because no evidence of it is to be found, and I would say that Guarini had misunderstood."[16]

In 1735, however, the Ferrarese historian Ferrante Borsetti (1682–1764), in his *Historia almi ferrariae gymnasii*, simply restated Guarini's text by writing, "Giovanni Bellini Ferrarese, celebrated painter, different from the Venetian, and teacher of Benedetto Coda."[17] In 1782, the Ferrarese historian Cesare Cittadella (1732–1809) was apparently the first to embellish Guarini's account in his *Catalogo istorico dei pittori e scultori ferraresi* by writing, without offering additional evidence, that "Giovanni Bellini Ferrarese lived in 1450."[18] He then summarized Guarini's 1621 text but noted that there was no further information about the artist to add, a seemingly curious statement given that he had provided the apparently fictitious artist with a date of activity. In his entry on Benedetto Coda, however, Cittadella corrected Guarini by asserting that Coda was the student of the Venetian Giovanni Bellini rather than of "Giovanni Bellini Ferrarese."[19]

In 1804, the author Luigi Ughi (1749–1823) combined Guarini's and Cittadella's accounts in his *Dizionario storico degli uomini illustri ferraresi* by repeating Guarini's biography and asserting that "Giovanni Bellini Ferrarese" had "lived in ca. 1450."[20] However, in assessing whether "Giovanni Bellini Ferrarese" was indeed the teacher of Benedetto Coda, Ughi agreed with Cittadella that Coda was taught by the famous artist Giovanni Bellini of Venice, because "Giovanni Bellini Ferrarese . . . has never been known, not by any other writer [aside from Guarini], nor by any of his paintings."[21]

In 1820, the writer Pietro Zani (1748–1821) also highlighted, in his *Enciclopedia metodica critico-ragionata delle belle arti*, the absence of any documentation on "Giovanni Bellini Ferrarese." After repeating Guarini's account and noting that Borsetti and Cittadella had "echoed" Guarini, Zani stated that the evidence for such a painter was "rather curious," and that, although he would like to discuss the artist, he was "completely devoid of any necessary documents to be able to do so."[22] Scholars who would later assert that "Giovanni Bellini Ferrarese" was in fact "documented" in Ferrara rarely mention Zani or his statement that he was unaware of any documentation.[23]

In 1938, Luisa Becherucci wrote in *Mostra di Melozzo e del Quattrocento romagnolo* that "Baruffaldi, in order to accept Vasari's statement [that Benedetto Coda of Ferrara was taught by Giovanni Bellini], invented a Giovanni Bellini Ferrarese, his hypothetical master."[24] In fact, Baruffaldi rather skeptically repeated Guarini. And in 1979, Daniela Scaglietti Kelescian stated in *Pittura a Rimini tra gotico e manierismo . . .* that Guarini and those Ferrarese historians who repeated him "made a series of errors of a truly regional nature, such as the invention of a Giovanni Bellini Ferrarese, who would have been the master of Coda."[25]

In summary, Guarini described and apparently invented a "Giovanni Bellini Ferrarese" in two brief entries in his 1621 *Compendio historico.* His reasons for doing so are unclear. Guarini's entries are made even more problematic by their errors: taken together, they incorrectly described "Giovanni Bellini Ferrarese" both as the master of Benedetto Coda and as the "Giovanni Bellini" praised by Ariosto. Other than Guarini in 1621, no early sources described an artist named Giovanni Bellini from Ferrara or buried in Ferrara, and there remains no known documentary or pictorial evidence supporting such an artist's existence, a fact published by later scholars, beginning with Cittadella in 1782. Nevertheless, several subsequent Ferrarese writers, including Cittadella himself, repeated and embellished Guarini's account, stating without evidence that "Giovanni Bellini Ferrarese" either had "lived in ca. 1450," was active from ca. 1440–1460, or was buried in ca. 1460. However, some scholars began to argue that Guarini had erred and that "Giovanni Bellini Ferrarese" was an invented figure, as the available evidence would seem to suggest.

Giovanni Bellini il Vecchio

In 1929, the Italian art historian Pietro Paoletti published excerpts from the 1440 *divisio* between Giovanni and Jacopo Bellini (see Chapters 1 and 3, and Appendix A) that described the two as "brothers and sons of the deceased Nicolò Bellini."[26] Paoletti did not recognize this Giovanni Bellini as the famous artist and instead identified him as a "hitherto unknown offspring of Nicolò" since no known documents had previously indicated that Jacopo had a brother (the *divisio* remains the only known document to identify Giovanni Bellini as Jacopo Bellini's brother or as Nicolò Bellini's son).[27] Paoletti, noting that Giovanni and Jacopo both lived in the parish of San Geminiano, presumably together, suggested that this Giovanni might have been a painter.

In 1973, Eugenio Billanovich, in his article in *Italia Medioevale e Umanistica,* sought to build upon Paoletti's hypothesis that the Giovanni Bellini of the 1440 *divisio* was an artist distinct from the famous Giovanni Bellini. Billanovich called the Giovanni Bellini mentioned in the *divisio* "Giovanni Bellini Vecchio" to distinguish between the two.[28] Billanovich then tentatively identified this figure as "Giovanni Bellini Ferrarese," who, Billanovich asserted, was active in Ferrara around 1440, and died there in 1460.[29] These unsupported dates would be repeated by later scholars.[30] As discussed above, however, "Giovanni Bellini Ferrarese" appears to have been a fiction invented by Guarini in 1621, and his purported years of activity were unsubstantiated embellishments added to Guarini's text by eighteenth-century Ferrarese writers as well as by Billanovich.

Billanovich also cited a 1436 document in which one Zohanne Bellino was paid for delivering "a bushel of wheat and a small cart of wine" from Ferrara to Venice (see fig. 114).[31] Billanovich imagined this event as similar to Jacopo Bellini's visit to the court of Ferrara in ca. 1440–41, after which Leonello d'Este, on behalf of his father, Marchese Niccolò III d'Este, sent "two bushels of wheat" to Jacopo in Venice.[32] As discussed above, however, a number of individuals named "Giovanni Bellini" lived in Italy during the fifteenth century. No profession or patronymic name is provided for Zohanne Bellino, who was apparently a simple merchant or conveyer of goods. He could not, however, have been the same Giovanni Bellini mentioned in the 1440 *divisio*, because, as discussed in Appendix A, that Giovanni Bellini was almost certainly born between 1424 and 1426 and would have been no older than 12 in 1436.

Lastly, Billanovich quoted the 1790 *Diario di Asola*, which describes the cathedral in Asola as "decorated with many unique panels and paintings, by Moretto, Romanino, Lattanzio Gambara, Zambellin Vecchio, Palma and so on."[33] Zambellin was a Venetian nickname for Giovanni Bellini, and Billanovich tentatively suggested that this "Zambellin Vecchio" might have been "Giovanni Bellini Vecchio."[34] It is difficult, however, to imagine that the author of the Asolan diary, who was listing well-known painters in an effort to celebrate the cathedral decorations, was speaking of any artist other than the famous Giovanni Bellini. When Guglielmo Pacchioni first cited the same diary in *Bollettino d'arte* (1914), he wrote that "the Asolan tradition . . . wants the painting to be a gift from the Venetian Republic and ascribes its authorship to old Giovanni Bellini" (meaning the Venetian artist in his old age).[35] Most subsequent scholars likewise interpreted "Zambellin Vecchio" as referring to the Venetian.[36] Another interpretation is that "Zambellin Vecchio" might have been a punctuation or transcription error, and that the original intended text was either "Zambellin, Vecchio Palma," or "Zambellin, Palma Vecchio." This might make sense, because Palma had been known as "Palma Vecchio" to distinguish him from his great-nephew, "Palma Giovane," since at least 1581.[37]

Thus in 1973, when Billanovich identified the so-called "Giovanni Bellini il Vecchio" as the so-called "Giovanni Bellini Ferrarese," he apparently merged two fictional individuals into one. Numerous subsequent scholars have cited Billanovich to assert, incorrectly, that "Giovanni Bellini Ferrarese" or "Giovanni Bellini il Vecchio" was documented in Ferrara between 1440 and 1460.[38] No documentation, however, exists for either of these figures, and none has surfaced since Billanovich published his article.

Attributing a Corpus to Giovanni Bellini il Vecchio

In 1977, Natalia Valli, heir of the Contessa Alma Gulinelli, donated a fifteenth-century *Coronation of the Virgin* (see Chapter 4, fig. 25) to the Pinacoteca Nazionale in Ferrara in memory of the contessa. The painting's earlier provenance is unknown. Restored in 1980, the Ferrara *Coronation* was first published without attribution in 1981 in *Un palazzo, un museo: La Pinacoteca Nazionale di Palazzo dei Diamanti*, edited by Jadranka Bentini.[39] The work bears a signature that was determined during restoration to be original: "*Iohannes Belinus me fecit*" [Giovanni Bellini made me] (fig. 26, see Chapter 4 for discussion of the Ferrara *Coronation* as Giovanni Bellini's earliest known work).

In 1990, the art historian Shigetoshi Osano proposed that the Ferrara *Coronation* was executed by "Giovanni Bellini il Vecchio" whose existence, as we have seen, had been

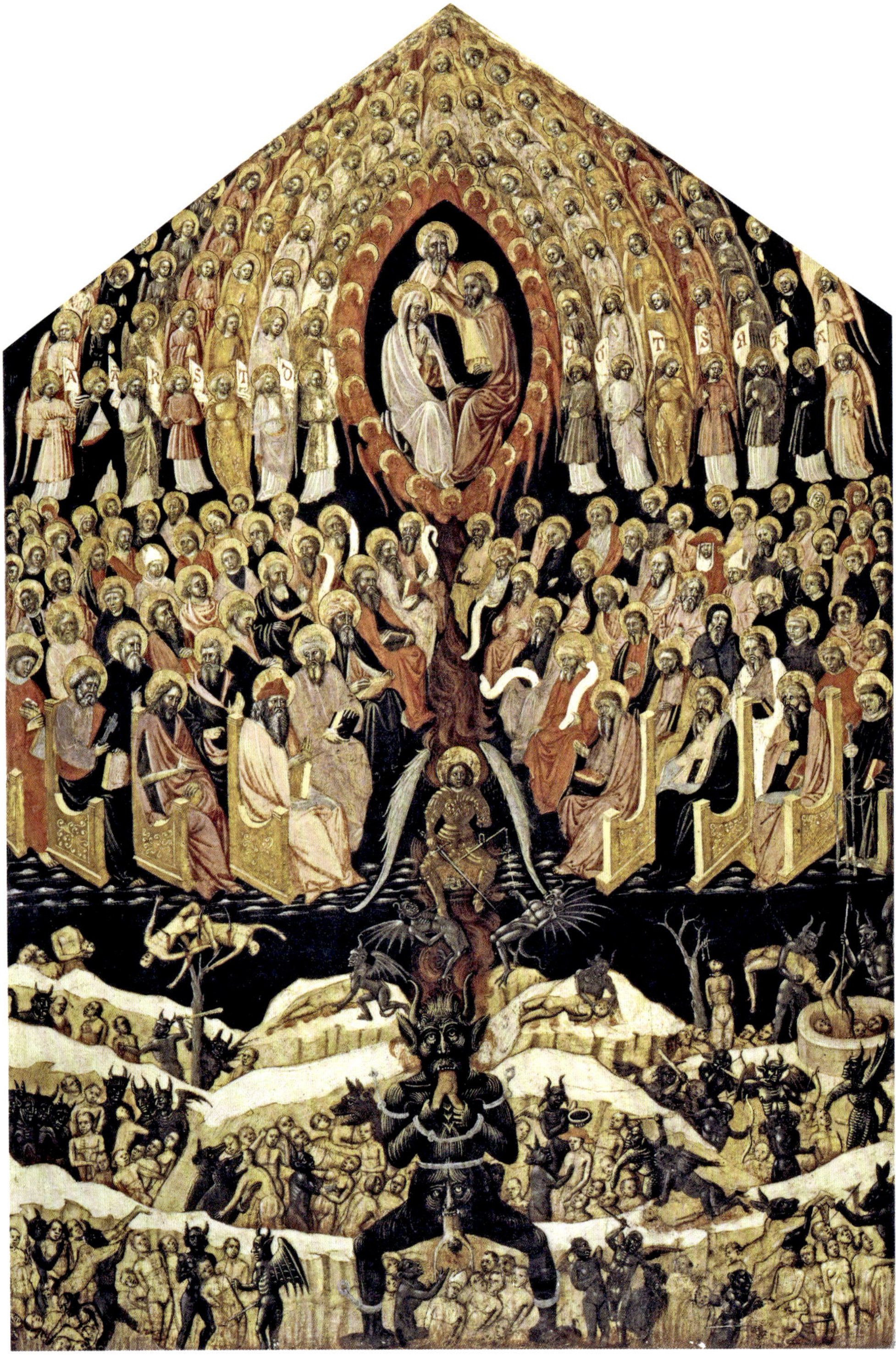

FIGURE 115 Attributed to the Master of the Avicenna, *Heaven and Hell*, ca. 1435. Panel, 111 × 78.5 cm. Pinacoteca Nazionale, Bologna

advanced by Billanovich in 1973. Through various motifs in the painting, such as the particular facial type of the Virgin, Osano also linked the Ferrara *Coronation* to the work of Jacopo Bellini and the Bellini workshop.[40] He tentatively agreed with Billanovich that "Giovanni Bellini il Vecchio" was the same artist as "Giovanni Bellini Ferrarese," and suggested that, after the signing of the Bellini *divisio* of 1440, "Giovanni Bellini il Vecchio" might have relocated to Ferrara.

In 1992, Emanuela Fiori followed Osano in *La Pinacoteca Nazionale di Ferrara: Catalogo generale*, tentatively attributing the Ferrara *Coronation* to "Giovanni di Nicolò Bellini" ("Giovanni Bellini il Vecchio"). Fiori wrote: "[Osano] connects a series of documents relating to a Giovanni Bellini, brother of Jacopo . . . that attest to the presence in Ferrara, between 1440 and 1460, of a Giovanni Bellini, painter from Ferrara, his death, and his burial in the Church of San Nicolò in Ferrara."[41] This is one of many examples of scholars incorrectly stating that there is documentation indicating that another Giovanni Bellini had lived and was buried in Ferrara in the mid-fifteenth century. But as we have seen, this information derives solely from Guarini, whose questionable assertions, published in 1621, did not provide any documentation or dates.

In 2004, Massimo Medica in the *Pinacoteca Nazionale di Bologna: Catalogo generale* accepted that the Ferrara *Coronation* was executed by "Giovanni di Nicolò Bellini" ("Giovanni Bellini il Vecchio"), who, he proposed, was also the same artist known as the Master of the Avicenna.[42] The Master of the Avicenna, whose identity is unknown, was an apparently Bolognese artist to whom a group of paintings and miniatures had already been attributed, including the illuminations in the Hebrew translation of Avicenna's *Canon medicinae*, Biblioteca Universitaria di Bologna, and a *Heaven and Hell* in the Pinacoteca Nazionale di Bologna that Medica dated to ca. 1435 (fig. 115).[43] Medica based his proposal on a stylistic analysis that likened the "four prophets placed high inside medallions" and the "numerous angels" of the Ferrara *Coronation* to various motifs in the works attributed to the Master of the Avicenna. Thus, in identifying the Master of the Avicenna as "Giovanni di Nicolò Bellini," Medica attributed an entire corpus of works to the latter.

It is difficult to accept Medica's attribution, however, since the defining stylistic characteristics of the Ferrara *Coronation*—its fanciful architecture, motifs that derive from Jacopo's Paris sketchbook, other motifs that derive from artists working in and around Venice, and centralized linear perspective—are demonstrably absent from the other works attributed to the Master of the Avicenna. Medica does mention, however, a miniature of *Saint Petronius Enthroned* in Bologna, dated 1443 (fig. 116), which indeed appears to have been inspired by the Ferrara *Coronation*. Yet this miniature is clearly by a different hand and may be a very early work by the miniaturist Leonardo Bellini, Jacopo Bellini's nephew, who would have seen the Ferrara *Coronation* in the Bellini workshop in ca. 1441–42.

In 2012, Medica published an article reiterating his identification of "Giovanni di Nicolò Bellini" as the Master of the Avicenna. No new attributions were made, but he proposed that "Giovanni di Nicolò Bellini" might have lived in Bologna, rather than in Ferrara, since

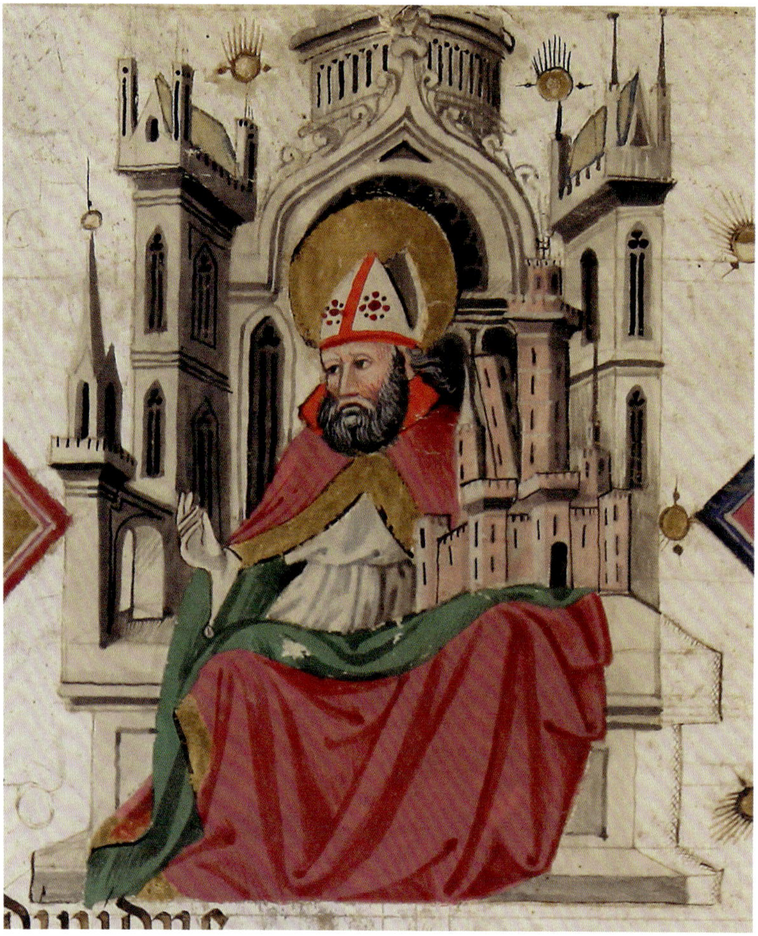

FIGURE 116 Unknown, possibly Leonardo Bellini, *Saint Petronius Enthroned,* 1443. Vellum. Archivio di Stato di Bologna

several of the works attributed to the Master of the Avicenna are Bolognese in origin.[44] To this end, Medica suggested that "Giovanni di Nicolò Bellini" ("Giovanni Bellini il Vecchio") might be identified "with that 'Master Giovanni of Venice, painter,' who was recorded by a few Bolognese documents between 1459–60."[45] Yet, since "Giovanni" was a very common name in Venice and the documents do not mention the artist's surname, it is doubtful that "Giovanni of Venice, painter" referred to Giovanni Bellini.

In 2014, in *Rivista d'arte,* Chiara Guerzi attributed the miniatures in a *Biblia pauperum* to the Master of the Avicenna, whom she identified as "Giovanni di Nicolò Bellini" ("Giovanni Bellini il Vecchio"). Guerzi expressed reservations regarding the "unquestionable weakness of some aspects of the research" on this so-called artist, including the identification of "Giovanni di Nicolò Bellini" as "Zohanne Bellino," mentioned in the 1436 Ferrarese document, and as "Giovanni Bellini Ferrarese," which was proposed by Billanovich.[46]

As recently as 2019, Anchise Tempestini wrote an essay in which he argued that there had existed a "Giovanni di Nicolò Bellini" distinct from the famous artist Giovanni Bellini. He stated that "history has identified Giovanni di Nicolò Bellini as a painter documented in Ferrara" and that it was probable that he "died in Ferrara in 1460 and was buried in the Church of San Nicolò."[47] Tempestini stated that the *Coronation of the Virgin* was painted in Ferrara, although the work's provenance is unknown.[48] The essay also cited the work of Medica and Guerzi to support the identification of the Master of the Avicenna as "Giovanni di Nicolò Bellini."[49] Finally, Tempestini sought to identify "Giovanni di Nicolò Bellini" with a painter called Giovanni fu Nicolò who witnessed a testament in Venice on April 29, 1457, but the Venetian document would have almost certainly recorded the surname had the artist been a member of the Bellini family.[50]

To conclude, *Young Bellini* interprets the 1440 *divisio* as referring to Giovanni Bellini, the famous artist, and identifies the Ferrara *Coronation* as his earliest known work. These two primary sources, the *divisio* and the Ferrara *Coronation,* are the two central pillars cited by scholars to hypothesize the existence of a so-called "Giovanni Bellini il Vecchio" and to reconstruct his corpus of works. Once these two sources are properly linked to the famous Giovanni Bellini, however, the house of cards falls: no other credible sources remain to support the existence of "Giovanni Bellini il Vecchio." No documents, inscriptions, or signatures prove his existence or the existence of "Giovanni Bellini Ferrarese." Indeed, no primary sources exist to suggest that Jacopo Bellini had a second close relative named "Giovanni Bellini." Rather, the existing evidence strongly indicates that art historians invented "Giovanni Bellini il Vecchio," a fantastical figure who was created through a series of misinterpretations, overreaching embellishments, and incorrect attributions.

Chronology for Giovanni Bellini

CA. 1393 Birth of Jacopo Bellini to Nicoletto Bellini and his first wife, Giovannina (Zanina)

1393–94 Nicoletto Bellini serves as *nonzolo* at the Scuola Grande della Misericordia

BEFORE 1424 Death of Jacopo Bellini's mother, Zanina

1424–26 Birth of Giovanni Bellini to Nicoletto Bellini and Nicoletto's second wife, Franceschina Vendramin

BEFORE 1429 Death of Nicoletto Bellini; probable death of Franceschina Vendramin

BEFORE 1429 Jacopo Bellini establishes a workshop in the parish of San Geminiano, Venice; Jacopo raises his half-brother, Giovanni, as his own son

1429–CA. 1435 Birth of Gentile Bellini

AFTER 1429 Birth of Nicolosia, Nicolò, and Leonello Bellini (their birth order is unknown)

CA. 1431 Birth of Andrea Mantegna

CA. 1441–42 Giovanni paints the Ferrara *Coronation* (see Chapter 4 and fig. 25)

1443–44 Giovanni paints predella panels for Jacopo's Brescia Annunciation (see Chapter 5 and fig. 45)

1444–50 Giovanni continues working as Jacopo's assistant, presumably helping execute the now-lost Scuola Grande di San Marco *albergo* cycle (see Chapter 6); nearly all works executed by the Bellini workshop during this period are lost

CA. 1449 Giovanni and Jacopo design the Mascoli Chapel *Visitation* mosaic (see Chapter 7 and fig. 73)

CA. 1450 Giovanni paints Birmingham *Saint Jerome* (see Chapter 7 and fig. 79)

CA. 1453 Marriage of Nicolosia Bellini and Andrea Mantegna

1459 Giovanni documented as living in the parish of San Lio, Venice

CA. 1455–65 Marriage of Giovanni and Ginevra Bocheta

1460 Giovanni, Gentile, and Jacopo Bellini complete now-lost Gattamelata Altarpiece in Padua

CA. 1464–69 Birth of Giovanni and Ginevra's son, Alvise Bellini

1470–71 Death of Jacopo Bellini and Nicolosia Bellini

1471 Death of Jacopo Bellini's wife, Anna Rinversi

1481 Giovanni documented as living in the parish of Santa Marina, Venice

CA. 1489 Death of Giovanni Bellini's wife, Ginevra Bocheta

1498–99 Death of Giovanni Bellini's son, Alvise

1506 Death of Andrea Mantegna

1507 Death of Gentile Bellini

1516 Death of Giovanni Bellini between the ages of 90 and 92 years old

Abbreviations

ABBREVIATIONS OF ARCHIVES

APVe – Archivio Patriarcale di Venezia

ASFi – Archivio di Stato di Firenze

ASMn – Archivio di Stato di Mantova

ASMo – Archivio di Stato di Modena

ASVe – Archivio di Stato di Venezia

ARCHIVAL ABBREVIATIONS AND SOURCES

ANT – Archivio Notarile, Testamenti

CIN – Cancelleria inferiore, Notai

SGSGE – Scuola Grande di San Giovanni Evangelista

SGSM – Scuola Grade di San Marco

SGSMM – Scuola Grande di Santa Maria della Misericordia (o della Valverde)

Notes

FAMILY TREE

Family Tree and notes compiled by Daniel Wallace Maze with the assistance of Rielle Jones-Teske, whom I thank. Names are ordered alphabetically, men by surname and women by maiden name. Individuals without known surnames are listed either by the identifiers employed in the cited documents, e.g. Francesco (da Pesaro), or by the family to whom they are most closely associated, e.g. Alixeta (Bellini). The references identify the individual's relationship to other family members and, when possible, provide birth and death dates. The references are not intended to be exhaustive.

1. Caterina Baresina: first wife of Gentile Bellini; presumably died soon after her last will of October 19, 1494 (ASVe, ANT, Andrea Scala, b. 878, docs 80–81 [draft and corrected versions]; Meyer zur Capellen, 1985, p. 115, doc. 45).
2. Alixeta (Bellini): daughter of Nicoletto Bellini's adopted daughter, Menega, and a potential beneficiary of Nicoletto's will of 1424 (ASVe, ANT, Lorenzo Buscarino, b. 545, doc. 63, fol. 10r–v; Barausse, 2020, pp. 19–20, doc. 3).
3. Alvise Bellini: only known child of Giovanni Bellini; beneficiary in his mother Ginevra Bocheta's will (ASVe, ANT, Lorenzo Stella, b. 877, doc. 829; Barausse, 2020, pp. 43–44, doc. 51); presumably died soon after his will of 1498 (ASVe, ANT, Lorenzo Stella, b. 877, doc. 755; Barausse, 2020, pp. 48–49, doc. 63). For Alvise's possible birthdate and further references, see Maze, 2013a, pp. 798–99 n. 64.
4. Elena Bellini: sister of Jacopo Bellini and half-sister of Giovanni Bellini; daughter of Nicoletto Bellini and Zanina; beneficiary in Nicoletto's will of 1424 (ASVe, ANT, Lorenzo Buscarino, b. 545, doc. 63, fol. 10r–v; Barausse, 2020, pp. 19–20, doc. 3); gave consent for her son Leonardo to enter a contract with Jacopo Bellini in 1443 (ASVe, CIN, Francesco Elmis, bb. 74–75, reg. XXVIII, fol. 20r; Barausse, 2020, p. 26, doc. 14).
5. Gentile Bellini: son of Jacopo Bellini and Anna Rinversi; born after Anna's will of 1429 (ASVe, ANT, Enrico Salomon, b. 946/c, doc. 313; Barausse, 2020, pp. 20–21, doc. 4; also see Chapter 2); died in 1507 (Sanudo, 1879–1903, 6: p. 552 [February 23, 1507]). For further references, see Meyer Zur Capellen, 1985, pp. 105–22.
6. Giovanni Bellini: son of Nicoletto Bellini and Franceschina Vendramin; born between mid-1424 and September 13, 1426 (see Chapter 1 and Appendix A). For further references, see Barausse, 2020; Maze, 2013a.
7. Jacopo Bellini: son of Nicoletto Bellini and Zanina; Gentile da Fabriano's assistant by 1412 (Mazzalupi, 2006a, p. 69, doc. 4); alive in July 1470 (Barausse, 2020, pp. 35–36, doc. 33); deceased by the time of his wife Anna Rinversi's will of November 25, 1471 (ASVe, ANT, Francesco Elmis, b. 361, fol. 65v, doc. 163; Barausse, 2020, pp. 36–37, doc. 35). For further references, see Eisler, 1989, pp. 530–33.
8. Leonardo (Bellini): son of Elena Bellini and Paolo (Remarius); lived with Jacopo Bellini from 1431 and entered into a contract with Jacopo (with approval from Elena and his unnamed brothers) in 1443 (ASVe, CIN, Francesco Elmis, b. 74, reg. XXVIII, fol. 20r; Barausse, 2020, p. 26, doc. 14); served as a deacon in the Scuola Grande di San Rocco in 1484 (Moretti, 1958, p. 63 n. 1). For Leonardo, see Ludwig, 1911, p. 168; Mariani Canova, 1968; Moretti, 1970; Bauer-Eberhardt, 1989; Marcon, 2001; Cattaneo, 2003; Szépe, 2018.
9. Leonello Bellini: son of Jacopo Bellini; husband of Elisabetta Michiel (dowry receipt of 1466: ASVe, CIN, Tomeo Tomei, b. 212, fasc. 2, fol. 33v; see fig. 14); born after Anna Rinversi's will of 1429 (ASVe, ANT, Enrico Salomon, b. 946/c, doc. 313; Barausse, 2020, pp. 20–21, doc. 4; also see Chapter 2); possibly named after Leonello d'Este and therefore born ca. 1440?; apparently deceased by Anna's will of 1471

(ASVe, ANT, Francesco Elmis, b. 361, fol. 65v, doc. 163; Barausse, 2020, pp. 36–37, doc. 35).

10. Menega (Bellini): adopted daughter of Nicoletto Bellini (ASVe, ANT, Lorenzo Buscarino, b. 545, doc. 63, fol. 10r–v; Barausse, 2020, pp. 19–20, doc. 3).

11. Nicoletto Bellini: father of Giovanni and Jacopo Bellini (ASVe, CIN, Vittore Pomino, b. 149, reg. "Protocollum mei Victoris Pomino Notarii de 1439," fol. 55v; Maze, 2013a, pp. 817–18, doc. 1); deceased by July 23, 1429 (ASVe, CIN, Tommaso de Tomei, b. 212, 23 luglio 1429; Maze, 2013a, p. 819, doc. 2). For further references, see Chapter 1 and Appendix A.

12. Nicolò Bellini: son of Jacopo Bellini and Anna Rinversi (ASVe, ANT, Francesco Elmis, b. 361, fol. 65v, doc. 163; Barausse, 2020, pp. 36–37, doc. 35); born after Anna's will of 1429 (ASVe, ANT, Enrico Salomon, b. 946/c, doc. 313; Barausse, 2020, pp. 20–21, doc. 4; also see Chapter 2); deceased after 1512 (C. Brown, 1969).

13. Nicolosia Bellini: daughter of Jacopo Bellini and Anna Rinversi; born after Anna's will of 1429 (ASVe, ANT, Enrico Salomon, b. 946/c, doc. 313; Barausse, 2020, pp. 20–21, doc. 4; also see Chapter 2); dowry subvention for her marriage to Mantegna received in 1453 (ASVe, SGSGE, vol. 72, fol. 199r; Barausse, 2020, pp. 28–29, doc. 17); apparently deceased by the time of Anna's will of 1471 (ASVe, ANT, Francesco Elmis, b. 361, doc. 163, fol. 65v; Barausse, 2020, pp. 36–37, doc. 35). For her death, see Maze, 2013a, p. 800 n. 68.

14. Zanina or Giovannina (Bellini): mother of Jacopo Bellini; first wife of Nicoletto Bellini; deceased by the time of Nicoletto's will of 1424 (ASVe, ANT, Lorenzo Buscarino, b. 545, doc. 63, fol. 10r–v; Barausse, 2020, pp. 19–20, doc. 3).

15. Alvise Bocheta: brother of Lucia Bocheta (ASVe, ANT, Lorenzo Dalla Torre, b. 1062, doc. 12; [unpublished]); member of Scuola Grande di San Marco in 1466 (Barausse, 2020, pp. 31–32, doc. 25); possibly the father of Ginevra, Francesco, Lucrezia, and Giovanni Bocheta (see Chapter 2). For further references, see D. Romano, 2007, pp. 278–92.

16. Francesco Bocheta: brother of Ginevra Bocheta; son of Alvise Bocheta(?); possibly father of Sebastiano; later a priest (ASVe, ANT, Lorenzo Stella, b. 877, doc. 829; Barausse, 2020, pp. 43–44, doc. 51); entered Scuola Grande di San Marco in 1465, expelled in 1468 (ASVe, SGSM, b. 3, "F" [unpublished]; ASVe, SGSM, 16 bis, "Notatorio 1428–1503" [unpublished]; also see Barausse, 2020, pp. 31–32, doc. 25); died after 1510 (Barausse, 2020, p. 44).

17. Ginevra Bocheta: only known wife of Giovanni Bellini (dowry receipt of 1485: ASV, ANT, Lorenzo Stella, b. 877, protocollo, fol. 28; Barausse, 2020, p. 42, doc. 47); married Giovanni probably in the late 1450s or early 1460s (Maze, 2013a, p. 798 n. 4); presumably died soon after her will of 1489 (ASVe, ANT, Lorenzo Stella, b. 877, doc. 829; Barausse, 2020, pp. 43–44, doc. 51); deceased by 1498 (ASVe, ANT, Lorenzo Stella, b. 877, doc. 755; Barausse, 2020, pp. 48–49, doc. 63).

18. Giovanni Bocheta: half-brother of Ginevra Bocheta; son of Alvise Bocheta(?); apparently illegitimate (ASVe, ANT, Lorenzo Stella, b. 877, doc. 829; Barausse, 2020, pp. 43–44, doc. 51).

19. Lucia Bocheta: mother-in-law of Samaritana Vendramin, who was Giovanni Bellini's maternal aunt; drew up her will in 1457 (ASVe, ANT, Lorenzo Dalla Torre, b. 1062, doc. 12 [unpublished]; I thank Paula Clarke for this reference).

20. Lucrezia Bocheta: sister of Ginevra Bocheta; daughter of Alvise Bocheta(?); an executor of Alvise Bellini's will of 1498 (ASVe, ANT, Lorenzo Stella, b. 877, doc. 755; Barausse, 2020, pp. 48–49, doc. 63).

21. Sebastiano Bocheta: nephew of Ginevra Bocheta; possibly son of Francesco Bocheta; under age 20 in 1489 (ASVe, ANT, Lorenzo Stella, b. 877, doc. 829; Barausse, 2020, pp. 43–44, doc. 51); beneficiary of Alvise Bellini's will of 1498 and called Alvise's nephew (*nepoti*), but appears to have been his first cousin (ASVe, ANT, Lorenzo Stella, b. 877, doc. 755; Barausse, 2020, pp. 48–49, doc. 63).

22. Francesco (da Pesaro): maternal uncle of Anna Rinversi; an executor of her will of 1429 (ASVe, ANT, Enrico Salomon, b. 946/c, doc. 313; Barausse, 2020, pp. 20–21, doc. 4).

23. Maria (di Antonio Trevisano): second wife of Gentile Bellini; drew up her will in 1503 (ASVe, ANT, Andrea Scala, b. 879, doc. 243; Meyer zur Capellen, 1985, p. 117, doc. 61); an executor of Gentile's will of 1507 (ASVe, ANT, Bernardo Cavanis, b. 271, doc. 307; Barausse, 2020, pp. 67–68, doc. 111).

24. Elena (di Giorgio): niece of Giovanni Bellini; daughter of Lucrezia Bocheta and Gabriele (di Giorgio); wife of Matteo Mondo (dowry receipt of 1481: ASVe, CIN, Giovanni Antonio Mando, b. 124, fol. 22r; Barausse, 2020, p. 40, doc. 43).

25. Gabriele (di Giorgio): husband of Lucrezia Bocheta, who was Ginevra Bocheta's sister (ASVe, ANT, Lorenzo Stella, b. 877, doc. 755; Barausse, 2020, pp. 48–49, doc. 63); identified as Ginevra's *consobrinus* (in this case, probably "relation") in Ginevra's

will of 1489 (ASVe, ANT, Lorenzo Stella, b. 877, filza cart., doc. 829; Barausse, 2020, pp. 43–44, doc. 51; also see Molmenti and Ludwig, 1907, p. 75 n. 1).

26. Fiornovella Dominici: beneficiary in her mother Lucia Bocheta's will of 1457; wife of Giovanni Musiolim (Musolin?) (ASVe, ANT, Lorenzo Dalla Torre, b. 1062, doc. 12 [unpublished]).
27. Giobbe Dominici: husband of Samaritana Vendramin, who was Giovanni Bellini's maternal aunt (ASVe, ANT, Nicolò Moravio, b. 677, doc. 897; D. Brown and Pizzati, 2014, p. 152); beneficiary in his mother Lucia's will of 1457 (ASVe, ANT, Lorenzo Dalla Torre, b. 1062, doc. 12 [unpublished]); probably died in August–September 1459, and certainly by March 1462 (according to Paula Clarke, who is currently writing an article about Giobbe and whom I thank).
28. Giovanni Dominici: husband of Lucia Bocheta; deceased by the time of her will of 1457 (ASVe, ANT, Lorenzo Dalla Torre, b. 1062, doc. 12 [unpublished]).
29. Giovanni Dominici: son of Giobbe Dominici (ASVe, ANT, Lorenzo Dalla Torre, b. 1062, doc. 12 [unpublished]); died in 1463 (Orvieto, 1969, p. 229 n. 4).
30. Lucrezia Dominici: daughter of Giobbe Dominici (ASVe, ANT, Lorenzo Dalla Torre, b. 1062, doc. 12 [unpublished]); not mentioned in Samaritana Vendramin's will of 1509 and thus presumably deceased (ASVe, ANT, Nicolò Moravio, b. 677, doc. 897; D. Brown and Pizzati, 2014, p. 152).
31. Andrea Mantegna: husband of Nicolosia Bellini; for documents related to birth and death dates, see Lightbown, 1986; Shaw and Boccia, 2016.
32. Elisabetta Michiel: wife of Leonello Bellini; daughter of (deceased) nobleman Giovanni Michiel (dowry receipt of 1466: ASVe, CIN, Tomeo Tomei, b. 212, fasc. 2, fol. 33v; see fig. 14).
33. Matteo Mondo: husband of Elena (di Giorgio); son of (deceased) Giovanni Mondo (dowry receipt of 1481: ASVe, CIN, Giovanni Antonio Mando, b. 124, fol. 22r; Barausse, 2020, p. 40, doc. 43).
34. Caterina (Remarius): daughter of Elena Bellini; potential beneficiary in her grandfather Nicoletto Bellini's will of 1424 (ASVe, ANT, Lorenzo Buscarino, b. 545, doc. 63, fol. 10r–v; Barausse, 2020, pp. 19–20, doc. 3).
35. Paolo (Remarius): husband of Elena Bellini; an executor of Nicoletto Bellini's will of 1424 (ASVe, ANT, Lorenzo Buscarino, b. 545, doc. 63, fol. 10r–v; Barausse, 2020, pp. 19–20, doc. 3); deceased by 1443 (ASVe, CIN, Francesco Elmis, bb. 74–75, reg. XXVIII, fol. 20r; Barausse, 2020, p. 26, doc. 14). "Remarius" was either a surname or his occupation, an oar-maker.
36. Anna Rinversi: wife of Jacopo Bellini; pregnant in 1429 (ASVe, ANT, Enrico Salomon, b. 946/c, doc. 313; Barausse, 2020, pp. 20–21, doc. 4); presumably died soon after her will of 1471 (ASVe, ANT, Francesco Elmis, carta sciolta, b. 361, doc. 2; Barausse, 2020, pp. 36–37, doc. 35). Also see Barausse, 2020, p. 30, doc. 20; Maze 2013a, p. 819, doc. 2.
37. Branca Rinversi: father of Anna Rinversi; deceased by 1429 (ASVe, CIN, Tommaso de Tomei, b. 212, 23 luglio 1429). Also see Barausse, 2020, p. 30, doc. 20. For additional documents on Branca and other members of the Rinversi family, see Molà, 1994, p. 188 n. 145.
38. Gera (Rinversi): mother of Anna Rinversi; an executor of Anna's will of 1429 (ASVe, ANT, Enrico Salomon, b. 946/c, doc. 313; Barausse, 2020, pp. 20–21, doc. 4); drew up her will in 1469 (ASVe, ANT, Pietro Rossi, b. 870, doc. 111; Barausse, 2020, p. 30, doc. 20); deceased by 1471 (ASVe, ANT, Francesco Elmis, b. 361, carta sciolta, doc. 2; Barausse, 2020, pp. 36–37, doc. 35).
39. Nicolò Rinversi: brother of Anna Rinversi; Servite friar; beneficiary in Anna Rinversi's will of 1429 (ASVe, ANT, Enrico Salomon, b. 946/c, doc. 313; Barausse, 2020, pp. 20–21, doc. 4); executor of his mother Gera's will of 1469 (ASVe, ANT, Pietro Rossi, b. 870, doc. 111; Barausse, 2020, p. 30, doc. 20).
40. Franceschina Vendramin: mother of Giovanni Bellini; second wife of Nicoletto Bellini; an executor of Nicoletto's will of 1424 (ASVe, ANT, Lorenzo Buscarino, b. 545, doc. 63, fol. 10r–v; Barausse, 2020, pp. 19–20, doc. 3).
41. Giovanni Vendramin: brother of Samaritana; deceased by 1509 (ASVe, ANT, Nicolò Moravio, b. 677, doc. 897; D. Brown and Pizzati, 2014, p. 152).
42. Marina Vendramin: daughter of Giovanni Vendramin; potential beneficiary in her aunt Samaritana Vendramin's will of 1509 (ASVe, ANT, Nicolò Moravio, b. 677, doc. 897; D. Brown and Pizzati, 2014, p. 152).
43. Samaritana Vendramin: maternal aunt of Giovanni Bellini; an executor of her mother-in-law Lucia Bocheta's will of 1457 (ASVe, ANT, Lorenzo Dalla Torre, b. 1062, doc. 12 [unpublished]); presumably died soon after her will of 1509 (ASVe, ANT, Nicolò Moravio, b. 677, doc. 897; D. Brown and Pizzati, 2014, p. 152).

INTRODUCTION

1. The Venetian calendar year began on March 1, a system known as *more veneto* (m.v, meaning "according to the customs of Venice"). Thus a Venetian document dated February 6, 1428 (e.g., the first will of Jacopo Bellini's wife, Anna) corresponds to February 6, 1429 in the Gregorian calendar. In this book, unless noted, dates are not given as m.v. The dates proposed for Jacopo Bellini's drawings derive primarily from the compelling research of Degenhart and Schmitt (1990, II-5: pp. 252–66).
2. See Appendix A for a detailed discussion. Agosti, 1993, p. 52 n. 29.
3. Maze, 2013a.
4. See Appendix A for a detailed analysis.
5. Vasari, 1966–87, 3: p. 441.
6. For Mantegna's year of birth as possibly being earlier than 1431, see Shaw and Boccia, 2016.
7. For instance, Bätschmann, 2008, pp. 13–16, begins with an examination of Giovanni's Birmingham *Saint Jerome*. See also Lucco, 2008b, p. 136; Gasparotto, 2017c, p. 63.
8. For a summary of the various opinions on these paintings, see Lucco, 2008b, pp. 146–47, 148–50, 182–84; Villa, 2008; Di Lorenzo, 2012; Lucco, 2020.

CHAPTER 1

1. The episode is described in ASFi, Diplomatico Normali Camera Fiscale, 1424.11.28, and ASFi, Provvisioni, 115 (serie registri), fols 8r–9r. Both are transcribed by Venturi in Vasari, 1896, 1: pp. 11–14, and the latter also in Mazzalupi, 2006a, pp. 79–81, doc. 73.
2. The date is reported by Crowe and Cavalcaselle (1871, 1: p. 101), Milanesi (Vasari, 1878–85, 3: p. 150), Venturi (Vasari, 1896, 1: p. 10), and others as the feast day of San Barnaba, which fell on June 11, 1423. The source for the date was presumably a now-lost document cited by Crowe and Cavalcaselle (1871, p. 102 n. 1).
3. The Palazzo dello Strozzino was likely built on the land once occupied by Gentile's workshop; see Davisson, 1980, pp. 759–60; De Marchi, 1992, pp. 135, 184 n. 1; Bernacchioni, 2006, pp. 121–22. For the Palazzo dello Strozzino and its surroundings, see Elam, 1985; Belli, 1998.
4. For Gentile's arrival in Florence, see Bernacchioni, 2006, pp. 121, 130 n. 4. On the identity of Gentile's assistants, see De Marchi, 1992, pp. 136–53, 186–87 nn. 30–33; De Marchi, 2006c.
5. ASFi, Provvisioni, 115 (serie registri), fol. 8r: "*certa scultilia et picture maxime importantie.*" "*Scultilia*" can refer to polychrome sculptures, picture frames, or some other type of painted object (see Davisson, 1980, p. 760 n. 11), perhaps even the reverse of the Pisa *Madonna of Humility* that represents polychrome inlaid marble (see Frosinini, 2006, p. 250; De Marchi, 2010, p. 196). For a discussion of the role of sculptures in Gentile da Fabriano's workshop practice and production, see De Marchi, 2006c, p. 14.
6. For the Frick's *Virgin and Child, with Saints Lawrence and Julian*, see Becker et al., 2003, pp. 351–56. For Gentile's *Madonna of Humility* in Pisa, see Frosinini, 2006; De Marchi, 2010.
7. ASFi, Provvisioni, 115 (serie registri), fol. 8: "*prescriptus Iacobus de precepto dicti magistri Gentilini redarguit ipsum Bernardum.*"
8. ASFi, Diplomatico Normali Camera Fiscale, 1424.11.28: ". . . *sub descriptione Iacobi de Venetiis famuli et discipuli magistri Gentilini pictoris de Fabbiano habitatoris in populo Sancte Marie Ugonis de Florentia in domo et habitatione dicti magistri Gentilini.*" This identification of "Jacopo of Venice" as Jacopo Bellini is generally accepted and supported by a range of sources. For instance, Jacopo Bellini described himself as Gentile da Fabriano's disciple (*discipulus*; see Eisler, 1989, p. 517), as did Vasari (*discepolo*; Vasari, 1966–87, 3: p. 419); the Florentine document cited in note 1 above (ASFi, Provvisioni, 115 (serie registri), fols 8r–9r) and dated April 3, 1425, describes Jacopo of Venice as Gentile's disciple (*discipulus*), and, as discussed by De Marchi (1992, pp. 186–87 n. 33), no compelling evidence suggests that Gentile had more than one longstanding assistant and disciple named "Jacopo of Venice." However, the Florentine documents also call him "Jacopo di Piero," and the name of Jacopo Bellini's father was Nicolò or Nicoletto. Christiansen (1982, p. 4) speculated that Jacopo di Piero should "be identified with the young Jacopo Bellini," and that perhaps Jacopo either "lie[d] to protect himself" or his name was "incorrectly transcribed" (see also Christiansen, 2006, p. 49 n. 45). This latter possibility was also advanced by De Marchi, 2006c, pp. 13, 48 n. 40. Fletcher (1998, pp. 150–51 n. 33) noted that such errors were not uncommon in legal documents of the period.
9. De Marchi, Laureati, and Mochi Onori, 2006, pp. 57–109; Pizzati, 2006. According to an entry in the *mariegola* (matricula) of the Scuola of San Cristoforo dei Mercanti, Gentile resided in the parish of Santa Sofia, in the *sestiere* of Cannaregio ("Maistro Zentil da Fabriano S[ancta] Sofia").

See ASVe, Scuole piccole e suffragi, b. 406 (Mariegola della Scuola di S. Maria e di S. Cristoforo dei Mercanti alla Madonna dell'Orto), fol. 76r; see also Cicogna, 1853, VI.2: p. 871; Mazzalupi, 2006a, p. 68, doc. 2; Humphrey, 2015, pp. 258–64. As discussed by Pizzati (2006, pp. 110–11 n. 6), it is not possible to date Gentile's membership in the *scuola*, although Mazzalupi (2006a, p. 68, doc. 2) tentatively placed it before 1414.

10. Lametti, 2001, p. 428; Mazzalupi, 2006a, pp. 68–78; De Marchi, 2006c; Maze, 2017, p. 43. On August 27, 1411, Gentile received 225 florins from Ugolino III da Trinci, Lord of Foligno, for "*quasdam picturas*" he had made in the "*sala imperatorum in camera rosarum* [and] *in loggia*." Five months later, on January 12, 1412, Gentile was paid 93 florins "*per quasdam picturas*" and a "*parvam conam imaginis Virginis Mariae*" that he had painted with the aid of four assistants, including "*magistro Iacopo de Venezia*." On September 18, 1419, Gentile requested from Pandolfo III Malatesta safe passage from Brescia for eight people and eight horses (Mazzalupi, 2006a, p. 77, doc. 66), and presumably Jacopo was among this group. On March 23, 1420, Gentile was documented as being in Fabriano (Mazzalupi, 2006a, p. 77, doc. 67), and later the same year he was residing in Florence (Mazzalupi, 2006a, p. 78, doc. 69).

11. At the beginning of the sixteenth century, Marcantonio Michiel (2000, pp. 30–31) saw Jacopo's painting in the Paduan collection of Pietro Bembo: "*In casa di Misser Pietro Bembo . . . Il ritratto in profilo di Gentil da Fabriano fu di mano di Jacomo Bellino*." For the relationship between the Bellini and the Bembo, see Fletcher, 2004, pp. 30–31. In 1815 the portrait was in Venice, at the Palazzo Gradenigo. Cornelia Dolfin, wife of Vincenzo Gradenigo (the last descendant of Elena Bembo and Pietro Gradenigo), willed her possessions to one of her servants, including a portrait of Pietro Bembo by Titian and Jacopo Bellini's portrait of Gentile (Eiche, 1983, p. 358).

12. Vasari, 1966–87, 3: pp. 427–28: "*Ebbe* [Jacopo] *due figliuoli inclinatissimi all'arte, e di bello e buon ingegno: l'uno fu Giovanni, e l'altro Gentile; al quale pose così nome per la dolce memoria che teneva di Gentile da Fabriano, stato suo maestro e come padre amorevole*." The name "Gentile" is so rare in Venice that, among the thousands of noblemen who served in elected office in Venice between 1340 and 1524 and are recorded in the Rulers of Venice Database, there appears to be only one—"Gentile di Andrea Contarini"—and only a few officeholders with a father named "Gentile" (Kohl, Mozzato, and O'Connell, "The Rulers of Venice, 1332–1524," accessed August 6, 2020, www.rulersofvenice.org).

13. The fresco was painted for the chapel of Bishop Giulio Memmo and destroyed in 1759. The inscription had read: "In the year 1436 Jacopo Bellini painted this with his slight talent to the extent his artistic skill [could] reach. His teacher was Gentile, a man renowned in the Venetian world, an outstanding man in whom his native city of Fabriano rejoices" ("*Mille quadrigentos sex et triginta per annos Jacobus haec pinxit, tenui quantam attigit artem / Ingenio Bellinus. Idem praeceptor et illi. Gentilis veneto fama celeberrimus orbe Quo Fabriana viro praestanti urbs patria Gaudet*"). For this translation and a discussion, see Maze, 2013b, pp. 114–18. For a slightly different translation, see Eisler, 1989, pp. 346, 525.
See also Marinelli, 1987, p. 62; Degenhart and Schmitt, 1990, 5: pp. 106–09 n. 4. Earlier, Jacopo had signed his first documented work of ca. 1430, a now-lost painting of Saint Michael for the Church of San Michele Arcangelo in Padua, with the words: "Jacopo of Venice, disciple of Gentile da Fabriano, painted it" (JACOBUS DE VENETIIS DISCIPULUS GENTILE DA FABRIANO PINXIT; Eisler, 1989, p. 517). See also Rigoni, 1929; Land, 1982. In his early independent career, Jacopo also used such inscriptions to elevate his own artistic status by associating his work with Italy's most renowned practitioner of the International Gothic style. For the function of signatures in Renaissance paintings, see Matthew, 1998, pp. 616–48; Gilbert, 2000; Rubin, 2006; Pincus, 2008; Rawlings, 2009, pp. 108–57.

14. Vasari, 1966–87, 3: p. 428; see note 12 above.

15. ASFi, Provvisioni, 115 (serie registri), fol. 8r: "*Tu fai una grande villania a gittare, essendo oggimai grande come uno huomo*." The transcription of this document, here and below, is based on that of Venturi (Vasari, 1896, 1: pp. 10–14); see also Ricci, 1908, 1: p. 49, doc. 4.

16. ASFi, Provvisioni, 115 (serie registri), fol. 8r: "*Quibus equidem verbis iratus prefatus Bernardus multa verba iniuriosa et derisoria protulit contra eum, invitans ipsum ad faciendum secum ad pusillos. Qui Iacobus tante iniurie impatiens respondit quod sic et ita vicissim ad pugnos bellarunt manibus vacuis nullaque alia interveniente percussione*."

17. Ibid.: "*Bernardum ser Silvestri ser Tommasii notarii et civis florentini et de populo Sancte Trinitatis de Florentia*."

18. Ruggiero, 2015, pp. 98–99; D. Romano, 2014.
19. ASFi, Provvisioni, 115 (serie registri), fol. 8r–v: "*Et quod ipse Iacobus credens de narratis commissis per eum nullam fiendam esse condempnationem super vestris galeis ad servitia vestre comunitatis accessit.*"
20. G. Guarnieri, 1967, p. 139; Tazzara, 2017, p. 22.
21. Mallett, 1967, pp. 25–39. Florence apparently owned "11 great galleys and 15 long ones" not long after purchasing the seaports (ibid., p. 24).
22. The ship that Jacopo boarded might have been one of the Florentine "*ghalee grosse*" that set sail for the Levant on July 26, 1423, and returned to Porto Pisano on November 28 of the same year (Sapori, 1956, p. 81). Since Jacopo evidently did not return to Florence until October of the following year, perhaps he sought work on another ship. See also Yousefzadeh, 2018.
23. ASFi, Provvisioni, 115 (serie registri), fol. 8r.
24. Ibid.: "*Iacobus intentione infrascriptum malleficium commictendi armatus quodam bastone ligneo, re acta ad infrascripta maleficia commictendum dolose et appensate assalivit Bernardum ser Silvestri [. . .] et cum dicto bastone pluribus vicibus admenando percussit una percussione ipsum Bernardum in brachio sinistro sine sanguinis effuxione contra voluntatem dicti Bernardi.*"
25. Ibid., fol. 8v: "*Et quod supradictus ser Silvester videns quod prefatus Iacobus erat absens, ipsum notificari fecit in condempnatione narrata commisisse prelibato executori, qui erat valde ipsius ser Silvestri familiaris [. . .] una condempnatione librarum quadrigentarum quinquaginta flor. parv. cum quarto pluris.*"
26. Ibid.: "*Et demum die vigesimo quarto mensis octobris anni millesimi quadrigentesimi vigesimi quarti fuit ex parte tunc domini protestatis civitatis Florentie recommendatus in carceribus Stincarum Vestri Communis.*" For the origin of the prison's name, see Wolfgang, 1960; Wolfgang, 1990, p. 569.
27. ASFi, Provvisioni, 115 (serie registri), fol. 8v: "*Et quod pauperimus est et non videt modum a tanta miseria liberari. . . .*" For debtors in Le Stinche, see Geltner, 2008, p. 19. Wolfgang (1960, pp. 149, 151–52) and Wolfgang (1990, pp. 569–70) identified several prominent Florentines who had been imprisoned there, including the poets Dino di Tura and Francesco Berni, the chronicler Giovanni Villani, and the historian Giovanni Cavalcanti.
28. Records in the *Archivio delle Stinche* are missing for the period of Jacopo Bellini's incarceration (that they are missing was confirmed in correspondence from Carla Zarrilli, Director of the ASFi, September 24, 2015).
29. For an overview of the prison, which was located where Teatro Verdi stands today, see Wolfgang, 1990.
30. Geltner, 2008, p. 21.
31. Ibid., pp. 19–22. For a description of the inmates' condition, see the poem by Niccolò Macchiavelli reprinted in Wolfgang, 1960, p. 151.
32. Bernacchioni, 2006.
33. At the time of the will, Lorenzo Buscarino was the *plebanus* (parish priest) of the Church of San Giacomo dall'Orio. For Nicoletto's will, see ASVe, ANT, Lorenzo Buscarino, b. 545, n. 63, fol. 10r–v; Barausse, 2020, pp. 19–20, doc. 3. Unless otherwise cited, the biographical information concerning the Bellini presented in this section derives from this document.
34. Pedani Fabris, 1996.
35. For the tinsmith's craft in Renaissance Venice, see Garzoni, 1996, pp. 740–41.
36. A number of *batistagni* (or *stagneri*) had their workshops on the Calle dei Stagneri, a narrow alley that still connects Campo San Bartolomeo with Campo della Fava (see Tassini, 1964, p. 647; DeLancey, 2011).
37. Zanina is described as deceased in Nicoletto's 1424 will (see also Maze, 2013a, p. 790 n. 23, p. 791).
38. For Leonardo and his career as a miniaturist, see Mariani Canova, 1968; Moretti, 1970; Bauer-Eberhardt, 1989; Marcon, 2001; Cattaneo, 2003; Fletcher, 2004, pp. 21, 33; Szépe, 2018.
39. Mazzalupi, 2006a, p. 69, doc. 4.
40. Maze, 2013a, p. 791.
41. On the relationship of artisans to their parish church in Venice, see D. Romano, 1987, pp. 77–130.
42. Later, in 1477, a group of *batistagni* and *peltreri* (pewterers) founded the Scuola Piccola di San Giovanni Evangelista in the Church of San Salvador; due to a disagreement with the Augustinian Regular Canons of San Salvador over the ownership of the altar of San Giovanni, which had been given to the D'Anna family in 1559, the Scuola moved to the nearby Basilica of San Bartolomeo in 1571 (Tassini, 1964, p. 647; Finocchi Ghersi, 1997; Vio, 2004, pp. 397–98; Pichi, 2009, pp. 52–54). The altar, located on the Gospel side, is currently dedicated to St. Anthony the Great, patron of the Scuola dei Luganegheri (sausage makers), and was renovated between 1582 and 1603 (Pichi, 2009, pp. 54–55).
43. ASVe, ANT, Lorenzo Buscarino, b. 545, n. 63, fol. 10r–v: "*Item dimitto Scole Sancti Leonardi posite in Sancto Salvatore ducatum unum auri pro anima mea. Item dimitto Scolle Sancti Theodori ducatum unum auri pro anima mea.*" For the Scuola of San Leonardo,

see Vio, 2004, pp. 392–93; Humphrey, 2015, pp. 380, 382 nn. 2–3. Many *batistagni* joined the Scuola Grande di San Teodoro, which, before being elevated to a *scuola grande* on March 25, 1552, met at the Church of San Salvador (Gallo, 1961–62; Gramigna and Perissa, 2008, pp. 27–36).

44. APVe, Parrocchia di Santissimo Salvatore di Venezia, Registri dei battesimi, b.1.
45. ASVe, SGSMM, b. A., reg. 2 (LXXVI/11), fol. 80v: "*ser Nicholeto belin bati stagno de san Salvador.*" His is the second-to-last name entered under the letter "N," and the *mariegola* appears to have ended in ca. 1390.
46. The *scuola* was founded in the Church of Santa Maria Gloriosa dei Frari on September 8, 1261. In 1290, it had 320 members. In 1308, it was refounded in Cannaregio, and in 1310, it obtained from the friars of the Abbazia della Misericordia the right to build a meeting house adjacent to the abbey church. See Pullan, 1971, p. 38; Howard, 1999, p. 18; Gramigna and Perissa, 2008, pp. 125–27.
47. For the membership figures, see Pullan, 1971, pp. 33–34, 86–87. For the *scuole grandi* in general, see Pullan, 1971; Pullan, 1981; Maschio, 1981; Mackenney, 1987; Wurthmann, 1989; Fortini Brown, 1996a; D. Romano, 1996b; Glixon, 2003.
48. ASVe, SGSMM, b. 11, March 13, 1393 – March 1394: "*Mccclxxxxiii. di. 13. Março . . . Oficiali de meço Ano . . . Ser Nicoleto belim* [*ni?*]. *Nonçolo . . . Mccclxxxxiiii. di de Março . . . Nonçioli Ser Nicholeto belom* [sic] *San Salvador.*" Despite the latter misspelling, this must be Nicoletto Bellini because the other *nonzoli* who started on the half-year are listed in the next year as well. The position of *nonzolo* in this *scuola* disappeared after 1457, evidently replaced by the *masseri*, although both positions existed in the year 1455. For the duties performed by *nonzoli*, see ASVe, SGSM, b. 41, fol. 4v, *Capitolo decimo*; Glixon, 2003, p. 21.
49. Pullan (1971) remains the standard text on membership and benefits in the *scuole*.
50. Nicoletto is not listed again in ASVe, SGSMM, b. 11.
51. For the transcription of Nicoletto's will, see Barausse, 2020, pp. 19–20, doc. 3. For a discussion of the document, see Maze, 2013a, p. 791 n. 29.
52. ASVe, ANT, Lorenzo Buscarino, b. 545, n. 63, fol. 10r–v: "*Item dimitto [Cha]tarucie filie Helene, filie mee, ducatos decem auri pro suo maritate,*" and ibid., fol. 10r–v: "*Item dimitto Helene filie mee ducatos viginti quatuor auri* [. . .] *Item volo quod Iacobus pictor filius meus solvere debeat commissarie mee one id et totum quod michi dare tenetur, de quo debito sibi remittantur ducati viginti quatuor aur, qui sibi spectare possent pro repromissa quondam matris sue.*"
53. Cessi, 1938, 4:27: pp. 207–08, including glosses.
54. Barausse, 2020, p. 26, doc. 14; Maze, 2017, p. 41. In Nicoletto's will, "Remarius" likely signifies the vocation of Elena's husband, Paolo, rather than his surname. *Remèr* means oarmaker in Venetian, and Paolo's son, Leonardo, does not use Remarius as his surname in known documents. See the Bellini Family Tree, pp. 6–7.
55. Mazzalupi, 2006a, p. 68, doc. 1; Pizzati, 2006, p. 108.
56. For arguments and evidence, see Maze, 2013a. Franceschina's last name can be determined from her sister Samaritana's will (ASVe, ANT, Nicolò Moravio, b. 677, n. 897, transcribed in D. Brown and Pizzati, 2014, p. 152: "*Samaritana relicta ser Iob Dominici de confinio Sancte Marine.*") Also see Appendix A.
57. ASVe, ANT, Lorenzo Buscarino, b. 545, n. 63, fol. 10r–v; Barausse, 2020, pp. 19–20, doc. 3: "*Franceschine uxori mee dilecte.*"
58. ASVe, ANT, Nicolò Moravio, b. 677, n. 897, transcribed in D. Brown and Pizzati, 2014, p. 152. See also Appendix A; Maze, 2017, pp. 40–41, 54 n. 56.
59. This can be inferred from a passage in Samaritana's will: "*Marinam neptem meam filiam quondam ser Ioannis Vendramini fratris mei*" (ASVe, ANT, Nicolò Moravio, b. 677, n. 897).
60. For the Vendramin family branches, see D. Brown and Pizzati, 2014, p. 152. For Andrea Vendramin's social climbing and his inclusion in Gentile Bellini's *Miracle of the Relic of the Holy Cross at the Bridge of San Lorenzo*, see Petkov, 2014, pp. 27–46; Fortini Brown, 1988, pp. 79, 139–42, 155, 222.
61. D. Brown and Pizzati, 2014, p. 152 n. 43, arrived at a similar conclusion about Samaritana (also personal correspondence with Pizzati, April 2015).
62. ASVe, ANT, Lorenzo Buscarino, b. 545, n. 63, fol. 10r–v, Barausse, 2020, pp. 19–20, doc. 3: "*uxor mea Franceschina sit pro maiore parte.*"
63. ASVe, ANT, Lorenzo Buscarino, b. 545, n. 63, fol. 10r–v: "*In quo quidem meo testamento volo et esse constituto mee fidei comissarios Franceschinam uxorem meam dilectam, Paulum Remarium generum meum, Petrum Musolino, olim filium ser Pauli ab Astis, et Iacobum Belino pictorem filium meum.*" For deciphering problematic surnames, see also Lowe, 2013, pp. 416–18, 434–35.
64. ASVe, ANT, Lorenzo Buscarino, b. 545, n. 63, fol. 10r–v; Barausse, 2020, pp. 19–20, doc. 3: "*Et quod ab aliquo commissariorum meorum non possit neque valeat mollestari modo aliquo vel ingenio et si*

quis ex meis commissariis vellet ipsam molestare volo quod sit privatus et extra meam commissariam et de dicta commissaria se modo aliquo non impediat et quod ipsa sit sola commissaria in eadem casu in quocumque contractu persisterit."

65. ASVe, ANT, Lorenzo Buscarino, b. 545, n. 63, fol. 10r–v: *"Et si ipsa Hellena petere vellet commissarie mee, tunc nichil percipere debeat de legato per me sibi facto. Item volo quod Iacobus pictor filius meus solvere debeat commissarie mee omne id et totum quod michi dare tenetur, de quo debito sibi remittantur ducati viginti quatuor auri, qui sibi spectare possent pro repromissa quondam matris sue. Et in casu quo non esset contentus, solvere debeat totum debitum in quo michi tenetur, et sit privatus legato per me ipsi facto."*
66. For the argument and supporting evidence, see Appendix A; Maze, 2013a.
67. The title of the relevant Venetian law is "No one can disinherit their son." Cessi, 1938, 4:35: p. 213. See also Appendix A; Maze, 2013a, p. 792 n. 30.
68. ASVe, CIN, Vittore Pomino, b. 149, reg. "Protocollum mei Victoris Pomino notarii de 1439," fol. 55v. The document is transcribed and translated in Maze, 2013a, pp. 817–18. For the argument for being at least 14, see Cessi, 1938, 2:2: p. 103; Griphio, 1606, 6:24:98: ". . . and nobody male shall be able to cease his guardianship unless he is 14 years of age" (*. . . quod nemo masculus deinceps de tutoria possit exire, nisi 14. annum excesserit aetatis suae*). Humfrey (1984, p. 4; following Botteon and Aliprandi, 1893, pp. 30–31) used the same law to determine the birth year of the artist Giovanni Battista Cima.
69. Vasari, 1966–87, 3: p. 441: *"Finalmente Giovanni essendo pervenuto all'età di novanta anni, passò di male di vecchiaia di questa vita."* For the date of Giovanni's death, see Sanudo, 1879–1903, 23: p. 256 (November 29, 1516): *"Se intese, questa matina esser morto Zuan Belin optimo pytor, havia anni. . . ."* For an analysis of the documents concerning Giovanni's birth, see Appendix A.
70. ASVe, CIN, Vittore Pomino, b. 149, reg. "Protocollum mei Victoris Pomino notarii de 1439," fol. 55v; Maze, 2013a, pp. 817–18: *"Hinc est quod nos Iohannes Belino et Iacobus Belino fratres ac filii quondam ser Nicolai."*
71. Maze, 2013a, pp. 789–90.
72. Barausse, 2020, pp. 19–20, doc. 3.
73. For the Venetian laws, see Cessi, 1938, book 4; Griphio, 1606, book 4. For an overview of the Roman law, see Buckland and Stein, 2007, pp. 334–404; Robinson, 1905, p. 270: "[A] testament may be totally null from the very beginning because it failed to meet the complete requirement of a valid instrument, e.g. . . . by passing over a *suus heres* [a person under the paternal power of the deceased]." For disinheritance, see Maze, 2013a, p. 792 nn. 30–33.
74. This is from Roman law; see Buckland, 1953, p. 202. For the Venetian law, see Griphio, 1606, "Nove Leggi," M.Cons.1418.29.Marzo, fol. 6r–v: *"Che li figlioli, nasciuti dopo il testamento delli loro padre, rompino esso testamento."*
75. Ibid.; Buckland and Stein, 2007, p. 332. See also Berger, 1953, p. 640 (*Postumus suus*), p. 735 (*Testamentum ruptum*).
76. Barausse, 2020, pp. 19–20, doc. 3.
77. ASVe, CIN, Tommaso de Tomei, b. 212, 23 luglio 1429: "Jacopo Bellini, a painter residing in the parish of San Geminiano and son of the deceased ser Nicoletto Bellini." For a complete transcription and translation, see Maze, 2013a, p. 819.
78. For Franceschina, see Appendix A. See also Maze, 2013a, pp. 791 n. 29, 792 n. 33, 794–95; Maze, 2017, p. 40.
79. ASVe, CIN, Vittore Pomino, b. 149, reg. "Protocollum mei Victoris Pomino notarii de 1439," fol. 55v. Maze, 2013a, pp. 817–18: *"Iohannes Belino et Iacobus Belino fratres ac filii quondam ser Nicolai de confinio Sancti Iuminiani."*
80. On communal identity, see Maze, 2013a, pp. 806–07.
81. When Giovanni Bellini's wife, Ginevra, drew up her will on September 23, 1489, she was gravely ill and presumably died soon afterward; see Barausse, 2020, pp. 43–44, doc. 51: *"Ego Zenevra, uxor egregii viri ser Ioannis Bellini pictoris de confinio Sancte Marine, mente sana licet corpore languens."* Giovanni Bellini's son, Alvise, was also gravely ill when he drew up his will on December 14, 1498 (in which his mother Ginevra is described as deceased), and he died soon afterward (Barausse, 2020, pp. 48–49, doc. 63).

CHAPTER 2

1. Cappelli, 1930, pp. 11–12.
2. As described in ASFi, Provvisioni, 115 (serie registri), fols 8r–9r; Mazzalupi, 2006a, pp. 79–81, doc. 73: *"Iacobus in die Pascatis Resurrectionis Domini nostri Yhesu Christi, quod celebrabitur die octavo presentis mensis aprilis anni millesimi quadringentesimi vigesimiquinti, possit et debeat offeri ad ecclesiam Sancti Iohannis Baptiste civitatis Florentie in dicta civitate et more solito duci capite discoperto cum torchieto in manibus et horis consuetis et cum tubis precedentibus ad oblationem predictam."* For the symbolism of the procession, see Trexler, 1980, pp. 260–61.

3. ASFi, Diplomatico Normali Camera Fiscale, 1424.11.28; Mazzalupi, 2006a, p. 80, doc. 73: "*Et quod ipse Iacobus die vigesimo ottavo mensis novembris anno millesimo quadringentesimo vigesimo quarto pacem habuit de predictis a supradicto Bernardo, ut constat per instrumentum inde confectum per ser Bartholomeum Iohannis Dini de Laterino notarium publicum florentinum.*"
4. Leonardo Bellini earned 12 ducats the first year, and 14 ducats the next, as Jacopo's assistant (Barausse, 2020, 26, doc. 14). According to Stahl (2008, pp. 67–68) and Rossi (2012, pp. 70–73), a Venetian gold ducat weighed 3.545 grams and a gold florin weighed 3.53 grams. Spufford (1989, p. 332) notes that the weight of the florin varied from 3.52 to 3.54 grams, while the weight of the ducat remained constant.
5. Brackett, 2002, p. 43 n. 53; Trexler, 1980, p. 267 n. 173: "The government absorbed the prisoners' past jail costs, which prisoners normally paid before they could be released, and paid the debts of prisoners as well." Mellyn, 2014, pp. 67–68: "Only the poorest and most wretched were usually granted freedom and only 50 could be released at any time." This type of amnesty was not limited to Florence; see Koenig, 2001.
6. Brackett, 2002, p. 43 n. 53.
7. Cecchi, 2005, pp. 59–69, 71–73; Bernacchioni, 2006.
8. Brackett, 2002, p. 122. For the date of the painting, once visible on the original frame ("OPUS GENTILIS DE FABRIANO MCCCCXXV MENSE MAII"), see Richa, 1762, X/2: p. 270 n. 21.
9. De Marchi, 2006b; Mazzalupi, 2006b, pp. 133–34.
10. Riccetti, 2006.
11. De Marchi, 2006b.
12. Mazzalupi, 2006b, pp. 140–41.
13. Mazzalupi, 2006a, p. 84, doc. 88.
14. Christiansen, 1982, p. 156, doc. 3, 160, doc. 4.
15. ASFi, Provvisioni, 115 (serie registri), fols 8r–9r: "*Et quod pauperrimus est . . .*"
16. See Appendix A; Maze, 2013a, pp. 785–89.
17. Ibid.
18. Ibid., pp. 796–800.
19. As stated in the *Glossa ordinaria*, "*etiam sexagenarius . . . in potestate est*": Kuehn, 1982, p. 177 n. 8.
20. Novellus, 1564, Index 'f' and 4:3: p. 41: "*Fratres emancipati non sunt in fraterna compagnia.*"
21. Maze, 2013a, pp. 796–800.
22. Ibid.
23. Allen, 2008, p. 19.
24. On the class of Venetian-born citizens, see Casini, 1992; Zannini, 1993; Grubb, 2000; Bellavitis, 2001.
25. For example, the Venetian painter Giovanni Mansueti, after his apprenticeship with the Bellini family (ca. 1479–89), opened his own workshop by virtue of a 200-ducat dowry that he received from his wife, Laura Longini: Matino, 2010, pp. 18–19, 33 n. 53.
26. Chojnacki, 2000, pp. 95–114; Bellavitis, 1995; Bellavitis, 2012; Bellavitis, 2014, pp. 328–32. In Venice, a 1420 Senatorial act allowed the husband to keep the corredo, which was one-third of the entire marriage gift, with the remaining two-thirds considered the wife's dowry proper (Chojnacki, 2000, pp. 82–3).
27. Pullan, 1971, pp. 183–84; D. Romano, 2007, p. 5; Lanaro and Varanini, 2009, p. 93.
28. ASVe, ANT, Enrico Salomon, b. 946/c, n. 313; Barausse, 2020, pp. 20–21, doc. 4.
29. Molà, 1994, p. 188 n. 145. On the term *sanser* (or *senser*), see Boerio, 1998, p. 644; Cortellazzo, 2007, pp. 1160–61. The *Scuola dei sanseri* met at the Church of the Ognissanti in the *sestiere* of Dorsoduro (Zorzi, 1972, II: pp. 485–86; Manno, 1995, p. 127; Cecchini, 2000, p. 221). On January 22, 1435, the Council of Ten decreed that "*chi vuol esser Sanser bisogna o che sia Cittadin originario o che abbia moglie Veneziana, ovver abbia abitato 10 anni in Venezia, eccetto però nelle Sanserie di Formenti, Zuje, Cambi nelle quali ognuno benché Forestier possa esercitarsi,*" and on June 26, 1487, the Council stated that *sanseri* must be "*Venetus vel subditus Terrarum et Locorum Nostrorum*": Vercellin, 1980, pp. 51–52 n. 24.
30. Branca Rinversi was "a business agent . . . in contact with many silk weavers from Lucca" (Molà, 1994, p. 188 n. 145). On the Amadi and Sandei families, see Molà, 1994; Pizzati, 2006.
31. ASVe, CIN, Tommaso de Tomei, b. 212, 23 luglio 1429; Maze, 2013a, pp. 819–20. This was less than Giovanni's wife's dowry of 500 ducats. The increase in dowries perhaps reflects the social elevation of the Bellini across generations. For the increase in the amount of dowries in early Renaissance Venice, see Chojnacki, 2000, pp. 132–52.
32. Ibid.
33. ASVe, CIN, Tomeo Tomei, b. 212, fasc. 2, fol. 33v: "*Die octo iulii 1466, indicione 14, Rivoalti. Plenam et irrevocabilem securitatem dotis et repromisse facio cum heredibus et successoribus meis ego Leonellus Bellino natus ser Iacobi Bellino pictor tibi Isabette filie quondam nobilis viri ser Iohannis Michael olim de confinio Sancte Marine dillecte uxori mee et successoribus tuis de ducatis ducentis quinquaginta quod michi parte dari promissi fuerunt tempore contracti et matrimonii nostri nunc autem quia tempores huius et cetera, obligans*

omnia mea bona et cetera. / Testes presbiteri Lazarus, Iohannis et Georgius Isidori Sancte Sophie." I am grateful to Stanley Chojnacki for sharing this previously unpublished document. I thank Mario Rosso for the transcription.

34. Jacopo received a payment, presumably for his work in Ferrara, on August 26, 1441 (Eisler, 1989, p. 53). His trip evidently overlapped with the trip of Pisanello, who returned from Ferrara to Mantua on August 16, 1441 (Cordellier, 1996, p. 502; Cicinelli, 1994–95, p. 65).
35. Cessi, 1938, 3:5–6: pp. 125–26: "*De possessionibus dividendis inter fratres. V. Decernimus quod, cum hactenus sit Veneciis consuetum quod maior frater possessionem patris dividebat et minor sive minores fratres partes a maiori fratre disignatas accipiebant, de cetero volumus quod omnes fratres in dividendis paternis possessionibus sint equales, et sic de omnibus habentibus possessiones comunes undecumque. Pro illis, qui possessionem indivisam habuerint, et aliquis eorum eam dividere voluerit et cognoscere partem suam. VI. Dicimus quod, si plures fuerint, qui possessionem indivisam habuerint, et fuerint omnes presentes in Veneciis, et aliquis illorum, qui fuerit Veneciis, voluerit dividere possessionem ipsam et cognoscere partem suam, debeat vocare eum vel omnes illos, qui habent partem in ipsa possessione, et denunciare ei vel eis quod possessionem ipsam velit dividere, et hoc facto debeant inter se possessionem illam dividere: quod si facere recusaverint vel non potuerint concordare inter se, iudices debeant possessionem ipsam dividere et sortes ponere.*" See also ibid., 4:14: pp. 200–05.
36. Maze, 2013a, pp. 793–96. For the meaning of the word *tutore*, see S. Battaglia, 2002, p. 471.
37. For the probable marriage date, see Maze, 2013a, pp. 798–99 n. 64.
38. ASVe, ANT, Nicolò Moravio, b. 677, n. 897; transcribed in D. Brown and Pizzati, 2014, pp. 152: "*Samaritana relicta ser Iob Dominici de confinio Sancte Marine.*" For Giobbe (Iopo) Dominici, see Sopracasa, 2011, pp. 159–60 n. 474; D. Brown and Pizzati, 2014, p. 152 n. 42. Della Pugliola (1731, p. 701) described him as living in Pera (Istanbul).
39. ASVe, ANT, Lorenzo Dalla Torre, b. 1062, n. 12, February 17, 1456 [m.v.] I thank Paula Clarke for this reference and Mario Rosso for its transcription. Lucia's will describes her husband, Giovanni Dominici, as deceased, and Lucia names three executors to her will: her brother Alvise; her daughter Fiornovella, wife of Giovanni Musolini; and her daughter-in-law Samaritana. It describes her son Giobbe as being in Constantinople.
40. I previously speculated that Alvise Bocheta was the father of Ginevra (Maze, 2017, p. 54 n. 56). See Appendix A and the Bellini Family Tree, for more information on Alvise.
41. See the Bellini Family Tree.
42. That Giobbe Dominici died in 1459 was presented in an unpublished paper by Paula Clarke, "Venetian Merchants in Constantinople in the 1450s," at the Renaissance Society of America Conference, Toronto, March 18, 2019. In personal correspondence on May 25, 2020, Clarke wrote that Giobbe probably died in August–September 1459, and certainly by March 1462. I thank Clarke, who is currently writing an article about Giobbe, for this information. For the death of Samaritana's son, Giovanni Dominici, see Orvieto, 1969, p. 229 n. 4.
43. Lucrezia was named in the will of her paternal grandmother, Lucia Bocheta (ASVe, ANT, Lorenzo Dalla Torre, b. 1062, n. 12, February 17, 1456 [m.v.]).
44. ASVe, ANT, Nicolò Moravio, b. 677, n. 897; transcribed in D. Brown and Pizzati, 2014, p. 152: "*Ioannem Bellinum . . . qui me semper eque ac matrem et amore et beneficiis prosecutus est.*" One may presume that Giovanni cared for Samaritana because her husband and son had died and because she and Giovanni are recorded as living in the same parish, presumably in the same household. See also Appendix A.
45. Vasari, 1966–87, 3: p. 428: "*Quando dunque furono alquanto cresciuti i detti due figliuoli [Giovanni and Gentile], Iacopo stesso insegnò loro con ogni diligenza i principi del disegno.*"
46. Although it is odd that Vasari (ibid., p. 549) described Jacopo Bellini's daughter, Nicolosia Bellini, who would marry Andrea Mantegna, only as "Gentile Bellini's sister" (*sorella di Gentile*), which she was, rather than as Giovanni Bellini's sister or as Giovanni and Gentile Bellini's sister, which indeed she was not. Biologically, she was Giovanni's niece.

CHAPTER 3

1. Hills, 1999a; Hills, 1999b; Savoy, 2012.
2. When we consider early Netherlandish art or paintings by Gentile da Fabriano or Antonello da Messina as pedagogical models for Giovanni's use of light, we should also note, perhaps first and foremost, Giovanni's artistic sensibility as fashioned by sunlight illuminating the city of Venice, which is often characteristic of how Giovanni treats light in his paintings.
3. Zorzi, 1972, II: pp. 332–37; Salomon, 2017.
4. For a period in 1464, probably while painting the

organ doors for the Basilica of San Marco, Gentile Bellini lived in an apartment in the Procuratie Vecchie, adjacent to the church and in his home parish of San Geminiano: ASVe, ANT, Nicolò [de] Avanzo, b. 46, doc. 116, February 29, 1463 [m.v.]; published in Ludwig, 1911, p. 89. See Maze, 2013a, p. 798 n. 62.

5. For instance, see Goffen, 1986.
6. Heyd, 1913, pp. 3–102; Cessi, 1953; Lane, 1973; Ashtor, 1983; Howard, 2000, pp. 12–35; Crouzet-Pavan, 2005, pp. 138–228; O'Connel, 2009; Arbel, 2013.
7. Barausse, 2020, p. 59, doc. 93 (including further references).
8. Hope, 2012; Dalla Costa, 2020, pp. 192–93.
9. Hope, 2012; Dalla Costa, 2020, pp. 192–93. Note that Bellini's letter is certainly not a forgery, as it is located among the Gonzaga papers in the state archives in Mantua (ASMn, Archivio Gonzaga, Autografi, b. 7, fol. 44).
10. I thank Alessio Assonitis, Director of the Medici Archive Project, for this observation and a discussion of Bellini's letters. Debra Pincus, however, is fairly certain that "this is a notary document with the notary signing for Giovanni" (personal correspondence, January 28, 2021).
11. Barausse, 2020, p. 35, doc. 32. Giovanni would later join the *scuola* and be elected *degano de tutto l'anno* in 1486 and *degano mezo anno* in 1494 (ibid., p. 42, doc. 48, p. 45, doc. 54). For the documents on Giovanni's paintings for the narrative cycle of the Sala dell'Albergo, see Barausse, 2020, pp. 67–68, docs 111–12, pp. 76–77, docs 132–33. For a discussion of the commissions, see Matino, 2017 (including further references).
12. The secondary evidence of Giovanni's literacy, namely, his inscriptions on paintings that were typically written in Latin, was presumably the product of consultations with humanist colleagues. See Olszaniec, 2009.
13. Wang, 2004; Smith, 2014.
14. For a discussion of the meaning and use of the term *studia humanitatis*, see Kohl, 1992; Chavasse, 2003.
15. Grendler, 1989, pp. 111–271; Grendler, 2013, pp. 677–78.
16. Ibid.
17. Grendler, 1982, p. 43; Grendler, 2013, pp. 676–77. A useful example is provided by Benedetto Cotrugli's *Libro dell'arte di mercatura*, written in 1458 but published in 1573. See Cotrugli Raguseo, 1990; Howard, 2000, pp. 19–22.
18. For a translation of Fibonacci's *Liber abaci*, see Sigler, 2002.
19. Grendler, 1982, pp. 44–47. The first illustrated Venetian edition of *Fior di virtù* was published in 1478 (Cline Horowitz, 1998, p. 103).
20. Cavalca, 2009.
21. Grendler, 1982, p. 47. In Venice, the *Legenda aurea* was published 27 times between 1474 (first edition) and 1516 (Giovanni Bellini's death), with six of the editions in Latin. See Pagnotta, 2005, pp. 87–94, 96–106, 403–04.
22. Grendler, 1989, pp. 323–25.
23. Vasari, 1966–87, 3: p. 428.
24. Maze, 2013a, p. 797.
25. There is no evidence indicating that Nicolò and Leonello were artists. For Nicolò, see C. Brown, 1969.
26. Gentile da Fabriano is recorded as being in Brescia by January 10, 1414 (Mazzalupi, 2006a, p. 69, doc. 5).
27. C. Guarnieri, 2016, p. 10, p. 33 n. 19 (including further references). Prior to January 11, 1412, Jacobello received 100 ducats annually from the Signoria (a sum that was then reduced) perhaps for executing frescoes in the Great Council Hall (ASVe, Deliberazioni Miste 1411–1415, reg. 49, fol. 71r, partially transcribed in Paoletti, 1893, I: p. 4 n. 6). See also De Marchi, 1992, pp. 63–64; De Marchi, 2006a, pp. 90–91.
28. For Jacobello's *Justice*, see Marconi, 1955, pp. 28–29 n. 26; Sinding-Larsen, 1974, pp. 55–56, pp. 174–75; Symeonides, 1977, pp. 50–52; Rosand, 1984, pp. 207–08; Manieri Elia, 2010.
29. For Giambono's *Saint Chrysogonus on Horseback* (ca. 1450), see R. Battaglia, 2016 (including further references).
30. For Giambono, see Pesaro, 1992; Franco, 2016. For a discussion of Giambono's style, see Land, 1974, pp. 6–16. Giambono sometimes infused recent innovations with a *retardataire* style; for example, the signature on his *Saint James* polyptych is a rare quattrocento example of a *cartellino* inscribed with Gothic rather than humanist-inspired lettering (Rawlings, 2009, p. 85).
31. On the Vivarini, especially regarding running perhaps the leading Venetian painting workshop of the 1440s, see Holgate, 1998, p. 91 ff.; Ceriana, 2016. For the *Madonna of the Rosary* polyptych, see Aikema, 2000.
32. For a discussion of these strategies, see Maze, 2013b, pp. 114–34.
33. Ibid., pp. 114–18.
34. On Giovanni's signatures, see Pincus, 2008 (including further references).

35. For Jacopo's strategies, see Maze, 2013b, pp. 114–20. For the relationship with Ulisse degli Aleotti, see B. Brown, 2011, p. 32 (including further references). For Bragadin's contract, see Barausse, 2020, p. 24, doc. 11; Maze, 2013a, p. 789; and Appendix A. For Jacopo's relationship with Giambono, see Franco, 1998, pp. 104, 134 n. 148.
36. Fletcher, 2004, pp. 32–41. For an overview of Giovanni's workshop and artistic practice, see Gentili, 1991; Golden, 2004; Mancuso and Gallone, 2004.
37. The two major studies of Jacopo's drawings are Eisler, 1989; Degenhart and Schmitt, 1990. In my opinion, the most consistently accurate dating for Jacopo's drawings is that by Degenhart and Schmitt, 1990, II-5: pp. 252–66. For a different dating, see Chapman, 2010.
38. Paris, Musée du Louvre, Département des Arts Graphiques, Inv. RF 1475–1556; London, British Museum, no. 1855, 0811.
39. Eisler, 1989; Humfrey, 1993, pp. 167–68.
40. Joost-Gaugier, 1974; Eisler, 1989, pp. 183–211; Fortini Brown, 1992.
41. Jacopo Bellini, *Dead Christ in Frame* (ca. 1455, Musée du Louvre, Paris, RF 1475, 3, fol. 7v; Eisler, 1989, pp. 352–53, 360, 494, pl. 219; Degenhart and Schmitt, 1990, II-6: pp. 303–10), and Jacopo Bellini, *Saint John the Baptist Standing in a Niche* (ca. 1438, Musée du Louvre, Paris, RF 1500, 37, fol. 32r; Eisler, 1989, pp. 403–14, 498; Degenhart and Schmitt, 1990, II-6: pp. 351–54). For a discussion of these works, see Humfrey, 1993, pp. 167–68.
42. Joost-Gaugier, 1975; Joost-Gaugier, 1977; Degenhart and Schmitt, 1990, II-5: pp. 59–94.
43. A documented exception to this is when, in 1441 in Venice, Jacopo apparently restored or executed the altarpiece for the high altar in the Church of San Fantin, a short walk from his workshop: Barausse, 2020, pp. 25–26, doc. 13.
44. Eisler, 1989, p. 23.
45. Jacopo's 1444 *Annunciation* for the Church of Sant'Alessandro was shipped to Brescia (Humfrey, 1994, p. 143).
46. Eisler, 1989, p. 525.
47. Most evidence documenting the age at which *garzoni* in Renaissance Venice began their apprenticeships derives from the sixteenth century. See Lazzarini, 1928–29, pp. 877–78; Favaro, 1975, pp. 57–58; Moncada, 1988, pp. 109–10; Hochmann, 2017, p. 52. Hochmann notes that the documents of Venice's *Giustizia vecchia* show that "the age of *garzoni* varies from 8 to 24 years," with the "great majority between age 10 and 15," although it is unclear when they began their apprenticeship.
48. For a brief overview of the tasks performed by apprentices in early Renaissance Italian workshops, see Cassanelli, 1998.
49. As compellingly shown by Calogero (2019), Eisler's (1985) proposed identification and partial reconstruction of the Gattamelata Altarpiece of 1460 appear to be incorrect. The whereabouts of the Gattamelata Altarpiece panels are thus unknown, and they may indeed no longer exist.
50. The unsigned partnership was written on September 24, 1440 (Barausse, 2020, p. 24, doc. 11).
51. See Chapter 2.
52. Jacopo shared the office with a certain Francesco dagli Elmi, or Elmis, a notary who drew up most of the currently known documents on Jacopo (Barausse, 2020, pp. 24–25, doc. 12).
53. Eisler, 1989, pp. 38–43, 512–13, 518.

CHAPTER 4

1. Osano (1990) and others (Fiori, 1992; Marinelli, 1996, pp. 67–69) have attributed the work to "Giovanni Bellini il Vecchio," also known as "Giovanni di Nicolò Bellini," who, I argue in Appendix B, did not exist.
2. The Ferrara *Coronation* was donated to the museum in 1977 by Natalia Valli in memory of the Contessa Alma Gulinelli (see Appendix B), restored in 1980, and first published in Bentini and Sarti, 1981.
3. There is no well-established scholarly methodology for identifying childhood paintings by Renaissance masters prior to the development of their identifiable style. A recognizable style takes time to develop, and a young artist might execute one or more works prior to its formation. A modern example is that of Salvador Dalí, whose earliest identifiable style, as seen in *The Great Masturbator* (1929), bears little resemblance to the style of his adolescent paintings. Dalí later recalled that, as a child, he thought of himself as an "impressionist painter" (Dalí, 2013, p. 86).
4. In Giovanni's Ferrara signature, the overline running from "o" to "h" is an abbreviation for the second "n". The verb "fecit" was not uncommon in signatures of the period: see Juřen, 1974; Matthew, 1998; Goffen, 2001 with further references. Beginning in the 1480s, some Italian artists instead began to sign their paintings using the Plinian "*faciebat*": see McHam, 2013, pp. 183–203 with further references.

5. Paintings executed by Renaissance masters during their childhood are extremely rare. *The Torment of Saint Anthony* in the Kimbell Museum was apparently executed by Michelangelo at age 12 or 13 (Bambach, 2017, pp. 30–36; Barry, 2017). Much has been written about Dürer's *Self-Portrait at Age 13* (1484, Albertina Museum, Vienna), which is not a painting but a silverpoint drawing on paper (Kemperdick, 2013). A painting of the Madonna and Child formerly in the Hugh Lane collection and now untraced includes a signature proclaiming that it was executed by Bartolomeo Vivarini at age 16 (Borenius, 1911, pp. 192–98), but scholars such as John Steer consider the inscription to be "almost certainly faked" (Steer, 2000, II: p. 1784). Mantegna's now-lost *Madonna and Child with Saints* (ca. 1448), formerly in the Church of Santa Sofia in Padua, apparently also bore an inscription—the authenticity of which has also been questioned—stating that the artist was 17 years old when he completed the work (Shaw and Boccia-Shaw, 1989; De Nicolò Salmazo, 1990, II: p. 534 n. 71). Parmigianino's *Baptism of Christ* (ca. 1519) and his Bardi Altarpiece (ca. 1521) were both apparently executed when the artist was younger than 18 (Ekserdjian, 2006, pp. 3–4, 22, 26, 44, 165, 192, 195, 258). Sofonisba Anguissola's birth year is uncertain, as are the birth years of many other Renaissance artists, and her earliest extant works might have been executed when she was an adolescent (Gamberini, 2016, pp. 29, 36 n. 1; Tramelli, 2016, p. 44 n. 7; Cole, 2019, pp. 2, 10).
6. Voragine, 1969, p. 457.
7. Bentini and Sarti, 1981.
8. Jacopo Bellini, *Departure for the Hunt* (ca. 1435–40, Musée du Louvre, Paris, RF 1510, 49, fol. 42v; Degenhart and Schmitt, 1990, II-6: pp. 363–67).
9. Jacopo Bellini, *Death of the Virgin* (ca. 1435–40, Musée du Louvre, Paris, RF 1495, 30, fol. 27r; Eisler, 1989, pp. 353, 367; Degenhart and Schmitt, 1990, II-6: pp. 343–44). For the Venetian balcony, see Concina, 1988, pp. 70, 91; Trincanato, 1997, pp. 30–31; Balistreri Trincanato, 2009.
10. Jacopo Bellini, *The Judgment of Solomon* (ca. 1435–40, Musée du Louvre, Paris, RF 1492, 27, fol. 24v–RF 1493, 28, fol. 25r; Degenhart and Schmitt, 1990, II-6: p. 340).
11. Jacopo Bellini, *Christ among the Doctors* (ca. 1440–45, Musée du Louvre, Paris, RF 1484, 14, fol. 16v–RF 1485, 15, fol. 17r; Degenhart and Schmitt, 1990, II-6: pp. 325–26).
12. Osano (1990, p. 11) made the same observation about Jacopo's *Madonna and Child* for the Parish Church of Legnaro, Padua. For the *Virgin and Child with Donor (Leonello d'Este?)*, see Eisler, 1989, pp. 38–43, 512–13, 518. For the Legnaro *Madonna*, see Marconi, 1955, p. 25 n. 22.
13. Christiansen, 1992b; Ceriana and Daffra, 1993.
14. See Chapter 3.
15. Bellazzecca, 2011, pp. 9–10. The attribution of the *Coronation* to Miretto is uncertain. Bellazzecca (2011, p. 10) attributes it to Stefano da Ferrara. Lucco (1989, pp. 83, 86) attributes it to an unspecified "*pittore altichieresco*." See Lucco, 1989, pp. 97–99 n. 25 for a brief summary of previous attributions. See also Flores d'Arcais, 1998, pp. 17–18.
16. Spiazzi, 2008, pp. 315–18.
17. Richards, 2000, pp. 211–16 (including further references).
18. A. Schulz, 1978; Goy, 2006, pp. 102–19. The contract for the Porta della Carta, dated November 10, 1438, was signed by both Giovanni and Bartolomeo Bon (Lorenzi, 1868, pp. 68–69, doc. 159); however, only Bartolomeo signed the work: "OP[U]S BARTOLOMEI."
19. Pope-Hennessey (1986, p. 222) argued that *Justice* was completed by 1441, but it might have been completed slightly later. See Goy, 2006, pp. 115, 280 n. 36 (including further references).
20. See also, for example, Jacopo's *Madonna and Child* at the Gallerie dell'Accademia in Venice (ca. 1450) and at the Uffizi (ca. 1450), and the *Annunciation of the Virgin* in the Church of Sant'Alessandro in Brescia (1443–44).
21. The quotation of Bembo is from his well-known letter to Marchesa Isabella d'Este of Mantua (Barausse, 2020, pp. 63–64, doc. 105): "*La invenzione, che mi scrive vostra signoria che io truovi al dissegno, bisognerà che s'accomodi alla fantasia di lui che l'ha a fare, il quale ha piacere che molto signati termini non si diano al suo stile, uso, come dice, di sempre vagare a sua voglia nelle pitture che, quanto è in lui, possano sodisfare a chi le mira.*" ("The invention, for which Your Excellency wrote me to find a design, will need to be adjusted according to the imagination of the man executing it [Bellini], who is pleased when many stipulations do not limit his brush, it being accustomed, as he says, always to wander according to his will in paintings so that, insofar as he is able, they may satisfy whoever admires them.") For a discussion of this passage, see Goffen, 2000, pp. 14–15; Fletcher, 2004, p. 31; Nagel, 2011, p. 57.
22. Gasparotto, 2017b, pp. 14–15.

23. On the Pesaro Altarpiece, see Wilson, 1977; Lucco, 2008b, pp. 190–94 (including further references).
24. Wilson, 2019.
25. See Manieri Elia, 2010, p. 66. The painting has also been attributed to Lorenzo da Venezia (ibid). "*Testes . . . ser Hercules quondam ser Iacobi de Flore pictoris de confinio Sancte Agnetis*" (Maze, 2013a, p. 817).
26. For the Correr *Crucifixion*, see Lucco, 2008b, pp. 182–84 (including further references).
27. For Raphael, see Wood, 2005, pp. 17–19.
28. By 1459, however, Giovanni was living in the nearby parish of San Lio, apart from Jacopo: Barausse, 2020, pp. 29–30, doc. 19.
29. Bambach, 2017, pp. 30–36; Barry, 2017, pp. 266–67. Although unusual in the Renaissance, artists occasionally produced works for themselves for a number of possible reasons. For instance, see S. Campbell, 2016, p. 71.
30. On signatures in Italian Renaissance art, see Matthew, 1998; Gilbert, 2000; Rubin, 2006. On Giovanni's signatures, see Pincus, 2008.
31. I thank Debra Pincus for her observations on this point.
32. For Giovanni's interest in the art of his contemporaries, see Christiansen, 2004a; Howard, 2004; Lucco, 2004; Pincus, 2004; Wilson, 2004. See also C. Campbell et al., 2018.

CHAPTER 5

1. Christiansen (1987, p. 141) suggested that the main and predella panels were sent to Brescia and reassembled there in the Church of Sant'Alessandro. Humfrey (1994, p. 143) argued that the entire polyptych, frame included, was sent in one piece to Vicenza by boat and then to Brescia. As discovered during its restoration, the main panels extend to the exact length of the predella, strongly suggesting that they were conceived as a whole and executed at the same time (Gnaccolini, 2002).
2. The friars were accompanied by a prior from San Salvador, Antonio da Vicenza (Marchese, p. 410, doc. VII; Gnaccolini, 2002, pp. 69, 82 n. 31). Andrea De Marchi (2003, p. 75) argued that the separate "payment to the masters who made the predella" was likely for a wooden base or platform to support the altarpiece and on which it was placed. Indeed, the word "predella" has multiple definitions relating to altars during the period.
3. Humfrey, 1994, pp. 144–45; Gnaccolini, 2002, pp. 67, 77 n. 9.
4. By the end of the nineteenth century, there was already a consensus among specialists that Jacopo had executed the main panels. For a detailed summary of the scholarship on the subject, see Eisler, 1989, pp. 510–12; G. Romano, 2003. For an attribution of the predella panels to Jacopo Bellini and Lorenzo da Venezia, see De Marchi, 2003.
5. Meyer zur Capellen, 1985, pp. 11–12, 140.
6. In 1457, Leonardo illustrated a manuscript for Leonardo Sanudo (Szépe, 2018, p. 88). See also Mariani Canova, 1968; Moretti, 1970; Bauer-Eberhardt, 1989; Marcon, 2001; Cattaneo, 2003.
7. Goldenberg et al., 2017, p. 48 n. 16; Moench, 1993, p. 78 n. 35. See also Sandberg-Vavalà, 1929. Another painting, the *Birth of Saint Eligius* (ca. 1397–1400), attributed to Martino da Verona, may also be based on the lost work by Altichiero (Longhi, 1958; Strehlke, 2004, pp. 237–41, fig. 42.1). A *Birth of the Virgin* (ca. 1369–1393) in the Princeton University Art Museum, attributed to Altichiero, has a similar composition, but it is doubtful that this is the original on which the Strasbourg *Birth of the Virgin* is based (Mather, 1936, 50–52).
8. In Jacopo's Paris sketchbook see, for example, *Dead Christ in Frame* (ca. 1455, Musée du Louvre, Paris, RF 1475, 3, fol. 7v), *Presentation of the Virgin in the Temple* (ca. 1445, Musée du Louvre, Paris, RF 1491, 25, fol. 23r), and *Saint John the Baptist Standing in a Niche* (ca. 1438, Musée du Louvre, Paris, RF 1500, 37, fol. 32r), among others.
9. Apparently, divine force bends the tree in Bellini's *Saint Francis* in the Frick (Rutherglen and Hale, 2015, p. 99).
10. For this strategy, see Chapter 4, p. 60.
11. For the use of light in early Italian art preceding Giovanni, see Hills, 1987.
12. Ibid., pp. 118–23.
13. Jacopo Bellini, *Death of the Virgin* (ca. 1435–40, Musée du Louvre, Paris, RF 1495, 30, fol. 27r; Eisler, 1989, pp. 353, 367; Degenhart and Schmitt, 1990, II-6: pp. 343–44).
14. Voragine, 1993, 2: p. 152.
15. Psalms 120–34 are called the Gradual Psalms or the Songs of Ascents or the Song of Steps, perhaps sung by pilgrims on the ascent to Jerusalem or by the Levite singers ascending 15 steps at the Temple in Jerusalem (Booij, 2010).
16. Jacopo Bellini, *Urban Square with Church Façade* (ca. 1440–45, Musée du Louvre, Paris, RF 1537, 86, fol. 69v; Degenhart and Schmitt, 1990, II-5: p. 85 and II-6: pp. 407–09. Degenhart and Schmitt date the drawing to 1450–55; if they are correct and I am

wrong about the date, then Giovanni presumably relied on Jacopo's *Judgment of Solomon* (1435–40) for the motifs of the staircase and *altana* (see fig. 31; see note 17 below). Both motifs also appear in the Louvre painting *Presentation of the Virgin* of ca. 1445, one of 12 *Scenes from the Life of the Virgin* attributed to Giovanni Francesco da Rimini.

17. Jacopo Bellini, *The Judgment of Solomon* (1435–40, Musée du Louvre, Paris, RF 1492, 27, fol. 24v–RF 1493, 28, fol. 25r). For the unusual staircase see, in Jacopo's London sketchbook, *Princess Taking Shelter in Castle Entry* (British Museum, London, 1855,0811.8), *Venetian Courtyard* (British Museum, London, 1855,0811.11v); *Courtyard with Sculptor at Work* (British Museum, London, 1855,0811.68v), and the *Beheading of St. John the Baptist* (British Museum, London, 1855,0811.74r).
18. Jacopo Bellini, *Presentation of the Virgin in the Temple* (early 1460s, British Museum, London, 1855, 0811.57r; Eisler, 1989, p. 292, pl. 157; Degenhart and Schmitt, 1990, II-5: pp. 39–41; Helas, 2016, pp. 55–57).
19. Schiller, 1971, I: pp. 55–56.
20. Richards, 2000, pp. 135–76.
21. Jacopo Bellini, *Stigmatization of Saint Francis* (ca. 1440–45, Musée du Louvre, Paris, RF 1532, 80, fol. 64v; Eisler, 1989, pp. 392–93, pls 255–56; Degenhart and Schmitt, 1990, II-6: pp. 399–401). Degenhart and Schmitt date the drawing to "about 1445."
22. Jacopo Bellini, *Lamentation/Entombment* (ca. 1430, Musée du Louvre, Paris, RF 1522, 68, fol. 54r; Eisler, 1989, pp. 352–53, pl. 218; Degenhart and Schmitt, 1990, II-6: pp. 381–86).
23. The legend was perhaps first described by Fra Bartolomeo da Trento in his *Liber epilogorum in gesta sanctorum* (ca. 1244–54).
24. Strehlke and Tucker, 2002; Strehlke, 2004, pp. 259–60; Joannides, 1993, pp. 414–22.
25. Jacopo Bellini, *Saint John the Baptist Preaching in a Harbor City* (ca. 1440, Musée du Louvre, Paris, RF 1477, 5, fol. 9r; Eisler, 1989, pp. 403–14). Degenhart and Schmitt (1990, II-5: pp. 134) linked this drawing to the Brescia *Miracle of the Snow* predella panel.
26. Voragine, 1993, 2: pp. 77–97.
27. For an excellent discussion of the iconography, including further references, see Field, 2003, pp. 89–90.
28. Jacopo Bellini, *The Judgment of Solomon* (ca. 1435–40, Musée du Louvre, Paris, RF 1492, 27, fol. 24v–RF 1493, 28, fol. 25r; Eisler, 1989, p. 286; Degenhart and Schmitt, 1990, II-6: p. 340).
29. Jacopo Bellini, *Death of the Virgin* (1435–40, Musée du Louvre, Paris, RF 1495, 30, fol. 27r; Eisler, 1989, pp. 353, 367; Degenhart and Schmitt, 1990, II-6: pp. 343–44).
30. See, for example, Godla and Allen, 2015.
31. See Goffen, 1995.
32. See Kristeva, 1980.
33. Christiansen, 1998; Aikema, 2003; Lucco, 2004; Gasparotto, 2017b, pp. 13–18; L. Campbell, 1981.
34. For Giovanni's use of light, especially in landscapes, see Blass-Simmen, 2015.

CHAPTER 6

1. For Leonardo Bellini, see Mariani Canova, 1968; Moretti, 1970; Bauer-Eberhardt, 1989; Marcon, 2001; Cattaneo, 2003; Szépe, 2018. For Gentile, whose first independent paintings were probably in the early 1460s, see Meyer zur Capellen, 1985, pp. 11–12, 140.
2. Steer, 1982, pp. 3–4.
3. McHam, 1994, pp. 38–39, 159 n. 72. For the argument that Antonio was born in the late 1460s, see Maek-Gérard, 1980, pp. 122–23.
4. Meyer zur Capellen, 1985, pp. 11–12, 140.
5. The hypothetical reconstruction by Eisler (1985) of the Gattamelata Altarpiece appears to be incorrect: see Calogero, 2019 (including further references). Giovanni continued to help Jacopo into the 1460s by contributing, for instance, to Jacopo's commission of four triptychs for the Church of the Scuola Grande di Santa Maria della Carità in Venice (1460–64). See also Humfrey, 1993, p. 341; Goffen and Scirè, 2000, pp. 26–35, 122–26; Christiansen, 2004a, p. 67; Lucco, 2008a, p. 37 n. 20; Maze, 2017, p. 45.
6. Fortini Brown, 1988, pp. 266–68 n. vii.
7. For Giovanni d'Alemagna and Antonio Vivarini, see Holgate, 1998; Ceriana, 2016.
8. For the *scuole grandi* as patrons of art, see Wurthmann, 1975. On Jacopo's membership and participation in the activities of the Scuola Grande di San Giovanni Evangelista, see Barausse, 2020, p. 22, doc. 7, pp. 24–25, doc. 12, pp. 28–29, docs 17–18. On Jacopo's narrative cycle for this *scuola*, see Fortini Brown, 1988, pp. 266–68 nn. vi–vii; Barausse, 2020, p. 19, docs 1–2; Hammond, 2016; Mazzotta, 2018.
9. Jacopo would later execute three *teleri* (large paintings on canvas), lost in the fire of 1485, for the Scuola Grande di San Marco (Fortini Brown, 1988, pp. 267–69 n. vii; Barausse, 2020, pp. 31–33, docs 24–26), among other commissions for the *scuole*.
10. Jacopo made a *gonfalone* (processional banner) for the Scuola Grande di Santa Maria della Carità (Barausse, 2020, pp. 26–28, docs 15–16).

11. The original four *scuole grandi* had been established in the mid-to-late thirteenth centuries as brotherhoods devoted to cleansing communal sins through pious acts of self-flagellation during public processions. They were initially called the *scuole dei battuti* (confraternities of the beaten), and only much later, by ca. 1467 (Pullan, 1981, p. 10), were they known as the *scuole grandi* (great confraternities), distinguishing them from Venice's numerous smaller confraternities, the *scuole piccole*. In Venice, by 1521, there were about 120 *scuole piccole* (Pullan, 1971, p. 34). In 1797, at the fall of the Venetian Republic, there were over 900 *scuole piccole* in the city (Gietz, 2017, p. 139). During the fourteenth century, the devotional focus of the *scuole grandi* shifted away from self-flagellation, while still maintaining traditions of frequent public processions, and toward dispensing charity to the poor, including and especially the *scuole*'s own brothers who had fallen on hard times or were in need of medical care. Thus, a *scuola grande* offered its members an enormously desirable social safety net if business ventures failed and families became impoverished, along with other welcome benefits, such as opportunities to network, perform good deeds, and have a well-attended funeral. Largely for these reasons, the popularity of the *scuole grandi* escalated. Membership numbers soon reached the limits of between five and six hundred brothers per *scuola* and sometimes more, set by the Venetian government.
12. The *scuole grandi* eventually amassed extensive holdings of local real estate, which might serve as poorhouses for the destitute, be inexpensively rented to members, or be leased for income, among other charitable and also revenue-producing uses. See Guidarelli, 2011; Guidarelli, 2017b.
13. Orlando, 2017, pp. 16–18. See also the chronological document list in Sohm, 1982, pp. 251–57, docs 1–11.
14. "*Fo dato lizenza amiser lovardian e compagni di far istoriar el nostro albergo dela schola de misser san marcho per lo mior modo li parera, ttuttj fono di questo parere*" (as first published in Wurthmann, 1975, p. 147 n. 2). Wurthmann stated that the project was left "entirely in the hands of the guardian grande," but the document names the "*lovardian e compagni*," and thus includes the officers of the governing board. For the cycle, see Humfrey, 1985, p. 137 n. 33.
15. Wurthmann, 1975, p. 143 n. 2; Fortini Brown, 1988, pp. 266–68 n. vii. It was only in July 1414 that the Scuola Grande di San Giovanni Evangelista occupied the entire building in its final location, soon after which a period of reconstruction began (Sohm, 1982, pp. 72–76).
16. Fortini Brown, 1988, p. 268.
17. As reported by Domenico Malipiero (1843–44, p. 675), "*la sera del Zuoba Santo* [March 31, 1485], *i fradeli della Scuola de S. Marco reduti in la so sala per andar a S. Antonio, se partì, e lassete impiadi i candeloti sull'altar, e el vento averse una finestra da ponente, tal che la cortina passete su i candeloti e se accese, e se brusete l'altar e 'l colmo, in modo che in quattr'hore se brusò tutta; e puoco ha mancà che no se habbia anche brusà la gesia de San Zuan Polo*." For the reconstruction of the meeting house, see Guidarelli, 2017a, pp. 46–60.
18. "*Inspiradi da inspiration divina pivi presto che humana, i nostri chari et amatissimi fradeli, messer Zentil Bellin al presente nostro dignissimo vardian da matin, etiam per nome de messer Zuane suo fradelo che al presente non ben se habet simul et semel, desiderosi et avidi de dar principio a le laudevel virtù et opere de l'arte soa de pictoria, ne i tellari deno esser fatti nel albergo de questa nostra bene[de]ta Schuola et questo sì per soa devotion et memoria, como etiam del quondam maistro Jacomo Bellin olim suo padre de le cui opere avanti l'incendio del bruxar de essa Schuola in esso albergo iaceva*" (Barausse, 2020, p. 44, doc. 53). Note that Giovanni was described as Gentile's brother, which was his communal rather than his biological identity; see Appendix A. At that time Gentile was the *scuola*'s Guardian da Matin, the third-highest administrative position, and Giovanni was also a member of the Scuola Grande di San Marco. For Gentile's and Giovanni's official positions at the *scuola* and how those positions helped them obtain the commission for decorating the Sala dell'Albergo, see Matino, 2017, pp. 118–22.
19. Fortini Brown, 1988, p. 268 n. vii.
20. In 1504, Gentile Bellini began the first work in the repainted cycle, *Saint Mark Preaching in Alexandria*, Pinacoteca Brera, Milan, 347 × 770 cm, which was completed by Giovanni Bellini after Gentile's death in 1507. On the narrative cycle for the new *albergo*, see Fortini Brown, 1988, pp. 291–95; Matino, 2017, pp. 117–33. Regarding the dimensions of the Sala dell'Albergo, Sohm (1982, p. 81) argued that the size cannot be determined; however, Fortini Brown (1988, p. 292) wrote, "The size and location of the *albergo* remained the same."
21. Fortini Brown, 1988, pp. 39–41, 261–65 n. iv; De Marchi, 1992, pp. 63–85.
22. Fortini Brown, 1988, pp. 261–65.
23. See Chapter 1.

24. On *cittadini* artistic taste, see Howard, 2013 (including further references).
25. Fortini Brown, 1988, pp. 31–32, 51–56, 272–78.
26. Thorndike, 1934, pp. 150–82; Mariani Canova, 1972, pp. 21–23; Clagett, 1976, pp. 8, 24 passim. Although lost, Fontana's treatise was mentioned in a volume published in Venice in 1544 (Mariani Canova, 1972, pp. 22–23). We can only speculate whether Fontana conceived his book as a response to Alberti's own treatise describing linear perspective (Alberti and Fontana had attended the University of Padua together in ca. 1417–18), or intended to praise Jacopo as Northern Italy's answer to Brunelleschi, the dedicatee of the Tuscan vernacular version of Alberti's text (ca. 1435).
27. "*Meministis nuper Pisanum* [Pisanello] *Venetumque* [Bellini], *optimos aevi nostri pictores, in mei* [Leonello d'Este] *vultus descriptione varie dissensisse, cum alter macilentiamcandori meo vehementioremadiecerit, alter pallidioremtamen licet non graciliorem vultum effigerent*," as transcribed in Baxandall (1963, p. 315, with an English translation on p. 314).
28. "*Quando il Pisan fra le famose imprese / sargumento cuntender cum natura / e convertir limmagine in pictura dil nuovo Illustre lionel marchexe, / Gia consumato havea il sexto mese / per dare propria forma ala figura, / alor fortuna sdegnosa che fura lumane glorie cum diverse onfexe, / Strinse che da la degna e salsa riva / se mose il Belin summo pictore, / novelo fidia al nostro ziecho mondo, / Che la sua vera effige feze viva / ala sentencia del paterno amore: / onde lui primo et poi il pisan secondo. / Quanto che gloriar te puoy, Bellino, / che quel che sente il tuo chiaro intellecto / la mano industriosa il proprio effecto / mostra di fuora gaio et pelegrino, / Sì che ad ogni altro insegni il ver camino / del divo Apelle et nobel Policleto, / che se natura t'ha facto perfecto / questa è gratia dal ciel e tuo destino / Però, se a la tua fama è degno nome, / il vulgo invidioso de onor privo / alcuna volta stimola et contende; / Habi pietà de lo suo grave some / e prendi omai questo exempio vivo / che qualche nebia il sol talor ofende*," as transcribed in Eisler (1989, p. 531, with an English translation on p. 512).
29. Maze, 2013b, pp. 124–28 (including further references).
30. Use of trecento models during the quattrocento was hardly novel. Both Donatello and Mantegna apparently adapted trecento models to create modern versions of narrative histories. Donatello's patrons probably indicated two sources as models for the Santo altar's narrative reliefs: the trecento fresco cycle by Stefano da Ferrara in the same church and a series of miniatures by Cristoforo Cortese in a manuscript recounting the legend of St. Anthony. Similarly, the executors of the Ovetari Chapel must have referred their commissioned artists to trecento fresco cycles; see McHam, 1994, p. 13 nn. 82–84, 91–94 (including further references).
31. In Florence, Jacopo might have had the opportunity to study works executed in linear perspective by Masaccio, such as his *Trinity* (ca. 1425–27, the Church of Santa Maria Novella) and *Tribute Money* (ca. 1425–27, Brancacci chapel), among others (Edgerton, 2009, pp. 77–116; Joannides, 1993, pp. 125–51, 174–83). In Siena, Jacopo might have seen Donatello's *Feast of Herod* (1424–27, Cathedral of Siena), which was executed in linear perspective (Edgerton, 2009, pp. 90–93).
32. Jacopo Bellini, *An Architectural Setting with the Presentation of Our Lady* (ca. 1435–40, Musée du Louvre, Paris, RF 1496, 31, fol. 28r); Maze, 2013b, pp. 127–31.
33. Degenhart and Schmidt, 1990, II-5: p. 39: "*Diese ist durch zehn Blätter getrennt von der reifen Lösung des anderen, das Geschehen ins Innere des 'Temples' verlegenden Typus des 'Tempelgang' (London fol. 68, Abb. 4b), die in ihrer Verdichtung auf Wesentliches eine Abkehr von der Willkür perpektivischer Experimente der Frühzeit bedeutete (Paris fol. 23, 28, Abb. 2–3).*"
34. Alberti, 1972, p. 54 n. 19: "*Huiusque ipsius hominis longitudinem in tres partes divido, quae quidem mihi partes sunt proportionales cum ea munsura quam vulgus brachium nuncupat. Nam ea trium brachiorum, ut ex symmetria membrorum hominis patet, admodum communis humani corporis longitudo est*" (English translation, p. 55 n. 19). Degenhart and Schmitt (1984, pp. 13–15) observed that Jacopo developed his drawings in the 1430s from traditional iconographies in which smaller-scale Gothic forms were often disjointedly placed within an "excessive . . . *spatial perspective*," whose recession was unsystematically divided by eye, and later moved toward compositions of creatively interpreted subjects that featured "Renaissance-like large-scale forms" harmoniously situated within a systemized perspectival space approaching that described by Alberti. Degenhart and Schmitt (ibid., p. 13) also argued that Jacopo's initial interest in individual antique forms led to the creation of entire compositions reflecting the "spirit of antiquity," of which only drawings and no paintings exist.
35. On Jacopo's stay in Ferrara, see Chapter 2; on Alberti's, see Grafton, 2002, pp. 189–224.

36. According to Grafton (ibid., p. 215), the artists of the Ferrarese court "had become familiar with Alberti's book." See also Rothlisberger, 1958–59, pp. 72–73; Mariani Canova, 1972, p. 14; Edgerton, 1966, pp. 375–76; Osano, 1981, pp. 11–12 n. 9; Eisler, 1989, pp. 46, 194, 443–52.
37. Jacopo Bellini, *Urban Square with Church Façade* (ca. 1440–45, Musée du Louvre, Paris, RF 1537, 86, fol. 69v; Degenhart and Schmitt, 1990, II-5: p. 85 and II-6: pp. 407–09). Jacopo's drawing *Presentation of the Virgin in the Temple* (ca. 1445, Musée du Louvre, Paris, RF 1491, 25, fol. 23r) depicts an imposing church in which a priest stands at the high altar, but Jacopo has positioned the priest's head lower than the heads of the figures in the middle ground—a perspectival impossibility, given the rising staircase and position of the viewer.
38. Fortini Brown, 1988, pp. 258–66.

CHAPTER 7

1. Gasparotto, 2017c, pp. 58–63; Vowles, 2018.
2. Humfrey (2004c) speculated that the patron might have been a humanist.
3. Christiansen, 2013. See also Rosand, 1972; Rogers, 1992; Holberton, 1999; S. Campbell, 2010.
4. Degenhart and Schmitt, 1990, II-5: pp. 135–42. Fiocco (1920, p. 228–29) interpreted the partial inscription "*. . . chobo . . . ro de la . . . pela de San Marco*" as indicating Jacopo Bellini's authorship, but cf. Hartt, 1959, p. 236.
5. Muraro, 1961. For a summary of the attributions, see Rossi Scarpa, 1997, pp. 233–34 n. 21; Rearick, 2002.
6. Sanudo, 1999, pp. 651–52; Rossi Scarpa, 1997, p. 223 (including further references).
7. My opinion is that the Bellini workshop was probably responsible for the design of the mosaics on the right wall, with Jacopo and Giovanni designing the *Visitation*, and Jacopo and his future son-in-law, Mantegna, designing the *Death of the Virgin*, where Mantegna is likely responsible for the two figures of Peter and Paul on the left and God the Father above, evidently inspired by Nicolò Pizzolo's *God the Father* (1449) in the Church of the Eremitani, Padua, and well known to Mantegna. For Pizzolo's *God the Father*, see Shaw, 1994, p. 233; Spiazzi, Toniolo, and Zanuso, 2006. Eisler (1989, pp. 54–55) earlier suggested that Jacopo and Mantegna might have worked together. See also Thode, 1898; Fiocco, 1959, pp. 103–20; Hartt, 1959; Muraro, 1961; Merkel, 1973; Rossi Scarpa, 1991; Rearick, 2002; B. Brown, 2007, p. 102 n. 64.
8. In this case, the mosaicist might have been Matteo Tibaldi (Rearick, 2002, p. 344).
9. Jacopo Bellini, *Flagellation of Christ* (ca. 1440–45, Musée du Louvre, Paris, RF 1483, 11, fol. 15r).
10. For framing architecture, see Jacopo Bellini, Paris sketchbook, fols 8r, 9r, 25r, and 35r. For barrel vaults, see ibid., fols 27r, 52r, 70r.
11. See, for instance, Marco Zoppo's *Saint Jerome in the Desert* (ca. 1450–45, mixed media on panel, 39 × 29 cm, Museo Nacional Thyssen-Bornemisza, Madrid).
12. See Chapter 4, n. 21.
13. Fortini Brown, 1988, pp. 266–68 n. vii.
14. Barausse, 2008, p. 334, doc. 15. Jacopo had already been elected *degano* in 1441.
15. Longhi (1978, pp. 48–49) argued for Giovanni's contribution to the Galleria Sabauda paintings. For their possible dating, see Mazzotta, 2018.
16. This last observation was made by Mazzotta (2018, p. 286), who ascribed all nine paintings to Giovanni Bellini while acknowledging that he did not examine firsthand the five works in the U.K., which are in a private collection.
17. See Hammond, 2016. Two of the works were recently sold by Christie's (Sale 17147, Old Masters, New York, May 1, 2019, LOT27, Formerly property of Stanley Moss, New York). I would attribute neither these two works nor the five paintings in the U.K. to Giovanni, although Giovanni seems to have contributed elements of the background landscape and perhaps other motifs to some of these seven works. Presumably, Gentile Bellini also made contributions. All nine paintings are quite damaged, although the U.K. group was recently restored. Note that after examining each of the nine works in person, I have revised the opinion expressed in Maze, 2017, p. 41.
18. Rebenich, 2002, pp. 1–60.
19. See Kaftal, 1952, pp. 477–506.
20. Calvalca, 2009, 2:4: p. 39; Rice, 1985, p. 23.
21. Voragine, 1993, 2: p. 213. See the letter in Wright, 1933, pp. 66–67.
22. Rice, 1985, p. 39.
23. Voragine, 1993, 2: pp. 213–14.
24. Ibid., p. 211. The etymology is fanciful.
25. Schiller, 1971, 1: pp. 78–79.
26. Dunkerton and Spring, 2018, p. 9, fig. 6.
27. Jacopo Bellini, *Saint Jerome Reading in the Wilderness* (ca. 1445, Musée du Louvre, Paris, RF 1486, 17, fol.18v; Eisler, 1989, pp. 159, 347, 369, 403; Degenhart and Schmitt, 1990, II-6: pp. 327–28).
28. Kleinbub, 2015.

29. Lightbown, 1986, pp. 394–96; Shaw, 1994, pp. 152, 238–39. Scholars have pointed to the similarity between the rock formations (e.g., Humfrey, 2004c, including further references). Previously, I shared my insights on the close compositional similarities between Giovanni's and Mantegna's paintings with Davide Gasparotto (2017c, p. 62).
30. Degenhart and Schmitt, 1990, II-6: p. 458: "*Noch nicht hat Mantegnas Einfluss auf den jungen Giovanni Bellini hier seinen Niederschlag gefunden*" (trans. mine). Robertson (1968, p. 16) held a similar opinion.
31. For the relationship between Mantegna and Giovanni Bellini, see the essays in C. Campbell et al., 2018 (including further references).
32. For the various dates that scholars ascribe to the Birmingham *Saint Jerome*, see Lucco, 2008b, pp. 136–38.
33. Crowe and Cavalcaselle, 1871, 1: p. 140 n. 1; see also Levi, 1988, p. 66. For the drawing, see Jacopo Bellini, *Seven Lions and Three Stags* (ca. 1450, Musée du Louvre, Paris, RF 1540, 91, fol. 72v; Eisler, 1989, 79; Degenhart and Schmitt, 1990, II-6: pp. 413–15). Degenhart and Schmitt date the drawing to 1450–55.
34. Jacopo Bellini, *Saint Jerome in the Wilderness* (ca. 1440, Musée du Louvre, Paris, RF 1490, 24, fol. 22v; Eisler, 1989, pp. 396, 403; Degenhart and Schmitt, 1990, II-6: p. 337).
35. The signature was first accepted as Giovanni's autograph by Crowe and Cavalcaselle (1871, 1: p. 140), and as "likely . . . original" by Herbert Lank in his conservation report dated October 13, 1973. I thank Robert Wenley and Debra Pincus for making this report and a condition report available to me. The signature has been rejected by Debra Pincus (2008, p. 114 n. 17), along with the "pseudo-cartellino," as "a botched attempt to look old" (personal correspondence, March 1, 2016).
36. My thanks to Marco Albertario for making a photographic detail of the Tadini signature available to me on May 4, 2016. I shared my insights concerning the Tadini signature with Gasparotto, who later published the signature comparison in Gasparotto, 2017c.
37. Pincus, 2008, pp. 89–119.

CONCLUSION

1. See, for example, Battisti, 1980; Fleming, 1982; Coltellacci, 1991; Gentili, 2004; Hills, 2004; Di Vito, 2015; Rutherglen and Hale, 2015; Gasparotto, 2017b; Belting, 2017.
2. Christiansen, 2004b, pp. 13, 20.
3. On the artistic relationship between Giovanni Bellini and Sebastiano del Piombo in the Church of San Giovanni Crisostomo, Venice, for example, see Luca, 2000 (including further references).
4. Cennini, 1933, pp. 14–15. For the Italian, see Cennini, 2004, p. 80; Cennini, 2015, p. 47. Cennini's text was dedicated to Saint Anthony of Padua and employed a number of Venetian terms. In the sixteenth century, Dürer would likewise advise the aspiring artist to "copy much of the work of good artists until he attains a free hand" (see Porras, 2013, pp. 66–67, 71 n. 59).
5. Milanesi and Milanesi, 1859, p. IX: "*finito libro, referamus gratias Xpo. 1437. A dì 31 di luglio ex Stincarum.*" The scholars argue that "*il libro fu finito di copiare nel 31 luglio del 1437, da un ignoto che tacque il suo nome, e che era sostenuto (per debiti civili) nelle Carceri delle Stinche di Firenze*" (Milanesi and Milanesi, 1859, p. X).
6. ASVe, ANT, Francesco Elmis, b. 361, carta sciolta, doc. 2: "*laboreria de zessio, de marmore et de relevijs.*"
7. See Maze, 2013b, pp. 168–72, for a full discussion. For the organ doors, Gentile's borrowings include the tear-duct eyes, contoured jowls, and half-open mouth of Jerome's lion, which was inspired by Jacopo's Paris sketchbook fol. 59v; see Degenhart and Schmitt, 1990, II-6: p. 393. The dramatic perspective of Gentile's barrel vaults, resting on pillars, coffered five rows deep, and drawn with a vanishing point under the picture plane was inspired directly from Mantegna's famous barrel vault in his *Saint James Led to Martyrdom* in the Eremitani. For the organ door shutters, see Bisson, 2012, pp. 51–57.
8. For evidence that Giovanni kept sketchbooks, see Christiansen, 2004b, pp. 13, 53 n. 11.
9. Jacopo Bellini, *Saint John the Baptist Standing in a Niche* (ca. 1438, Musée du Louvre, Paris, RF 1500, 37, fol. 32r); Eisler, 1989, pp. 403–14, 498; Degenhart and Schmitt, 1990, II-6: pp. 351–52.
10. Maze, 2013b, pp. 12–34.
11. This observation is from Humfrey, 1993, pp. 167–68.
12. Jacopo Bellini, *The Adoration of the Magi* (ca. 1435–40, Musée du Louvre, Paris, RF 1499, 36, fol. 31r).
13. Ibid., pp. 131–32. The fresco is part of a cycle in the Oratorio di San Giorgio, Padua (see Richards, 2000, pp. 177–211; Baggio, Colalucci, and Bartoletti, 1999).
14. King, 1994, pp. 61, 110, 287 (including further references). According to King, Jean Cossa received the manuscript on René's behalf.
15. For instance, see Meiss, 1957; Vowles and Korbacher, 2018 (including further references).

16. Robertson, 1960, p. 47; Bellosi, 2008, pp. 103–4. Also see Conti, 1994, pp. 262–68; De Marchi, 2018, pp. 33–34.
17. Ziliotto 1950, 78:28, 164:269; Fletcher, 1991, pp. 153–57; Pontone, 2014.
18. Humfrey, 2004c (including further references).
19. Jacopo Bellini, *King David Conquering Goliath* (ca. 1450, Musée du Louvre, Paris, RF 1544, 96, fol. 76v; Degenhart and Schmitt (1990, II-6: pp. 417–18) date the drawing to "about 1455," but there is no question that it served as a model for *Saint Maurice* (1452–53).
20. Jacopo Bellini, *Warriors Combat a Dragon* (ca. 1430, Musée du Louvre, Paris, RF 1517, 60, fol. 49r); Jacopo Bellini, *Galloping Horseman and Warrior on Foot* (ca. 1440, Musée du Louvre, Paris, RF 1552, 106, fol. 84r).
21. One can also observe the stark differences between Maurice's face and those of any of Jacopo's soldiers in any of his drawings. See Bellosi, 2008, pp. 103–04.
22. Robertson, 1960, p. 47.
23. Aikema and Brown, 1999a, pp. 202–07.
24. Lucco and Pontani, 1997.
25. Jacopo Bellini, *Crucifixion with the Virgin and Saint John* (ca. 1435–40, Musée du Louvre, Paris, RF 1523, 69, fol. 55r; Robertson, 1968, pp. 31–32).
26. For instance, see Jacopo Bellini's Paris sketchbook, fols 18, 34, and 37 (Degenhart and Schmitt, 1990, II-7, pls 17, 41, 44).
27. Degenhart and Schmitt, 1990, II-7, pls 44, 51, 87, 96. Lucco (2008b, p. 182) suggests that Giovanni's trio of soldiers might have been inspired by folio 15r in Marco Zoppo's album in the British Museum, executed after 1465. Zoppo's drawing, however, seems to postdate Giovanni's motif. For the dating of Zoppo's album, see Chapman, 1998, pp. 64–67, cat. 15.
28. Giovanni's use of this motif was noticed by Lucco (2008b, p. 182) and Weston (2009, p. 65). The motif was later used by Giovanni in his École des Beaux-Arts, Paris, drawing (ca. 1475) and Bristol painting (ca. 1475) of *The Descent into Limbo* (Ekserdjian, 1992, pp. 261–63 [here attributed to Mantegna]; pp. 267–68). For a compelling discussion, see Weston (2009, pp. 63–71), who argues that Lucco's proposed chronology for the works is untenable.
29. For instance, see Jacopo Bellini's Paris sketchbook, fols 21, 54, and 64v (Degenhart and Schmitt, II-7, pls 22, 70, 82). For a consideration of the Netherlandish influence on Giovanni's work, see Lucco, 2004, pp. 75–94.
30. Aikema and Brown, 1999a, pp. 202–07; Lucco, 2004, p. 78 (including further references).
31. Bomford, Roy, and Smith, 1986, p. 41. For a reconstruction, see Koch, 1988, pp. 509–16. For the polyptych's Venetian provenance, see Humfrey, 1993, pp. 159–60; L. Campbell, 1998, pp. 42–44; Aikema and Brown, 1999b, pp. 177–78 n. 11.
32. I previously shared my argument that Giovanni used Bouts's *Crucifixion* as an important model with Gasparotto (2017c, pp. 68–69). Scholars continue to debate over the reconstruction of the polyptych and whether Bouts's *Crucifixion* formed its central image. See Koch, 1988, pp. 512–16; L. Campbell, 1998, pp. 42–44; Wolfthal and Metzger, 2014, pp. 46–55, 76–82 (including further references).
33. Christiansen (2004a, pp. 56, 283 n. 16) argued that the fissures in the rocky plateau, along with the figure of Christ, derived from the predella panel of the Crucifixion from Mantegna's 1457–59 San Zeno Altarpiece in Verona. However, this does not appear to have been the case: Mantegna's fissured plateau is more likely an elaboration of the crevices in Giovanni's *Crucifixion*. Thus, Giovanni's *Crucifixion* seems to predate the San Zeno Altarpiece.
34. Christiansen (2004a, p. 56) observed that Bouts's *Entombment* (ca. 1450s, National Gallery, London), which apparently formed the top right wing of the polyptych, depicts a river (or perhaps a road) meandering to the horizon, and trees much like those represented in Giovanni's painting. For the influence of the proposed altarpiece on Giovanni's work, see Lucco, 1997; Gasparotto, 2017b.
35. For Giovanni's use of oils, see Whitehouse, 2012, pp. 22–26; Rutherglen and Hale, 2015, p. 196 n. 7. For Giorgione and Titian inspiring Giovanni, see Anderson, 2006, pp. 172–75; Ferino-Pagden, 2006, pp. 219–23, cat. 41; McHam, 2008.
36. See Chapter 4, note 32.
37. Space prevents a full examination here, but works in question include, for example, a paliotto, now dispersed, that is sometimes attributed to Giovanni Bellini's earliest years (see Cavanna, 2003; Tempestini, 2003; Longhi, 1978, pl. 45 (attributed to Antonio Vivarini); Volpe, 1978; Pallucchini, 1959, pp. 13–14, 127, pl. 6). The paliotto originally comprised 23 panels: a central scene of the Nativity with Saints Claire and Nicholas (now in Museo Amedeo Lia, La Spezia); 16 scenes from the Passion of Christ; 4 scenes depicting saints; and 2 scenes, one of the angel Gabriel and the other of the Virgin Annunciate, that together depict the Annunciation. Vincenzo Buonocore (2011a; 2011b) cited primary

source evidence to argue that the paliotto was executed by the Vivarini workshop. I fact-checked this evidence: at the Archivio Patriarcale di Venezia, the pastoral visits to Santa Chiara di Murano do describe an altar dedicated to San Nicolò, with an altarpiece made of wood and having images of San Nicolò, but no pastoral visits state that the altarpiece was executed by a painter named Antonio or by the Vivarini, and it is unclear whether the paliotto is the altarpiece mentioned. Also, Buonocore (2011a, p. 92 n. 25) cited "Le cose, 1707, p. 236," but no such text exists; and he cited *Il ritratto, overo le cose più notabili di Venezia* from 1705, but it does not include any reference to the Vivarini. After checking all of Buonocore's supporting citations and corresponding with Buonocore on February 28, 2017, to clarify them, I still could not locate any evidence linking the paliotto to the Vivarini workshop. In my view, the paliotto is almost certainly a product of the Bellini workshop. Whether its authorship should be ascribed to Giovanni, however, is an open question. One problem with attributing the work to Giovanni in the 1440s is that the paliotto's scene of *Saint Francis* (now in the Accademia) appears to be based directly on Jacopo Bellini's drawing of *Saint Francis* in the London sketchbook, folio 42r, which dates to the late 1450s. If the paliotto dates to ca. 1460, then it cannot be by Giovanni. It also does not suggest the style of Gentile Bellini. The remaining candidates are Leonardo Bellini, the miniaturist, and Leonello Bellini, about whom little is known. I thank Anna Cavanna for our discussions about the paliotto and for accompanying me to visit four of its panels in a private collection in Florence.

38. For Mantegna's year of birth as possibly being before 1431, see Shaw and Boccia, 2016.
39. For instance, a painting of Saint Jerome in São Paulo, attributed to Mantegna, appears to be a direct response to Giovanni's Birmingham *Saint Jerome*: it is set not during the day but at dusk, with an oil lamp lit within the cave, and Giovanni's hare at the bottom of the composition turns into an owl crowning the São Paulo *Saint Jerome*. In this case, Giovanni's composition seems to have been the point of departure, including the aperture in the outcropping, a device Giovanni probably invented. Cf. Vowles, 2018.

APPENDIX A

1. Agosti, 1993, p. 52, n. 29.
2. On February 25, 1453, Francesco of Lorenzo received on behalf of Jacopo Bellini 20 ducats toward Nicolosia Bellini's dowry in her marriage to Andrea Mantegna (ASVe, SGSGE, vol. 72, fol. 199r; Barausse, 2020, pp. 28–29, doc. 17).
3. Maze, 2013a.
4. Sanudo, 1879–1903, 23: p. 256 (November 29, 1516): "*Se intese, questa matina esser morto Zuan Belin optimo pytor, havia anni . . . .*"
5. Vasari, 1966–87, 3: p. 441.
6. Paoletti, 1894, pp. 5–6.
7. The will is dated February 6, 1428 [m.v.], which is February 6, 1429 on the Gregorian calendar: ASVe, ANT, Enrico Salomon, b. 946/c, doc. 313; Barausse, 2020, pp. 20–21, doc. 4: " . . . *sed gravida et propinquans partui volo hoc meum esse ultimum testa[me]ntum.*" Since Anna provided for her unborn child and for no other sons or daughters, it is understood that she did not yet have children.
8. Fry, 1899, p. 12. Anna Rinversi's will (ASVe, ANT, Francesco Elmis, b. 361, doc. 163, fol. 65v,) is transcribed in Barausse, 2020, pp. 36–37, doc. 35.
9. Fiocco, 1949.
10. Ibid.: "*La nascita del pittore doveva quindi cadere intorno al 1425, e certamente prima del 1429, quando la moglie di Jacopo era già gravida del primo figlio Gentile.*"
11. Longhi, 1949, pp. 277–78.
12. This shift may have begun with Lucco, 1990, pp. 410–13.
13. For instance, Lucco (2008a, p. 21) situated Giovanni's birth in 1438/40 and Humfrey (2004b, p. 6) situated it in 1435/38.
14. See, for instance, Christiansen (2004a, p. 53), who placed Giovanni's birth in ca. 1435 or later. For Mantegna's birth year as possibly being earlier than 1431, see Shaw and Boccia, 2016.
15. "Saint Jerome in the Wilderness," The Barber Institute of Fine Arts, accessed June 12, 2020, https://barber.org.uk/giovanni-bellini-about-1430-1516, which is in agreement with Lucco (2008b, pp. 136–38: "*una data in qualche modo ancorata al 1459*"), but in my opinion this is roughly ten years too late.
16. "Giovanni Bellini," The National Gallery, London, accessed June 12, 2020, www.nationalgallery.org.uk/artists/giovanni-bellini.
17. "Giovanni Bellini," National Gallery of Art, Washington, DC, accessed June 12, 2020, www.nga.gov/collection/artist-info.936.html.
18. For Gentile's portrait and trip to Istanbul, see Chong, 2005.

19. Foresti, 1503, Liber XVI, p. 427. In 1503, Foresti retitled his book to *Novissime hystoriarum omnium repercussiones . . . Mcccccii*. According to Worthen (2015), Foresti published four variant texts on the Bellini family, each version corrected and updated from the previous one, with some of the new information possibly supplied by Gentile Bellini himself. Later editions of the 1503 version were printed in 1506, 1513, and 1535 (Worthen, 2015, p. 48).
20. Vasari, 1966–87, 3: p. 435: *"Onde egli vi lavorò molte storie in compagnia di Gentile, più di lui giovane."* Ibid., 3: p. 436: *"Onde considerando il Senato che per essere Giovanni in età che male poteva sopportare disagi – senzaché non volevano privare di tant'uomo la loro città, avendo egli massimamente allora le mani nella già detta sala del Gran Consiglio –, si risolverono di mandarvi Gentile suo fratello, considerato ch'e' farebbe il medesimo che Giovanni."* Here, of course, Vasari was mistaken, because Giovanni had not yet commenced work in the Great Council Hall.
21. Ibid., p. 435: *"Finalmente, vicino già alla età di anni LXXX, passò all'altra vita; e da Giovanni suo fratello gli fu dato onorato sepolcro in San Giovanni e Paulo l'anno MDI."* The original manuscripts for both editions of Vasari's *Lives* no longer exist, and so it is unknown whether Vasari might have initially written the correct year of 1507 for Gentile's death, although the error was not corrected in the second version.
22. Ridolfi, 1648, 1: p. 39.
23. Vasari, 1832–38, p. 361 n. 1: *"Dei due Fratelli, Gentile era il maggiore, essendo egli nato nel 1421, e Giovanni nel 1426."*
24. Sanudo, 1879–1903, 6: p. 552 (February 23, 1507): *"ozi fo sepulto a San Zane Polo Zentil Belin, optimo pytor."*
25. Moschini, 1834, p. 23: *"Giovanni Bellini nacque in Venezia l'anno 1426,"* and p. 38: *"[C]osì, se vero fosse ch'egli compiesse la vita nell'anno ottantesimo di sua età, ne sarebbe nato l'anno 1427, e il suo fratello Giovanni ne sarebbe stato egli il primogenito".*
26. For a transcription, see Morelli, 1800, pp. 98–99 n. 7. There are two manuscript copies of Negri's *Peri Archon*: one in Vatican City (Biblioteca Apostolica Vaticana, Vatic. Lat. 4033, fol. 86: Gentile *maior natu*), and the other in Venice (Biblioteca Nazionale Marciana, ms. Lat VI 6 (=2753), fol. 109r: Gentile *maior natu*). Pattini (2013) notes that the former, dedicated to Doge Agostino Barbarigo, dates to ca. 1493–94 (see also Agosti, 1993, p. 52 n. 29; Agosti, 2009, p. 97 n. 37), and that the latter, dedicated to Doge Leonardo Loredan, dates to ca. 1510–12. When assessing Negri's testimony, it should be borne in mind that contemporary Renaissance accounts were often inaccurate. For example, the Venetian Franciscan friar Francesco Suriano (1450–1529: Suriano, 1900, p. 95; Chong, 2005, pp. 107, 111, 133 n. 32, including further references) wrote that Giovanni Bellini, rather than Gentile, had been sent by the Signoria to the Ottoman court and that Giovanni himself had told the friar about his trip after returning to Venice. Fra Bartolomeo da Foligno likewise reported in ca. 1482, approximately two years after Gentile had returned from Constantinople, that it had been Giovanni who had undertaken the journey (see Suriano, 1900, p. 95 n. A; Chong, 2005, p. 133 n. 32). In a book published in Rome in ca. 1507, Raffaele Maffei also misstated that it was Giovanni who had visited the Ottoman court (see Agosti, 2009, pp. 15, 55–56 n. 18).
27. Crowe and Cavalcaselle, 1871, p. 117 n. 1.
28. Cessi, 1938, 4:24: 201: p. 139: *"Dic legittimos, qui nati sunt de legittimo matrimonio et parentibus liberis, sed de aliis filiis nichil cavetur in statuto Veneciarum."* On this question, see Lucco, 2008a, pp. 21–23; Christiansen, 2004a, pp. 52–54; Fletcher, 2004, p. 25; Humfrey, 2004b, pp. 5–6; Lucco, 1990, pp. 411–13; Meyer zur Capellen, 1985, p. 10; Fiocco, 1949; Longhi, 1949, pp. 277–78; Paoletti, 1929, p. 70; Fry 1899, p. 12, among others.
29. Regarding Giovanni, residing in San Lio in 1459, see ASVe, ANT, Giuseppe Moisis, b. 727, doc. 32, fols 1v–2v, no. 32; Barausse, 2020, pp. 29–30, doc. 19. For arguments in favor of Giovanni's illegitimacy based on this document, see, for instance, Lucco, 2008a, pp. 20–21.
30. Robertson, 1968, p. 11; Goffen, 1989, pp. 3–4.
31. Robertson, 1968, p. 11.
32. Maze, 2013a.
33. Lightbown, 1986, pp. 15–29; Shaw and Boccia, 2016.
34. Vasari, 1966–87, 3: p. 441.
35. ASVe, CIN, Vittore Pomino, b. 149, reg. "Protocollum mei Victoris Pomino Notarii de 1439," fol. 55v; Maze, 2013a, pp. 817–18.
36. Paoletti, 1929, p. 68. For the document's generally accepted interpretation see, for instance, Eisler, 1989, p. 33.
37. See, for instance, Tempestini, 2019, pp. 26–27 (including further references).
38. ASVe, CIN, Vittore Pomino, b. 149, reg. "Protocollum mei Victoris Pomino Notarii de 1439," fol. 55v; Maze, 2013a, pp. 817–18: *"Licet divisio que sit inter fratres et cetera."* Connell (1988, p. 45) also considers the document an example of a *carta divisionis*.

Other *divisiones* in Pomino's register begin similarly. In a copy of the Bellini *divisio* made by the same notary, Pomino, and located in a different register within the same *busta* (folder), the "*et cetera*" received full standard expression: ASVe, CIN, Vittore Pomino, b. 149, reg. 1439–44, fol. 11r–v; this is cited in Barausse, 2020, p. 24, but unpublished.

39. Cessi, 1938, 3:4: pp. 124–25: "*Chapter concerning the fraternal partnership. 4.* We decree that, once the father is dead, the brothers remain in a fraternal partnership . . . unless they themselves make a division. However, if a father or any ancestor has bequeathed to a son or any descendent some specific thing, it will not be included in the fraternal partnership" (*Capitulum de fraterna compagnia. IIII. Volumus quod, mortuo patre, fratres maneant in fraterna compagnia . . . nisi et ipsi divisionem fecerint. Sed si pater vel aliquis de ascendentibus aliqua specialiter dimiserit filio vel alicui de inferioribus, illud non erit in fraterna compagnia*). The members of a fraternal partnership communally shared not only the inheritance of their father's (or grandfather's) estate, but also all other property not specifically omitted from the partnership: Cessi, 1938, 3:4: p. 124 n. 19. Here Venetian law differed from Roman law, which required that brothers, after their father died, enter voluntarily into a contract: Cessi, 1938, 3:4: p. 124 n. 20. For the fourteenth-century law eliminating the date of expiration of *fraterne compagnie*, see Griphio, 1606, 6:9: pp. 90–91.

40. Lane, 1944, pp. 178–80.

41. Jacoby, 2006, pp. 199–200 passim.

42. Cessi, 1938, 3:5–6: pp. 125–26: "*On dividing estates between brothers. 5.* We decree that, although it has hitherto been customary in Venice that the older brother divided the father's estate and that the younger brother or brothers received shares assigned by the older brother, henceforth we decree that, when dividing their father's estate, all brothers are equal. *For those who have an undivided estate and one of them desires to divide it and know his share. 6.* We decree that, if several persons together own an undivided estate, and they are all present in Venice, and any one of them who has been in Venice desires to divide this estate and know his share, then he should call the other or others who also have a share in this estate and announce to the other or others that he wishes to divide the estate; and by this act they should divide this estate among themselves: but if they refuse or have been unable to agree among themselves, the judges must divide this estate and cast lots" (*De possessionibus dividendis inter fratres. V. Decernimus quod, cum hactenus sit Veneciis consuetum quod maior frater possessionem patris dividebat et minor sive minores fratres partes a maiori fratre disignatas accipiebant, de cetero volumus quod omnes fratres in dividendis paternis possessionibus sint equales, et sic de omnibus habentibus possessiones comunes undecumque. Pro illis, qui possessionem indivisam habuerint, et aliquis eorum eam dividere voluerit et cognoscere partem suam. VI. Dicimus quod, si plures fuerint, qui possessionem indivisam habuerint, et fuerint omnes presentes in Veneciis, et aliquis illorum, qui fuerit Veneciis, voluerit dividere possessionem ipsam et cognoscere partem suam, debeat vocare eum vel omnes illos, qui habent partem in ipsa possessione, et denunciare ei vel eis quod possessionem ipsam velit dividere, et hoc facto debeant inter se possessionem illam dividere: quod si facere recusaverint vel non potuerint concordare inter se, iudices debeant possessionem ipsam dividere et sortes ponere).* For the standard form of a *divisio*, with examples, see Connell, 1988, pp. 45–46.

43. ASVe, CIN, Francesco Elmis, b. 74, reg. XX, fol. 216r; Barausse, 2020, p. 24, doc. 11.

44. The notary Francesco Elmis left a block of space directly after Jacopo and Donato's partnership contract, presumably for the names of the witnesses, which were never entered. The other acts in the same register offer no such space, and most were witnessed.

45. Connell (1988, p. 50) interprets the two documents in the same way. Supporting this view is a marginal note inscribed by the notary on a copy of the *divisio*: Pomino wrote that a duplicate of the *divisio* had been made for Jacopo (*exemplata una carta pro ser Jacobo*). The copy was presumably drawn up for Bragadin and the other notary, Francesco Elmis, to serve as proof of Jacopo's legal independence. For the copy of the 1440 *divisio*, see ASVe, CIN, Vittore Pomino, b. 149, reg. 1439–44, fols 11r–v; it is cited in Barausse (2020, p. 24), but unpublished.

46. See any *divisio* from ASVe, *Cancelleria inferiore, Miscellanea, notai diversi*, bb. 32–33.

47. ASVe, CIN, Vittore Pomino, b. 149, reg. 1439–1444, fols 3v–4r.

48. Maze, 2013a, pp. 817–18.

49. The unspecific text of the Bellini *divisio* can also be compared with the detailed terms separating the painters Ludovico and Francesco, sons of Mantegna, in their *divisio* of January 27, 1507 (see Signorini, 1996, p. 105 n. 20).

50. Cessi, 1938, 2:1: p. 102: "Since nobody is considered

able to act in contracts or judgments unless he or she is of legal age, we decree that it is suitable to define something about the age of mind. Therefore, we state that any person, either male or female, after he or she has turned 12, should be considered of proper age" (*Quoniam nullus idoneus intelligitur in iudiciis vel contractibus, nisi legittimam etatem compleverit, optimum esse decrevimus de mentis etate aliquid diffinire. Ideoque sanctimus quod quicumque, sive masculus sive femina fuerit, post XII annos completos etatem congruam habere censeantur*). The age of 12 derived from Lombard, rather than Roman, law; see Crescenzi, 1997, pp. 413–14. For age 14, see Cessi, 1938, 2:2: p. 103; and Griphio, 1606, 6:24:98: ". . . and nobody male shall be able to cease his guardianship unless he is 14 years of age" (. . . *quod nemo masculus deinceps de tutoria possit exire, nisi 14. annum excesserit aetatis suae*). This is the law that Peter Humfrey (1984, p. 4) cites, following Botteon and Aliprandi, 1893, pp. 30–31, to determine the birth year of the artist Giovanni Battista Cima: "The earliest record of Giambattista's existence dates from 1473, when his name is first mentioned in his father's tax returns. This signifies that he must have attained the majority age of 14 in the same year, and his birth-date can accordingly be fixed at 1459 (or possibly 1460)."

51. ASVe, CIN, Tommaso de Tomei, b. 212, 23 luglio 1429; Maze, 2013a, pp. 819–20.
52. In Roman legal practice, "[b]y the terms of civil law all illegitimate children were *sui iuris*—that is, not subject to *patria potestas*, which could issue only from marriage, or from judicial acts such as adoption and legitimation" (Kuehn, 2002, p. 34). In Renaissance Venice, however, adoption did not confer *patria potestas* to the adoptive father (Cessi, 1938, 4:24: p. 201 n. 139). See Maze, 2013a, pp. 789–90. Also see Novellus, 1564, "Index F": "*Fratres emancipati non sunt in fraterna compagnia*" (Emancipated brothers are not in fraternal partnerships).
53. ASVe, ANT, Lorenzo Buscarino, b. 545, fols 10r–v, doc. 63; Barausse, 2020, pp. 19–20, doc. 3.
54. Tiepolo's law of book 4, rubric 35 (Cessi, 1938, 4:35: p. 213) is titled "No one can disinherit his or her son" (*Nemo potest disheredare filium suum. XXXV*). Disinheritance was rare and predicated on the child committing at least one of 14 grave transgressions, such as plotting against the life of his or her parents, as enumerated in Cessi (1938, 4:35: p. 214 n. 207). Kuehn (2002, pp. 20–21) describes the disinheritance of legitimate sons under medieval law: "Yet the *pater* was not free to act with regard to *dos* and *patrimonium* . . . . He was bound by social expectations, intestacy rules, rights of legitim, and fideicommissary stipulations handed down from preceding generations. Only with the greatest difficulty could he disinherit a child, if he so chose."
55. On the legal obligations of Venetian notaries, see Cassandro, 1936, pp. 112–44; Pedani Fabris, 1996, pp. 3–16, 101–03. In Venice, "for the disinheritance to be valid, a legitimate reason must be included in the testament" (Kirshner, 2000, p. 135). Kuehn (2002, p. 26) notes that, according to medieval law, a legitimate son could be disinherited only by an included statement of cause in a father's testament: "like any direct heir (*suus heres*), he had to be expressly disinherited." Numerous jurists have commented on the legal difficulties of disinheriting a legitimate son; see Kirshner, 2000.
56. ASVe, CIN, Tommaso de Tomei, b. 212, 23 luglio 1429; Maze, 2013a, pp. 819–20: "*Jacobus Belino pictor filius quondam ser Nicoleti Belino de confinio Sancti Geminiani.*" Jacopo was married sometime before February 6, 1429, the date of Anna's will, in which she was described as Jacopo's wife and pregnant: ASVe, ANT, Enrico Salomon, b. 946/c, doc. 313; Barausse, 2020, pp. 20–21, doc. 4. Jacopo's *carta securitatis* of July 23, 1429, was drawn up several months later, which was not unusual; see Guzzetti, 2002, pp. 444–45.
57. ASVe, CIN, Vittore Pomino, b. 149, reg. "Protocollum mei Victoris Pomino notarii de 1439," fol. 55v; Maze, 2013a, pp. 817–18: "*Iohannes Belino et Iacobus Belino fratres ac filii quondam ser Nicolai de confinio Sancti Iuminiani.*" Both Giovanni and Jacopo resided in the parish of San Geminiano, for otherwise the parish of each would have been specified. Jacopo had been living in San Geminano at least since Anna's February 6, 1429, will; see ASVe, ANT, Enrico Salomon, b. 946/c, doc. 313; Barausse, 2020, pp. 20–21, doc. 4: "I, Anna, wife of Jacopo Bellini, painter in the parish of San Geminiano." Nicoletto and Franceschina lived in San Salvador; see ASVe, ANT, Lorenzo Buscarino, b. 545, fol. 10r–v; Barausse, 2020, pp. 19–20, doc. 3: "*Nicoletus Belin batistagno de confinio Sancti Salvatoris.*" According to Chojnacki (2000, p. 100), "most widows remained in their marital residence for many years"; but see also Guzzetti (2002, pp. 441, 461), who notes that only widows who swore not to remarry could remain in the homes of their deceased husbands. Franceschina and/or Nicoletto might also have died of the plague: in October 1427, Filelfo described plague-ridden

Venice as nearly deserted of patricians; see Robin, 1991, pp. 12–13, 22. Also see Maze, 2013a, pp. 794–95 for additional support for Franceschina's death having occurred during or soon after Giovanni's birth.

58. Maze, 2013a, p. 801.
59. Tiepolo's book 2 statutes delineating guardianships were applicable to Jacopo and Giovanni's circumstance. It is possible but doubtful that Franceschina, rather than Jacopo, became Giovanni's guardian upon Nicoletto's death: see Bellavitis, 2008, pp. 81–85. For brief discussions of adoption in Renaissance Venice, see D. Romano, 1996a, pp. 99–101; Bellavitis, 2008, pp. 42–44.
60. Cessi, 1938, 4:24: p. 201 n. 139.
61. Ibid., 4:8: pp. 184–86. Although the earnings of an unemancipated son were the property of his father, many jurists allowed general exceptions to be made, and unemancipated sons were often allowed to keep payment for their labor; see Kuehn, 1982, p. 20.
62. Sons might remain unemancipated for the majority of their lives, and, as stated in the *Glossa ordinaria*, a man in his sixties could still very well be under the authority of his father: "*etiam sexagenarius . . . in potestate est*"; see Kuehn, 1982, p. 177 n. 8.
63. Ibid., p. 12.
64. ASVe, ANT, Giuseppe Moisis, b. 727, doc. 32, fols 1v–2v; Barausse, 2020, pp. 29–30, doc. 19.
65. Lucco (2008a, p. 21) hypothesized that Giovanni was living in San Lio in 1459 with his biological mother. Fletcher (2004, p. 25) speculated that Giovanni was illegitimate, which "must have precipitated his departure from home." Both Goffen (1989, p. 262) and Robertson (1968, pp. 11–12) view Giovanni's living in San Lio, apart from Jacopo, as suggesting that he was already married by 1459.
66. Such a document is not housed where one might expect to find it, in ASVe, *Cancelleria inferiore, Miscellanea, notai diversi*, bb. 32–33. However, the absence of a document from the Venetian archives should not be used as negative proof of its existence. It should be mentioned that Gentile, perhaps while painting the organ doors for the Basilica of San Marco in Venice, lived for a period of time in 1464 in an apartment in the Procuratie Vecchie, adjacent to the church and in his home parish of San Geminiano; see ASVe, ANT, Niccolò [de] Avanzo, b. 46, doc. 116, February 29, 1463 [m.v.], which is published in Ludwig, 1911, p. 89. It is unlikely that the procuratorial apartment was either Jacopo's or Gentile's permanent place of residence. Cf. Bätschmann, 2008, p. 19; Fletcher, 2004, p. 15, perhaps from an ambitious reading by J. Schulz, 1982, p. 91, who relies on the aforementioned testament of February 29, 1463 [m.v.] witnessed by Gentile for his conclusions.
67. Connell, 1988, p. 39: "Sons who remained in business with their fathers were unlikely to be emancipated from them."
68. Lucco (2008a, p. 30) interpreted the omission of Giovanni from Anna's will as evidence that he was not Anna's son, and thus illegitimate; Humfrey (2004b, p. 5) did not believe the omission proves illegitimacy; Eisler (1989, p. 532) wrote that his "name is omitted for either his illegitimacy, or the unlikely possibility of his being the issue of an earlier, unknown marriage of Jacopo's"; and Goffen (1989, p. 3) described his absence merely as a "sin of omission" that did not necessarily mean that he was not her son.
69. According to a contract dated August 23, 1443, some 12 years earlier, in 1431, Jacopo Bellini had taken his nephew Leonardo (born ca. 1424) into his home and raised him (ASVe, CIN, Francesco Elmis, bb. 74–75, reg. XXIII, fol. 20r; Barausse, 2020, p. 26, doc. 14). Unlike Giovanni, however, Leonardo was neither described nor known as Jacopo's son, presumably for several reasons, including the fact that Leonardo's mother, Elena, Jacopo's sister, was alive in 1443 when Leonardo reached adulthood (see Bellini Family Tree). Jacopo's wife, Anna, was not unusual in omitting affines from her will; Chojnacki (2000, p. 298 n. 40) notes in a study of 50 married Venetian women's wills from 1305–1450 that only 5.6 percent of the 215 total bequests to relatives went to affines. The percentage would likely have been even lower in widows' wills. Anna also did not mention her daughter, Nicolosia, in her will. Had Anna died intestate, Nicolosia, although married, would have been entitled to an equal share of her mother's property. Emancipated and unemancipated sons also succeeded to their intestate mothers' property (Cessi, 1938, 4:27: pp. 207–08, including glosses). Thus, Mantegna's wife, Nicolosia, had probably died prior to Anna's November 25, 1471, will and after or during the birth of her son Ludovico in ca. 1470 (Signorini, 1996, p. 103 n. 3). Regarding Nicolosia, see Iotta, 2006; Lightbown, 1986, pp. 244, 248.
70. ASVe, ANT, Giuseppe Moisis, b. 727, doc. 32, fols 1v–2v; Barausse, 2020, pp. 29–30, doc. 19: "*ser Iohannes filius magistri Iacobi Bellini Sancti Leonis*." In the 1459 testament, Giovanni's name and that of his co-witness were crossed off and replaced with the

names of two other witnesses; Barausse (2020, p. 29) plausibly proposes that Giovanni had testified to a first version of the will drawn up on January 30, 1459, and that several clauses were subsequently added on April 2, 1459, thus requiring the document to be witnessed a second time by attestors who were not the original two.

71. The 1485 *securitatis carta* (ASVe, ANT, Lorenzo Stella, b. 877, protocollo, fol. 28; Barausse, 2020, p. 42, doc. 47): *"Ioannes Bellino quondam domini Iacobi."* The 1487 contract (Barausse, 2020, p. 42, doc. 48): *"Iohanne Bellino pictore quondam domini Iacobi."* Although the altarpiece signature is lost, it was recorded in 1590 by Fra Valerio Polidoro (see Callegari, 1997, p. 30): *"Iacobi Bellini Veneti Patris, ac Gentilis, & Ioannis Natorum opus. MCCCCIX."* Gentile Bellini's will of 1507 (ASVe, ANT, Bernardo Cavagnis, b. 271, doc. 307; Barausse, 2020, pp. 67–68, doc. 111): *"Iohannes frater meus carissimus."*
72. When Gentile Bellini was buried on February 23, 1507, Sanudo (1879–1903, 6: p. 552) wrote, "He is survived by his brother Giovanni Bellini" (*è restato il fratello, Zuan Belim*). When Giovanni died, Sanudo (1879–1903, 23: p. 256) referred to "Gentile Bellini his brother" (*Zentil Belin suo fradelo*), and on two other occasions, Sanudo (1980, pp. 34, 146) referred to Gentile and Giovanni as *fratelli* (brothers).
73. For an example of an adopted son who is identified as being a son in legal documents, see the Bellini *divisio* itself (ASVe, CIN, Vittore Pomino, b. 149, reg. "Protocollum mei Victoris Pomino Notarii de 1439," fol. 55v; Maze, 2013a, p. 818), witnessed by Ercole, the adopted son of the artist Jacobello del Fiore: "ser Ercole, son of the deceased ser Jacobello del Fiore, painter of the parish of Sant'Agnese" (*ser Hercules quondam ser Iacobi de Flore pictoris de confinio Sancte Agnetis*). See also Fogolari (1944, pp. 49–50): *"Herculi filio magistri Jacobelli de Flore"*; but he is identified as adopted in Jacobello's will, in Mas-Latrie (1869, p. 199): *"Herculi filio meo adoptivo."*
74. The bibliography on Renaissance communal and civic identity is large; for instance, see Martin, 2004, pp. 1–20, 161–76. Examples of altering one's own name in Renaissance Venice are numerous, even among painters, and include Girolamo Dente, who was attached to Titian's workshop and called himself Girolamo di Tiziano, although he was not Titian's son. For Girolamo di Tiziano, see Tagliaferro et al., 2009, pp. 102–06.
75. Paolo's last name, Remarius, appears in Nicoletto Bellini's will (April 11, 1424): *"Paulum Remarium generum meum"* (ASVe, ANT, Lorenzo Buscarino, b. 545, doc. 63, fol. 10; transcriptions in Barausse, 2020, pp. 19–20, doc. 3). "Remarius," or *remèr* in Venetian, meant oar maker (*"colui che fa i remi"*; Boerio, 1998, p. 563; Paoletti, 1929, p. 69; Moretti, 1958, p. 63 n. 1; Mariani Canova, 1969, p. 103), and it is unclear whether "Remarius" was Paolo's surname or merely a description of his profession. Leonardo signed a document dated September 7, 1469, as *"ser lunardo bellino quondam ser pauli de Venetiis"* (Paoletti, 1929, p. 69), thus using both his father's Christian name and his uncle's surname.
76. Paoletti, 1894, pp. 19–20. For Vittore Belliniano, see Rearick, 1998 (including the bibliography).
77. See note 73 above.
78. ASVe, ANT, Francesco Elmis, b. 361, reg. "Testamentorum," doc. 163, fol. 65v; Barausse, 2020, pp. 36–37, doc. 35.
79. See note 71 above.
80. See note 71 above.
81. It is also possible that the notary took it upon himself, in rendering Gentile's last wishes into the legal language of a testament, to append to Giovanni's name "my dearest brother," a not uncommon formulaic apposition in Renaissance Venetian wills (see Chojnacki, 2000, p. 162).
82. D. Brown and Pizzati, 2014 (the document is transcribed on p. 152). In Samaritana's will, Giovanni Bellini is described as Samaritana's *"nipote,"* meaning nephew or grandson. Since she was too old to have been his grandmother, and since her maiden name was not Bellini but Vendramin, she was almost certainly his maternal aunt. For a similar opinion, see D. Brown and Pizzati, 2014, p. 151 n. 36, but the authors' suggestion that Giovanni was either illegitimate or the son of Jacopo from an earlier marriage appears to be incorrect.
83. Maze, 2017, p. 40.
84. D. Brown and Pizzati (2014, p. 152 n. 43) arrived at a similar conclusion about Samaritana (also personal correspondence with Pizzati).
85. ASVe, ANT, Nicolò Moravio, b. 677, doc. 897; transcribed in Brown and Pizzati, 2014, p. 152: *"Ioannem Bellinum . . . qui me semper eque ac matrem et amore et beneficiis prosecutus est."* See also Appendix B. Note that Samaritana's wishes were rendered into legal language by the notary, making the interpretation of her intent more problematic.
86. This information on Giobbe (Iopo) Dominici's death was provided by Paula Clarke, who is researching the merchant, in email correspondence on May 25,

2020. For his son Giovanni Dominici's death, see Orvieto, 1969, p. 229 n. 4. I thank Paula Clarke for the reference and for sharing her research.

87. D. Brown and Pizzati, 2014, p. 152.
88. In his study of Venetian patrician wills, Chojnacki (2000, p. 141) concluded that "in the fourteenth and fifteenth centuries, the preferred nuptial age for patrician girls was 13 to 15." See also Chojnacki, 2000, pp. 186–93, 314–15 n. 15. Ruggiero (1985, p. 13) stated that "in Venice females seem to have married earlier than in Florence, usually shortly after they reached puberty. Marriages are reported for 11- and 12-year-olds, but the norm appears to have been 13 and 14."
89. Beltrami, 1954, p. 92 passim. On the significant numbers of centenarians in seventeenth- and eighteenth-century Venice, see Bamji, 2018, pp. 5–6 passim.
90. ASVe, ANT, Lorenzo Dalla Torre, b. 1062, n. 12 [unpublished]; I thank Paula Clarke for this reference.
91. Maze, 2017, p. 54 n. 56.
92. Rutherglen and Hale (2015, p. 81) were among the first to mention the new genealogy.
93. Wilson, 2015.
94. Bayer, 2017.
95. Gentili, 2017, p. 108: *"Intanto anagraficamente, perché è morto a novant'anni—come sapeva già Vasari, seguito dai vecchi maestri del secolo scorso e invece contraddetto dai maestrini più recenti, che per lui hanno inventato date di nascita sempre più avanzate. La questione è stata definitivamente chiarita da uno studio esemplare, su basi rigorosamente documentarie, pubblicato ormai tre anni fa da Daniel Wallace Maze e tenacemente ignorato, per davvero o per finta, soprattutto tra gli italiani. Tanto più per questo sarà opportuno che io lo riassuma, in estrema sintesi, per la parte specificamente biografica."*
96. Ibid.
97. Pincus, 2019: "Entering into the assessment of their early relationship is the much-debated question of Giovanni's birth date, opened up again by Daniel Wallace Maze (*Renaissance Quarterly* 66, no. 3, Fall 2013); Maze makes a persuasive case for Giovanni and Jacopo being sons of the same father but different mothers, and he places Giovanni Bellini's birth date between 1424 and 1428. This would put Mantegna, considered to have been born around 1431, almost a contemporary of Bellini. (Maze's new dating proposal is not addressed in the exhibition.)"
98. D. Brown, 2019, p. 34 n. 19. See also Vowles and Korbacher, 2018, p. 270 n. 1.
99. Blass-Simmen and Weppelmann, 2017. Vinco (2014, p. 102 n. 21) stated that he believed that there was a separate individual who was Jacopo's brother and an artist himself.
100. Brown and Pizzati, 2014, p. 152.
101. Villa, 2017, p. 86 n. 21.
102. Vinco, 2019, p. 61 n. 2.
103. Tempestini (2019) also discussed the new research at length, largely to argue that "Giovanni il Vecchio" was a real person with a corpus of works. On this point, see Appendix B. Lucco (2020, pp. 276–79) also hypothesized both the existence of an artist named "Giovanni di Nicolò Bellini" who was different from Giovanni Bellini, and that Samaritana Vendramin was significantly older than her nephew, Giovanni Bellini, who therefore must have been born not in ca. 1425 but towards 1440. Both hypotheses appear to be incorrect and are discussed above and in Appendix B.
104. Grave, 2018, pp. 46–47.
105. See Callegari, 1997, p. 30.
106. *Oxford Latin Dictionary* 1976, V:1160, s.v. "natus": "A son."
107. *Metamorphoses*, 15.819: *"tu facies natusque suus, qui nominis heres."* In this passage, Jupiter tells Venus that she will deify Caesar with help from Caesar's son, who is Augustus. For this topic, see Wheeler, 2000, p. 142.
108. In email correspondence on June 23, 2020, Stanley Chojnacki wrote: "As for the quote, I agree with your surmise that 'natorum' is basically a fancy way of saying 'filiorum.'"

APPENDIX B

1. Tempestini, 2019, pp. 25–26.
2. Varanini, 1990, p. 5 n. 2; Biblioteca Civica Tartarotti di Rovereto, *Archivio storico comunale di Rovereto*, Ms. 75. 6 (29), fol. 3r: *"Magister Ioannes Petrus Belinus pictor filius ser Stefani de Venetiis."*
3. Varanini, 1990, p. 7: *"il patronimico impedisce di collegare questo Giovanni Pietro Bellini alla ben nota dinastia di artisti veneziani."* See also Varanini, 1990, p. 7 n. 1.
4. ASMo, *Camera Ducale, Mandamenti in volume*, reg. 4, 1436–38, fol. 61v.
5. Ludwig, 1911, p. 87.
6. Tassini, 1888, 1: p. 142; Ludwig, 1911, p. 88; Paoletti, 1929, p. 67; Meyer zur Capellen, 1980, p. 108 and n. 31.
7. *Annali della Fabbrica del Duomo di Milano*, 1880, pp. 255, 275, 277–78, 283–84 passim; Boito, 1889, p. 248; Gronau, 1909; Bora, 1976, p. 65 n. 3; Repishti, 2004, p. 108 n. 14. Also see Lanciani (1903, p. 223), who, quoting a letter by Pirro Ligorio to Fulvio

Orsini, wrote of a Giovanni Bellini who may not have been the famous artist (Billanovich, 1973, p. 370).

8. Paoletti, 1894, p. 19; Ludwig, 1911, p. 88.
9. Cecchetti, 1887b, p. 204. Billanovich (1973, p. 370) believed that this Giovanni Bellini was the one from Modena. See also Tempestini, 2019, p. 29.
10. Guarini, 1621, p. 78: "*Si seppellirono per un tempo in questa Chiesa li Bellini, tra' quali vi fù quel Giovanni Bellino celebratissimo Pittore, che meritò per il molto suo valore, di essere mentovato dal . . . . poeta Lodovico Areosti, nel trentesimoterzo Canto del suo Poema, mentre dice. E quei, che furo a' nostri dì, ò son'hora, / Leandro, Andrea Mantegna, Gioan Bellino.*"
11. Gallo, 1963; Renosto, 1963.
12. Guarini, 1621, p. 359: "*Seppellivansi anche in questa chiesa i Codi uno de' quali che fù Benedetto, riuscì Pittore eccellentissimo, e fù alievo di Giovanni Bellino Ferrarese, da me descritto nella chiesa di San Nicolò, hò detto Ferrarese a distinzione di Giovanni Bellino Viniziano.*"
13. Vasari, 1966–87, 3: p. 441: "*Stette con esso [Giovanni] lui ancora, sebben non fece molto frutto, Benedetto Coda da Ferrara, che abitò in Arimini, dove fece molte pitture.*"
14. See Scaglietti Kelescian, 1982, pp. 556–57, who disagreed with earlier writers such as Guarini and Baruffaldi who "*sostengono che [Benedetto Coda] fosse di origine ferrarese giungendo a supporre l'esistenza di un Giovanni Bellini Ferrarese.*"
15. Baruffaldi, 1844, p. 162: "*Marco Antonio Guarino, scrittore ferrarese . . . annovera fra i pittori ferraresi un altro Giovanni, pure Bellino, e ad esso lui attribuisce quella lode che dall'Ariosto vien data con tanta giustizia ad uno di simil nome nel suo Furioso. . . . Io trovo in non pochi autori venire appropriati a lode di Bellino veneziano, come si può chiaramente vedere nel Borghini, nel Vasari, nel Ridolfi, e soprattutto nel Fornari.*"
16. Ibid., pp. 162–63: "*Dalla scuola del Bellino ferrarese (del quale io non darò verun conto, per non trovarne menzione, e piuttosto dirò avere il Guarini avere equivocato).*"
17. Borsetti, 1735, 2: p. 432: "*JOANNES BELLINI Ferrariensis, Pictor celebris, quem à Veneto alterum, & Benedicti Codi Praeceptorem fuisse afferit Marcus Ant. Guarini, Chiese di Ferrara, lib. 5, fol. 359.*"
18. Cittadella, 1782, 1: p. 71: "*Gian Bellini Ferrarese. Viveva nel 1450. Un Gian Bellini ancora tra Pittori Ferraresi si annovera diverso dal Veneto famosissimo Dipintore, e ce lo fa avvertire il nostro Istorico delle Chiese di Ferrara Marc. Antonio Guarini lib. 5 fol. 359. . . . Ma siccome di Lui non si ha più di questa, per altro autorevole, notizia, così non abbiam luogo a parlarne più oltre.*"
19. Ibid., 1: p. 72: "*Benedetto Codi. Viveva circa il 1460 . . . e trovo che studiasse, non già, siccome disse il nostro Guarini, da Gian Bellini Ferrarese, ma dal Veneto celebre Gian Bellini.*"
20. Ughi, 1804, 1: p. 38: "*Marc'Antonio Guarini . . . ricorda certo Gian Bellini pittore antico, e diverso dal famoso Bellini Veneziano: fu Precettore, dic'egli, di Benedetto Codi, e viveva circa il 1450.*"
21. Ibid., 1: p. 131: "*Secondo l'opinione di Cittadella . . . egli fu allievo di Giambellino il Veneto e secondo quella di Marc'Antonio Guarini egli fu scolaro d'un altro Giambellini Ferrarese, pittore, dic'egli, di que' tempi. Dal non essere mai stato conosciuto quest'ultimo nè da qualche altro Scrittore, nè da alcun suo quadro, che per sua memoria ci abbia lasciato convien dedurre, che Benedetto Codi riuscito un pittore di gran merito, e di gran riputazione avesse appresa l'arte da Gio. Bellini Veneziano famoso pittore di quel tempo, che unitamente a Gentile suo Fratello dipinsero gli eccellenti quadri, che sono nella Sala del Consiglio a Venezia.*"
22. Zani, 1820, 3: p. 315: "*Ecco un altro Gio: Bellini affatto curioso, che io fo conoscere più per apparire fedele storico che altro. D. Marcantonio Guarini nelle Chiese di Ferrara, date alla stampa nel 1621, parlando egli di quella di S. Nicolò «Si seppellirono per un tempo in questa Chiesa li Bellini, tra' quali vi fù quel Giovanni Bellino celebratissimo Pittore, che meritò per il molto suo valore, di essere mentovato dal . . . . poeta Lodovico Areosti, nel trentesimoterzo Canto del suo Poema, mentre dice. E quei, che furo a' nostri dì, ò son'hora, / Leandro, Andrea Mantegna, Gioan Bellino». Indi parlando della Chiesa di San Vitale, segue a dire che «Benedetto Codi riuscì Pittore eccellentissimo, e fù alievo di Giovanni Bellino Ferrarese, da me descritto nella chiesa di San Nicolò, hò detto Ferrarese a distinzione di Gio: Bellino Viniziano». Il Borsetti e il Cittadella fanno eco al Guarini; ed il Frisi, per non entrare in brighe, non parla né del Bellini Ferrarese né del Veneziano. Questa notizia è, come ho detto da principio, affatto curiosa. Vorrei pur io farvi sopra qualche riflessione, ma trovandomi completamente privo dei documenti necessarii per ben riuscirvi, taciuti, non so dire il perché, dai primi tre accennati Scrittori.*"
23. For instance, neither Billanovich (1973), nor Osano (1990), nor Tempestini (2019) mention Zani.
24. Becherucci, 1938: "*Benedetto Coda . . . altri [documents] ancora, dal 1512 al 1524, lo dicono invece di Ferrara, e ferrarese lo suppone il Baruffaldi, che per accettare la notizia vasariana inventa un Giovanni Bellini ferrarese suo ipotetico maestro.*"
25. Scaglietti Kelescian, 1979, p. 74: "*I quali incorrono in una serie di equivoci di schietto carattere campanilistico, come ad esempio l'inventare un Giovanni Bellini ferrarese, che sarebbe stato maestro del Coda, o il farlo morire a Ferrara,*

dove sarebbe stato sepolto nella chiesa di S. Vitale, nel 1520."

26. Maze, 2013a, pp. 817–18, doc. 1.
27. Paoletti, 1929, p. 68.
28. Billanovich, 1973, p. 359.
29. Ibid.
30. See, for instance, Tempestini, 2019, pp. 26–27.
31. Billanovich, 1973, p. 359. The document was first published by Bertoni, 1921, p. 101 n. 2.
32. Billanovich, 1973, p. 359. On this document, see Venturi, 1884, pp. 604–05.
33. Ibid., pp. 361–62. Billanovich noted that his transcription came from a manuscript copy of what he called the *Diario di Asola* located in the Biblioteca del Seminario di Mantova (see Billanovich 1973, p. 362 n. 1). A printed copy of the book, titled *Diario per quest'anno MDCCXC ad uso della città e diocesi di Asola*, is located in the Biblioteca Queriniana di Brescia. It reads: "*La Cattendrale-Abbaziale sotto li gloriosi titoli di M.V. Assunta al Cielo, e di S. Andrea Apostolo, Chiesa di maestosa antica Architettura, e decorata di molte Tavole, e Pitture singolari, delli Moretto, Romanino, Lattanzio Gambara, Zambellin Vecchio, Palma ec*" (pp. 58–59).
34. Billanovich (1973, p. 362) wrote: "*Si potrebbe quindi, tutt'al più, aggiungere alla conoscenza ancora molto lacunosa dell'attività di Giovanni di Nicolò Bellini questa sua presenza vicino al confine del territorio veneto. Però, benchè si abbia solo un accenno tanto vago, non si può escludere a priori che la pala di Asola, in cui i critici scorgono echi delle scuole padovana, muranese e ferrarese, sia dovuta al fratello di Iacopo. Appaiono anche ovvi i ricordi stilistici ferraresi, sia volendo identificare il pittore nel Giovanni Bellini del documento edito dal Bertoni, sia ammettendo che Marcantonio Guarini ed il Diario asolano alludano ad una sola persona.*"
35. Pacchioni, 1914, p. 403: "*La tradizione asolana, raccolta anche dal vecchio Diario della città e diocesi di Asola, vuole che il dipinto sia dono della Repubblica veneta e ne ascrive la paternità a Zambellin vecchio, l'artista che, insieme al Mantegna, nella tradizione ha, come un eroe mitico, assorbito in sè ogni personalità artistica secondaria del quattrocento veneziano.*"
36. Besutti, 1915, p. 125; Longhi, 1995, p. 385; Voltini, 1958, p. 9; Garini et al., 2015, p. 30.
37. Sansovino, 1581, "*Tavola Quarta*": "*Iacopo Palma Vecchio Pittore*" and "*Iacopo Palma giovane.*" See also Sansovino, 1581, VI:97: "*Iacopo Palma il vecchio.*"
38. These subsequent scholars include Osano (1990, p. 13), Fiori (1992, p. 41), Cordellier (1995, pp. 97–98, doc. 38), Franco (1996, p. 16 n. 23), Marinelli (1996, p. 68), and Tempestini (2019, p. 26).
39. Bentini and Sarti, 1981.
40. Osano, 1990, pp. 14–16.
41. Fiori, 1992, p. 41: "*Lo studioso [Osano] mette in connessione una serie di documenti relativi ad un Giovanni Bellini fratello di Jacopo . . . che attestano la presenza a Ferrara tra il 1440 e il 1460 di un Giovanni Bellini pittore 'ferrarese', la sua morte e la sua sepoltura nella chiesa di San Nicolò a Ferrara (Guarini, 1621; Billanovich, 1973).*"
42. Medica, 2004.
43. Ibid.
44. Medica, 2012, p. 222: "*nel documento del 1436 non si fa alcuna menzione della professione specifica del personaggio citato a Ferrara, da dove del resto non è affatto certo, come invece fino ad ora si è supposto, provenga fin dall'origine la tavola in questione.*"
45. Ibid., p. 225: "*con quel 'Magister Iohannes de Venetiis pictor' ricordato da alcuni documenti bolognesi tra il 1459–60.*" The documents were partially published in Filippini and Zucchi, 1968, p. 77: "*1459. – Magister Iohannes de Venetiis pictor è padrino in un atto battesimale. 1460. – Idem. (schede Fillipini). A.B. – Libri battesimali, ad ann[um].*"
46. Guerzi, 2014, p. 36: "*seppur riconoscendo l'indiscutibile labilità di alcuni fronti della ricerca . . . ma anche, d'altro canto, come non sia affatto ancora scontata la possibilità di sovrapporre questo con quel «Zohan Bellino» documentato in ambito estense da un documento del 2 ottobre 1436.*" Ibid., p. 37 n. 22: "*i documenti ferraresi tacciono relativamente al patronimico, fatto che evidentemente impedisce di verificare fino in fondo la tenuta dell'ipotesi di Billanovich.*"
47. Tempestini, 2019, p. 26: "*La storia dell'arte ha identificato Giovanni di Nicolò Bellini con un pittore documentato a Ferrara.*" Ibid., p. 27: "*È probabile che Giovanni di Nicolo Bellini si sia trasferito nella città Estense dopo la divisione dei beni fatta a Venezia con il fratello Jacopo nel 1440 e che sia il Giovanni Bellini morto a Ferrara nel 1460 e ivi sepolto nella chiesa di San Nicolo.*"
48. Ibid., p. 26: "*a Ferrara, dove esegue e firma una Incoronazione di Maria oggi conservata nella locale Pinacoteca Nazionale.*" Cf. Guerzi, 2014, p. 36: "*Medica ha infatti rilevato come . . . non esistono a oggi prove per legare ab origine alla città di Ferrara la tavola con l'Incoronazione della Vergine della Pinacoteca Nazionale di Ferrara.*"
49. Medica, 2012, p. 222; Guerzi, 2014, pp. 36–37.
50. Tempestini, 2019, p. 27: "*Sembra però che Giovanni non avesse tagliato tutti i ponti con Venezia, se si deve identificare con il Giovanni fu Nicolò testimone il 29 aprile 1457 in un atto notarile nella citta lagunare*" (document first published by Cecchetti, 1887a, p. 64).

Bibliography

ARCHIVAL SOURCES

APVe, *Parrocchia di Santissimo Salvatore di Venezia, Registri dei battesimi*, b.1.

ASFi, *Diplomatico Normali Camera Fiscale*, 1424.11.28.

ASFi, *Provvisioni*, 115 (serie registri).

ASMn, *Archivio Gonzaga, Autografi*, b. 7.

ASMo, *Camera Ducale, Mandamenti in volume*, reg. 4, 1436–38.

ASVe, ANT, Bernardo Cavagnis, b. 271.

ASVe, ANT, Francesco Elmis, b. 361.

ASVe, ANT, Giuseppe Moisis, b. 727.

ASVe, ANT, Lorenzo Buscarino, b. 545.

ASVe, ANT, Lorenzo Stella, b. 877.

ASVe, ANT, Niccolò [de] Avanzo, b. 46, no. 116.

ASVe, ANT, Nicolò Moravio, b. 677, no. 897.

ASVe, ANT, Enrico Salomon, b. 946/c, no. 313.

ASVe, ANT, Lorenzo Dalla Torre, b. 1062, no. 12.

ASVe, *Cancelleria inferiore, Miscellanea, notai diversi*, bb. 32–33.

ASVe, CIN, Francesco Elmis, bb. 74–75.

ASVe, CIN, Vittore Pomino, b. 149, reg. "Protocollum mei Victoris Pomino notarii de 1439".

ASVe, CIN, Tommaso de Tomei, b. 212.

ASVe, *Deliberazioni Miste 1411–1415*, Reg. 49.

ASVe, SGSGE, vol. 72.

ASVe, SGSM, b. 41.

ASVe, SGSMM, b. A., reg. 2 (LXXVI/11).

ASVe, SGSMM, b. 11.

ASVe, *Scuole piccole e suffragi*, b. 406 (Mariegola della Scuola di S. Maria e di S. Cristoforo dei Mercanti alla Madonna dell'Orto).

Biblioteca Civica Tartarotti di Rovereto, *Archivio storico comunale di Rovereto*, Ms. 75. 6 (29).

MANUSCRIPT SOURCES

Tassini, Giuseppe, 1888, *Cittadini veneziani*, Venice, Biblioteca del Museo Correr, ms. P.D. c. 4 1/5.

PRINTED PRIMARY AND SECONDARY SOURCES

Agosti, Giovanni, 1993, "Su Mantegna, 1. (All'ingresso della mostra del 1992, a Londra)," *Prospettiva*, 71, pp. 42–52.

——, 2009, *Un amore di Giovanni Bellini* (Milan: Officina Libraria).

Aikema, Bernard, 1999, "12. Giovanni Bellini. *The Crucifixion*," "10. Collaborator or Follower of Jan van Eyck. *The Crucifixion*," in Bernard Aikema and Beverly Louise Brown (eds), *Renaissance Venice and the North: Crosscurrents in the Time of Bellini, Dürer, and Titian*, exh. cat. (New York: Rizzoli; London: Thames and Hudson), pp. 202–03, 206–07.

——, 2000, "La Cappella d'oro di San Zaccaria: Arte, religione e politica nella Venezia del doge Foscari," *Arte veneta*, 57, pp. 23–41.

——, 2003, "I crocifissi di Giovanni Bellini. Genesi e significato di un tema pittorico nel Quattrocento fra Nord e Sud," in Fernando Rigon (ed.), *Bellini e Vicenza: Capolavori che ritornano*, exh. cat. (Cittadella: Biblos), pp. 39–43.

—— and Beverly Louise Brown (eds), 1999a, *Renaissance Venice and the North: Crosscurrents in the Time of Bellini, Dürer, and Titian*, exh. cat. (New York: Rizzoli; London: Thames and Hudson).

—— and Beverly Louise Brown, 1999b, "Painting in Fifteenth-Century Venice and the *ars nova* of the Netherlands," in Bernard Aikema and Beverly Louise Brown (eds), *Renaissance Venice and the North: Crosscurrents in the Time of Bellini, Dürer and Titian*, exh. cat. (New York: Rizzoli; London: Thames and Hudson), pp. 176–83.

Alberti, Leon Battista, 1972, *On Painting and On Sculpture: The Latin Text of De Pictura and De Statua*, Cecil Grayson (ed. and trans.), (London: Phaidon).

Allen, Denise, 2008, "Riccio's Bronze Narratives," in Denise Allen and Peta Motture (eds), *Andrea Riccio, Renaissance Master of Bronze*, exh. cat. (New York: The Frick Collection), pp. 15–40.

Anderson, Jaynie, 2006, "Allegories and Mythologies," in David A. Brown and Sylvia Ferino-Pagden (eds), *Bellini, Giorgione, Titian, and the Renaissance of Venetian Painting*, exh. cat. (New Haven and London: Yale University Press), pp. 147–87.

Annali della Fabbrica del Duomo di Milano. Dall'origine fino al presente, 1880, vol. 3 (Milan: G. Brigola).

Arbel, Benjamin, 2013, "Venice's Maritime Empire in the Early Modern Period," in Eric R. Dursteler (ed.), *A Companion to Venetian History, 1440–1797* (Leiden and Boston: Brill), pp. 125–253.

Armstrong, Lilian, 1976, *Paintings and Drawings of Marco Zoppo* (New York: Garland).

Ashtor, Eliyahu, 1983, *Levant Trade in the Later Middle Ages* (Princeton: Princeton University Press).

Baggio, Luca, Gianluigi Colalucci, and Daniela Bartoletti (eds), 1999, *Altichiero da Zevio nell'Oratorio di San Giorgio: Il restauro degli affreschi* (Padua: Centro Studi Antoniani; Rome: De Luca).

Balistreri Trincanato, Corrado, 2009, "Liagò, logge," in *Venezia città mirabile. Guida alla veduta prospettica di Jacopo de' Barbari* (Caselle di Sommacampagna: Cierre), pp. 211–24.

Bambach, Carmen C., 2017, "Michelangelo: Divine Draftsman and Designer," in Carmen C. Bambach (ed.), *Michelangelo: Divine Draftsman and Designer*, exh. cat. (New York: The Metropolitan Museum of Art), pp. 15–265.

Bamji, Alexandra, 2018, "Marginalia and Mortality in Early Modern Venice," *Renaissance Studies*, 33.5, pp. 808–31.

Barausse, Manuela, 2008, "Giovanni Bellini. I documenti," in Mauro Lucco and Giovanni Carlo Federico Villa (eds), *Giovanni Bellini*, exh. cat. (Milan: Silvana Editore), pp. 327–59.

——, 2020, "Giovanni Bellini. I documenti," in Mauro Lucco (ed.), *Giovanni Bellini: Catalogo ragionato* (Ponzano Veneto: ZeL Edizioni), pp. 12–78.

Barry, Claire, 2017, "Examining Michelangelo's *Torment of Saint Anthony*: New Revelations," in Carmen C. Bambach (ed.) *Michelangelo: Divine Draftsman and Designer*, exh. cat. (New York: The Metropolitan Museum of Art), pp. 266–67.

Baruffaldi, Girolamo, 1844, *Vite de' pittori e scultori ferraresi*, vol. 1 (Ferrara: Domenico Taddei).

Bätschmann, Oskar, 2008, *Giovanni Bellini* (London: Reaktion Books).

Battaglia, Roberta, 2016, "8. Michele Giambono, *San Crisogono*," in Matteo Ceriana and Valeria Poletto (eds), *Il Paradiso riconquistato. Trame d'oro e colore nella pittura di Michele Giambono*, exh. cat. (Venice: Marsilio), pp. 161–64.

Battaglia, Salvatore, 2002, *Grande dizionario della lingua italiana*, vol. 21 (Turin: Unione Tipografico-Editrice Torinese).

Battisti, Eugenio, 1980, "Le origini religiose del paesaggio veneto," *Esistenza mito ermeneutica. Scritti per Enrico Castelli. Archivio di filosofia*, 50.1, pp. 227–46.

Bauer-Eberhardt, Ulrike, 1989, "Lauro Padovano und Leonardo Bellini als Maler, Miniatoren, und Zeichner," *Pantheon*, 47, pp. 49–82.

Baxandall, Michael, 1963, "A Dialogue on Art from the Court of Leonello d'Este: Angelo Decembrio's *De Politia Litteraria Pars LXVIII*," *Journal of the Warburg and Courtauld Institutes*, 26, pp. 304–26.

Bayer, Andrea, 2017, "Review of *Examining Giovanni Bellini: An Art 'More Human and More Divine'* by Carolyn C. Wilson," *Renaissance Quarterly*, 70.3, pp. 1059–60.

Becherucci, Luisa, 1938, "Benedetto Coda," in Cesare Gnudi and Luisa Becherucci, *Mostra di Melozzo e del Quattrocento romagnolo*, exh. cat. (Bologna: Poligrafici de Il Resto del Carlino), p. 141.

Becker, David P., et al. (eds), 2003, *The Frick Collection: An Illustrated Catalogue*, vol. 9, *Drawings, Prints and Later Acquisitions* (New York: The Frick Collection).

Bellavitis, Anna, 1995, "La famiglia 'cittadina' veneziana nel XVI secolo: Dote e successione. Le leggi e le fonti," *Studi veneziani*, 30, pp. 55–68.

——, 2001, *Identité, mariage, mobilité sociale: Citoyennes et citoyens à Venise au XVIe siècle* (Rome: École Française de Rome).

——, 2008, *Famille, genre, transmission a Venise au XIVe siècle* (Rome: École Française de Rome).

——, 2012, "La dote a Venezia tra medioevo e prima età moderna," in Anna Bellavitis, Nadia Maria Filippini, and Tiziana Plebani (eds), *Spazi, poteri, diritti delle donne a Venezia in età moderna* (Verona and Bolzano: QuiEdit), pp. 5–20.

——, 2014, "Family and Society," in Eric R. Dursteler (ed.), *A Companion to Venetian History, 1400–1797* (Leiden and Boston: Brill), pp. 319–52.

Bellazzecca, Enrico, 2011, "Miretto, Nicolò," in *Dizionario biografico degli italiani*, vol. 75 (Rome: Istituto della Enciclopedia Italiana), pp. 9–10.

Belli, Gianluca, 1998, "Il Palazzo dello Strozzino," in Gabriele Morolli (ed.), *Michelozzo. Scultore e architetto (1396–1472)* (Florence: Centro D), pp. 35–44.

Bellosi, Luciano, 2008, "Giovanni Bellini e Andrea Mantegna," in Giovanni Agosti and Dominique Thiébaut (eds), *Mantegna 1431–1506*, exh. cat. (Paris: Musée du Louvre), pp. 103–49.

Belting, Hans, 2017, "Poetry and Painting: *Saint Jerome in the Wilderness*," in Davide Gasparotto (ed.), *Giovanni Bellini: Landscapes of Faith in Renaissance Venice*, exh. cat. (Los Angeles: J. Paul Getty Museum), pp. 25–35.

Beltrami, Daniele, 1954, *Storia della popolazione di Venezia dalla fine del secolo XVI alla caduta della Repubblica* (Padua: CEDAM).

Bennett, Richard, 1900 (ed.), *A Catalogue of the Early Printed Books and Illuminated Manuscripts Collected by Richard Bennett* (Manchester: R. Bennett).

Bentini, Jadranka and Marco Sarti, 1981, "Pittore veneziano della prima metà del sec. XV," in Jadranka Bentini (ed.), *Un palazzo, un museo. La Pinacoteca Nazionale di Palazzo dei Diamanti*, exh. cat. (Bologna: Alfa), pp. 109–10.

Berger, Adolf, 1953, "Encyclopedic Dictionary of Roman Law," *Transactions of the American Philosophical Society*, 43.2, pp. 333–809.

Bernacchioni, Annamaria, 2006, "Firenze," in Andrea De Marchi, Laura Laureati, and Lorenza Mochi Onori (eds), *Gentile da Fabriano. Studi e ricerche* (Milan: Electa), pp. 121–32.

Bertoni, Giulio, 1921, *Guarino da Verona fra letterati e cortigiani a Ferrara (1429–1460)* (Geneva: Olschki).

Besutti, Antonio, 1915, "La chiesa cattedrale di Asola," *Brixia sacra. Bollettino bimestrale di studi e documenti per la storia ecclesiastica di Brescia*, no. 4.3, pp. 120–55.

Billanovich, Eugenio, 1973, "Note per la storia della pittura nel Veneto," *Italia medioevale e umanistica*, 16, pp. 359–89.

Bisson, Massimo, 2012, *Meravigliose macchine di giubilo. L'architettura e l'arte degli organi a Venezia nel Rinascimento* (Venice: Fondazione Giorgio Cini).

Blass-Simmen, Brigit, 2015, "'Qualche lontani': Distance and Transcendence in the Art of Giovanni Bellini," in Carolyn C. Wilson (ed.), *Examining Giovanni Bellini: "An Art More Human and More Divine"* (Turnhout: Brepols, 2015), pp. 77–91.

——, and Stefan Weppelmann (eds), 2017, *Padua and Venice: Transcultural Exchange in the Early Modern Age* (Berlin and Boston: de Gruyter).

Boerio, Giuseppe, 1998, *Dizionario del dialetto veneziano*, 2nd edn (Florence: Giunti).

Boito, Camillo, 1889, *Il duomo di Milano e i disegni per la sua facciata* (Milan: Tipografia di Luigi Marchi).

Bomford, David, Ashok Roy, and Alistair Smith, 1986, "The Techniques of Dieric Bouts: Two Paintings Contrasted," *National Gallery Technical Bulletin*, 10, pp. 39–57.

Booij, Th., 2010, "Psalms 120–136: Songs for a Great Festival," *Biblica*, 91.2, pp. 241–255.

Bora, Giulio, 1976, "Note cremonesi, II: L'eredità di Camillo e I Campi," *Paragone*, 311, pp. 49–74.

Borenius, Tancred, 1911, "Three Paintings by Bartolomeo Vivarini," *The Burlington Magazine for Connoisseurs*, 19.100, pp. 192–98.

Borsetti, Ferrante, 1735, *Historia almi Ferrariae Gymnasii*, 2 vols (Ferrara: Typis Bernardini Pomatelli).

Botteon, Vincenzo and Antonio Aliprandi, 1893, *Ricerche intorno alla vita e alle opere di Giovanni Battista Cima* (Conegliano: Tipo-Litografia Francesco Cagnani).

Brackett, John K., 2002, *Criminal Justice and Crime in Late Renaissance Florence, 1537–1609* (Cambridge: Cambridge University Press).

Braghirolli, Willelmo, 1877, "Carteggio d'Isabella d'Este Gonzaga intorno ad un quadro di Giambellino," *Archivio veneto*, 13, pp. 370–83.

Brown, Beverly Louise, 2007, "Titian's 'Christ and the Adulteress,'" *Artibus et historiae*, 28.56, pp. 73–105.

——, 2011, "Portraiture at the Courts of Italy," in Keith Christiansen and Stefan Weppelmann (eds), *The Renaissance Portrait from Donatello to Bellini*, exh. cat. (New York: The Metropolitan Museum of Art; London: Yale University Press), pp. 26–47.

Brown, Clifford Malcolm, 1969, "Una testa de Platone antica con la punta dil naso di cera: Unpublished Negotiations between Isabella d'Este and Niccolò and Giovanni Bellini," *The Art Bulletin*, 51.4, pp. 372–77.

——, 1982, *Isabella d'Este and Lorenzo da Pavia: Documents for the History of Art and Culture in Renaissance Mantua*, with the collaboration of Anna Maria Lorenzoni (Geneva: Droz).

Brown, David A., 2019, *Giovanni Bellini: The Last Works* (Milan: Skira).

——, and Anna Pizzati, 2014, "'Meum amantissimum nepotem': A New Document Concerning Giovanni Bellini," *The Burlington Magazine*, 156.1332, pp. 148–52.

Buckland, William W., 1953, *A Manual of Roman Private Law*, 2nd edn (Cambridge: Cambridge University Press).

——, and Peter Stein, 2007, *A Text-Book of Roman Law: From Augustus to Justinian*, 3rd edn (Cambridge: Cambridge University Press).

Buonocore, Vincenzo, 2011a, "Alvise Vivarini rivisitato: Problemi di committenza (parte I)," *Arte cristiana*, 99.863, pp. 81–94.

——, 2011b, "Alvise Vivarini rivisitato: Problemi di committenza, (parte II)," *Arte cristiana*, 99.864, pp. 161–76.

Callegari, Raimondo, 1997, "Su due polittici di Giorgio Schiavone," *Arte veneta*, 50, pp. 24–37.
Calogero, Giacomo Alberto, 2019, "Il problema della pala Gattamelata e gli esordi di Giovanni Bellini," *Paragone*, 3rd series, 70.147 (835), pp. 3–31.
Campbell, Caroline et al. (eds), 2018, *Mantegna and Bellini*, exh. cat. (London: National Gallery).
Campbell, Lorne, 1981, "Notes on Netherlandish Pictures in the Veneto in the Fifteenth and Sixteenth Centuries," *The Burlington Magazine*, 123.941, pp. 467–73.
——, 1998, *National Gallery Catalogues: The Fifteenth-Century Netherlandish Schools* (London: National Gallery).
Campbell, Stephen J., 2010, "Naturalism and Venetian 'Poesia': Grafting, Metaphor, and Embodiment in Giorgione, Titian, and the Campagnolas," in Alexander Nagel and Lorenzo Pericolo (eds), *Subject and Aporia in Early Modern Art* (Brookfield: Ashgate), pp. 115–43.
——, 2016, "Titian's *Flaying of Marsyas*: Thresholds of the Human and the Limits of Painting," in Joseph Campana and Scott Maisano (eds), *Renaissance Posthumanism* (New York: Fordham University Press), pp. 64–98.
Cappelli, Adriano, 1930, *Cronologia, cronografia e calendario perpetuo* (Milan: U. Hoepli).
Casini, Matteo, 1992, "La cittadinanza originaria a Venezia tra i secoli XV e XVI. Una linea interpretativa," in *Studi veneti offerti a Gaetano Cozzi* (Venice: Il Cardo), pp. 133–50.
Cassandro, Giovanni, 1936, "La curia di petizion," *Archivio veneto*, 19, pp. 72–144.
Cassanelli, Roberto, 1998, "Artisti in bottega. Luoghi e prassi dell'arte alle soglie della modernità," in Roberto Cassanelli (ed.), *La bottega dell'artista tra Medioevo e Rinascimento* (Milan: Jaca Book), pp. 7–29.
Cattaneo, Angelo, 2003, "God in His World: The Earthly Paradise in Fra Mauro's 'Mappamundi' Illuminated by Leonardo Bellini," *Imago mundi*, 55, pp. 97–102.
Cavalca, Domenico, 2009, *Vite dei Santi Padri*, Carlo Delcorno (ed.) (Florence: Galluzzo).
Cavanna, Anna Maria, 2003, "Un paliotto della metà del Quattrocento e il problema degli esordi di Giovanni Bellini," *La Diana*, 6/7, pp. 97–113.
Cecchetti, Bartolomeo, 1887a, "Nomi di pittori e lapicidi antichi," *Archivio veneto*, 33, pp. 43–65.
——, 1887b, "Saggio di cognomi e autografi di artisti in Venezia, secoli XIV–XVIII," *Archivio veneto*, 34, pp. 203–14.
Cecchi, Alessandro, 2005, "Il 'trittico' Quaratesi da San Nicolò Oltrarno agli Uffizi"; "I Quaratesi di San Nicolò Oltrarno e Gentile da Fabriano," in Alessandro Cecchi (ed.), *Gentile da Fabriano agli Uffizi* (Milan: Silvana Editore), pp. 59–69, 71–73.
Cecchini, Isabella, 2000, *Quadri e commercio a Venezia durante il Seicento. Uno studio sul mercato dell'arte* (Venice: Marsilio).
Cennini, Cennino, 1933, *The Craftsman's Handbook. The Italian "Il libro dell'arte,"* Daniel V. Thompson, Jr. (trans.) (New York: Dover Publications; New Haven: Yale University Press).
——, 2004, *Il libro dell'arte di Cennino Cennini*, Fabio Frezzato (ed.) (Vicenza: Neri Pozza).
——, 2015, *Il libro dell'arte*, Lara Broecke (trans.) (London: Archetype Publications).
Ceriana, Matteo, 2016, "'Paradisi' veneziani: Michele Giambono, Giovanni d'Alemagna e Antonio Vivarini," in Matteo Ceriana and Valeria Poletto (eds), *Il Paradiso riconquistato. Trame d'oro e colore nella pittura di Michele Giambono*, exh. cat. (Venice: Marsilio), pp. 39–87.
—— and Emanuela Daffra (eds), 1993, *Gentile da Fabriano. Il Polittico di Valle Romita*, exh. cat. (Milan: Charta).
—— and Valeria Poletto (eds), 2016, *Il Paradiso riconquistato. Trame d'oro e colore nella pittura di Michele Giambono*, exh. cat. (Venice: Marsilio).
Cessi, Roberto (ed.), 1938, *Gli statuti veneziani di Jacopo Tiepolo del 1242 e le loro glosse* (Venice: Officine Grafiche Carlo Ferrari).
——, 1953, *La Repubblica di Venezia e il problema adriatico* (Naples: Edizioni Scientifiche Italiane).
Chapman, Hugo, 1998, *Padua in the 1450s: Marco Zoppo and His Contemporaries* (London: The British Museum Press).
——, 2010, "A Tournament: From an Album of 99 Folios," in Hugo Chapman and Marzia Faietti (eds), *Fra Angelico to Leonardo, Italian Renaissance Drawings* (London: The British Museum Press), pp. 122–29.
Chavasse, Ruth, 2003, "The *studia humanitatis* and the Making of a Humanist Career: Marcantonio Sabellico's Exploitation of Humanist Literary Genres," *Renaissance Studies*, 17.1, pp. 27–38.
Chojnacki, Stanley, 2000, *Women and Men in Renaissance Venice: Twelve Essays on Patrician Society* (Baltimore, MD, and London: The Johns Hopkins University Press).
Chong, Alan, 2005, "Gentile Bellini in Istanbul: Myths and Misunderstandings," in Caroline Campbell

and Alan Ching (eds), *Bellini and the East*, exh. cat. (London: National Gallery; New Haven: Yale University Press), pp. 106–29.

Christiansen, Keith, 1982, *Gentile da Fabriano* (London: Chatto and Windus).

——, 1987, "La pittura a Venezia e nel Veneto nel primo Quattrocento," in Federico Zeri (ed.), *La pittura in Italia. Il Quattrocento*, 2 vols, vol. I (Milan: Electa), pp. 119–46.

——, 1992a, "3. Andrea Mantegna, *St Jerome in the Wilderness*"; "8. Andrea Mantegna, *The Adoration of the Shepherds*," in Jane Martineau (ed.), *Andrea Mantegna*, exh. cat. (London: Royal Academy of Arts; New York: The Metropolitan Museum of Art), pp. 115–17, 126–27.

——, 1992b, "Gentile da Fabriano," in *Pinacoteca di Brera. Scuole dell'Italia centrale e meridionale* (Milan: Electa), pp. 131–37.

——, 1998, "The View from Italy," in Maryan Ainsworth and Keith Christiansen (eds), *From Van Eyck to Bruegel: Early Netherlandish Painting in the Metropolitan Museum of Art*, exh. cat. (New York: The Metropolitan Museum of Art), pp. 39–61.

——, 2004a, "Bellini and Mantegna," in Peter Humfrey (ed.), *The Cambridge Companion to Giovanni Bellini* (Cambridge: Cambridge University Press), pp. 48–74.

——, 2004b, "Giovanni Bellini and the Practice of Devotional Painting," in Rhonda Kasl (ed.), *Giovanni Bellini and the Art of Devotion* (Indianapolis: Indianapolis Museum of Art), pp. 7–57.

——, 2006, "L'arte di Gentile da Fabriano," in Laura Laureati and Lorenza Mochi Onori (eds), *Gentile da Fabriano e l'altro Rinascimento*, exh. cat. (Milan: Electa), pp. 19–51.

——, 2013, "Bellini and the Meditational 'Poesia,'" *Artibus et historiae*, 67.34, pp. 9–20.

Cicinelli, Aldo, 1994–95, "Pisanello a Mantova: Nuovi studi," *Studi di storia dell'arte*, 5–6, pp. 55–92.

Cicogna, Emmanuele Antonio, 1853, *Delle inscrizioni veneziane*, 6 vols (Venice: Andreola).

Cittadella, Cesare, 1782, *Catalogo istorico de' pittori e scultori ferraresi e delle opere loro*, 4 vols (Ferrara: Francesco Pomatelli).

Clagett, Marshal, 1976, "The Life and Works of Giovanni Fontana," *Annali dell'Istituto e Museo di Storia della Scienza*, 1, pp. 5–28.

Cline Horowitz, Maryanne, 1998, *Seeds of Virtue and Knowledge* (Princeton: Princeton University Press).

Cole, Michael W., 2019, *Sofonisba's Lesson: A Renaissance Artist and Her Work* (Princeton: Princeton University Press).

Coltellacci, Stefano, 1991, "*Oboedite praepositis vestris, et subiacete illis*. Fonti letterarie e contesto storico della *Derisione di Noè* di Giovanni Bellini," *Venezia cinquecento*, 1.2, pp. 119–56.

Concina, Ennio, 1988, *Pietre parole storia. Glossario della costruzione nelle fonti veneziane (secoli XV–XVIII)* (Venice: Marsilio).

Connell, Susan, 1988, *The Employment of Sculptors and Stonemasons in Venice in the Fifteenth Century* (New York: Garland).

Conti, Alessandro, 1994, "Giovanni nella bottega di Jacopo Bellini," in *Hommage à Michel Laclotte. Études sur la peinture du Moyen Age et de la Renaissance* (Milan: Electa; Paris: Réunion des Musées Nationaux), pp. 260–71.

Cordellier, Dominique, 1995, "Documenti e fonti su Pisanello (1395–1581 circa)," *Verona illustrata*, 8, pp. 3–282.

——, 1996, "Cronologia," in Paola Marini (ed.), *Pisanello* (Milan: Electa), pp. 499–506.

Cortelazzo, Manlio, 2007, *Dizionario veneziano della lingua e della cultura popolare nel XVI secolo* (Limena: La Linea).

Cotrugli Raguseo, Benedetto, 1990, *Il libro dell'arte di mercatura*, Ugo Tucci (ed.) (Venice: Arsenale).

Crescenzi, Victor, 1997, "Il diritto civile," in Girolamo Arnaldi, Giorgio Cracco, and Alberto Tenendi (eds), *Storia di Venezia dalle origini alla caduta della Serenissima*, vol. 3, *La formazione dello stato patrizio* (Rome: Istituto della Enciclopedia Italiana), pp. 409–74.

Crouzet-Pavan, Èlisabeth, 2005, *Venice Triumphant: The Horizons of a Myth*, Lydia Cochrane (trans.), (Baltimore, MD: The Johns Hopkins University Press).

Crowe, Joseph A. and Giovanni Battista Cavalcaselle, 1871, *A History of Painting in North Italy: Venice, Padua, Vicenza, Verona, Ferrara, Milan, Friuli, Brescia from the Fourteenth to the Sixteenth Century*, 2 vols (London: John Murray).

Dalí, Salvador, 2013, *The Secret Life of Salvador Dalí*, Haakon M. Chevalier (trans.) (New York: Dover Publications).

Dalla Costa, Thomas, 2020, "The *Poesie* in Correspondence," in Matthias Wivel (ed.), *Titian: Love, Desire, Death*, exh. cat. (London: National Gallery; New Haven: Yale University Press), pp. 192–203.

Davisson, Darrell D., 1980, "New Documents on Gentile da Fabriano's Residence in Florence,

1420–22," *The Burlington Magazine*, 122.932, pp. 759–63.

Degenhart, Bernhard and Annegrit Schmitt, 1984, *Jacopo Bellini. L'album dei disegni del Louvre* (Milan: Jaca Book).

——, 1990, *Corpus der italienischen Zeichnungen, 1300–1450*, 3 vols (Berlin: G. Mann).

DeLancey, Julia A., 2011, "'In the Streets Where They Sell Colors': Placing '*vendecolori*' in the Urban Fabric of Early Modern Venice," *Wallraf-Richartz-Jahrbuch*, 72, pp. 193–232.

De Marchi, Andrea, 1992, *Gentile da Fabriano. Un viaggio nella pittura italiana alla fine del gotico* (Milan: F. Motta).

——, 2003, "'Lorenzo e Jachomo da Venexia': Un percorso da Zanino a Jacopo Bellini e un enigma da risolvere," *Saggi e memorie di storia dell'arte*, 27, pp. 71–100.

——, 2006a, *Gentile da Fabriano. Un viaggio nella pittura italiana alla fine del gotico*, 2nd edn (Milan: F. Motta).

——, 2006b, "A Siena e a Roma, al servizio di Papa Martino V," in Laura Laureati and Lorenza Mochi Onori (eds), *Gentile da Fabriano e l'altro Rinascimento*, exh. cat. (Milan: Electa), pp. 296–97.

——, 2006c, "Gentile e la sua bottega," in Andrea De Marchi, Laura Laureati, and Lorenza Mochi Onori (eds), *Gentile da Fabriano. Studi e ricerche* (Milan: Electa), pp. 9–53.

——, 2010, "Cat. C.7: Gentile da Fabriano, *Madonna dell'Umiltà*," in Max Seidel (ed.), *Le arti a Siena nel primo Rinascimento. Da Jacopo della Quercia a Donatello*, exh. cat. (Milan: F. Motta), pp. 196–97.

——, 2018, "Mantegna/Bellini: Invention vs. Poetry," in Caroline Campbell et al. (eds), *Mantegna and Bellini*, exh. cat. (London: National Gallery) pp. 28–39.

——, Laura Laureati, and Lorenza Mochi Onori (eds), 2006, *Gentile da Fabriano. Studi e ricerche* (Milan: Electa).

De Nicolò Salmazo, Alberta, 1990, "Padova," in Mauro Lucco (ed.), *La pittura nel Veneto. Il Quattrocento*, 2 vols, vol. II (Milan: Electa), pp. 481–54.

Denifle, Heinrich and Emile Chatelaine, 1897, *Chartularium Universitatis Parisiensis. Sub auspiciis consilii generalis facultatum parisiensium*, vol. 4, *Ab anno MCCCLXXXXIIII usque ad annum MCCCCII*, (Paris: Apud Fratres Delalain), reprint (Cambridge: Cambridge University Press, 2014).

Diario per quest'anno MDCCXC ad uso della città e diocesi di Asola, 1790 (Venice: Domenico Pompeati).

Desportes, Pierre and Hélène Millet, 1996, *Fasti Ecclesiæ Gallicanæ. Répertoire prosopographique des évêques, dignitaires et chanoines de France de 1200 à 1500*, vol. 1, *Diocese d'Amiens* (Turnhout: Brepols).

Di Lorenzo, Andrea, 2012, "Imago Pietatis," in Andrea De Marchi, Andrea Di Lorenzo, and Lavinia Galli Michero (eds), *Giovanni Bellini dall'icona alla storia*, exh. cat. (Turin: Allemandi), pp. 56–59.

Di Vito, Mauro, 2015, "'Per lo quale ennallumini la nocte'. Il verbasco fiorito del San Francesco che riceve le stimmate di Giovanni Bellini alla Frick Collection ed altri appunti di storia naturale," in Carolyn C. Wilson (ed.), *Examining Giovanni Bellini: An Art "More Human and More Divine"* (Turnhout: Brepols), pp. 113–25.

Dunkerton, Jill, and Marika Spring (eds), 2018, "Giovanni Bellini's Painting Technique," *National Gallery Technical Bulletin*, 39, Jill Dunkerton and Marika Spring, with R. Billinge and C. Higgitt, and contributions from D. A. Peggie and C. Campbell, pp. 4–25.

Edgerton, Samuel Y., 1966, "Alberti's Perspective: A New Discovery and a New Evaluation," *The Art Bulletin*, 48.3/4, pp. 367–78.

——, 2009, *The Mirror, the Window, and the Telescope: How Renaissance Linear Perspective Changed Our Vision of the Universe* (Ithaca, NY: Cornell University Press)

Eiche, Sabine, 1983, "On the Dispersal of Cardinal Bembo's Collections," *Mitteilungen des Kunsthistorischen Institutes in Florenz*, 27, pp. 353–59.

Eisler, Colin, 1985, "*Saints Anthony Abbot and Bernardino of Siena*, Designed by Jacopo and Painted by Gentile Bellini," *Arte veneta*, 39, pp. 32–40.

——, 1989, *The Genius of Jacopo Bellini: The Complete Paintings and Drawings* (New York: H. N. Abrams).

Ekserdjian, David, 1992, "10. Andrea Mantegna. *Life and Passion of St Maurice*," "66. Andrea Mantegna. *Descent into Limbo*," "69. Giovanni Bellini. *Descent into Limbo*," in Jane Martineau (ed.), *Andrea Mantegna*, exh. cat. (London: Royal Academy of Arts; New York: The Metropolitan Museum of Art), pp. 129–33, 261–63, 267–68.

——, 2006, *Parmigianino* (New Haven and London: Yale University Press).

Elam, Caroline, 1985, "Two Drawings by Baccio d'Agnolo and the Problems of a Private Renaissance Square," *I Tatti Studies in the Italian Renaissance*, 1, pp. 105–35, 274–86.

Favaro, Elena, 1975, *L'arte dei pittori in Venezia e i suoi statuti* (Florence: Olschki).

Ferino-Pagden, Sylvia, 2006, "Pictures of Women–Pictures of Love," in David A. Brown and Sylvia

Ferino-Pagden (eds), *Bellini, Giorgione, Titian, and the Renaissance of Venetian Painting*, exh. cat. (New Haven and London: Yale University Press), pp. 189–235.

Field, Richard S., 2003, "A Fifteenth-Century Woodcut of the Death of the Virgin in a Manuscript of *Der Stachel der Liebe*," *Studies in Iconography*, 24, pp. 71–137.

Filippini, Francesco and Guido Zucchi, 1968, *Miniatori e pittori a Bologna. Documenti del secolo XV* (Rome: Accademia Nazionale dei Lincei).

Finocchi Ghersi, Lorenzo, 1997, "Artisti e committenti a San Salvador," *Arte veneta*, 51, pp. 21–39.

Fiocco, Giuseppe, 1920, "Michele Giambono," *Venezia studi di arte e storia*, 1, pp. 206–36.

——, 1949, "Giovanni e la famiglia dei Bellini alla luce di nuovi documenti," *Vernice: Rassegna d'arte*, 4.33–34, p. 6.

——, 1959, *L'arte di Andrea Mantegna* (Venice: Neri Pozza).

Fiori, Emanuela, 1992, "Giovanni di Nicolò Bellini (?)," in Jadranka Bentini (ed.), *La Pinacoteca Nazionale di Ferrara. Catalogo generale* (Bologna: Nuova Alfa), pp. 40–42.

Fleming, John V., 1982, *From Bonaventure to Bellini: An Essay in Franciscan Exegesis* (Princeton: Princeton University Press).

Fletcher, Jennifer M., 1971, "Isabella d'Este and Giovanni Bellini's *Presepio*," *The Burlington Magazine*, 113.825, pp. 703–13.

——, 1991, "The Painter and the Poet: Giovanni Bellini's *Portrait of Raffaele Zovenzoni* Rediscovered," *Apollo*, 134, pp. 153–57.

——, 1998, "I Bellini," in Roberto Cassanelli (ed.), *La bottega dell'artista tra Medioevo e Rinascimento* (Milan: Jaca Book), pp. 131–53.

——, 2004, "Bellini's Social World," in Peter Humfrey (ed.), *The Cambridge Companion to Giovanni Bellini* (Cambridge: Cambridge University Press), pp. 13–47.

Flores d'Arcais, Francesca, 1998, "Note sulla decorazione a fresco del Palazzo della Regione di Padova," in Anna Maria Spiazzi (ed.), *Il Palazzo della Ragione di Padova. Indagini preliminari per il restauro – studi e ricerche* (Treviso: Canova), pp. 11–22.

Fogolari, Gino, 1944, "Jacobello del Fiore e la sua famiglia (nuovi documenti)," *Archivio veneto*, 5th series, 34–35, pp. 33–50.

Foresti, Jacopo Filippo, 1503, *Novissime hystoriarum omnium repercussiones. Nouiter a Reuerendissimo patre Iacobophilippo Bergomense, . . . edite: que Supplementum supplementi Cronicarum nuncupantur. Incipiendo ab exordio mundi, vsque in Annum salutis nostre 1502* (Venice: Albertinum De Lissona Vercellensem).

Fortini Brown, Patricia, 1988, *Venetian Narrative Painting in the Age of Carpaccio* (New Haven and London: Yale University Press).

——, 1992, "The Antiquarianism of Jacopo Bellini," *Artibus et historiae*, 13.26, pp. 65–84.

——, 1996a, "Le «Scuole»," in Alberto Tenenti and Ugo Tucci (eds), *Storia di Venezia dalle origini alla caduta della Serenissima*, 7 vols, vol. V, *Il Rinascimento: Società ed economia* (Rome: Istituto della Enciclopedia Italiana), pp. 307–54.

——, 1996b, *Venice and Antiquity: The Venetian Sense of the Past* (New Haven and London: Yale University Press).

Franco, Tiziana, 1996, "Intorno al 1430: Michele Giambono e Jacopo Bellini," *Arte veneta*, 48, pp. 7–17.

——, 1998, *Michele Giambono e il monumento a Cortesia da Serego* (Padua: Il Poligrafo).

——, 2016, "'Michael Çambono pinxit': Note su un pittore veneziano tra Gotico e Rinascimento," in Matteo Ceriana and Valeria Poletto (eds), *Il Paradiso riconquistato. Trame d'oro e colore nella pittura di Michele Giambono*, exh. cat. (Venice: Marsilio), pp. 13–37.

Frosinini, Cecilia, 2006, "Cat. VI.1: Gentile da Fabriano: *Madonna dell'Umiltà*," in Laura Laureati and Lorenza Mochi Onori (eds), *Gentile da Fabriano e l'altro Rinascimento*, exh. cat. (Milan: Electa), pp. 248–51.

Fry, Roger E., 1899, *Giovanni Bellini* (London: At the Sign of the Unicorn).

Gallo, Rodolfo, 1961–62, "La Scuola Grande di San Teodoro," in *Atti dell'Istituto Veneto di Scienze, Lettere e Arti*, 118, pp. 461–95.

——, 1963, "La Scuola di Sant'Orsola, i teleri di Carpaccio e la tomba di Gentile e Giovanni Bellini," *Bollettino dei Musei Civici Veneziani*, 8.2–3, pp. 1–24.

Gamberini, Cecilia, 2016, "Sofonisba Anguissola at the Court of Philip II," in Sheila Barker (ed.), *Women Artists in Early Modern Italy: Careers, Fame, and Collectors* (Turnhout: Harvey Miller), pp. 29–38.

Garini, Michele et al. (eds), 2015, *La cattedrale di Asola* (Asola: Gilgamesh).

Garzoni, Tommaso, 1996, *La piazza universale di tutte le professioni del mondo*, Paolo Cherchi and Beatrice Collina (eds), 2 vols (Turin: Einaudi).

Gasparotto, Davide (ed.), 2017a, *Giovanni Bellini: Landscapes of Faith in Renaissance Venice*, exh. cat.

(Los Angeles: J. Paul Getty Museum).
——, 2017b, "Giovanni Bellini and Landscape," in Davide Gasparotto (ed.), *Giovanni Bellini: Landscapes of Faith in Renaissance Venice*, exh. cat. (Los Angeles: J. Paul Getty Museum), pp. 11–23.
——, 2017c. "1. Giovanni Bellini. *Saint Jerome in the Wilderness*"; "2. Giovanni Bellini. *Crucifixion with the Virgin and Saint John the Evangelist*," in Davide Gasparotto (ed.), *Giovanni Bellini: Landscapes of Faith in Renaissance Venice*, exh. cat. (Los Angeles: J. Paul Getty Museum), pp. 58–63, 64–69.
Gaye, Giovanni, 1839–40, *Carteggio inedito d'artisti dei secoli XIV. XV. XVI.*, 3 vols (Florence: Giuseppe Molini).
Geltner, Guy, 2008, "*Isola non isolata*: Le Stinche in the Middle Ages," *Annali di storia di Firenze*, 3, pp. 7–28.
Gentili, Augusto, 1991, "Giovanni Bellini, la bottega, i quadri di devozione," *Venezia cinquecento*, 1.2, pp. 27–60.
——, 2004, "Bellini and Landscape," in Peter Humfrey (ed.), *The Cambridge Companion to Giovanni Bellini* (Cambridge: Cambridge University Press), pp. 167–81.
——, 2017, "Devote meditazioni," in *Bellini e i Belliniani. Dall'Accademia dei Concordi di Rovigo* (Venice: Marsilio), pp. 108–35.
Gietz, Nora, 2017, "The Scuole Grandi and Venetian Charitas during and after the Napoleonic Suppression (1806)," in Gabriele Matino and Nora Gietz (eds), *"Ebbi fame e mi deste da mangiare." Luoghi, principi e funzioni della* charitas *veneziana, 1260–1806* (Modena: Franco Cosimo Panini), pp. 137–50.
Gilbert, Creighton E., 2000, "A Preface to Signatures (with Some Cases in Venice)," in Mary Rogers (ed.), *Fashioning Identities in Renaissance Art* (Aldershot: Ashgate), pp. 79–89.
Glixon, Jonathan, 2003, *Honoring God and the City: Music at the Venetian Confraternities, 1260–1806* (Oxford: Oxford University Press).
Gnaccolini, Laura Paola, 2002, "L'*Annunciazione* di Jacopo Bellini in Sant'Alessandro a Brescia: Considerazioni in margine a un restauro," in Massimo Cappella, Ida Gianfranceschi and Elena Lucchesi Ragni (eds), *Vincenzo Foppa. Tecniche d'esecuzione, indagini e restauri* (Milan: Skira), pp. 69–70.
Godla, Joseph and Denise Allen, 2015, "*St. Francis in the Desert* and the Art of Linear Perspective," in Susannah Rutherglen and Charlotte Hale (eds), *In a New Light: Giovanni Bellini's "St. Francis in the Desert" at the Frick Collection* (New York: The Frick Collection), pp. 132–53.
Goffen, Rona, 1986, "Bellini, S. Giobbe and Altar Egos," *Artibus et historiae*, 7.14, pp. 57–70.
——, 1989, *Giovanni Bellini* (London and New Haven: Yale University Press).
——, 1995, "Giovanni Bellini's Half-Length Madonna," *The Art Bulletin*, 57.4, pp. 487–518.
——, 2000, "Giovanni Bellini: Il Rinascimento visto da Rialto," in Rona Goffen and Giovanna Nepi Scirè (eds), *Il colore ritrovato. Bellini a Venezia*, exh. cat. (Milan: Electa), pp. 3–23.
——, 2001, "Signatures: Inscribing Identity in Italian Renaissance Art," *Viator*, 32, pp. 303–70.
—— and Giovanna Nepi Scirè (eds), 2000, *Il colore ritrovato. Bellini a Venezia*, exh. cat. (Milan: Electa).
Golden, Andrea, 2004, "Creating and Re-Creating: The Practice of Replication in the Workshop of Giovanni Bellini," in Ronda Kasl (ed.), *Giovanni Bellini and the Art of Devotion* (Indianapolis: Indianapolis Museum of Art), pp. 91–127.
Goldenberg, Paula et al. (eds), 2017, *De Giotto à Goya. Peintures italiennes et espagnoles du Musée des Beaux-Arts de Strasbourg*, exh. cat. (Strasbourg: Musées de la Ville de Strasbourg).
Goy, Richard J., 2006, *Building Renaissance Venice: Patrons, Architects and Builders c. 1430–1500* (New Haven and London: Yale University Press).
Grafton, Anthony, 2002, *Leon Battista Alberti: Master Builder of the Italian Renaissance* (Cambridge, MA: Harvard University Press).
Gramigna, Silvia and Annalisa Perissa, 2008, *Scuole grandi e piccole a Venezia tra arte e storia. Confraternite di mestieri e devozione in sei itinerari* (Venice: Grafiche 2am).
Grave, Johannes, 2018, *Giovanni Bellini: The Art of Contemplation* (Munich, London, and New York: Prestel).
Grendler, Paul F., 1982, "What Zuanne Read in School: Vernacular Texts in Sixteenth Century Venetian Schools," *The Sixteenth Century Journal*, 13, pp. 41–54.
——, 1989, *Schooling in Renaissance Italy: Literacy and Learning, 1330–1600* (Baltimore, MD, and London: The Johns Hopkins University Press).
——, 2013, "Education in the Republic of Venice," in Eric R. Dursteler (ed.), *A Companion to Venetian History, 1440–1797* (Leiden and Boston: Brill), pp. 675–99.
Griphio, D. Rizzardi (ed.), 1606, *Volumen statutorum, legum ac iurium d[ominii] Venetorum* (Venice: Joannem Zenarium).
Gronau, Georg, 1909, "Bellini, Giovanni II," in Ulrich Thieme and Felix Becker (eds), *Allgemeines*

Lexikon der bildenden Künstler von der Antike bis zur Gegenwart, vol. 3 (Leipzig: W. Engelmann), p. 266.

Grubb, James S., 2000, "Elite Citizens," in John Martin and Dennis Romano (eds), *Venice Reconsidered: The History and Civilization of an Italian City-State, 1297–1797* (Baltimore: The Johns Hopkins University Press), pp. 339–64.

Guarini, Marc'Antonio, 1621, *Compendio historico dell'origine, accrescimento, e prerogatiue delle chiese, e luoghi pij della città, e diocesi di Ferrara* (Ferrara: Heredi di Vittorio Baldini).

Guarnieri, Cristina, 2016, "Una pala ribaltabile per l'esposizione delle reliquie: Le *Storie di Santa Lucia* di Jacobello del Fiore a Fermo," *Arte veneta*, 73, pp. 9–35.

Guarnieri, Giuseppe Gino, 1967, *Da Porto Pisano a Livorno città, attraverso le tappe della storia e della evoluzione geografica: Studio storico-critico* (Pisa: Giardini).

Guerzi, Chiara, 2014, "Una *Biblia pauperum* di Giovanni di Nicolò Bellini (già Maestro dell'Avicenna," *Rivista d'arte*, 5.48, pp. 31–46.

Guidarelli, Gianmario, 2011, "Le Scuole Grandi veneziane nel XV e XVI secolo: Reti assistenziali, patrimoni immobiliari e strategie di governo," *Mélanges de l'École Française de Rome*, 123.1, pp. 59–81.

——, 2017a, "L'architettura della scuola grande di San Marco," in Gherardo Ortalli and Salvatore Settis (eds), *La Scuola Grande di San Marco a Venezia* (Modena: Franco Cosimo Panini), pp. 43–66.

——, 2017b, "Pietre come pane. L'architettura e la politica assistenziale delle scuole grandi veneziane," in Gabriele Matino and Nora Gietz (eds), *"Ebbi fame e mi deste da mangiare." Luoghi, principi e funzioni della* charitas *veneziana, 1260–1806* (Modena: Franco Cosimo Panini), pp. 63–73.

Guzzetti, Linda, 2002, "Dowries in Fourteenth-Century Venice," *Renaissance Studies*, 16.4, pp. 430–73.

Hammond, Joseph, 2016, "Five Jacopo Bellinis: The Lives of Christ and the Virgin at the Scuola Grande di S. Giovanni Evangelista, Venice," *The Burlington Magazine*, 158.1361, pp. 601–09.

Hartt, Frederick, 1959, "The Earliest Works of Andrea Castagno: Part Two," *The Art Bulletin*, 41.3, pp. 225–36.

Helas, Philine, 2016, "Sui gradini del tempio. Il tempio e la scala nell'architettura picta tra il XIV e il XVI secolo," in Sabine Frommel and Gerhard Wolf (eds), *Architettura picta nell'arte italiana da Giotto a Veronese* (Modena: Franco Cosimo Panini), pp. 43–67.

Heyd, Guglielmo, 1913, *Storia del commercio del Levante nel Medioevo*, 5th series, 10 (Turin: Unione Tipografico-Editrice Torinese. Biblioteca dell'Economista).

Hills, Paul, 1987, *The Light of Early Italian Painting* (New Haven and London: Yale University Press).

——, 1999a, "Marble and Water: Patterns of Venetian Colour," *Art Quarterly: National Art Collection Fund* (autumn), pp. 34–41.

——, 1999b, *Venetian Colour: Marble, Mosaic, Painting and Glass 1250–1550* (New Haven and London: Yale University Press).

——, 2004, "Bellini's Colour," in Peter Humfrey (ed.), *The Cambridge Companion to Giovanni Bellini* (Cambridge: Cambridge University Press), pp. 182–94.

Hochmann, Michel, 2017, "La formazione del pittore a Venezia durante il Cinquecento," in Anna Bellavitis, Martina Frank, and Valentina Sapienza (eds), *Garzoni. Apprendistato e formazione tra Venezia e l'Europa in età moderna* (Mantua: Universitas Studiorum S.r.l.), pp. 49–64.

Holberton, Paul, 1999, "La critica e la fortuna di Giorgione: Il conflitto delle fonti," in Mauro Lucco (ed.), *La pittura nel Veneto. Il Cinquecento*, 3 vols, vol. III (Milan: Electa), pp. 1015–40.

Holgate, Richard I., 1998, *The Vivarini Workshop and Its Patrons*, unpublished PhD thesis (St Andrews: University of St Andrews).

Hope, Charles, 2012, "La paternità delle lettere di Tiziano," in Lionello Puppi and Charles Hope (eds), *Tiziano. L'epistolaio* (Florence: Alinari 24 ore), pp. 345–49.

Howard, Deborah, 1999, "La Scuola Grande della Misericordia di Venezia," in Gianni Fabbri (ed.), *La Scuola Grande della Misericordia di Venezia. Storia e progetto* (Milan: Skira), pp. 13–70.

——, 2000, *Venice and the East: The Impact of the Islamic World on Venetian Architecture 1100–1500* (New Haven and London: Yale University Press).

——, 2004, "Bellini and Architecture," in Peter Humfrey (ed.), *The Cambridge Companion to Giovanni Bellini* (Cambridge: Cambridge University Press), pp. 143–66.

——, 2013, "Contextualising Titian's *Sacred and Profane Love*: The Cultural World of the Venetian Chancery in the Early Sixteenth Century," *Artibus et historiae*, 34.67, pp. 185–99.

Humfrey, Peter, 1984, *Cima da Conegliano* (Cambridge: Cambridge University Press).

——, 1985, "The Bellinesque *Life of St. Mark* Cycle

for the Scuola Grande di San Marco in Venice in Its Original Arrangement," *Zeitschrift für Kunstgeschichte*, 48.2, pp. 225–42.

——, 1993, *The Altarpiece in Renaissance Venice* (New Haven and London: Yale University Press).

——, 1994, "The Bellini, the Vivarini and the Beginnings of the Renaissance Altarpiece in Venice," in Eve Borsook and Fiorella Superbi Gioffredi (eds), *Italian Altarpieces* (Oxford: Clarendon Press).

——(ed.), 2004a, *The Cambridge Companion to Giovanni Bellini* (Cambridge: Cambridge University Press).

——, 2004b, "Introduction," in Peter Humfrey (ed.), *The Cambridge Companion to Giovanni Bellini* (Cambridge: Cambridge University Press), pp. 1–11.

——, 2004c, "2. *St Jerome in the Desert*," in Peter Humfrey et al. (eds), *The Age of Titian: Venetian Renaissance Art from Scottish Collections*, exh. cat. (Edinburgh: National Galleries of Scotland), p. 60.

Humphrey, Lyle, 2015, *La miniatura per le confraternite e le arti veneziane. Mariegole dal 1260 al 1460* (Venice: Fondazione Giorgio Cini – Cierre Edizioni).

Iotta, Roberta, 2006, "Un cammeo per Nicolosia," *Civiltà mantovana*, 41.122, pp. 162–73.

Jacoby, David, 2006, "Marco Polo, His Close Relatives, and His Travel Account: Some New Insights," *Mediterranean Historical Review*, 21.2 (December), pp. 193–218.

Joannides, Paul, 1993, *Masaccio and Masolino: A Complete Catalogue* (London: Phaidon Press).

Joost-Gaugier, Christiane L., 1974, "Considerations Regarding Jacopo Bellini's Place in the Venetian Renaissance," *Arte veneta*, 28, pp. 21–38.

——, 1975, "Jacopo Bellini's Interest in Perspective and Its Iconographical Significance," *Zeitschrift für Kiunstgeschichte*, 38, pp. 1–28.

——, 1977, "The Tuscanization of Jacopo Bellini," *Acta historiae artium*, 23, pp. 95–112, 291–313.

Juřen, Vladimir, 1974, "Fecit-faciebat," *Revue de l'Arte*, 26, pp. 27–30.

Kaftal, George, 1952, *Saints in Italian Art: Iconography of the Saints in the Paintings of North East Italy* (Florence: Sansoni).

Kasl, Ronda (ed.), 2004, *Giovanni Bellini and the Art of Devotion* (Indianapolis: Indianapolis Museum of Art).

Kemperdick, Stephan, 2013, "'Rendered According to My Own Image': Portraits and Selfportraits," in Jochen Sander (ed.), *Dürer: His Art in Context*, exh. cat. (Frankfurt am Main: Stadel Museum; Munich, London, and New York: Prestel), pp. 93–99.

King, Margaret L., 1994, *The Death of the Child Valerio Marcello* (Chicago and London: The University of Chicago Press).

Kirshner, Julius, 2000, "Baldus de Ubaldis on Disinheritance: Contexts, Controversies, Consilia," *Ius commune: Zeitschrift für europäische Rechtsgeschichte*, 27, pp. 119–214.

Kleinbub, Christian K., 2015, "Jacopo Bellini and the Drawing of Idolatry," in Jodi Cranston (ed.), *Venetian Painting Matters, 1450–1750* (Turnhout: Brepols), pp. 21–34.

Koch, Robert A., 1988, "The Getty '*Annunciation*' by Dirk Bouts," *The Burlington Magazine*, 130.1024, pp. 509–22.

Koenig, John, 2001, "Prisoner Offerings, Patron Saints and State Cults at Siena and Other Italian Cities from 1250 to 1550," *Bullettino senese di storia patria*, 108, pp. 222–96.

Kohl, Benjamin G., 1992, "The Changing Concept of the *studia humanitatis* in the Early Renaissance," *Renaissance Studies*, 6, pp. 185–202.

——, Andea Mozzato, and Monique O'Connell, "The Rulers of Venice, 1332–1524: Interpretation, Methods, Database," www.rulersofvenice.org (accessed August 6, 2020)

Korbacher, Dagmar, 2018, "In Close Artistic Dialogue," in Caroline Campbell et al. (eds), *Mantegna and Bellini*, exh. cat. (London: National Gallery), pp. 108–25, 270–71.

Kristeva, Julia, 1980, "Motherhood According to Giovanni Bellini," in *Desire in Language*, Thomas Gora and Alice Jardine (trans.), Leon S. Roudiez (ed.) (New York: Columbia University Press), pp. 237–70.

Kuehn, Thomas, 1982, *Emancipation in Late Medieval Florence* (New Brunswick, NJ: Rutgers University Press).

——, 2002, *Illegitimacy in Renaissance Florence* (Ann Arbor: The University of Michigan Press).

Laderchi, Camillo, 1837, *La pittura ferrarese. Memorie* (Ferrara: Servadio).

Lametti, Laura, 2001, "Il manoscritto intitolato 'Appunti sopra la città di Foligno. Scritti da Ludovico Coltellini accademico fulginio. Parte nona. 1770–1780,'" in Giordana Benazzi and Francesco Federci Mancini (eds), *Il palazzo Trinci di Foligno* (Perugia: Quattroemme), pp. 427–46.

Lanaro, Paola, and Gian Maria Varanini, 2009, "Funzioni economiche della dote nell'Italia centro-settentrionale (tardo medioevo/inizi età moderna)," in Simonetta Cavaciocchi (ed.), *La famiglia nell'economia europea secc. XIII–XVIII / The*

Economic Role of the Family in the European Economy from the 13th to the 18th Centuries (Florence: Firenze University Press), pp. 81–102.

Lanciani, Rodolfo, 1903, *Storia degli scavi di Roma e notizie intorno le collezioni romane de antichità*, vol. 2 (Rome: Tipografia della R. Accademia dei Lincei).

Land, Norman E., 1974, *Michele Giambono: A Catalogue Raisonné*, unpublished PhD thesis (Charlottesville: University of Virginia).

——, 1982, "A Note on Jacopo Bellini's Lost St. Michael and a Possible Date for Pisanello," *Zeitschrift für Kunstgeschichte*, 45.3, pp. 283–86.

Lane, Frederic C., 1944, "Family Partnerships and Joint Ventures in the Venetian Republic," *The Journal of Economic History*, 4.2, pp. 178–96.

——, 1973, *Venice: A Maritime Republic* (Baltimore, MD, and London: The Johns Hopkins University Press).

Laureati, Laura and Lorenza Mochi Onori (eds), 2006, *Gentile da Fabriano e l'altro Rinascimento*, exh. cat. (Milan: Electa).

Lazzarini, Vittorio, 1928–29, "Antichi ordinamenti veneziani a tutela del lavoro dei garzoni," *Atti del Reale Istituto Veneto di Scienze, Lettere ed Arti*, 88, pp. 873–94.

Levi, Donata, 1988, *Cavalcaselle. Il pioniere della conservazione dell'arte italiana* (Turin: Giulio Einaudi).

Lightbown, Ronald, 1986, *Mantegna: With a Complete Catalogue of the Paintings, Drawings and Prints* (Oxford: Phaidon and Christie's).

Longhi, Roberto, 1949, "The Giovanni Bellini Exhibition," *The Burlington Magazine*, 91, pp. 277–83.

——, 1952, *Viatico per cinque secoli di pittura veneziana* (Florence: Sansoni).

——, 1958, "Due pannelli del seguito di Altichiero," *Paragone*, 107, pp. 64–65.

——, 1978, *Ricerche sulla pittura veneta, 1946–1969: Viatico per cinque secoli di pittura veneziana, Calepino veneziano, Giovanni Bellini, Guariento, da Altichiero a Pisanello, l'Amico friulano del Dosso, Antonio Vivarini, Crivelli e Mantegna, Squarcione, Zanino di Pietro, Giusto de' Menabuoi, Tiziano, Alvise Vivarini* (Florence: Sansoni).

——, 1995, *Il palazzo non finito. Saggi inediti 1910–26*, Francesco Frangi and Cristina Montagnani (eds) (Milan: Skira).

Lorenzi, Giambattista, 1868, *Monumenti per servire alla storia del Palazzo Ducale di Venezia; ovvero, Serie di atti pubblici dal 1523 al 1797, che variamente lo riguardano tratti dai veneti archivi e coordinati* (Venice: Tipografia del Commercio di M. Visentini).

Lowe, Kate, 2013, "Visible Lives: Black Gondoliers and Other Black Africans in Renaissance Venice," *Renaissance Quarterly*, 66.2, pp. 412–52.

Luca, Francesca de, 2000, "37. Giovanni Bellini. *Pala dei santi Cristoforo, Girolamo e Ludovico*," in Rona Goffen and Giovanna Nepi Scirè (eds), *Il colore ritrovato. Bellini a Venezia*, exh. cat. (Milan: Electa), pp. 164–65.

Lucco, Mauro, 1989, "Padova," in Mauro Lucco (ed.), *La pittura nel Veneto. Il Quattrocento*, 2 vols, vol. I (Milan: Electa), pp. 80–101.

——, 1990, "Venezia 1450–1500," in Mauro Lucco (ed.), *La pittura nel Veneto. Il Quattrocento*, 2 vols, vol. II (Milan: Electa), pp. 395–480.

——, 1997, "Un'eco fiamminga in Giovanni Bellini," in Cristina Acidini Luchinat et al. (eds), *Scritti per l'Istituto Germanico di Storia dell'Arte di Firenze* (Florence: Le Lettere), pp. 199–204.

——, 2004, "Bellini and the Flemish Painting," in Peter Humfrey (ed.), *The Cambridge Companion to Giovanni Bellini* (Cambridge: Cambridge University Press), pp. 75–94

——, 2008a, "La primavera del Mondo tuto, in ato de Pitura," in Mauro Lucco and Giovanni Carlo Federico Villa (eds), *Giovanni Bellini*, exh. cat. (Milan: Silvana Editore), pp. 19–37.

——, 2008b, "2. Giovanni Bellini. *San Girolamo in penitenza*"; "5. Giovanni Bellini. *Madonna con il Bambino dormiente sul parapetto*"; "6. Giovanni Bellini. *Trasfigurazione*"; "12. Giovanni Bellini. *San Girolamo in penitenza*"; "15. Giovanni Bellini. *Crocifissione*"; "17. Giovanni Bellini. *Pala Pesaro*," in Mauro Lucco and Giovanni Carlo Federico Villa (eds), *Giovanni Bellini*, exh. cat. (Milan: Silvana Editore), pp. 136–38, 146–47, 148–50, 182–84, 190–94.

——, 2020, "Gli anni giovanili (circa 1460–1480)," in Mauro Lucco (ed.), *Giovanni Bellini: Catalogo ragionato* (Ponzano Veneto: ZeL Edizioni), pp. 268–85.

—— and Anna Pontani, 1997, "Greek Inscriptions on Two Venetian Renaissance Paintings," *Journal of the Warburg and Courtauld Institutes*, 60, pp. 111–29.

—— and Giovanni Carlo Federico Villa (eds), 2008, *Giovanni Bellini*, exh. cat. (Milan: Silvana Editore).

Ludwig, Gustav, 1911, "Archivalische Beiträge zur Geschichte der venezianischen Kunst," *Aus dem Nachlass G. Ludwigs*, W. von Bode, G. Gronau, and D. von Hadeln (eds) (Berlin: Bruno Cassirer).

Mackenney, Richard, 1987, *Tradesmen and Traders: The World of the Guilds in Venice and Europe, c. 1250–c. 1650* (London and Sidney: Croom Helm).

Maek-Gérard, Michael, 1980, "Die 'Milanexi' in Venedig: Ein Beitrag zur Entwichlungsgeschichte der Lombardi-Werkstatt." *Wallraf-Richartz-Jahrbuch*, 41, pp. 105–30.

Malipiero, Domenico, 1843–44, "Annali veneti dall'anno 1457 al 1500, ordinati e abbreviati dal senatore Francesco Longo," *Archivio storico italiano*, 7.2, pp. 589–720.

Mallett, Michael E., 1967, *The Florentine Galleys in the Fifteenth Century* (Oxford: Clarendon Press).

Mancuso, Cinzia Maria and Antonietta Gallone, 2004, "Giovanni Bellini and His Workshop: A Technical Study of Materials and Working Methods," in Ronda Kasl (ed.), *Giovanni Bellini and the Art of Devotion* (Indianapolis: Indianapolis Museum of Art), pp. 129–51.

Manieri Elia, Giulio (ed.), 2010, *Capolavori restaurati. Le Gallerie dell'Accademia e Save Venice Inc.* (Venice: Marsilio).

Manno, Massimo, 1995, *I Mestieri di Venezia. Storia, arte e devozione delle corporazioni dal XIII al XVIII secolo*, 2nd edn (Cittadella: Biblos).

Marchese, Vincenzo, 1854, *Memorie dei più insigni pittori, scultori e architetti domenicani*, 2 vols, vol. I (Florence: Felice le Monnier).

Marcon, Susy, 2001, "Il *Mappamondo* di Fra' Mauro e il miniatore Leonardo Bellini," in Mario Pianotti and Laura De Rossi (eds), *Per l'arte da Venezia all'Europa. Studi in onore di Giuseppe Maria Pilo*, vol. 1. *Dall'antichità a Caravaggio* (Venice: Edizioni della Laguna), pp. 103–108.

Marconi, Sandra Moschini, 1955, *Gallerie dell'Accademia di Venezia. Opere d'arte dei secoli XIV e XV* (Rome: Istituto Poligrafico dello Stato).

Maresti, Alfonso, 1678, *Teatro genealogico et historico dell'antiche, & illustri famiglie di Ferrara*, 3 vols (Ferrara: Stampa Camerale).

Mariani Canova, Giordana, 1968, "Per Leonardo Bellini," *Arte veneta*, 22, p. 9–20.

——, 1969, *La miniatura veneta del Rinascimento* (Venice: Alfieri).

——, 1972, "Riflessioni su Jacopo Bellini e sul libro dei disegni del Louvre," *Arte veneta*, 26, pp. 9–30.

——, 1995, "La miniatura a Venezia dal Medioevo al Rinascimento," in Rodolfo Pallucchini (ed.), *Storia di Venezia. Temi: L'arte*, 3 vols, vol. II (Rome: Istituto della Enciclopedia Italiana), pp. 769–843.

Marinelli, Sergio (ed.), 1987, *Proposte e restauri. I musei d'arte negli anni ottanta*, exh. cat. (Verona: Museo di Castelvecchio).

——, 1996, "Ferrara, tra Venezia e Modena," in Jadranka Bentini, Sergio Marinelli, and Angelo Mazza (eds), *La pittura veneta negli stati estensi* (Verona: Banca Popolare di Verona – Banco S. Geminiano e S. Prospero), pp. 65–94.

Martin, John J., 2004, *Myths of Reniassance Individualism* (New York: Palgrave Macmillan).

Martinelli, Domenico, 1705, *Il ritratto, overo Le cose più notabili di Venezia* (Venice: Lorenzo Baseggio).

Maschio, Ruggero, 1981, "Le scuole grandi a Venezia," in Girolamo Arnaldi and Manlio Pastore Stocchi (eds), *Storia della cultura veneta*, 6 vols, vol. III, *Dal primo Quattrocento al Concilio di Trento* (Vicenza: Neri Pozza), pp. 193–206.

Mas-Latrie, Louis de, 1869, "Testaments d'artistes vénitien. Jacobello del Fiore, Gentile Bellini, Palma Vecchio," *Bibliothèque de l'École des Chartes*, 30, pp. 195–211.

Mather, Frank Jewett, Jr., 1936, "Veronese Primitives in the Cannon Collection," *Art in America* 24, pp. 49–58.

Matino, Gabriele, 2010, "Gentile Bellini, Giovanni Mansueti e il *Riconoscimento del miracolo della reliquia della Croce al ponte di San Lio*: chiarimenti e proposte," *Venezia cinquecento*, 40.2, pp. 5–34.

——, 2017, "Il ciclo dell'Albergo della Scuola Grande di San Marco: Una nuova prospettiva," in Gherardo Ortalli and Salvatore Settis (eds), *La Scuola Grande di San Marco a Venezia* (Modena: Cosimo Panini Editore), pp. 117–33.

Matthew, Louisa C., 1998, "The Painter's Presence: Signatures in Venetian Renaissance Pictures," *The Art Bulletin*, 80.4, pp. 616–48.

Maze, Daniel W., 2013a, "Giovanni Bellini: Birth, Parentage, and Independence," *Renaissance Quarterly*, 66.3, pp. 783–823.

——, 2013b, *The Bellini Workshop: Emancipations, Enterprises, and Cittadini Originari*, unpublished PhD thesis (Los Angeles: University of California).

——, 2017, "The Life of Giovanni Bellini," in Davide Gasparotto (ed.), *Giovanni Bellini: Landscapes of Faith in Renaissance Venice*, exh. cat. (Los Angeles: J. Paul Getty Museum), pp. 37–55.

Mazzalupi, Matteo, 2006a, "Regesto," in Andrea De Marchi, Laura Laureati, and Lorenza Mochi Onori (eds), *Gentile da Fabriano. Studi e ricerche* (Milan: Electa), pp. 68–84.

——, 2006b, "Siena"; "Roma," in Andrea De Marchi, Laura Laureati, and Lorenza Mochi Onori (eds), *Gentile da Fabriano. Studi e ricerche* (Milan: Electa), pp. 133–34, 140–41.

Mazzotta, Antonio, 2018, "In His Father's Workshop:

Giovanni Bellini's Paintings for the Scuola Grande di S. Giovanni Evangelista, Venice," *The Burlington Magazine*, 160, pp. 283–89.

McHam, Sarah Blake, 1994, *The Chapel of St. Anthony at the Santo and the Development of Venetian Renaissance Sculpture* (Cambridge: Cambridge University Press).

——, 2008, "Reflections of Pliny in Giovanni Bellini's *Woman with a Mirror*," *Artibus et Historiae*, 29, no. 58, pp. 157–71.

——, 2013, *Pliny and the Artistic Culture of the Italian Renaissance: The Legacy of the Natural History* (New Haven and London: Yale University Press).

Medica, Massimo, 2004, "66. Maestro dell'Avicenna. *Paradiso e Inferno*," in Jadranka Bentini, Gian Piero Cammarota, and Daniela Scaglietti Kelescian (eds), *Pinacoteca Nazionale di Bologna. Catalogo generale*, vol. 1, *Dal Duecento a Francesco Francia* (Venice: Marsilio), pp. 187–90.

——, 2012, *Sull'attività bolognese di Giovanni di Nicolò Bellini, pittore e miniatore veneziano*, in Federica Toniolo and Gennaro Toscano (eds), *Miniatura: Lo sguardo e la parola. Studi in onore di Giordana Mariani Canova* (Milan: Silvana Editore), pp. 222–26.

Meiss, Millard, 1957, *Andrea Mantegna as Illuminator* (Gluckstadt and Hamburg: Verlag von J. J. Augustin).

Mellyn, Elizabeth W., 2014, *Mad Tuscans and Their Families: A History of Mental Disorder in Early Modern Italy* (Philadelphia: University of Pennsylvania Press).

Merkel, Ettore, 1973, "Un problema di metodo: La 'Dormitio Virginis' dei Mascoli," *Arte veneta*, 27, pp. 65–80.

Meyer zur Capellen, Jürg, 1980, "Bellini in der Scuola Grande di San Marco," *Zeitschrift für Kunstgeschichte*, 43.1, pp. 104–08.

——, 1985, *Gentile Bellini* (Stuttgart: Franz Steiner Verlag).

Michiel, Marcantonio, 2000, *Notizia d'opere del disegno*, Theodor Frimmel (ed.) (Florence: Edifir).

Milanesi, Gaetano (ed.), 1879, *Le opere di Giorgio Vasari con nuove annotazioni e commenti*, 9 vols (Florence: Sansoni).

——and Carlo Milanesi, 1859, "Prefazione," in Cennino Cennini, *Il libro dell'arte o Trattato della pittura*, Gaetano Milanesi and Carlo Milanesi (eds) (Florence: Felice Le Monnier), pp. III–XXIX.

Minardi, Mauro, 2007, "Gotico padano e gotico internazionale. Ferrara attorno al 1450," in Mauro Natale (ed.), *Cosmè Tura e Francesco del Cossa. L'arte a Ferrara nell'età di Borso d'Este*, exh. cat. (Ferrara: Ferrara Arte), pp. 183–91.

Moench, Esther, 1993, *Les primitifs italiens du Musée des Beaux-Arts de Strasbourg* (Strasbourg: Musées de la Ville de Strasbourg).

Molà, Luca, 1994, *La comunità dei lucchesi a Venezia: Immigrazione e industria della seta nel tardo Medioevo* (Venice: Istituto Veneto di Scienze, Lettere ed Arti).

Molmenti, Pompeo, 1888, "I pittori Bellini: Documenti e ricerche," *Archivio veneto*, 36.1, pp. 221–34.

——and Gustav Ludwig, 1907, *The Life and Works of Vittorio Carpaccio*, Robert H. Hobart Cust (trans.) (London: John Murray).

Moncada, Valentina, 1988, "The Painters' Guild in the Cities of Venice and Padua," *Anthropology of Aesthetics*, 15, pp. 105–21.

Morelli, Giovanni, 1890 [under the pseudonym Ivan Lermolieff], *Kunstkritische Studien über italienische Malerei. Die Galerien Borghese und Doria Panfili in Rom* (Leipzig: Brockhaus).

Morelli, Jacopo (ed.), 1800, *Notizia d'opere di disegno nella prima metà del secolo XVI. Esistenti in Padova, Cremona, Milano, Pavia, Bergamo, Crema e Venezia* (Bassano: s.n.).

Moretti, Lino, 1958, "Di Leonardo Bellini, pittore e miniatore," *Paragone*, 99, pp. 58–66.

——, 1970, "Bellini, Leonardo," in *Dizionario biografico degli italiani*, vol. 7 (Rome: Istituto della Enciclopedia Italiana), pp. 712–13.

Moschini, Giannantonio, 1834, *Giovanni Bellini e pittori contemporanei, almanacco per l'anno 1834* (Venice: Giuseppe Orlandelli).

Muraro, Michelangelo, 1961, "The Statutes of the Venetian *Arti* and the Mosaics of the Mascoli Chapel," *The Art Bulletin*, 43.4, pp. 263–74.

Nagel, Alexander, 2011, *The Controversy of Renaissance Art* (Chicago and London: The University of Chicago Press).

Novellus, Iacobus, 1564, *Volumen statutorum, legum ac iurum D. Venetorum, cum amplissimo indice omnium materiarum* (Venice: Comin da Trino al Segno della Fontana).

O'Connel, Monique, 2009, *Men of Empire: Power and Negotiation in Venice's Maritime State* (Baltimore, MD: The Johns Hopkins University Press).

Olszaniec, Wlodzimierz, 2009, "The Latin Inscription in Giovanni Bellini's *Pietà*," *Journal of the Warburg and Courtauld Institutes*, 72, pp. 233–36.

Orlando, Ermanno, 2017, "La Scuola Grande di San Marco a Venezia. La storia e le fonti," in Gherardo Ortalli and Salvatore Settis (eds), *La Scuola Grande di San Marco a Venezia* (Modena: Franco Cosimo Panini), pp. 13–31.

Orvieto, Paolo, 1969, "Un esperto orientalista del '400: Benedetto Dei," *Rinascimento*, 9, pp. 205–75.
Osano, Shigetoshi, 1981, "Rogier Van Der Weyden e l'Italia: Problemi, riflessioni e ipotesi (II)," *Antichità viva*, 20.5, pp. 5–14.
——, 1990, "'Johanes Belinus me fecit.' Ipotesi per un altro Giovanni Bellini veneziano," *Verona illustrata*, 3, pp. 9–16.
Oxford Latin Dictionary, 1976, vol. V (Oxford: Clarendon Press).
Pacchioni, Guglielmo, 1914, "Un ignoto vivarinesco a S. Andrea di Asola," *Bollettino d'arte*, 8, pp. 399–404.
Pagnotta, Linda, 2005, *Le edizioni italiane della "Legenda Aurea"* (Florence: Apax Libri).
Pallucchini, Rodolfo, 1959, *Giovanni Bellini* (Milan: A. Martello).
Panzer, Georg Wolfgang, 1797, *Annales typographici ab artis inventae origine ad annum MD*, vol. 5 (Nuremberg: Johannis Eberhardi Zeh).
Paoletti, Pietro, 1893, *L'architettura e la scultura del Rinascimento in Venezia*, 2 vols (Venice: Ongania-Naya).
——, 1894, *Raccolta di documenti inediti per servire alla storia della pittura veneziana nei secoli XV e XVI*, fasc. 1, *I Bellini* (Padua: Reale Stabilimento P. Prosperini).
——, 1929, *La Scuola Grande di San Marco* (Venice: Comune di Venezia).
Pattini, Dante, 2013, "Negri, Francesco," *Dizionario biografico degli italiani*, vol. 78 (Rome: Istituto della Enciclopedia Italiana), pp. 116–20.
Pedani Fabris, Maria Pia, 1996, *"Veneta Auctoritate Notarius": Storia del notariato veneziano, 1514–1797* (Milan: Giuffrè).
Pesaro, Cristina, 1992, "Michele Giambono," *Saggi e memorie di storia dell'arte*, 18, pp. 13–69.
Petkov, Kiril, 2014, *The Anxieties of a Citizen Class: The Miracles of the True Cross of San Giovanni Evangelista, Venice 1370–1480* (Leiden and Boston: Brill).
Pichi, Silvia, 2009, "Scuole di devozione, arti e mestieri nella chiesa di San Salvador," in Gianmario Guidarelli (ed.), *La chiesa di San Salvador. Storia, arte, teologia* (Padua: Il Prato), pp. 29–65.
Pincus, Debra, 2004, "Bellini and Sculpture," in Peter Humfrey (ed.), *The Cambridge Companion to Giovanni Bellini* (Cambridge: Cambridge University Press), pp. 122–42.
——, 2008, "Giovanni Bellini's Humanist Signature: Pietro Bembo, Aldus Manutius and Humanism in Early Sixteenth-Century Venice," *Artibus et historiae*, 29.58, pp. 89–119.
——, 2019, "Review of *Mantegna and Bellini*, exh. cat. Caroline Campbell, Dagmar Korbacher, Neville Rowley, and Sarah Vowles (eds)", July 31, 2019, www.caareviews.org/reviews/3563 (accessed December 11, 2020).
Pizzati, Anna, 2006, "Venezia," in Andrea De Marchi, Laura Laureati, and Lorenza Mochi Onori (eds), *Gentile da Fabriano. Studi e ricerche* (Milan: Electa), pp. 104–15.
Poldi, Gianluca and Giovanni Carlo Federico Villa, 2009, *Indagando Bellini* (Milan: Skira).
Pontone, Marzia, 2014, "Giovanni Bellini e Raffaele Zovenzoni. Un sodalizio artistico e letterario nella Venezia del Quattrocento," in Emanuela Daffra (ed.), *Giovanni Bellini. La nascita della pittura devozionale umanistica. Gli studi*, exh. cat. (Milan: Skira), pp. 89–93.
Pope-Hennessey, John, 1986, *Italian Gothic Sculpture* (Oxford: Oxford University Press).
Porras, Stephanie, 2013, "Dürer's Copies," in Stephanie Buck and Stephanie Porras (eds), *The Young Dürer: Drawing the Figure*, exh. cat. (London: The Courtauld Gallery), pp. 57–71.
della Pugliola, Bartolomeo, 1731, "Historia miscella bononiensis ab anno MCIV usque ad annum MCCCXCIV," in Lodovico Antonio Muratori (ed.), *Rerum italicarum scriptores*, vol. 18 (Milan: Ex Typographia Societatis Palatinae in Regia Curia), pp. 237–792.
Pullan, Brian, 1971, *Rich and Poor in Renaissance Venice: The Social Institutions of a Catholic State* (Oxford: Blackwell).
——, 1981, "Natura e carattere delle Scuole," in Terisio Pignatti (ed.), *Le Scuole di Venezia* (Milan: Electa), pp. 9–26.
Pungileoni, Luigi, 1831, "Alcune notizie intorno a Gentile e Giovanni Bellini," *Giornale araldico di scienze, lettere ed arti*, 50, pp. 287–94.
Rawlings, Kandice, 2009, *Liminal Messages: The "Cartellino" in Italian Renaissance Painting*, unpublished PhD thesis (New Brunswick: Rutgers, State University of New Jersey).
Rearick, William R., 1998, "The Drawings of Vittore Belliniano," in Anna Forlani Tempesti and Simonetta Prosperi Valenti Rodino (eds), *Per Luigi Grassi. Disegno e disegni* (Rimini: Galleria), pp. 48–63.
——, 2002, "The Dormitio Virginis in the Cappella dei Mascoli," in Tiziana Franco and Giovanna Valenzano (eds), *De lapidibus aententiae: Scritti di storia dell'arte per Giovanni Lorenzoni* (Padua: Il Poligrafo), pp. 343–62.

Rebenich, Stefan, 2002, *Jerome: The Early Church Fathers* (New York and London: Routledge).
Renosto, Renato, 1963, "La Cappella di S. Orsola a Venezia," *Bollettino dei Musei Civici Veneziani*, 8.2–3, pp. 37–50.
Repishti, Francesco, 2004, "La facciata del Duomo di Milano (1537–1657)," in Francesco Repishti and Richard Schofield, *Architettura e controriforma. I dibattiti per la facciata del Duomo di Milano* (Milan: Electa).
Riccetti, Lucio, 2006, "Orvieto," in Andrea De Marchi, Laura Laureati, and Lorenza Mochi Onori (eds), *Gentile da Fabriano. Studi e ricerche* (Milan: Electa), pp. 135–39.
Ricci, Corrado, 1897, "Un sonetto artistico del secolo XV," *Arte e storia*, XVI, pp. 27–28.
Rice, Eugene F., 1985, *Saint Jerome in the Renaissance* (Baltimore and London: The Johns Hopkins University Press).
——, 1908, *Jacopo Bellini e i suoi libri di disegni*, 2 vols (Florence: Fratelli Alinari).
Richa, Giuseppe, 1762, *Notizie istoriche delle chiese fiorentine*, 10 vols (Florence: Pietro Gaetano Viviani).
Richards, John, 2000, *Altichiero: An Artist and His Patrons in the Italian Trecento* (Cambridge: Cambridge University Press).
Ridolfi, Carlo, 1648, *Le maraviglie dell'arte, overo Le vite de gl'illustri pittori veneti, e dello stato*, 2 vols (Venice: Gio Battista Sgava).
Rigoni, Erice, 1929, "Jacopo Bellini a Padova nel 1430," *Rivista d'arte*, 11.7–9, pp. 261–64.
Robertson, Giles, 1960, "The Earlier Work of Giovanni Bellini," *Journal of the Warburg and Courtauld Institutes*, 23.1/2, pp. 45–59.
——, 1968, *Giovanni Bellini* (Oxford: Clarendon Press).
Robin, Diana, 1991, *Filelfo in Milan: Writings 1451–1477* (Princeton: Princeton University Press).
Robinson, James J., 1905, *Selections from the Public and Private Law of the Romans* (New York: American Book Company).
Rogers, Mary, 1992, "Decorum in Lodovico Dolce and Titian's *Poesie*," in Francis Ames-Lewis and Anka Bednarek (eds), *Decorum in Renaissance Narrative Art* (London: Birkbeck College, University of London), pp. 111–20.
Romano, Dennis, 1987, *Patricians and Popolani: The Social Foundations of the Venetian Renaissance State* (Baltimore, MD: The Johns Hopkins University Press).
——, 1996a, *Housecraft and Statecraft: Domestic Service in Renaissance Venice, 1400–1600* (Baltimore, MD: The Johns Hopkins University Press).
——, 1996b, "L'assistenza e la beneficenza," in Alberto Tenenti and Ugo Tucci (eds), *Storia di Venezia dalle origini alla caduta della Serenissima*, vol. 5, *Il Rinascimento: Società ed economia* (Rome: Istituto della Enciclopedia Italiana), pp. 355–406.
——, 2007, *The Likeness of Venice: A Life of Doge Francesco Foscari, 1373–1457* (New Haven and London: Yale University Press).
——, 2014, "The Limits of Kinship: Family Politics, Venedetta, and the State in Fifteenth-Century Venice," in Michael Knapton, John E. Law, and Alison A. Smith (eds), *Venice and the Veneto during the Renaissance: The Legacy of Benjamin Kohl* (Florence: Firenze University Press), pp. 87–102.
Romano, Giovanni, 2003, "1. Jacopo Bellini," in Giovanni Agosti, Mauro Natale, and Giovanni Romano (eds), *Vincenzo Foppa. Un protagonista del Rinascimento*, exh. cat. (Milan: Skira), pp. 82–83.
Rosand, David, 1972, "*Ut pictor poeta*: Meaning in Titian's *Poesie*," *New Literary History*, 3.3, pp. 527–46.
——, 1984, "Venezia e gli dei," in Manfredo Tafuri (ed.), *"Renovatio urbis." Venezia nell'età di Andrea Gritti (1523–1538)* (Rome: Officina), pp. 201–15.
Rossi, Franco, 2012, *"Melior ut est florenus". Note di storia monetaria veneziana* (Rome: Viella).
Rossi Scarpa, Giulia, 1991, "I mosaici della Cappella Mascoli," in Renato Polacco (ed.), *San Marco. La basilica d'oro* (Milan: Berenice), pp. 287–303.
——, 1997, "La Cappella dei Mascoli: Il trionfo dell'architettura," in Renato Polacco (ed.), *Storia dell'arte marciana: I mosaici* (Venice: Marsilio), pp. 222–34.
Rothlisberger, Marcel, 1958–59, "Studi su Jacopo Bellini," *Saggi e memorie di storia dell'arte*, 2, pp. 41–89.
Rowley, Neville, 2018, "When Bellini *Traced* Mantegna: Two Paintings of the Presentation of Christ in the Temple," in Caroline Campbell et al. (eds), *Mantegna and Bellini*, exh. cat. (London: National Gallery Company), pp. 140–47.
Rubin, Patricia, 2006, "Signposts of Invention: Artists' Signatures in Italian Renaissance Art," *Art History*, 29.4, pp. 563–99.
Ruggiero, Guido, 1985, *The Boundaries of Eros: Sex, Crime and Sexuality in Renaissance Venice* (New York and Oxford: Oxford University Press).
——, 2015, *The Renaissance in Italy: A Social and Cultural History of the Rinascimento* (Cambridge: Cambridge University Press).
Rutherglen, Susannah and Charlotte Hale (eds), 2015,

In a New Light: Giovanni Bellini's "St. Francis in the Desert" at the Frick Collection (New York: The Frick Collection).

Salomon, Xavier, 2017, "'A Ruby among the Pearls': The Lost Church of San Geminiano in Venice and Its Sixteenth-Century Decoration," in Benjamin van Beneden and Nicola Jennings (eds), *David Bowie's Tintoretto: Angel Foretelling the Martyrdom of Saint Catherine of Alexandria* (London: Colnaghi Foundation), pp. 54–69.

Sandberg-Vavalà, Evelyn, 1929, "A Chapter in Fourteenth-Century Iconography: Verona," *The Art Bulletin*, 11.4 (Dec), pp. 376–412.

Sansovino, Francesco, 1581, *Venetia citta nobilissima et singolare descritta in 14 libri* (Venice: Iacomo Sansovino).

Sanudo, Marin, 1879–1903, *I diarii di Marin Sanudo (1496–1533)*, 58 vols, Federico Stefani et al. (eds) (Venice: Tipografia del Commercio di Marco Visentini).

——, 1980, *De origine, situ et magistratibus urbis Venetae ovvero la città di Venezia (1493–1530)*, Angela Caracciolo Aricò (ed.) (Milan: Cisalpino-La Goliardica).

——, 1999, *Le vite dei dogi, 1423–1457*, Angela Caracciolo Aricò (ed.), Chiara Frison (transcription), vol. 1 (Venice: La Malcontenta).

Sapori, Armando, 1956, "I primi viaggi di Levante e di Ponente delle Galere Fiorentine," *Archivio storico italiano*, 114.1 (409), pp. 69–91.

Savoy, Daniel, 2012, *Venice from the Water: Architecture and Myth in an Early Modern City* (New Haven and London: Yale University Press).

Scaglietti Kelescian, Daniela, 1979, "Benadetto Coda," in Daniele Benati et al., *Pittura a Rimini tra gotico e manierismo. Recupero e restauro del patrimonio artistico riminese. Dipinti su tavola*, exh. cat. (Rimini: Museo Civico), pp. 74–75.

——, 1982, "Coda, Benedetto," in *Dizionario biografico degli italiani*, vol. 26 (Rome: Istituto della Enciclopedia Italiana), pp. 556–58.

Schiller, Gertrud, 1971, *Iconography of Christian Art*, Janet Seligman (trans.), 2 vols (London: Lund Humphries).

Schulz, Anne Markham, 1978, "The Sculpture of Giovanni and Bartolomeo Bon and Their Workshop," *Transactions of the American Philosophical Society*, 68, pp. 1–81.

Schulz, Juergen, 1982, "The House of Titian, Aretino, and Sansovino," in David Rosand (ed.), *Titian: His World and His Legacy* (New York: Columbia University Press), pp. 73–118.

Shaw, Keith V., 1994, *The Ovetari Chapel: Patronage, Attribution, and Chronology*, unpublished PhD thesis (Philadelphia: University of Pennsylvania).

—— and Theresa Boccia, 2016, "Andrea Mantegna Called Andrea Squarcione," in Molly Bourne and A. Victor Coonin (eds), *Encountering the Renaissance: Celebrating Gary M. Radke and 50 Years of the Syracuse University Graduate Program in Renaissance Art* (Ramsey, NJ: Wapaac Organization), pp. 317–24.

—— and Theresa M. Boccia-Shaw, 1989, "Mantegna's Pre-1448 Years Reexamined: The Santa Sofia Inscription," *The Art Bulletin*, 71.1, pp. 47–57.

Sigler, Laurence E., 2002, *Fibonacci's "Liber Abaci." A Translation into Modern English of Leonardo Pisano's Book of Calculation* (New York: Springer-Verlag).

Signorini, Rodolfo, 1996, "New Findings about Andrea Mantegna: His Son Ludovico's Post-Mortem Inventory (1510)," *Journal of the Warburg and Courtauld Institutes*, 59, pp. 103–18.

Sinding-Larsen, Staale, 1974, *Christ in the Council Hall: Studies in the Religious Iconography of the Venetian Republic* (Rome: L'Erma di Bretschneider).

Smith, Carl, 2014, *What's in a Name? Michelangelo and the Art of Signature* (Nashville, TN: The K Press).

Sohm, Philip L., 1982, *The Scuola Grande di San Marco 1437–1550: The Architecture of a Venetian Lay Confraternity* (New York and London: Garland).

Sopracasa, Alessio, 2011, "Les Marchands vénitiens à Constantinople d'après une tariffa inédite de 1482," *Studi veneziani*, LXIII, pp. 49–218.

Spiazzi, Anna Maria, 2008, "La decorazione del Salone," in Ettore Vio (ed.), *Il Palazzo della Ragione di Padova. La storia, l'architettura, il restauro* (Campodarsego: Signum), pp. 315–25.

——, Domenico Toniolo, and Camilla Zanuso, 2006, "Saggi di anastilosi dei frammenti degli affreschi della Cappella Ovetari nella chiesa degli Eremitani in Padova," in Davide Banzato, Albert De Nicolò Salmazo, and Anna Maria Spiazzi (eds), *Mantegna e Padova, 1445–1460* (Milan: Skira), pp. 178–79.

Spufford, Peter, 1989, *Money and Its Use in Medieval Europe* (Cambridge: Cambridge University Press).

Stahl, Alan M., 2008, *Zecca. La Zecca di Venezia nell'età medioevale* (Rome: Il Veltro)

Steer, John, 1982, *Alvise Vivarini: His Art and Influence* (Cambridge: Cambridge University Press).

——, 2000, "2. Bartolomeo Vivarini," in Jane Turner (ed.), *Encyclopedia of Italian Renaissance and Mannerist Art*, 2 vols, vol. II, *Macagnino to Zucchi* (London: MacMillan; New York: Grove).

Strehlke, Carl Brandon, 2004, *Italian Paintings 1250–1450 in the John G. Johnson Collection and the Philadelphia Museum of Art* (Philadelphia: Philadelphia Museum of Art).

—— and Mark Tucker, 2002, "The Santa Maria Maggiore Altarpiece," in Carl Brandon Strehlke and Cecilia Frosinini (eds), *The Panel Paintings of Masolino and Masaccio: The Role of Technique* (Milan: 5 Continents), pp. 111–29.

Suriano, Francesco, 1900, *Il trattato di Terra Santa e dell'Oriente di frate Francesco Suriano, missionario e viaggiatore del secolo XV*, Girolamo Golubovich (ed.) (Milan: Tip. Edit. Artigianelli, 1900).

Symeonides, Sibilla, 1977, *Fourteenth and Fifteenth Century Paintings in the Accademia Gallery, Venice* (Florence: L. S. Olschki).

Syson, Luke, 2009, "Reflections on the Mantegna Exhibition in Paris," *The Burlington Magazine*, 151, pp. 526–35.

Szépe, Helena Katalin, 2018, *Venice Illuminated: Power and Painting in Renaissance Manuscripts* (New Haven and London: Yale University Press).

Tagliaferro, Giorgio et al. (eds), 2009, *Le botteghe di Tiziano* (Florence: Alinari 24 Ore).

Tassini, Giuseppe, 1964, *Curiosità veneziane, ovvero Origini delle denominazioni stradali* (Venice: Filippi).

Tazzara, Corey, 2017, *The Free Port of Livorno and the Transformation of the Mediterranean World (1574–1790)* (New York: Oxford University Press).

Tempestini, Anchise, 2003, "Riflessioni su alcune opere di Giovanni Bellini o a lui attribuite," *Studi di storia dell'arte*, 14, pp. 89–108.

——, 2019, "La famiglia dei pittori Bellini. Precisazioni e novità," *Artibus et historiae*, 80.40, pp. 25–33.

Thode, Henry, 1895, "Neue archivalische Forschungen über venezianische Kunst," *Repertorium für Kunstwissenschaft*, 18, pp. 180–93.

——, 1898, "Andrea del Castagno in Venedig," in Karl Masner (ed.), *Festschrift für Otto Benndorf zu seinem 60. Geburtstage gewidmet von Schülern, Freunden und Fachgenossen* (Vienna: Hölder), pp. 307–17.

Thompson, Daniel V., Jr. (ed.), 1932, Cennino Cennini, *Il libro dell'arte*, 2 vols (New Haven: Yale University Press).

Thorndike, Lynn, 1934, *A History of Magic and Experimental Science*, 8 vols, vol. IV, *Fourteenth and Fifteenth Century* (New York: Columbia University Press).

Toffanello, Marcello, 2010, *Le arti a Ferrara nel Quattrocento. Gli artisti e la corte* (Ferrara: Edisai Edizioni).

Toscano, Gennaro, 2006–07, "40a–b. Vita e passione di San Maurizio," in Davide Banzato, Alberta De Nicolò Salmazo, and Anna Maria Spiazzi (eds), *Mantegna e Padova, 1445–1460*, exh. cat. (Milan: Skira), pp. 224–26.

Tramelli, Barbara, 2016, "Sofonisba Anguissola, 'Pittora de Natura': A Page from Van Dyck's Italian Sketchbook," in Sheila Barker (ed.), *Women Artists in Early Modern Italy: Careers, Fame, and Collectors* (Turnhout: Harvey Miller), pp. 39–45.

Trincanato, Egle Renata, 1997, *Su Venezia e la laguna veneta, e altri scritti di architettura, 1948–93* (Rome: Officina Edizioni).

Trexler, Richard C., 1980, *Public Life in Renaissance Florence* (New York: Academic Press).

Ughi, Luigi, 1804, *Dizionario storico degli uomini illustri ferraresi*, 2 vols (Ferrara: Eredi di Giuseppe Rinaldi).

Varanini, Gian Maria, 1990, "Un pittore veneziano a Rovereto nel 1470," *Verona illustrata*, 3, pp. 5–8.

Vasari, Giorgio, 1832–38, *Le opere di Giorgio Vasari pittore e architetto aretino, parte prima, contentente porzione delle vite dei più eccellenti pittori scultori e architetti*, Giovanni Masselli (ed.) (Florence: David Passigli e Soci).

——, 1878–85, *Le opere di Giorgio Vasari con nuove annotazioni e commenti*, Gaetano Milanesi (ed.), 9 vols (Florence: Sansoni).

——, 1896, *Le vite de' più eccellenti pittori, scultori e archittetori scritte da M. Giorgio Vasari pittore et architetto aretino*, Adolfo Venturi (ed.), vol. 1, *Gentile da Fabriano e Il Pisanello* (Florence: Sansoni).

——, 1966–87, *Le vite de' più eccellenti pittori, scultori e architettori: Nelle redazioni del 1550 e 1568*, Rosanna Bettarini and Paola Barocchi (eds), 6 vols (Florence: Sansoni).

Venturi, Adolfo, 1884, "I primordi del Rinascimento artistico a Ferrara," *Rivista storica italiana*, I, pp. 591–631.

Vercellin, Giorgio, 1980, "Mercanti turchi e sensali a Venezia," *Studi veneziani*, 4, pp. 45–78.

Villa, Giovanni Carlo Federico, 2008, "10. Giovanni Bellini. *Cristo morto compianto dalla Madonna e san Giovanni Evangelista (Pietà)*," in Mauro Lucco and Giovanni Carlo Federico Villa (eds), *Giovanni Bellini*, exh. cat. (Milan: Silvana Editore), pp. 164–66.

——, 2017, "Andrea Mantegna and Giovanni Bellini: The Hidden Dialogue," in Brigit Blass-Simmen and Stefan Weppelmann (eds), *Padua and Venice: Transcultural Exchange in the Early Modern Age* (Berlin and Boston: de Gruyter), pp. 79–92.

Vinco, Mattia, 2014, "*L'Istrias* di Raffaele Zovenzoni e Giovanni Bellini ante 1475," in Emanuela Daffra (ed.),

Giovanni Bellini: La nascita della pittura devozionale umanistica. Gli studi, exh. cat. (Milan: Skira), pp. 97–102.

——, 2019, "Frammenti innovativi: Le prime pale d'altare di Giovanni Bellini a Venezia," in Peter Humfrey et al. (eds), *Giovanni Bellini "... il migliore nella pittura"* (Venice: Lineadacqua, Fondazione Giorgio Cini), pp. 59–73.

Vio, Gastone, 2004, *Le scuole piccole nella Venezia dei dogi. Note d'archivio per la storia delle confraternite veneziane* (Costabissara (VI): A. Colla).

Volpe, Carlo, 1978, "Per gli inizi di Giovanni Bellini," *Arte veneta*, 32, pp. 56–60.

Voltini, Franco, 1958, "Antonio della Corona ad Asola," *Paragone*, 9, pp. 9–22.

Voragine, Jacobus de, 1969, *The Golden Legend of Jacobus de Voragine*, William Granger Ryan and Helmut Ripperger (eds and trans.) (New York: Arno Press).

——1993, *The Golden Legend: Readings on the Saints*, W. Granger Ryan (ed. and trans.), 2 vols (Princeton: Princeton University Press).

Vowles, Sarah, 2018, "Saint Jerome," in Caroline Campbell et al. (eds), *Mantegna and Bellini*, exh. cat. (London: National Gallery), pp. 126–29.

——and Dagmar Korbacher, 2018, "Jacopo Bellini and the Formation of Giovanni," in Caroline Campbell et al. (eds), *Mantegna and Bellini*, exh. cat. (London: National Gallery), pp. 104–07, 270.

Wang, Aileen June, 2004, "Michelangelo's Signature," *The Sixteenth Century Journal*, 35, pp. 447–73.

Weston, Hazel, 2009, *"Christ's Descent into Limbo" at the Bristol City Art Gallery and Museum: A Singular Work of Art*, unpublished MPhil thesis (Birmingham: University of Birmingham).

Wheeler, Stephen M., 2000, *Narrative Dynamics in Ovid's "Metamorphoses"* (Tübingen: Narr)

Whitehouse, Fiona Lucy, 2012, *The Influence of Netherlandish Paintings on Giovanni Bellini and Cima da Conegliano*, unpublished PhD thesis (London: Birkbeck College, University of London).

Wilson, Carolyn C., 1977, *Bellini's Pesaro Altarpiece: A Study in Context and Meaning*, unpublished PhD thesis (New York: New York University).

——, 2004, "Giovanni Bellini and the Modern Manner," in Peter Humfrey (ed.), *The Cambridge Companion to Giovanni Bellini* (Cambridge: Cambridge University Press), pp. 95–121.

——(ed), 2015, *Examining Giovanni Bellini: An Art "More Human and More Divine"* (Turnhout: Brepols).

——, 2019, "Moving Forward: Bellini's Pesaro Altarpiece in View of New Advances," in Peter Humfrey et al. (eds), *Giovanni Bellini "... il migliore nella pittura"* (Venice: Lineadacqua, Fondazione Giorgio Cini), pp. 89–102.

Wolfgang, Marvin E., 1960, "A Florentine Prison: Le Carceri delle Stinche," *Studies in the Renaissance*, 7, pp. 148–66.

——, 1990, "Crime and Punishment in Renaissance Florence," *The Journal of Criminal Law and Criminology*, 81.3, pp. 567–84.

Wolfthal, Diane and Cathy Metzger, 2014, *Los Angeles Museums*, vol. 22, *Corpus of Early Netherlandish Painting* (Brussels: Royal Institute for Cultural Heritage).

Wood, Jeryldene M., 2005, "Young Raphael and the Practice of Painting in Renaissance Italy," in Marcia B. Hall (ed.), *The Cambridge Companion to Raphael* (Cambridge: Cambridge University Press), pp. 15–35.

Worthen, Amy, 2015, "An Inconvenient Text: The *Supplementum Chronicarum* as a Source for Information about Gentile and Giovanni Bellini," in Carolyn C. Wilson (ed.), *Examining Giovanni Bellini: "An Art More Human and More Divine"* (Turnhout: Brepols, 2015), pp. 39–59.

Wright, Frederick Adam (ed. and trans.), 1933, *Select Letters of St. Jerome* (London: Heinemann; Cambridge, MA: Harvard University Press, The Loeb Classical Library).

Wurthmann, William B., 1975, *The Scuole Grandi and Venetian Art, 1260–c. 1500*, unpublished PhD thesis (Chicago: The University of Chicago).

——, 1989, "The Council of Ten and the Scuole Grandi in Early Renaissance Venice," *Studi veneziani*, 18, pp. 15–66.

Yousefzadeh, Mahnaz, 2018, *Florence's Embassy to the Sultan of Egypt: An English Translation of Felice Brancacci's Diary* (Cham: PalgraveMacmillan).

Yriarte, Charles, 1896, "Isabelle d'Este et les artistes de son temps, V. Relations d'Isabelle avec Giovanni Bellini," *Gazette des beaux-arts*, 38, 3rd series, 15, pp. 215–28.

Zani, Pietro, 1820, *Enciclopedia metodica critico-ragionata delle belle arti*, 28 vols (Parma: Tipografia Ducale).

Zannini, Andrea, 1993, *Burocrazia e burocrati a Venezia in età moderna: I cittadini originari (sec. XVI–XVIII)* (Venice: Istituto Veneto di Lettere, Scienze e Arti).

Ziliotto, Baccio, 1950, *Raffaele Zovenzoni. La vita, i carmi* (Trieste: Arti Grafiche Smolars).

Zorzi, Alvise, 1972, *Venezia scomparsa*, 2 vols (Milan: Electa).

Index

Page references in *italic* refer to the illustrations

adoption, in Bellini family, 23–24, 132, 133–34, 137
Aesop, 96
Alberti, Leon Battista, 85–88
Aleotti, Ulisse degli, 42, 85
Alixeta, granddaughter of Nicoletto Bellini, 6, 23–24, 150n2
altarpieces, Renaissance designs by Jacopo Bellini, 43, 108
Altichiero, 43, 47, 66–68, 85
  Chapel of San Giacomo, Basilica of Sant'Antonio, Padua, frescoes, 85
    Crucifixion, 72, *73*
  Church of the Eremitani, Padua, *Coronation of the Virgin* (destroyed), 56, *56*, 63
  Oratory of San Giorgio, Padua, frescoes, 85, 168n13
    Adoration of the Magi, 108, *109*
  Palazzo Scaligeri, Verona, frescoes, 85
Amadi family, 33
Angelico, Fra, 64
Anguissola, Sofonisba, 162n5
Anjou, Duke of *see* René I
antiquity, interest in, 43, 47, 98
Antonello da Messina, 159n2
architecture
  architectural settings
    Brescia altarpiece predella panels, 66, 68–70, 71, 76
    Ferrara *Coronation of the Virgin*, 48, 50–52, 56–58
  influence of Venetian architecture on Giovanni Bellini's paintings, 36–38, 56–58
  in Jacopo Bellini's Paris sketchbook, 50–52, 68, 71, 76, 85–88, 93, 108
  see also linear perspective; portal motif
Ariosto, Ludovico, 140, 141, 142
Asola, cathedral, 143
Avicenna, Master of the *see* Master of the Avicenna

Barbari, Jacopo de', *View of Venice*, *24*
Baresina, Caterina, wife of Gentile Bellini, 6, 150n1
Baruffaldi, Girolamo, 141
Bayer, Andrea, 135–36
Becherucci, Luisa, 141
Belin, Zovano de, da Modena, 138
Belin, Zuane, 138
Belinus, Johannes, 138
Bellini, Alvise, son of Giovanni, 7, 29, 135, 148, 150n3
Bellini, Elena, wife of Paolo Remarius, 6, 23, 25, 26, 130, 150n4
Bellini, Gentile
  in Bellini workshop, 45, 66, 80, 90, 107, 115, 167n17
  family tree and chronology, 6, 148, 150n5
  named after Gentile da Fabriano, 19
  parentage and relationship with Giovanni Bellini, 12, 33, 124, 125–28, 129, 132–34
  WORKS
  Basilica of San Marco, Venice, organ doors, 107, 160n4
  Ducal Palace, Venice, Great Council Hall, 84
  Procession in Piazza San Marco (Venice, Gallerie dell'Accademia), *83*
  Saint Mark Preaching in Alexandria (completed by Giovanni Bellini) (Milan, Pinacoteca di Brera), *83*, 165n20
  Scuola di San Marco, Venice, *sala capitolare*, 82, 135
  Sultan Mehmet II (London, National Gallery), 125, *126*
Bellini, Giovanni
  artistic style
    assimilation of motifs and ideas from other artists, 58, 63, 89, 106–7, 115–16, 121
    color contrasts, 60–62
    influence of Venetian architecture, 36–38, 56–58
    reuse of motifs from own work, 118
    visual empathy, 78
    see also landscape; light; linear perspective; portal motif
  in Bellini workshop
    artistic training, 41–47
    as Jacopo Bellini's assistant, 1440s, 80–89, 90–96
  birth and parentage, 11–12, 14, 26–29, 34, 124–37
  childhood and education, 14, 32, 34–35, 36–47
  death and burial, 140
    age at death, 125, 129
  and *divisio* (1440), 26, 45–47, 62, 129–31, 133, 142–43, 147
  family tree and chronology, 7, 148, 150n6
  illegitimacy, disproved, 26, 124, 128

Bellini, Giovanni (*cont.*)
as Jacopo Bellini's half-brother, 12, 26–29, 34–35, 125, 128–34
and Mantegna
artistic relationship, 12, 98–100, 125, 169n33, 170n39
older or younger?, 12, 121, 124, 125, 129
manuscript illuminations, 113
see also below, WORKS, Marcello Manuscript illuminations
namesakes, 138, 143
see also "Bellini, Giovanni, Ferrarese"; "Bellini, Giovanni, il Vecchio"
portrait, *10*
relationship with Gentile Bellini, 12, 124, 125–28, 129, 132–34
signature, 38–39, *39–40*, 42, 100–101, *103*
on *Coronation of the Virgin* (Ferrara), 48, 50, 58, *58*, 62, 143
WORKS
Agony in the Garden (London, National Gallery), 116
Annunciation (attributed) (Turin, Galleria Sabauda), 96
Birth of the Virgin (attributed) (Turin, Galleria Sabauda), *95*, 96
Brescia Altarpiece, predella panels, 14–16, 64–78, *65*
Birth of the Virgin, 14, 66–70, *67*, 78, 96
Death of the Virgin, 76, *77*
Miracle of the Snow, 74–76, *75*
Presentation of the Virgin, 14–16, 64–66, *65*, 70–71, *70*, 78
Visitation, 14–16, 72–74, *73*, 92, *92*
Coronation of the Virgin (Ferrara, Pinacoteca Nazionale), 14, 48–63, *49–51*, *54*, *57–58*, 116, 121, 147
attributed to "Giovanni Bellini il Vecchio", 143–45, 147
parallels with Brescia Altarpiece, predella panels, 64–66, *65*, 71, 72, 78
Coronation of the Virgin (Pesaro Altarpiece) (Pesaro, Museo Civico), *59*, 60, 93
Crucifixion with the Virgin and Saint John the Evangelist (Venice, Museo Correr), 16, *61*, 62, 116–21, *117*, *119–20*
Davis *Virgin and Child* (New York, Metropolitan Museum of Art), 12
Feast of the Gods (Washington, National Gallery of Art), 125
Imago Pietatis (Milan, Museo Poldi Pezzoli), 12
Marcello Manuscript illuminations (*Passion of St Maurice*) (Paris, Bibliothèque de l'Arsenal), 16, 108–16, *111*
Assembly of the Order of the Crescent, 93, *110*
Saint Maurice, *112*, 113–16, *114–15*
Pietà (Bergamo, Accademia Carrara), 12
Saint Francis in the Desert (New York, Frick Collection), *15*, 16, 68, 78, 90, 101
Saint Jerome in the Wilderness (Birmingham, Barber Institute of the Fine Arts), 12, 16, 90–105, *97*, *103–5*, 108, 116, 125
Saint Mark Preaching in Alexandria (with Gentile Bellini) (Milan, Pinacoteca di Brera), *83*, 165n20
Transfiguration of Christ (Venice, Museo Correr), 12, *13*, 118
Virgin and Child (Lochis Madonna) (Bergamo, Accademia Carrara), *79*
Visitation (Venice, Basilica of San Marco, Mascoli Chapel), 90–93, *91–93*, *104*
"Bellini, Giovanni, Ferrarese", 139–43, 145, 146
"Bellini, Giovanni, il Vecchio", 16, 129, 136, 138, 142–47
"Bellini, Giovanni di Nicolò", 145–47
Bellini, Giovanni Pietro, son of Stefano of Venice, 138, *139*
Bellini, Jacopo
artistic style, 78, 106–7, 116
birth and parentage, 23
as *degano* of Scuola Grande di San Giovanni Evangelista, 47, 95
and *divisio* (1440), 26, 45–47, 62, 129–31, 133, 142–43, 147
family tree and chronology, 6, 148, 150n7
and father's will, 23, 25, 26, 31
in Ferrara, 33, 45–47, 85, 88, 142
in Florence, 14, 18, 19–21, 22–23, 30–31, 106
as Gentile da Fabriano's assistant, 14, 18–23, 30–31, 33, 53, 80, 107
as Giovanni Bellini's half-brother, 12, 26–29, 34–35, 125, 128–34
London sketchbook, 42–43, 71, *72*, 164n17
and manuscript illumination, 108, 113
Paris sketchbook, 42–45, 69, 85–88, 107, 118
influence on Brescia Altarpiece predella panels, 68, 70, 71, *71*, 72–74, *74–75*, 76, *77*
influence on Ferrara *Coronation of the Virgin*, 48, 50–52, *51–53*, 63
see also below, WORKS, Paris sketchbook
signatures and inscriptions, 42, 100–101, *103*
workshop *see* Bellini workshop
WORKS
Annunciation (Brescia Altarpiece) (Brescia, Sant'Alessandro), 60, 64, *65*, 76, 162n20
Gattamelata Altarpiece (lost), 45, 81, 132, 134, 137
London sketchbook, *Presentation of the Virgin in the Temple*, 71, *72*
Madonna and Child (Venice, Gallerie dell'Accademia), 52, *54*, 162n20
Paris sketchbook (Louvre, Cabinet des dessins)
Adoration of the Magi, 108, *109*
Architectural Setting with the Presentation of Our Lady, 85, *86–87*

Christ among the Doctors, 52, *53*
Crucifixion with the Virgin and Saint John, 116–18, *118*
Death of the Virgin, 50, *51*, 76
Departure for the Hunt, 50, *51*
Flagellation of Christ, 93, *94*
Galloping Horseman and Warrior on Foot, 113–15, *114–15*
Judgment of Solomon, 50, *52*, 71, 76, *77*
King David Conquering Goliath, 113, *113–14*
Lamentation/Entombment of Christ, 74, *74*
Saint Jerome in the Wilderness, 100, *102*, *105*
Saint Jerome Reading in the Wilderness, 98, *99*, *104*
Saint John the Baptist Preaching in a Harbor City, *75*, 76
Saint John the Baptist Standing in a Niche, *107*, 108
Seven Lions and Three Stags, 100, *101*, *105*
Stigmatization of Saint Francis, 74, *74*
Urban Square with Church Façade, 71, *71*, 88
Warriors Combat a Dragon, 113–15, *114–15*
Penitent Saint Jerome (Verona, Museo di Castelvecchio), 98, *99*
Venice
Basilica of San Marco, Mascoli Chapel, 90–93, *91–93*, *104*
Scuola Grande di San Giovanni Evangelista, 81–82, 95–96
Scuola Grande di San Marco, 81–89, 90, 134
Scuola Grande di Santa Maria della Carità, 82, 164n5
Virgin and Child (Lovere, Galleria Tadini), 100–101, *103*
Virgin and Child with Donor (Paris, Musée du Louvre), *46*, 47, 52, 60
Bellini, Leonardo, 6, 23, 25, 132, 133, 150n8, 170n37
in Bellini workshop, 80, 90, 115
as miniaturist, 66, 145, *146*
Bellini, Leonello, 6, 41, 47, 148, 150–51n9, 170n37
dowry receipt, 33, *34*
Bellini, Nicoletto, 6, 23–28, 31–32, 128–33, 148, 151n11
will, 14, 23–25, 26–28, *27*, 130–31
wives *see* Vendramin, Franceschina; Zanina (Giovannina)
Bellini, Nicolò, 6, 33, 41, 125, 132, 148, 151n12
Bellini, Nicolosia, wife of Andrea Mantegna, 6, 33, 148, 150n12, 159n46, 174n69
marriage, 100, 124
Bellini workshop
establishment, 1420s, 30–35
Gentile Bellini in, 45, 66, 80, 90, 107, 115, 167n17
Giovanni Bellini's artistic training, 41–47
Leonardo Bellini in, 80, 90, 115
location, 41, 127, 129, 130
major commissions, 1440s, 80–89, 90–96
paliotto attributed to, 169–70n37
Belliniano, Vittore, 133
Portrait of a Man (Chantilly, Musée Condé), *10*
Bellino, Johannes, 138
Bellino, Zohanne, 138, *139*, 142–43, 146
Bellosi, Luciano, 108
Bembo, Pietro, 19, 60, 95
Benveduti, Romano de, 22
Bergamo, Accademia Carrara, Bellini, Giovanni
Pietà, *12*
Virgin and Child (Lochis Madonna), *79*
Bernardo, son of Silvestro, fight with Jacopo Bellini, 19–22, 30
Billanovich, Eugenio, 142–43, 145, 146
Birmingham, Barber Institute of the Fine Arts, Bellini, Giovanni, *Saint Jerome in the Wilderness*, 12, 16, 90–105, *97*, *103–5*, 108, 116, 125
Bocheta, Alvise, 7, 34, 135, 151n15
Bocheta, Francesco, 7, 135, 151n16
Bocheta, Ginevra, wife of Giovanni Bellini, 7, 29, 34, 135, 148, 151n17
Bocheta, Giovanni, 7, 151n18
Bocheta, Lucia, 7, 34, 135, 151n19
Bocheta, Lucrezia, 7, 151n20
Bocheta, Sebastiano, 7, 151n21
Bologna, 45, 145–46
Archivio di Stato di Bologna, *Saint Petronius Enthroned*, 145, *146*
Pinacoteca Nazionale, Master of the Avicenna (attributed), *Heaven and Hell*, *144*, 145
Bon, Bartolomeo, Porta della Carta (Venice, Ducal Palace), 56–58, *57–58*, 116
Bono, Luca and Vito, 130
Borbottoni, Fabio
Le Stinche Prison Seen from Via Ghibellina (Florence, Palazzo dell'Ente Cassa di Risparmio), *22*
View of Piazza delle Cipolle with the Church of Santa Maria degli Ughi (Florence, Palazzo dell'Ente Cassa di Risparmio), *19*
Borsetti, Ferrante, 141
Bouts, Dieric, *Crucifixion* (Royal Museums of Fine Arts, Brussels), 118–21, *119–20*
Bragadin, Donato, 42, 45, 130
Brescia, 18, 45
Sant'Alessandro, Bellini, Jacopo and Giovanni, Brescia Altarpiece, 14–16, 64–78, *65*
Annunciation, 60, 64, *65*, 76, 162n20
Birth of the Virgin, 14, 66–70, *67*, 78, 96
Death of the Virgin, 76, *77*
Miracle of the Snow, 74–76, *75*
Presentation of the Virgin, 14–16, 64–66, *65*, 70–71, *70*, 78
Visitation, 14–16, 72–74, *73*, 92, *92*
Bridget, Saint, vision of, 96
Brown, David Alan, 136
Brussels, Royal Museums of Fine Arts, Bouts, Dieric, *Crucifixion*, 118–21, *119–20*
Buscarino, Lorenzo, 23, 27–28

Canaletto, Antonio, *The Square of Saint Mark's and the Piazzetta, Venice* (Hartford, CT, Wadsworth Atheneum Museum of Art), *38*
Carpaccio, Vittore, 93
Castagno, Andrea del, 92
Cavalca, Domenico, *Vite dei Santi Padri*, 40, 96
Cavalcaselle, Giovanni Battista, 100, 127
Cellini, Benvenuto, *22*
Cennini, Cennino, 106–7
Chantilly, Musée Condé, Belliniano, Vittore, *Portrait of a Man*, *10*
children and adolescents, paintings by, 48, 62–63
Cittadella, Cesare, 141, 142
classical subjects *see* antiquity
Coda, Benedetto, 140, 141–42
color contrasts in Giovanni Bellini's paintings, 60–62
Crowe, Joseph Archer, 100, 127

Decembrio, Angelo, 85
d'Este, Isabella, Marchesa, letter to, 38, *39*, 41
d'Este, Leonello, Marchese, 33, *46*, 47, 85, 140
d'Este, Niccolò III, Marchese, 47, 140
d'Este court (Ferrara), 33, 45–47, 85, 88, 142
divisio (1440), 26, 45–47, 62, 129–31, 133, 142–43, 147
Dominici, Fiornovella, 7, 152n26
Dominici, Giobbe, 7, 34, 134, 135, 152n27
Dominici, Giovanni (d. by 1457), 7, 152n28
Dominici, Giovanni (d. 1463), 7, 34, 152n29
Dominici, Lucrezia, 7, 34, 152n30
Dominici, Samaritana *see* Vendramin, Samaritana
Donatello, 43, 88, 166n30–31
  Saint John the Baptist (Venice, Santa Maria dei Frari), *107*, 108
dowries in Renaissance Venice, 25, 32, 33, *34*, 130, 131, 132
Dürer, Albrecht, 162n5, 168n4

education in 15th-century Venice, 38–41
Elena (di Giorgio), wife of Matteo Mondo, 7, 151n24
Elmis, Francesco (Francesco dagli Elmi), 161n52, 172n44–45
emancipation, in Venetian law, 31–32, 62, 102, 129, 132
Ercole del Fiore, 60, 133
  Coronation of the Virgin (attributed) (Venice, Gallerie dell'Accademia), 60, *61*
Eyck, Jan van, 118

Fabriano, 18, 53
Ferrara
  "Giovanni Bellini Ferrarese", 139–43, 145, 146
  Jacopo Bellini visits d'Este court, 33, 45–47, 85, 88, 142
  Pinacoteca Nazionale *see* Bellini, Giovanni, WORKS, *Coronation of the Virgin*
  San Nicolò, 139–40, 145, 147
Fibonacci, Leonardo, 40
Fiocco, Giuseppe, 125
Fiori, Emanuela, 145
Florence
  Galleria degli Uffizi, Gentile da Fabriano
    Nativity, predella panel of Strozzi Altarpiece, 69, *69*, 98
    panels from Quaratesi Altarpiece, *32*
  Gentile da Fabriano's workshop, 18, *19*, 85
  Jacopo Bellini in, 14, 18, 19–21, 22–23, 30–31, 106
  Le Stinche, prison, 22–23, *22*, 30, 106
  Palazzo dell'Ente Cassa di Risparmio, Borbottoni, Fabio
    Le Stinche Prison Seen from Via Ghibellina, *22*
    View of Piazza delle Cipolle with the Church of Santa Maria degli Ughi, *19*
  Santissima Annunziata, 64
Foligno, 18
Fontana, Giovanni, 84–85

Foresti, Jacopo Filippo, 125, 130, 132
Foscari, Doge Francesco, 92
Francesco (da Pesaro), uncle of Anna Rinversi, 6, 151n22
fraterna compagnia (fraternal partnership), Jacopo and Giovanni Bellini, 31, 34, 45–47, 129–30, 133
  see also divisio
Fry, Roger, 125, 128

Gabriele (di Giorgio), 7, 151–52n25
garzoni, 45
Genoa, 21
Gentile da Fabriano
  influence on Giovanni Bellini, 53–56, 58, 159n2
  as Jacopo Bellini's master, 14, 18–23, 30–31, 33, 53, 80, 107
  in Venice, 18, 25, 41, 84
  workshop in Florence, 18, *19*, 85
  WORKS
  Coronation of the Virgin with Saints (Valle Romita Polyptych) (Milan, Pinacoteca di Brera), 53–56, *54*, 63
  Ducal Palace, Venice, Great Council Hall, 84
  Madonna and Child, with Saints Lawrence and Julian (New York, Frick Collection), 18, *20*
  Madonna of Humility (Pisa, Museo Nazionale di San Matteo), 18, *21*
  Nativity (predella panel of Strozzi Altarpiece) (Florence, Galleria degli Uffizi), 69, *69*, 98
  Quaratesi Altarpiece (Florence/London/Rome), 30–31, *32–33*
Gentili, Augusto, 136
Gera (Rinversi), 6, 152n38
Giambono, Michele, 42, 84, 88, 93
  Saint Chrysogonus on Horseback (Venice, San Trovaso), *43*
Giorgione, 78, 90, 121
Giotto di Bondone, Scrovegni Chapel frescoes, Padua, 66, *68*, 71
Giovanni d'Alemagna, 42, 81, 88
  and Antonio Vivarini, *Madonna*

of the Rosary (Venice, San Zaccaria), *44*
Goffen, Rona, 128
Golden Legend see Voragine, Jacobus de
Gonzaga, Marchese Ludovico, 100
Gothic style
late Gothic painting, 41–42, 60, 63, 81, 88, 102
Venetian architecture, 36–38
Grave, Johannes, 136–37
Guariento di Arpo, 63, 84
Guarini, Marc'Antonio, 139–42, 145
Guerzi, Chiara, 146, 147
Gulinelli, Contessa Alma, 143

Hartford, CT, Wadsworth Atheneum Museum of Art, Canaletto, *The Square of Saint Mark's and the Piazzetta, Venice*, *38*
humanism, 38, 42, 60, 84–85, 113
and education, 39–40

illuminated manuscripts *see* manuscript illuminations
Istanbul, Gentile Bellini visits, 125, 127

Jacobello del Fiore, 41–42, 84, 133
Justice Enthroned between the Archangels Gabriel and Michael (Venice, Gallerie dell'Accademia), 42, *42*
Jerome, Saint, 96
see also Bellini, Giovanni, WORKS, *Saint Jerome in the Wilderness*

landscape
in Birmingham *Saint Jerome*, 96, 98–100
in Brescia Altarpiece, *Visitation*, 72–74, *73*
in Correr *Crucifixion*, 116, 118–21
see also portal motif
Latin, artists' knowledge of, 40, 41, 137
Legenda Aurea see Voragine, Jacobus de
light, Giovanni Bellini's depiction of
in Birmingham *Saint Jerome*, 96–98, 108
in Brescia Altarpiece, predella panels, 16, 69, 71, 74, 76, 78, 116
influence of Venice, 36, *37*
use of a consistent light source, 16, 69, 71, 76, 98, 116
linear perspective
in Brescia Altarpiece, predella panels, 66, 70, 71, 76, 78, 89
in Jacopo Bellini's Paris sketchbook, 43–45, 50, 63, 85–88, *86–87*, 108
lions, 96, 98, 100, 101, *104–5*
Livorno, 21
Lombardo, Antonio, 80, *81*
Lombardo, Pietro, 80, *81*
London
British Museum, Bellini, Jacopo, London sketchbook, 42–43, 164n17
Presentation of the Virgin in the Temple, 71, *72*
National Gallery
Bellini, Gentile, *Sultan Mehmet II*, 125, *126*
Bellini, Giovanni, *Agony in the Garden*, 116
Gentile da Fabriano, panel from Quaratesi Altarpiece, *32*
Longhi, Roberto, 125
Lorenzo da Venezia, 163n4, 163n25
Lovere, Galleria Tadini, Bellini, Jacopo, *Virgin and Child*, 100–101, *103*
Lucca, 33

Machiavelli, Niccolò, *22*
Mantegna, Andrea
Church of the Eremitani, Padua, Ovetari Chapel, 166n30, 168n7
Calling of Saints James and John, 98–100, *100*, 102, *104*, 108, 116
family tree and chronology, 6, 148, 152n31
influence on Gentile Bellini, 107
marriage to Nicolosia Bellini, 100, 124
works attributed to, 92, 108, 167n7
relationship with Giovanni Bellini
artistic relationship, 12, 98–100, 125, 169n33, 170n39
older or younger?, 12, 121, 124, 125, 129
youthful work, 162n5
Mantua, 100
manuscript illuminations
by Giovanni Bellini, 113
see also Bellini, Giovanni, WORKS, Marcello Manuscript illuminations
by Leonardo Bellini, 66
Marcello, Jacopo Antonio, 108, *111*
see also Bellini, Giovanni, WORKS, Marcello Manuscript illuminations
Maria, wife of Gentile Bellini, 6, 151n23
Masaccio, 166n31
Masolino, *Founding of Santa Maria Maggiore* (Naples, Museo Nazionale di Capodimonte), *75*, 76
Masselli, Giovanni, 127
Master of the Avicenna, 145–46, 147
Heaven and Hell (attributed) (Bologna, Pinacoteca Nazionale), *144*, 145
mathematics, 40
see also linear perspective
Medica, Massimo, 145–46, 147
meditational paintings, 16, 90
Mehmet II, Sultan, 125, *126*, 127
Menega, adopted daughter of Nicoletto Bellini, 6, 23–24, 151n10
mercantesca script, 38, 39, 41
Michelangelo, 62, 162n5
Michiel, Elisabetta, wife of Leonello Bellini, 6, 152n32
Milan
cathedral, 138
Museo Poldi Pezzoli, Bellini, Giovanni, *Imago Pietatis*, 12
Pinacoteca di Brera
Bellini, Gentile and Giovanni, *Saint Mark Preaching in Alexandria*, *83*, 165n20
Gentile da Fabriano, *Coronation of the Virgin with Saints* (Valle Romita Polyptych), 53–56, *54*, 63

miniatures *see* manuscript illuminations
Miretto, Nicolò, *Coronation of the Virgin* (Padua, Palazzo della Ragione), *55*, 56, 58
model books, 14th-century, 43, 88
Mondo, Matteo, 7, 151n33
mosaics, Venice, Basilica of San Marco, Mascoli Chapel, 90–93, *91–93*, *104*
Moschini, Giannantonio, 127
Musolino, Pietro, 26

Naples, Museo Nazionale di Capodimonte, Masolino, *Founding of Santa Maria Maggiore*, *75*, 76
narrative painting, 81–82, 84, 85–88, 101, 102
natorum, meaning of, 137
Negri, Francesco, 127, 132, 134
Netherlandish art, 116, 118–21
New York
  Frick Collection
    Bellini, Giovanni, *Saint Francis in the Desert*, *15*, 16, 68, 78, 90, 101
    Gentile da Fabriano, *Madonna and Child, with Saints Lawrence and Julian*, 18, *20*
  Metropolitan Museum of Art, Bellini, Giovanni, Davis *Virgin and Child*, 12

oil painting, 121
Orvieto, 31
Osano, Shigetoshi, 143–45

Pacchioni, Guglielmo, 143
Padua
  Basilica of Sant'Antonio di Padova, Chapel of San Giacomo (now of San Felice), frescoes by Altichiero, 85
    Crucifixion, 72, *73*
  Church of the Eremitani
    Altichiero, *Coronation of the Virgin* (destroyed), 56, *56*, 63
    Ovetari Chapel, Mantegna frescoes, 166n30, 168n7; *Calling of Saints James and John*, 98–100, *100*, 102, *104*, 108, 116
  Donatello's influence, 88
  lost works by Jacopo Bellini, 154n13
    Gattamelata Altarpiece, 45, 81, 132, 134, 137
  Oratory of San Giorgio, frescoes by Altichiero, 85, 168n13
    Adoration of the Magi, 108, *109*
  Palazzo della Ragione, Nicolò Miretto, *Coronation of the Virgin*, *55*, 56, 58
  Scrovegni Chapel, Giotto frescoes, 66, *68*, 71
paliotto attributed to Bellini workshop, 169–70n37
Palma Vecchio, 143
Paoletti, Pietro, 124–25, 129, 142
Paolo "Remarius", husband of Elena Bellini, *see* Remarius
Paolo Veneziano, 63
Paris
  Bibliothèque de l'Arsenal, Bellini, Giovanni, *Passion of St Maurice* manuscript, 16, 108–16, *111*
    Assembly of the Order of the Crescent, 93, *110*
    Saint Maurice, *112*, 113–16, *114–15*
  Musée du Louvre, Bellini, Jacopo
    Paris sketchbook *see* Bellini, Jacopo, WORKS, Paris sketchbook
    Virgin and Child with Donor, *46*, 47, 52, 60
Parmigianino, 162n5
perspective *see* linear perspective
Pesaro, Museo Civico, Bellini, Giovanni, *Coronation of the Virgin*, *59*, 60, 93
Pincus, Debra, 136
Pisa, Museo Nazionale di San Matteo, Gentile da Fabriano, *Madonna of Humility*, 18, *21*
Pisanello, 84, 85
Pizzati, Anna, 136
poesie, 90
Polidoro, Fra Valerio, 137
Pomino, Vittore, 129, 130
portal motif, 93–95, *93*, 100
Porto Pisano, 21

Raphael, 62
Remarius, Caterina, 6, 25, 152n34
Remarius, Paolo, 6, 25, 26, 133, 152n35
René I, Duke of Anjou, Order of the Crescent, 108, 115
Riccio, Andrea, 32
Ridolfi, Carlo, 127, 128, 141
Rinversi, Anna, wife of Jacopo Bellini, 6, 14, 33–34, 125, 131, 148, 152n36
  will (1429), 33, 125, 127, 128
  will (1471), 107, 125, 128, 132, 133, 134
Rinversi, Branca, 6, 33, 152n37
Rinversi, Nicolò, 6, 152n39
Robertson, Giles, 108, 115, 128
Rome
  Basilica of San Giovanno in Laterano, 31
  Pinacoteca Vaticana, Gentile da Fabriano, panels from Quaratesi Altarpiece, *33*
  Santa Maria Maggiore, miracle of the snow, 74
Rovereto, 138, *139*

Sandei family, 33
Sanudo, Marin, 35, 124, 127, 132, 134
Scaglietti Kelescian, Daniela, 141
scuole grandi, 24–25, 82
  see also Venice, Scuola Grande di San Giovanni Evangelista; Venice, Scuola Grande di San Marco; Venice, Scuola Grande di Santa Maria della Carità
Sebastiano del Piombo, 168n3
Servite order, 64
Siena, 31
signatures
  Giovanni Bellini, 38–39, *39–40*, 42, 100–101, *103*
    on *Coronation of the Virgin* (Ferrara), 48, 50, 58, *58*, 62, 143
  Jacopo Bellini, 42, 100–101, *103*
Silvestro, son of Tommaso, 22
Strasbourg, Musée des Beaux-Arts, Anonymous (after

Altichiero?), *Birth of the Virgin*, 66, *67*
Strozzi, Palla, 23

Tempestini, Anchise, 147
tinsmiths, Venice, 23–25
Titian, 38, 78, 90, 121
Turin, Galleria Sabauda, Bellini, Giovanni, *Annunciation* and *Birth of the Virgin* (attributed), *95*, 96

Ughi, Luigi, 141

Valli, Natalia, 143
Varanini, Gian Maria, 138
Vasari, Giorgio
  on Bellini family, 19, 35, 41, 127
    Giovanni Bellini's birth date, 12, 26, 124–25, 127, 129
    Giovanni Bellini's parentage, 35, 127, 132, 134
  on Benedetto Coda, 140, 141
Vendramin, Franceschina, 7, 148, 152n40
  as wife of Nicoletto Bellini and mother of Giovanni Bellini, 14, 25–26, 28–29, 128, 131, 134–35
Vendramin, Giovanni, 7, 25, 152n41
Vendramin, Marina, 7, 25, 134, 152n42
Vendramin, Samaritana, wife of Giobbe Dominici, 7, 25, 34, 152n43
  will, 25, 134–35, 136
Vendramin family, 25–26, 134
Venice
  architecture and light effects, influence on Giovanni Bellini's visual aesthetic, 36–38, *37*, 56–58
  Basilica of San Marco, 34, 36, 56
    Bellini, Gentile, organ doors, 107, 160n4
    Mascoli Chapel, mosaics, 90–92; Bellini, Jacopo and Giovanni, *Visitation*, 90–93, *91–93*, *104*
  Ca' d'Oro, *Crucifixion* (anonymous, after Jan van Eyck?), 118, *118*
  Calle dei Stagneri, 23, *24*
  Ducal Palace, 36
    Great Council Hall, 41, 84
    Porta della Carta, 56–58, *57–58*, 116
  Gallerie dell'Accademia
    Bellini, Gentile, *Procession in Piazza San Marco*, *83*
    Bellini, Jacopo, *Madonna and Child*, 52, *54*, 162n20
    Ercole del Fiore (attributed), *Coronation of the Virgin*, 60, *61*
    Jacobello del Fiore, *Justice Enthroned between the Archangels Gabriel and Michael*, 42, *42*
  Museo Correr, Bellini, Giovanni
    Crucifixion with the Virgin and Saint John the Evangelist, 16, *61*, 62, 116–21, *117*, *119–20*
    Transfiguration of Christ, 12, *13*, 118
  Piazza San Marco, 36–38, *38*
  San Geminiano, church and parish, *35*, 36, *38*, 58
    Bellini workshop, 41, 129, 131, 132
    Giovanni Bellini's childhood home, 14, 29, 34, 36, 128, 129
  San Lio, parish, 128, 132, 148
  San Salvador, church and parish, 23, 24–25, *24*, 29, 131
  San Trovaso, Giambono, Michele, *Saint Chrysogonus on Horseback*, *43*
  San Zaccaria, Giovanni d'Alemagna and Antonio Vivarini, *Madonna of the Rosary*, *44*
  Santa Maria dei Frari, Donatello, *Saint John the Baptist*, *107*, 108
  Santa Marina, parish, 148
  Scuola di San Leonardo, 24
  Scuola di San Teodoro, 24
  Scuola di Santa Maria della Misericordia (della Valverde), 24–25, 82
  Scuola Grande di San Giovanni Evangelista, 47, 81–82, *81*, 88, 95–96, *95*
  Scuola Grande di San Marco, *81*, 88, 90
    albergo, 16, 81–89, *83*, 90
    contract for (1470), 38–39, *40*
    members of, 135, 138
    sala capitolare, 82, 135
  Scuola Grande di Santa Maria della Carità, 82, 164n5
Verona
  cathedral, Bellini, Jacopo, *Crucifixion* fresco, 19, 45
  Museo di Castelvecchio, Bellini, Jacopo, *Penitent Saint Jerome*, 98, *99*
  Palazzo Scaligeri, 85
Vicenza, 64
Villani, Giovanni, *22*
Vivarini, Antonio, 42, 80, 81
  and Giovanni d'Alemagna, *Madonna of the Rosary* (Venice, San Zaccaria), *44*
Vivarini, Bartolomeo, 162n5
Vivarini workshop, 80, 84, 88, 170n37
Voragine, Jacobus de, *Legenda Aurea (Golden Legend)*, 41, 48, 70, 76
  on Saint Jerome, 96, 98, 102, 108

wandering (*vagare*), Pietro Bembo on Giovanni Bellini's artistic strategy, 60, 69, 95
  see also portal motif
Washington, National Gallery of Art, Bellini, Giovanni, *Feast of the Gods*, 124
wills *see* Bellini, Nicoletto; Rinversi, Anna; Vendramin, Samaritana

"Zambellin Vecchio", 143
Zani, Pietro, 141
Zanina (Giovannina), wife of Nicoletto Bellini and mother of Jacopo Bellini, 6, 23, 25, 26, 128, 148, 151n14
Zoppo, Marco, 167n11, 169n27
Zovenzoni, Raffaele, 113

Picture Credits

© Accademia di Belle Arti Tadini, Archivio Fotografico (photo Da Re 2018): figs 85, 86, p. 104
© Archivio fotografico G.A.VE "su concessione del Ministero dei beni e delle attività culturali – Gallerie dell'Accademia di Venezia": figs 21, 33
Archivio di Stato di Mantova (State Archive of Mantua), Autographs, envelope 7, 44–45 cards recto and verso: fig. 19
Archivio di Stato di Modena (State Archive of Modena). Su concessione del Ministero per i beni e le attività culturali e per il Turismo – Archivio di Stato di Modena: fig. 114
Archivio di Stato di Venezia (State Archive of Venice): figs 10, 14, 20
Archivio di Stato, Bologna (State Archive of Venice): fig. 116

ART RESOURCE

Alfredo Dagli Orti/Art Resource, NY: fig. 57
Alinari/Art Resource, NY: fig. 42
Alinari/SEAT/Art Resource, NY: fig. 91
Photo: Gérard Blot/© RMN-Grand Palais/Art Resource, NY: figs 27, 28, 29, 31, 32, 54, 58, 59, 62, 64, 70, 71, 77, 81, 83, 84, 89, 92, 97, 98, 100, 101, 102, 103, 106, pp. 104–05
Mario Bonotto/Scala/Art Resource, NY: figs 45, 46, 49, 53, 56, 60, 63, 74
© The Trustees of the British Museum/Art Resource, NY: fig. 55
G. Dagli Orti/De Agostini Picture Library/Bridgeman Images: fig. 50
Erich Lessing/Art Resource, NY: fig. 65
Photo: Luciano Pedicini/Alinari/Art Resource, NY: fig. 61
Photo: Mathieu Rabeau/© RMN-Grand Palais/Art Resource, NY: fig. 24
© RMN-Grand Palais/Art Resource, NY: fig. 1
Scala/Art Resource, NY: figs 6, 7, 12, 13, 107
Scala/Ministero per i Beni e le Attività culturali/Art Resource, NY: figs 11, 52
The Henry Barber Trust, The Barber Institute of Fine Arts, University of Birmingham/Bridgeman Images: figs 79, 87, p. 104

Biblioteca Civica "Tartarotti" di Rovereto (TN – Italia), Manoscritti – MS 75.6 (29): fig. 113
Bibliothèque nationale de France: figs 93, 94, 95, 96, 99, 104, p. 4
© Cameraphoto Arte, Venezia: figs 2, 23, 36, 43, 44, 51, 66, 67, 68, 73, 75, 76, 80, 90, 105, 109, 111, p. 104
Cappella Dotto, Chiesa Eremitani, Padova: fig. 37
Collezione d'arte Fondazione CR Firenze: fig. 4
Illustration by Elisabetta Fava: figs 71, 72
© The Frick Collection: figs 3, 5
Photo: Minneapolis Institute of Art: fig. 9
Su concessione del Ministero per i Beni e le Attività Culturali e per il turismo – Direzione Musei Emilia Romagna. Further reproduction or duplication by any means is prohibited: fig. 115
Su concessione del Ministero per i Beni e le Attivita Culturali, Polo Museale dell'Emilia Romagna: figs 25, 26, 30, 34, 39, 41, 47, 48
© The National Gallery, London. Layard Bequest, 1916: fig. 112
Courtesy National Gallery of Art, Washington, D.C. Sebastiano Ricci, Lodovico Ughi, and Giovanni Antonio Faldoni, *Iconographic Representation of the Illustrious City of Venice*, 1729. Etching and engraving, 148.5 × 264.2 cm: pp. 8–9
Palazzo Ducale, Venice © Sarah Quill/Bridgeman Images: fig. 40
Photo: Pinacoteca di Brera: figs 35, 69
Royal Collection Trust/© Her Majesty Queen Elizabeth II 2021: fig. 11
© Royal Museum of Fine Arts Belgium, Brussels. Photo: J. Geleyns (Art Photography): figs 108, 110
Photo: Steven Varni: figs 16, 17
Venezia Romanica by Wladimiro Dorigo, Cierre, Caselle di Sommacampagna 2003. Map by Renza Calabrese: fig. 15
Allen Phillips/Wadsworth Atheneum: fig. 18
Wikimedia Commons: figs 8, 82, p. 104
CC0: fig. 78
Photo by Didier Descouens (CC BY SA 4.): fig. 22
Photo by Wolfgang Moroder (CC SA 3.): fig. 38

Acknowledgments

My greatest academic debt is to Joanna Woods-Marsden, my PhD supervisor at the University of California, Los Angeles, who invited me into her classroom and encouraged me to stay; I would not be an art historian without her generosity and guidance. I also thank her for reading a draft of this book. My colleague Gabriele Matino, who discussed crucial ideas in this study with me, also deserves special mention. I am grateful to Deborah Howard, who championed this project and offered critical suggestions. I am also thankful to Stephen Campbell and Geoffrey Symcox for supporting my scholarship over many years.

I thank the institutions that offered me research fellowships. As a Barbara Thom Postdoctoral Fellow at the Huntington, I reshaped my project into this book. Fellowships from the American Council of Learned Societies and the National Endowment for the Humanities supported crucial research on the Bellini workshop that provides the basis for this study. During my Fulbright Fellowship at the University of York, I was warmly embraced by the History of Art faculty, and I especially thank my gracious hosts Amanda Lillie and Michael White, as well as Elizabeth Prettejohn, Anthony Geraghty, and Teresa Kittler for our stimulating conversations. The Fulbright also allowed me to examine works of art related to this project that were spread throughout the U.K., and I am particularly thankful to Hugo Chapman for allowing me to spend a day with the Jacopo Bellini album at the British Museum. I also thank Dominique Cordellier for providing access to Jacopo's other sketchbook at the Louvre. In addition, Caroline Campbell and Matthias Wivel at the National Gallery, Neville Rowley at the Gemäldegalerie in Berlin, Vincent Delieuvin at the Louvre, and the welcoming Art History faculty at the University of Warwick—especially Louise Bourdua, Lorenzo Pericolo, and my dear friend Giorgio Tagliaferro—were immensely helpful during this period.

The University of Iowa has been tremendously supportive during the writing of this book. Funds from the School of Art and Art History along with a College of Liberal Arts and Sciences Book subvention helped support its publication. Funds from my Fountiene Lee Duda fellowship at Iowa contributed toward the image rights. The art history professors at Iowa—Craig Adcock, Björn Anderson, Robert Bork, Amy Huang, Dorothy Johnson, Joni Kinsey, Brenda Longfellow, Barbara Mooney, Joyce Tsai, and the late Christopher Roy, whom I miss—have been wonderful to work with. I have turned to them often for all sorts of advice. My colleagues in the School of Art and Art History have been equally kind, and I thank in particular Andrew Casto, Terry Conrad, Rachel Cox, T. J. Dedeaux-Norris, Andrew Evans, Troy Fitzpatrick, Ab Gratama, Griffin Idleman, David Johnson, Betsey Kosier, Lynne Lanning, Kevin McGlynn, Heather Parrish, Sara Pettit, Alice Phillips, Saralyn Richardson, Serina Sulentic, Jeremy Swanston, Rijn Templeton, and particularly Steve McGuire, who offered great support for this book.

A number of colleagues helped with different aspects of the research for this book. I thank Mario Russo for transcribing several documents for me at the Archivio di Stato di Venezia, Rielle Jones-Teske for helping prepare the Bellini Family Tree, Anna Pizzati for searching for Elisabetta Michiel in the historical archives, and Paula Clarke and Stanley Chojnacki for sharing their research with me. I am grateful to Debra Pincus, who provided important comments on a draft, and to Susannah Rutherglen, who made suggestions for the Introduction. I thank Alexandra Bamji, Andrea Bayer, Meryl Bailey, Lorenzo Buonanno, Molly Bourne, Brigit Blass-Simmen, Anna Cavanna, Lorenzo Calvelli, Matteo Casini, Matteo Ceriana, Donal Cooper, Tracy Cooper, Thomas Dalla Costa, Blake de Maria, Jill Dunkerton, Benita Eisler, Colin Eisler, Peter Fane-Saunders, Davide Gasparotto, Augusto Gentili, Nora Gietz, Joseph Godla, James Grubb, Joseph Hammond, Paul Hills, David Young Kim, Emanuele Lugli, Giulio Manieri Elia, Antonio Mazzotta, Luca Molà, Reinhold Mueller, Monika Schmitter, Edward Tuttle, and Amy Worthen for their advice and support while I was preparing this book.

It grieves me not to be able to thank in person two individuals who helped with the early research for this study: the late Tom Worthen and the late Carolyn Wilson. Tom was instrumental to the writing of my earlier article on this material in *Renaissance Quarterly*, which forms a section of Appendix A in this book. Carolyn reviewed the *Renaissance Quarterly* article and offered numerous helpful suggestions, and she and I later organized a series of panels on Giovanni Bellini at the Renaissance Society of America conference in Boston. I wish I could share this book with them.

In preparing the manuscript for publication, I owe special thanks to Mark Eastment of Yale University Press for his enthusiastic support of the project. Also at Yale, I warmly thank my editor Julie Hrischeva, superb copyeditor Jane Ace, and Grade Design. Fellowships and a subvention from the Gladys Krieble Delmas Foundation helped me conduct research for this study and supported the publication of this book. It was wonderful to work with Nina

Damavandi, who was responsible for the picture research and permissions, and I also thank Merrie Bergmann for her copyediting.

My family provided me with the greatest encouragement. My mother, Diane, introduced me to a love of art history, and my father, Judd, taught me to seek out the truth. My brilliant wife, Jenifer, was a constant source of love and inspiration; she also read every chapter numerous times. My son Montgomery lived for nearly four years in Venice and Florence while I conducted the dissertation research that underpins this book. My son Cosimo was born in Venice during this time and rode the vaporetto back from the hospital before he was a day old. I am grateful for all our adventures, and this book is dedicated to Diane, Judd, Jenifer, Montgomery, and Cosimo.

First published by Yale University Press 2021
302 Temple Street, P. O. Box 209040, New Haven CT 06520-9040
47 Bedford Square, London WC1B 3DP
yalebooks.com | yalebooks.co.uk

ISBN 978-0-300-23661-3 HB
Library of Congress Control Number: 2020952061

10 9 8 7 6 5 4 3 2 1
2025 2024 2023 2022 2021

Designed by Peter Dawson, gradedesign.com
Printed in Great Britain by Gomer Press Ltd, Llandysul, Ceredigion, Wales

Front cover: Giovanni Bellini, *Saint Maurice* (detail), 1453. Miniature from Jacopo Antonio Marcello's *Passion of Saint Maurice* manuscript. Tempera, gum, or glue on vellum, 18.7 × 14 cm. Bibliothèque de l'Arsenal, Paris. Bibliothèque nationale de France
Back cover: Giovanni Bellini, *Saint Jerome in the Wilderness*, ca. 1450. Tempera on panel, 44 × 22.9 cm. The Henry Barber Trust, The Barber Institute of Fine Arts, University of Birmingham/Bridgeman Images
Frontispiece: Giovanni Bellini, *Saint Francis in the Desert* (detail), ca. 1476–78. Oil on panel, 124.6 × 142 cm. © The Frick Collection, New York

Published with the support of the Gladys Krieble Delmas Foundation